WITHDRAWN

The Politics
of
School
Desegregation

norc

NATIONAL OPINION RESEARCH CENTER
MONOGRAPHS IN SOCIAL RESEARCH

The Politics
of
School
Desegregation

Comparative Case Studies
of Community Structure
and Policy-Making

By

ROBERT L. CRAIN

With the assistance of
MORTON INGER
GERALD A. McWORTER
JAMES J. VANECKO

ALDINE PUBLISHING COMPANY
Chicago

The research reported herein was
supported by the Office of Education,
Departmet of Health, Education, and Welfare,
Project No. 5-0641-2-12-1

First published 1968 by
ALDINE Publishing Company
529 South Wabash Ave.
Chicago, Illinois 60605

Library of Congress Catalog Card Number 67-27390
Designed by Greer Allen
Printed in the United States of America

SECOND PRINTING 1969

Preface

Money talks, as the saying goes, and public money talks with the accents of the political process. Nowhere is this process seen more clearly than in conflicts arising over the policies of local boards of education. Major decisions such as the location of new school buildings, curriculum changes, and the drawing of attendance areas involve the allocation of resources among various interest groups. Inevitably, as one group sees its interests subordinated to those of others, controversy arises and the members of the board of education find themselves involved in what are essentially political negotiations.

The nature of these controversies, the intensity of public reaction, and the bitterness of the contending factions vary considerably from time to time and from city to city. A decision to build a new school may pass without controversy at one time, while a similar decision may provoke prolonged and bitter dispute a few years later. In some cities, changes in attendance areas that affect the racial balance in schools may occur with little overt dispute, while in others an attempt to alter a boundary, even if it affects only a few students, may provoke long and hostile action on the part of the citizenry. The reasons for these variations in the nature and degree of political controversy surrounding school board decisions is of great interest to the student of the political process as well as the student of educational administration. How one goes about assessing the sources of variation in controversy is, however, difficult to determine.

One can start by asking: What are the variables involved in a school board decision that might influence the way in which the decision is made? An obvious beginning point is the content of the decision itself: Does it allocate some major portion of the school board's resources to the advantage of a particular interest group? If the change is of relatively small magnitude, does it imply a radical revision of the traditional pattern of distribution of resources among various subgroups of the population? Is there some new element in the decision which was previously considered to be outside the school board's scope of concern? Thus, one source of variation might arise from the decision itself and the historical conditions surrounding similar decisions in that particular city.

A second type of variable that would seem to be important on *a priori* grounds is related to the groups whose interests are directly affected by the decision. What sort of groups are these? How well organized are they? What resources do they have available to exert pressure on the school board? Are these groups tied in with larger political institutions so that decisions made by the school board either for or against their interests would have ramifications that would affect other city government agencies? Thus a school board may react differently to the demands of a group which is a major supporting group for the city administration than it would to a group which has been traditionally in opposition to, or has been unimportant in, local political elections.

A third type of variable, perhaps less obvious than the first two, concerns the characteristics of the school board members themselves. Here one would be concerned not only with the mode of selection of board members, but also with the question of their personal characteristics and beliefs. Are school board members elected by local citizens or are they appointed by some political official? Are they themselves political figures or are they drawn from non-political citizens' groups? What are the educational and occupational backgrounds of school board members? What are their general political and ideological positions on social questions that might be relevant to the kinds of decisions that the school board is called upon to make?

The research strategy adopted by Robert L. Crain in studying the relation of these three types of variables to school board decision making has been to concentrate on a detailed analysis of a single decision—the decision to desegregate the schools—as it was made by the school boards of fifteen cities. In some cities this decision was made at the school board's own initiative, while in others it was made (or refused) under intense pressure by civil rights groups and the courts. What the nature of these differences is, and how the interplay of historical, political, and sociological factors influence the decision-making process, is the subject of this monograph. Mr. Crain and his associates present a detailed analysis of the individual decisions made by the school boards, and then compares the behavior of different school boards, first in the North and then in the South. From this comparison, he is able to draw some inferences about the factors that influence the way in which decisions are handled and their eventual outcome. Even though his comparative analysis involves a small number of cases, Crain is able to separate out the common themes that cut across a variety of particular instances. In so doing, he has made a significant contribution to our understanding of the complexities of the political decision-making process in urban America.

NORMAN M. BRADBURN
Director
National Opinion Research Center

Acknowledgments

A study such as this owes a huge debt to the two hundred persons who permitted us to interview them and who graciously made their files available to us. We are especially conscious of the sacrifices they made since they were all very busy men and women —school board members, school administrators, public officials, newspapermen, and heads of civil rights groups. A number of them gave us confidential documents, permitted us to borrow their personal files, and helped us locate documents. Some of them permitted us interviews as long as eight hours. We remember several of these persons as especially helpful, considerate, or insightful; but we will not thank any of them here by name. To thank one or two would be an insult to twenty others who also went out of their way for us, and to thank twenty would be an improper recognition of our debt to a hundred more.

We will no doubt disappoint many of the respondents, who were hopeful that we would present a series of usable recommendations. But as responsible social scientists we are convinced that our duty is to report the facts and to give possible sociological explanations of these facts, and to let those who are qualified by experience or training develop specific proposals from them.

Many of our informants disagree with our interpretation of these data, of course; but in many respects those who disagreed were more helpful than the others. We are especially indebted to the many people in New Orleans who permitted us to interview them and who gave us access to their personal documents. Their exceeding graciousness is particularly gratifying, since our research was probing a deep and still healing wound in that community. The study put us in touch with a group of men and women who were called upon to perform courageous acts in a situation of great turmoil and in the face of real personal danger. Our study of New Orleans is concerned with explaining its inability to desegregate peacefully, but it is also a study of the way in which a city on the brink of total disaster managed to save itself. Although it is true that there was violence in New Orleans, it is equally true that the city avoided the serious tragedy that Birmingham suffered. The integrated schools were boycotted, but the public school system itself survived. As President Kennedy noted, all Americans should be grateful to the good people of New Orleans, and especially to the Orleans Parish school board.

We are indebted to June Shagaloff of the national office of the National Association for the Advancement of Colored People, who gave us valuable advice and information about the national picture. Anyone who attempts a study such as this has a great advantage if his cities are described in the City Politics Reports published by the Harvard-MIT Joint Center for Urban Studies, under the direction of Edward C. Banfield.

We are also thankful for the assistance of Warren Breed, of Tulane University's Department of Sociology, and G. William Foster, Jr., of the University of Wisconsin Law School. J. David Greenstone and Grant McConnell, of the University of Chicago's Department of Political Science, have read and commented on drafts of Chapter 15; their help is gratefully acknowledged.

W. Wayne Shannon, of the Louisiana State University Department of Political Science, prepared a special study of the desegregation of the Baton Rouge schools, which provided a valuable comparison with our study of New Orleans.

The research staff is also indebted to Lisa Paul, who handled most of the clerical work for the project, to Lillian Rochon and Rose Thomas, who typed the manuscript, Mary A. Spaeth, who edited the index, Bonnie McKeon, who edited the manuscript and did the artwork, and Elaine Richardson, who proofread it.

The study owes a large debt to Peter H. Rossi, who conceived the project and provided both moral support and technical advice throughout the study. Norman M. Bradburn gave the manuscript a critical reading and made numerous helpful comments.

This manuscript is very definitely a team effort. The members of the research staff were Morton Inger, Thomas M. Landye, Gerald A. McWorter, Paul Peterson, Robert T. Stout, and James J. Vanecko. They were responsible for the interviewing, and for preliminary drafts of many of the chapters.

Each chapter contains a footnote which identifies, in the case of the case studies, the staff members who were responsible for the interviewing, and in the analytic chapters, those responsible for the preliminary analysis. In addition, many chapters identify a member of the project as responsible for either the first draft or, in one case, for the complete writing of the chapter. The senior author is, however, responsible for the content.

The project was financed by the U.S. Office of Education, and we are very grateful for the academic freedom which they provided.

R. L. C.

Contents

Contents

List
of Tables

List of Tables

List
of Illustrations

Part I

Eight Northern Cities

1

Introduction

This is an analysis of the way in which fifteen American city school systems made decisions regarding school integration. Eight of these cities studied are northern ones that were faced with demands for the elimination of *de facto* segregation. The remaining seven are southern cities that desegregated their systems in compliance with the *Brown* decision of the Supreme Court.

The reader may wish to know why we collected these facts and ideas about school desegregation. The reasons are rather disparate, and we think that the findings will interest a number of different types of readers.

Politics, however it is defined, is mainly concerned with the process by which groups of people make decisions that are binding on the members of the group. Studies like this one, which focus on a single decision as it is made in different cities, are one way to approach the study of urban politics. Of course, no theory can be derived from studying a single issue, and therefore this sort of study will need to be repeated for other types of decisions. But this disadvantage is more than compensated for by the fact that concentrating on a single decision permits us to examine simultaneously a number of cities and to determine not only how the decision is made in each city, but also what factors cause cities to differ.

School integration is an interesting issue for our purposes because it is a new issue. Rigid decision-making techniques have not yet been developed, and the range of possible outcomes is large. Furthermore, decisions are made in highly ambiguous situations where there are no simple formulas to follow. Thus the decision will vary from one place to another, and we can expect this variation to be caused not by trivial differences in administrative structure, but by differences in basic political style. Our analysis suggests that this is indeed the case. Cities that resemble each other in their handling of school integration have fundamental political similarities. For example, the most important factor determining the behavior of the school boards we studied seems to be the amount of influence in the hands of the civic elite—the businessmen and others who participate in city decision making from outside the government and the political parties. Our analysis suggests partial explanation of why these civic elites have more influence in some cities than in others.

In addition, the study serves a quite different function. It describes one aspect of one of the most important social movements in recent American history. Some writers have seen the 1954 Supreme Court decision as the most important single cause of the "Negro revolution," and in the northern cities we studied, school integration has frequently been the leading edge of the civil rights movement. A good look at this issue, and the way it has been handled, may help us to understand and anticipate the future course of race relations in America.

In the past, most of our information about school integration has come from newspapers and news magazines, and they have presented a highly distorted picture. The national press usually portrays the school system and the civil rights movement as two uncompromising opponents. Newspapers report the conflicts in detail—the picketing, the boycotts, the resignations of superintendents, and the role of race in school board election campaigns. Conflict is news. Peace is not. The newspapers have not given the public a systematic picture—a census of where the news is good as well as where it is bad. This is also a goal of our study.

The fifteen cities studied give at least a preliminary picture of the state of school integration in the big cities throughout the country. The picture is not quite as dismal as might be expected. Of the eight northern cities, three have resolved the school integration issue in one way or another; demonstrations, if they ever occurred, are a thing of the past. In two cities, plans are now being implemented which show promise of settling the issue for a few years. In another, the issue has not been resolved, but at this writing is simmering quietly. Two other cities are facing demonstrations. There is a great deal of conflict in these cities, but it is clear that conflict is not unavoidable. And if Negro education has not changed radically, it is also true that each of our eight cities has taken some steps to improve the education of its Negro students. A social revolution of considerable importance is being handled gracefully in at least some cities.

But in this study we try to be more than systematic journalists. We also want to spell out more precisely the nature of the school desegregation issue. The prevailing myths—that civil rights leaders want total integration immediately and that they would rather demonstrate than negotiate, that school superintendents are narrow-minded autocrats, that school boards are representatives of a segregationist power structure, that white voters will rise up in arms at the first sign of a school bus—are, we think, simply not true. One of our main concerns is to estimate precisely what civil rights leaders expect from the schools and what they are willing to accept and how school boards, school administrators, and voters feel about the issue. Perhaps we only reflect the social scientist's faith that things look simpler when we understand them, but we think that the school integration issue is less complicated and less irrational than it has been made to look.

Another goal of the study is to explain differences between cities. Why was there so much controversy in San Francisco and so little in Baltimore? Since school desegregation decisions are made by groups of people (school boards) which are influenced by other groups of people (the civil rights movements), it therefore follows that differences in the kinds of decisions made will depend upon differences in the composition and interests of these groups. From this common-sense perspective, school integration is merely one of the many issues handled by local government. This study can then add to our general knowledge of the community and, conversely, the recent renaissance in the study of local governments and community structure can provide some conceptual tools to look at civil rights and the schools. This returns to the first goal of the study—by understanding the way in which many cities handled a common issue we can develop some general ideas about how American public schools and American cities are governed.

THE RESEARCH DESIGN

Unfortunately, there has been little systematic research on the politics of school integration. Williams and Ryan (1954) provided a valuable analysis of desegregation in border cities before the *Brown* decision; but the changes in the national climate since that time have been so great that school integration is in many ways not the same issue that it was then. Our reading of research done in schools of education has generally not been as useful as we had hoped. There are two reasons for this: first, the school system is seen from the administrator's perspective and in the frame of reference of the educational profession; second, much of the work consists of disparate research which has not been put into a useful conceptual scheme. One valuable exception is Kimbrough (1964).

Since we did not feel that the literature provided us with a set of hypotheses that we could test, we were forced to fall back on a case study technique. The great advantage of the case study is that it makes minimal restrictions on the research. The observer can feel free to pursue a particular hypothesis as far as his imagination and the cooperation of his respondents will permit. In each city, we tried to answer seven very general questions:

1. What is the issue? Who wants integration, and what do they mean? Who is opposed? Why? (Can we distinguish between the demands publicly made by the civil rights leaders and the philosophy which lies behind the demands? Similarly, can we find fundamental attitudes behind the position held by the other actors?)

2. Who are the actors? How many persons participate in developing a demand for integration? Who are the actors who decide how to reply to the demand? (Was the decision made by the school board, the superintendent, the power elite, the mayor?)

3. What are the channels of communication and influence that connect the actors to each other and to the holders of various kinds of power? (Is poor communication an important factor in the creation of controversy? Does the school board tend to go to influential persons for help?)

4. What resources did the various actors have at their disposal (votes, prestige, money, etc)?

5. What are the factors that placed the particular men in decision-making positions? (Does an appointed school board differ from an elected one? Under what conditions do militants take over leadership of a civil rights organization?)

6. Is there a relationship between the behavior of the actors in the school integration issue and the general structure of politics in the city?

7. What is the relationship between the behavior of elites and that of the masses? To what extent do the masses depend upon the leadership for

cues concerning when a "spontaneous" protest for or against desegregation should occur?

The other advantage to the case study approach is that it permits a "total analysis" of the particular issue. Since we were restricting ourselves to the study of only a particular aspect of desegregation, we set as the final goal of the project the complete explanation of the differences between cities on this issue—not only as complete a list of causal factors as possible, but also an estimate of the relative importance of each factor. We concluded, for example, that not only are the personal attitudes of school board members toward the civil rights movement important in determining the extent to which the school system will move to integrate schools, these attitudes seem to be by far the most important factor. Similarly, we concluded that the willingness and ability of the civil rights movement to engage in demonstration has relatively little effect on what the school board does. This is part of what we mean by total analysis.

We also tried to trace the causes of variation in school integration decisions back to fundamental characteristics of the city: its population composition, its economy, and its political structure. This would have been impossible if we had restricted ourselves to highly specific data. But instead, we tried to collect as much related, miscellaneous information as possible about each city.

The great disadvantage of the case study is that it is time consuming, and in the past this has meant that one social scientist studied only one city. The single case study has some serious drawbacks, since it is impossible to know whether the conditions reported are unique or whether they are representative. For this reason, it has outlived its usefulness. The three most valuable recent monographs on community decision-making all are based on comparisons between cities. Banfield and Wilson (1963) based their work on data collected by their students in a number of large cities. Williams and Adrian (1963) studied four middle-sized Michigan cities in an effort to match certain aspects of the cities in order to minimize unimportant differences. Agger, Goldrich, and Swanson (1964) also based their study on research in four communities.

Empirical research on the community is fundamentally no different from empirical research in any other area; it simply aims to establish relationships that exist between variables. To note that both competitive politics and large public expenditures for projects such as urban renewal are present in New Haven is not very helpful. We need to know whether these two variables are systematically linked in most cities. Even if we do not wish to establish correlations, but only to describe the American city, a comparative study is necessary. We cannot answer the question, "How militant is the northern civil rights movement?" while looking only at New York City.

Our research budget would have permitted a complete case study of one or two cities; but two cities would not be sufficient for this purpose. There would be a great risk of selecting a biased sample. We could have studied one hundred cities, if we had limited ourselves to the study of two or three variables. But we could not take chances on our ability to guess which were the crucial variables. Our solution to the dilemma was a rather novel research design. We selected fifteen cities, eight in the North and seven in the South, by a modified random sampling scheme, which is described in Appendix 1. In each city we made a case study. We then selected what we thought were the key variables and assigned each city scores on each variable, so that survey-style statistical analysis could be used. This design gave us the advantage of the case study, since we could search for the most important factors in each case, and also permitted at least a tentative demonstration that these factors were important in all our cities. We were able to stay within a research budget by taking the smallest number of cities that would permit comparative analysis and then economizing on data collection techniques.

The data were collected by a team of two or three interviewers who usually spent one week in each city. During that time they interviewed most of the members of the school board, the leaders of the civil rights movement, local informants such as newspapermen or social scientists who were familiar with the local situation, and, where possible, key elites such as the mayor or the most influential businessmen. We collected, on the average, twenty-two interviews per city, ranging from thirty minutes to eight hours in length. The interviews focused upon determining what was demanded by the civil rights movement, what the school system did in response, and what actions (demonstrations, suits, countersuits, etc.) took place or were threatened. In the process of collecting this data, we found out who the most important actors were. We interviewed these men to determine the pattern of communication and the channels of influence that connected them and to determine their personal characteristics—in particular their social origins and their political ideology. We then began tracing the reasons why these particular men were in decision-making positions by trying to find out how persons are recruited to these roles and obtaining information about the community's general political and civic structure. Finally, in each city the interviewers gathered several pounds of printed documents—school board minutes, reports, complete sets of newspaper clippings, and even copies of private correspondence.

Our fears that a week of interviewing in each city would not be enough time proved to be unfounded. We had no difficulty in learning the detailed story of the decision; there may be some well-kept secrets that we did not uncover, but we think that in almost every city we have a story complete enough for analysis. In addition, we found, as other researchers have noted, that a clear impression of the particular "tone" or "style" of a city is immediately apparent, although sometimes we were not successful in identifying all the factors that make up a city's "style" of action.

It would be pleasant to pretend that we had conducted a total analysis—one that considered every possible factor and then developed the relationship of each variable to the outcome of the integration controversy. Of course, one cannot design research that will do this. However, by the use of open-ended interviewing, a flexible data collection schedule, and a willingness to rewrite the questionnaires repeatedly, we were able to keep in mind many possible hypotheses. In addition, we often found that when a hypothesis developed from our study of one city, we could search the files and our memories for the necessary data to make at least a rough test of the hypothesis in the cities we had visited earlier.

School desegregation in the North may seem to have much in common with desegregation in the South; and this is no doubt true. However, from the point of view of this study, which is concerned solely with the way in which decisions were made—the political process—the two issues have almost nothing in common. For this reason, this volume is divided into five parts. In Part I, we report the case studies of the northern cities. Part II draws these case studies together into a comparative analysis. In Part III, we turn to the southern cities, and use six of our studies as a matrix in which to locate the one southern city in our sample that suffered severe disruption when it was called upon to desegregate. In Part IV, we turn our attention to the civil rights movement, and look at northern and southern civil rights movements in successive chapters. Part V contains two concluding chapters.

The case studies of the eight northern cities are presented very briefly in Chapters 2–9. Each chapter is simply a description of how the desegregation issue was raised, how it was debated, and how it was finally resolved. In writing the description, we have not attempted a thorough account of every action; instead we have stressed the key actions, and those that seemed particularly significant in setting that story apart from the others. In general, there is little in the stories which an informed resident of the city might not already know. We have also speculated about the factors that might have caused the city to take the particular course that it did, but mainly these chapters are descriptive, and most of the analysis is postponed to Part II. We have added brief descriptions in some cases of some of the actors, where we think this is helpful to the reader. Of course, we are not interested in singling out persons for praise or blame; but one of the reasons why cities differ in their actions is that they place different types of men in leadership positions.

We are not concerned with the technicalities of actions taken by schools to meet the demands of the civil rights movement. We do not intend to describe in detail or evaluate particular plans for school integration or various techniques for upgrading education of the "culturally deprived." Rather, our focus is upon the school integration issue as a political matter. Our concern is with the problems of communication, perception, influence, power, and ideology which are part of this story, just as they are part of any political decision.

After each chapter was written, copies were given to our respondents. They made many important criticisms. In two cases, a school board or a school superintendent objected strongly to our report and in these cases the city has been given a pseudonym in the report. In a third case, one school board member objected, and that person is not mentioned in the report.

In Chapter 10 we review the eight case studies and attempt to develop a general picture of the typical integration decision—what the basic demands of the civil rights movement are, how the school board and the superintendent respond, and how the mass of white citizens react. In effect, this chapter is an overview of the issue. The following three chapters then analyze the differences between the eight cities. Chapter 11 shows that much of the difference between cities can be explained by the composition of the school board. In Chapter 12 we pursue the two major variables— the liberalism of the school board members and the cohesion of the board—and conclude that the differences between boards lie in the differences in the way members are recruited to serve. Chapter 13 traces these differences in recruitment patterns to differences in the basic makeup of the city: its political structure, its population composition, and its economic base. These thirteen chapters make up the first two parts of the book.

We are somewhat surprised by our findings. For example, a great deal has been written about school superintendents and their role in the school integration decision; our case studies suggest that the superintendent plays a minor role in comparison to the school board. Much has also been written about the aggressiveness of the civil rights movement; our interviews suggest that the aggressive movements appear in relatively few cities in the North. We were more impressed by the weakness of the typical civil rights group. In addition, we did not find the typical civil rights movement to be engaged in "irresponsible" direct action; if a political strategist were called in to advise the civil rights groups in our cities, we think that he would generally advise more picketing, not less. Finally, we were somewhat surprised to find evidence that despite the pressures working on school board members, they did not seem to be learning to play new roles as full-time political actors; instead, their decisions about school integration seemed to be affected most by the personal prejudices for or against Negroes which they brought with them when they first joined the board.

Part III of this volume deals with one facet of school desegregation in the South. In contrast to the North, school desegregation in the South has been a simple issue; the school board is ordered to desegregate, either by the federal judiciary or, recently, by the executive branch; and some sort of desegregation, at least token, follows. There is, in this otherwise orderly game, a wild card that can disrupt the entire sequence of events—mob violence. We have therefore singled out one city—New Orleans—which, along with Little Rock and Birmingham, is a landmark in the history of southern desegregation. In Chapters 14 through 17, we study New Orleans, first putting it in a context of the diffusion of desegregation through the South, then reporting the story of this city's crisis, presenting an analysis and an explanation of the story, and finally testing our explanation by comparing New Orleans to the six other southern cities.

Part IV is concerned with civil rights movements and the way they differ from one northern city to another. This is an interesting opportunity to use some of the material developed earlier, since some of the factors that cause school boards to operate in certain ways have the same effect on civil rights movements, despite the fact that the former are governmental agencies governed by rather specific legislation and the latter are social movements which have no codified way of selecting leadership or defining membership and no legal limits upon the goals to be pursued.

Part V consists of two concluding chapters: Chapter 20 is concerned with trying to use our knowledge of school desegregation in the South to predict how the issue will change in the North. Chapter 21 focuses upon a few of the broader implications of the study for theories of community decision-making.

We think the report will be valuable to the persons involved in school desegregation. Certainly, we have no formula for either racial peace or racial progress, but the report may provide the reader with a useful account of the situation in other cities and, more important, a perspective on the whole matter that may help him to understand his own community. In addition, we hope that the analysis will provide useful data for the social scientists who are concerned with the government of the public schools. We especially hope that we can stimulate more research on school boards. In the years of work on the study of education, few writers have focused upon school boards as political bodies, and the results of this study indicate that more attention should be given to them. Finally, we hope that these new data will be of value to the

students of American local government and the American community. While we do not develop any general theories of community structure or community decision making, we hope that
this study brings us closer to the day when such theories can be
subjected to thorough empirical test.

2

St. Louis

Banfield (1965) introduces his description of St. Louis by observing that St. Louis does not have the middle-income population necessary to support "good government," but has it just the same. The St. Louis school segregation controversy is a good example of "good government" in action.

THE ST. LOUIS POLITICAL SYSTEM

The main political division in St. Louis can be referred to as South Side versus North Side. South St. Louis is German and was once Republican; north St. Louis is solidly Democratic and contains the remnants of a political machine based on Irish, Italian, and Negro votes. (Of course, politics does not follow exact geographic lines, but we will use these terms for descriptive purposes.)

During the school segregation crisis of 1963, southsider Raymond Tucker was in his last term as mayor of St. Louis. Previously he had been opposed in each Democratic primary by the North Side regular Democrats. He defeated them with the help of business support, an appeal to good government, and the votes of the South Side German wards. While in office, Tucker ran a "clean" administration (he had been an engineering school professor) and stressed civil promotion of the "Gateway to the West" and projects such as urban renewal and the Saarinen arch. The urban renewal project that contributed so much to building Tucker's image—Mill Creek—played an important role in the integration issue, as we shall see.

THE SCHOOL BOARD AND ITS SCHOOLS

The North Side Democrats never had much patronage in Republican St. Louis; in fact, only one Democratic mayor was

The interviewing in St. Louis was conducted by James J. Vanecko and Thomas M. Landye. The first draft of this chapter was prepared by James Vanecko.

elected before 1949. The exceedingly clean city charter made them dependent upon non-city jobs for their organizations. Some of these jobs came from the Democratic state capital, but many came from the school system. The party also benefitted from its control over school purchasing. An effort at reform began with the school board elections of 1951, but had relatively little success until, in 1958, one of the reform board members, a young executive named Daniel Schlafly, succeeded in breaking a scandal. One top school administrator had been removed from office and the board president was under fire when Schlafly stood for reelection in 1959. (In St. Louis the twelve board members serve staggered six-year terms, so that four members [or more, if there are any vacancies] are elected every two years.)

There had never been a Negro elected to city-wide office in St. Louis, although several men had tried. In the 1959 election, the Negro candidate for the school board was Reverend John Hicks. The Negro wards represented a sizable bloc of the North Side anti-reform votes, and Hicks and Schlafly reached an agreement for mutual support. Hicks took many votes away from the organization and threw some of these to Schlafly (many simply "bulleted" by voting only for Hicks). The result is that both of them, and a third "reform" candidate, were elected. During the next two years, two northsiders resigned, and Mayor Tucker made two blue-ribbon appointments. Two years later, in 1961, five more of the board's seats came up for reelection, and Schlafly and others organized a citizens' committee, composed primarily of businessmen, which found candidates and financed them. The committee slated another Negro, James Hurt, the son of a prominent physician and owner of a small loan company. The entire slate won rather handily. Now with a majority of the board, the reformers were able to reorganize the contracts and maintenance programs.

With the elimination of patronage, the usefulness of the schools to the organization Democrats was over, and since that time the citizens' committee candidates have been virtually unopposed. In 1963 the last seats of the board were swept by the slate, with one seat going to a Negro woman active in PTA and neighborhood work. Superintendent Philip Hickey retired because of health in 1963, and his deputy, William Kottmeyer, succeeded him as superintendent. Although both were committed to running a "clean" school system, the political involvement of the schools had given them a broad background in the political arts. Thus the school system had men with political "savvy" both on the board and in its top administrative offices.

Although the reorganization of the schools solved some of its problems, the schools were and are still in a series of binds. One of these is money. With the city's limited tax base as its main support, the school system has not been able to afford many new programs (property assessment has not been changed in a decade). The other bind on the schools is the combination of the Missouri state school law and a rural-dominated state legislature. The law sets the maximum tax rate at a very low level and requires that any school system operating above that level receive approval from the voters in referenda held at least every two years.

From 1955 to 1963, the civil rights issue lay dormant. The school system and Hickey had received much praise throughout the United States for the speed and success of their desegregation program immediately after the Supreme Court decision of 1954. But throughout this era of good feeling, there was an undercurrent of racial protest. The schools were *de facto* segregated, with over 90 per cent of the Negroes attending segregated schools.[1]

The Negro community was, during this time, split into an uneasy alliance between the professional politicians (who were affiliates of the North Side organization) and the Negro business elite. The ward political bosses were "welfare oriented," primarily concerned with obtaining their share of the jobs and favors to be distributed; the business elite represented an old St. Louis elite that was somewhat more militant on racial matters. By 1963, the left wing of the Negro community had become mobilized around a growing CORE chapter and the voice of a young turk politician, William Clay.

During this period, the basic racial ecology of the city was being drastically altered by the Mill Creek urban renewal project. In 1950 the Negro population was concentrated in the old center-city wards. As has happened in many cities, these wards were bulldozed. The Negro population was displaced into the West

[1]Throughout this report, we will use "segregated" to mean a school enrolling over 90 per cent of one race. Our conventional measure of segregation will be the percentage of Negroes attending such schools. (See Appendix 2 for a discussion of this particular measure, and a table comparing the school systems studied.)

End. In 1950 the West End area had a population of 83,000 people, and it was 99 per cent white. Ten years later, it was 30 per cent white. Now an influx of young, Protestant families filled the public schools far beyond capacity. School bond proposals were defeated repeatedly, so that by the time a bond issue was finally passed to build new elementary schools in the West End, the schools were already badly overcrowded. In 1955 the school system began transporting the excess children to empty classrooms in all corners of the city. However, the predominantly Negro students arrived in the all-white receiving schools in "contained units"—they arrived a few minutes later than other students and attended classes only with their bus-mates. In part, the contained units were a solution to a complex logistics problem involving bus schedules; also, in some schools the transportees heavily outnumbered the resident students so that the integrated schools would be racially imbalanced. And in the mid-1950's, when the entire bussing program was running great risk of segregationist opposition, contained units were probably the only realistic approach. By 1963, however, the civil rights leadership saw the segregation of transported students as a slap in the face.

This was but one of the factors that made the West End situation explosive. In addition, there was considerable complaint from parents who resented the overcrowded schools, and many parents objected to having their children bussed, whether in contained units or not. Most important, the white families who had stayed in the West End and organized to stabilize the area racially were losing the battle and unhappy about it.

In the election in the spring of 1963, the final third of the school board seats were filled by the reform slate. The school system also held its regular referendum to receive approval to levy taxes above the state maximum. They received the approval by fewer than three hundred votes this time. In the spring, the *de facto* segregation issue spread through much of the country and caught fire in St. Louis' West End.

THE WEST END COMMUNITY CONFERENCE REPORT

The West End Community Conference was an organization of middle-class whites and Negroes dedicated to maintaining stable integration. The group was led by Mrs. Ann Voss, a white housewife who succeeded her husband as president and who devoted tremendous energy to the organization.

On March 17, 1963, the Conference issued a report, charging that the schools in the West End were more segregated than could be accounted for by housing segregation. They specifically accused the board of permitting white students to transfer out of schools in the area while refusing Negroes the same privilege. They also charged that the school board's plan to move Harris Teachers College (the teachers college operated by the public schools) out of the West End would discourage whites from staying in the area, and they raised the issue of segregation of the transported pupils. They asked for the appointment of a committee to study the question. The school board met a few days later to discuss the report and consider appointing a commission. Immediately, the NAACP, a young turk Negro politician, William Clay, CORE, and other civil rights groups began to make statements.

The school board held a public hearing, at which these groups presented testimony. The meeting was long and the testimony disorganized. In response, the school administration prepared a document, replying, as its title said, to 136 charges made at the hearings. By merely presenting a long catalogue of charges made, this report had the effect of belittling the central issues, such as the teachers college and the transportation program, by surrounding them with more trivial charges. It lumped together statements made by everyone, including some by board vice-president Hicks. Finally, it produced a flat "no" as an answer to everything. Needless to say, the quality of the arguments used to demolish the charges varied considerably. Although the report served a useful function in rebutting some of the false charges, the tone of the document was such as to add fuel to the flames.

At the same time, the board itself was in the process of naming the commission requested by the West End Community Conference and the NAACP. In retrospect, one of the most important actions taken by the school board was the appointment of this commission. It was appointed at the very beginning of the controversy and instructed to report quickly; in addition, the commission was made up of persons acceptable to the civil rights movement. The Negro school board members had been consulted for names—not only Hicks, but the more militant James Hurt. The Catholic diocese, under the leadership of Cardinal Ritter and St. Louis University, has a liberal slant, and from this community the board selected as its chairman a man with impeccable credentials as an integrationist—Trafford Maher, S. J., of the education school of St. Louis University. The man primarily responsible for the selection of the committee was Schlafly, who was then board president.

The Maher committee had been asked to make an interim report on the Harris Teachers College question. Their report endorsed the move of the teachers college out of the West End. Hicks sharply criticized the report, and he, the other two Negroes, and a white Episcopal minister, Allan Zacher, voted against the motion to transfer the school. The weight of logic was on the side of the transfer. It seems unlikely that keeping the teachers college in its present location (a few doors from the residence of Mrs. Voss, the West End Conference leader) would encourage any of its white faculty or students to remain living in the area.

THE DEMONSTRATIONS

But it was unfortunate that this demand of the West End group had to be singled out and rejected at this time, since it led the civil rights leaders to expect more unfavorable rulings when the Maher commission completed its report. During the first week of June, Mrs. Voss met with Charles Oldham, a long-time labor lawyer and an ex-national chairman of CORE, Dr. Jerome Williams, and William Clay. These men were probably the most important leaders in the militant wing of the St. Louis civil rights movement. They decided to raise again the issue of the segregation of the bussing program and testified before the school board on June 5. When the board failed to respond to their testimony, they decided to blockade the buses which would pick up West End pupils. On June 7, the buses were blockaded by a small group of civil rights leaders. Two days later the schools recessed for the summer.

At this point Schlafly called for the board to obtain a court ruling on the legality of the bussing program. James McClellan made the motion, but Dr. Robert Rainey proposed an amendment that the ruling should be sought only if the Maher commission, whose report was due that month, recommended retaining bussing in contained units. Apparently Rainey's amendment was accepted by McClellan, although this vote is not a matter of record; the final motion read that the ruling would be requested after the Maher commission had reported. (The wording is important. If the board had asked for an immediate ruling, it would have appeared to commit the board to retaining contained units regardless of the Maher recommendations.)

By mid-June, the original demands had been broadened to include a general plea for a program of integration of both pupils and staff. At this point, the protesters announced that they would put on a demonstration outside the school board offices on the evening of June 20. Mayor Tucker publicly asked them to cancel the demonstrations. The protesters had three principal demands: (1) that the transported pupils be fully integrated at receiving schools; (2) that faculties be integrated; and (3) that school district boundaries be redrawn to insure maximum integration. On June 20, 1963, the protesters demonstrated, and the next evening the Board of Education met, the Maher commission reported, and the board voted to do two things—to submit the report to Superintendent Hickey for a reply, and to start holding public hearings on the report.

The Maher report, while avoiding any direct criticism of the school system, made a series of recommendations, including the integration of faculties, the integration of the transported students, and the adoption of an open enrollment program. The *Post-Dispatch* reported that unidentified members of the school administration viewed the recommendations as unrealistic. After the citizens' committee report, the Patrons Alliance, a city-wide organization, functioning somewhat in competition with the PTA and quite conservative in outlook, opposed the report.

Superintendent Hickey's health was already failing at this point, and Deputy Superintendent Kottmeyer, who had been instrumental in drawing up the "136 replies," was put in charge of preparing the administration's reaction to the Maher report. There was considerable change in tone between the two documents. Whereas the earlier one had made it clear that there was little at fault in the system, this one stated that the school system was going to do something. Still, it was not completely clear what that something was. The report promised to terminate the contained unit bussing device, but then proceeded to list statistics showing that the logistics of moving pupils across the city required that pupils arrive late, leave early, etc., so that this new policy could not be put in effect in the coming fall. The report also noted the problem of maintaining racial balance in receiving schools. Several new elementary schools would be opened during the next year; if this did not eliminate bussing entirely, it would simplify the logistics and racial balance problems. The report went on to list a series of other changes that would be made: more teaching staffs would be integrated, action would be taken on the vocational education program, and tactics would be adopted to prevent white transfers from high schools in the West End. When this somewhat ambiguous document was presented to the board, there was very little discussion, and the board voted (this time eight to three on racial lines) to accept the staff's recommendations. It was probably not clear to anyone when the school system actually intended to integrate all its receiving schools in the transportation program. It was possible when the new schools were opened, the bussing would be stopped completely. (In fact, it was going to integrate several, but not all, that fall. The following year the new schools were opened in the West End, and the bussing program was cut back to seven hundred students. With this reduction, it was possible to integrate all receiving schools. In 1965, it was increased again to 2,600 students, and all receiving schools were still integrated.)[2]

Meanwhile, the board was faced with a racial issue which was not a matter of administrative prerogative. The board presidency was about to be vacated, as Schlafly completed his turn in the revolving office in October. Traditionally, the board would elect its vice-president as the new president. But the vice-president was Hicks. Was St. Louis ready to see a Negro as its school board president? Was the middle of the integration squabble the right time? The board decided to find out and elected Hicks its new president.

[2]The school administration's position is that it is possible to integrate the bussed students only if the total number of transportees is small enough to permit short traveling distances and to maintain racial balance. They consider 2,600 to be very near the maximum possible number that can be integrated.

The next step in the civil rights battle was the NAACP's decision to file suit against what they called the Hickey-Kottmeyer plan. The board filed its suit to determine the legality of bussing by contained units. It also went to court to obtain an injunction to prevent a school boycott threatened by the NAACP. But in fact, although the civil rights leadership did not know it, the battle was over. More important, and this they also did not know, they had won. The segregated bussing program would be phased out, steps to increase faculty integration would be taken, and the board had committed itself to integration. One plausible interpretation of what happened here is that the school system decided to walk the tightrope between the civil rights groups and the segregationists by integrating the schools, but on a slow timetable, and without publicly advertising it more than necessary. In any case, the Negro board members, Hicks and Hurt, were now ready to oppose any attempt to boycott the schools.

SETTLEMENT

The uneasy coalition between the conservative NAACP and the direct action groups had already fallen to pieces by this time. During July, while the board was deciding what to do with the Maher report, Dr. Williams called for another conference meeting of all the interested community groups and involved individuals. According to one militant, this meeting was "stacked with NAACP people and the conservatives of the community." It was decided that the education issue should be left up to the Education Committee of the NAACP. The counterstrategy of the militant wing was simple. They formed a new organization called ACT, included some other organizations to legitimate their own claim to city-wide representation, and decided that the Education Committee of the NAACP would be required to report to them. The NAACP (and several Negro political leaders) took a stand against this power play.

With the Negro school board members now supporting the Hickey proposals, the militants were completely isolated. The militants picketed Hicks' home, but as they prepared to send pickets to Hickey's house, he suffered a severe stroke. These moves were only half-hearted in any case. Most of the militants were becoming involved in the picketing of the Jefferson Bank in support of a demand to hire Negroes. Meanwhile the NAACP continued to threaten a boycott; they scheduled a huge rally for the Sunday before the opening of school. But on the day of the rally, a demonstration at the Jefferson Bank resulted in the arrest of Oldham and other leaders. At the time of the rally, Mrs. Oldham and Clay were leading a huge march the other way, to picket the city jail. Needless to say, the school rally was a flop. Thus ended the school integration issue, six months after it had begun, and three months after the first demonstration.

The militants in the civil rights movement, including at least one of the Negro school board members, were unhappy with the outcome. During the following year, various efforts were made to reopen the issue, but this received little community support. The following year, all transported pupils were successfully integrated into receiving schools. (A segregationist protest during the fall of 1963 had been successfully squelched.)

There is little question that the school board survived the storm. In 1964, board president Hicks resigned to take a church in New York. Mayor Tucker appointed as his replacement another minister, Dr. Amos Ryce, who had led the boycott of the school busses. James McClellan, a corporation lawyer, became board president. In 1965, when Hicks' seat came up for election, the citizens' committee which had reformed the board attached Ryce to their slate. Only one opposition candidate (supported by the teachers union) ran against the four slate endorsees, and the slate was elected handily. Schlafly, running for reelection, ran very well in the Negro wards. Also in 1965, the board held its tax referendum. This time it was defeated. However, the electorate was not serious in its vote to push the school system over the brink; in a second election held a few weeks later, the tax rate was endorsed overwhelmingly. When the response of the wards to the tax in 1965 is compared to 1963, a general increase in support throughout the city is apparent. However, the most impressive increases were in the Negro wards, where the percentage voting "yes" increased from 74 per cent in 1963 to 89 per cent in 1965. Both Schlafly and the schools had received votes of confidence from the Negro voters. Meanwhile, the white voters had forgiven or forgotten the picketing done by Ryce. Whereas in 1961 only 69 per cent of the white voters who voted for the slate had voted for the Negro member, in 1965 Ryce received 76 per cent of their votes.

INTERPRETATION

The first question is, Who influenced the outcome of the desegregation decision? It seems clear to us that the general decision to look for ways to meet some of the demands of the civil rights movement was made by the board. The leaders of the bus boycott made an unsuccessful effort to involve Mayor Tucker, but he apparently played no significant role. None of the city's other elected officials were involved. While Superintendent Kottmeyer drew the actual plans, it also seems clear that the board both explicitly and implicitly let him know that he should "do something to let the steam out."

In the original reform the board members were dependent on a group of influential businessmen for the financing of their election campaigns.[3] But there is no evidence that these "angels," who had also helped support bond campaigns, influenced the board overtly. At most, various board members may have wondered a bit about their reaction to the situation, but it seems most likely that the elites felt they had "delegated" responsibility for making school decisions to their "representatives" on the board. (We must also remember that Schlafly had originally recruited their support, so that he, at least, was in no sense a delegate of theirs.)

The school board's decision was complicated by the apparent turn-around in the goals of the Negro community. In the middle 1950's the West End was concerned about the overcrowded schools, and there was objection to the bussing program. Of course, the West End voted heavily in favor of bonds to build new schools. However, before the schools were completed, the complaint was changed; bussing was now seen as a way of integrating schools, and the opposition was to the segregation of the transported pupils. After 1963 the most militant of the civil rights leaders were opposing the opening of what they were now calling ghetto schools. Actually, this seemingly complete reversal is not as peculiar as it appears in retrospect, and similar changes of course occurred in other cities as well.

[3]Some of our respondents argued that the "angels" played a minor role, with Schlafly almost single-handedly running the campaigns.

One possible thesis is that the school board did not satisfy the protesters; rather the fundamental split in the civil rights movement was not mendable, and regardless of the outcome of the issue, the movement would have collapsed from the weight of its internal struggles. There is some truth to this. When the militants lost control of the school integration movement, it would be logical for them to start hunting for another issue.[4] However, had the school board played the role of the villain, then all the members of the movement, including the Negro board members, would have been forced to follow public opinion and continue battling with the school. In a sense, the militants' feeling may have been one of futility—futility in that the school system was not making the concessions they wanted, but at the same time was making enough concessions to prevent the militants from gaining much community support. The rather progressive race relations in other aspects of the community also kept the Negro leadership from becoming more militant. The City Council was passing civil rights legislation, Negroes were being appointed to governmental positions, and the Catholic diocese was strongly committed to integration. In addition, Daniel Schlafly commented to us that the police department helped the situation by its judicious handling of the demonstrations.

The militants' position would have been much more sharply undercut if the board had chosen to give the symbols of victory to the civil rights movement. If they had clearly stated that they were going to capitulate, that the segregation of the transportation program was wrong and would stop, then the movement would have felt free to celebrate. In fact, many of the civil rights leaders did not know what they had won. There was no guarantee that the bussing program would ever be integrated, and there was the distinct possibility that rather than do that, the bussing program would be stopped entirely. (The board, after all, could have used portable classrooms to alleviate the overcrowding.) The wording of the Maher report, and the board's adoption of a policy statement committing it to integration, were important symbolic victories, but the rest was rather vague.

[4]Actually, there is a relationship between the Jefferson Bank and the schools. One reason why the bank was singled out is that the school system kept its funds there. More important, the Jefferson Bank has ties to St. Louis politics.

If we look at the reality, instead of the symbols, we see that the board actually should have angered the segregationists more than the civil rights movement. The board could have defended bussing by contained units (and, in starting to seek a court ruling on its legality, almost did this). It could have denied that the facilities were segregated. It could have rejected the Maher report. But the school system gave enough, so that if it did not satisfy the militants, it at least won the grudging approval of the Negro business elite, the Negro board members, and some of the grass roots. The board did meet many of the integrationist demands, but they also managed to prevent a segregationist explosion. They succeeded in getting offstage before the tightrope could break.

In none of the other cities will we find an administrative action that has had as much effect on the number of students in integrated schools as in St. Louis. In the absence of the bussing program, the schools would be quite segregated, with only 10 per cent of the Negro students and 14 per cent of the white students in integrated schools. However, during 1965–66 the bussing of 2,600 Negro students into predominantly white schools increased the percentage of Negroes and whites in integrated schools to 14 and 36 per cent, respectively. The bussing program has tripled the number of whites in integrated schools.[5]

Why did the board acquiesce as much as they did? One reason, quite simply, is that the major actors were basically liberal in their orientation toward racial issues. For example, McClellan, in comment on Hicks' election to the presidency, said that it was important to show the white community that the board members "weren't prejudiced." In saying this, McClellan reveals that his reference group is the liberal white community and the community elite. (He, like most of the board members, is a resident of the fashionable and reform-oriented Forest Park area.)

Similarly, although some of Schlafly's public remarks could be interpreted as hostile to the civil rights movement, Schlafly had been instrumental in appointing the liberal Maher committee (and the early appointment of this liberal committee virtually determined the outcome). Or to go back farther in time, Schlafly had attempted to recruit a Negro to the board, and he did not try to

[5]The St. Louis statistical data do not permit a precise calculation, but these figures should be reasonably accurate.

select an "Uncle Tom" in the place of Hicks or Hurt. One board member commented of William Kottmeyer that "He was the sort of man who could kick the door shut and say, 'You're right—that is discrimination and I know it. Here's what I want to do about it. . . .' " This sort of candidness would have also been valuable.

A second reason why the board was able to respond to the demands made on it was that its lines of communication to the Negro community were very good. Here, much of the credit must go to Hicks. During his time on the board, Hicks had managed to earn the wholehearted respect of the white board members, while at the same time retaining his position as an integrationist. In addition, the necessity of producing a Negro-reform coalition had forced the white board members to build relationships with important Negro community leaders—particularly the influential editor of the *Argus,* Howard Woods. The schools' public relations firm was also in close touch with Woods. In passing, we should observe that one uniting force in the Negro community is the highly developed Negro business elite. Neither militant nor conservative, they were an important couterweight to the more conservative Negro politicians. Standing in the middle of the Negro community, they were in touch with Hicks, Hurt, Mrs. Oldham (who is the daughter of a prominent St. Louis Negro family), and the NAACP.

The final major point we wish to make is that the decision-making authority was highly centralized, partly at least because of the interlocking web of "exchange" relations between the actors. Kottmeyer, for example, had several reasons to respect his board, for they had reformed the schools and recruited the business support for the tax referenda. The board members also owed debts to each other, and particularly to Schlafly, for organizing the slate and running the reform campaign. In turn, Schlafly could be grateful to Hicks and Hurt for their support of the reform movement.

The result was a highly unified decision-making structure that could hold the respect of diverse elements of the community. But ultimately, the centralizing force was money and prestige, contributed by the businessmen who had financed the reform. A question that will be raised in the analysis of all eight cities is the effect of having an elected, rather than appointed, school board. The St. Louis board members generally like serving on an elected board. And the board certainly handled the integration issue with more skill than some of the appointed boards we will examine. Nevertheless, it must be remembered that the slate is inherently an unstable force, because of the drain of the biennial election campaigns upon it. It is easier to recruit candidates and funds when the glamour of reform is in the air. In 1965, without this appeal, and with the race issue hovering in the background, the slate was able to function. (It recruited a lawyer with impressive credentials to fill a vacancy on the board, and it accepted Ryce as a slate member.) But it has not been in operation very long, and the future is always unpredictable.

If St. Louis handled the integration issue with more skill than some of the other appointed boards, our other two northern elected boards did not do as well. We shall look at those two boards next, and later try to make some generalizations about the effect of election and appointment on school board behavior.

3

Lawndale

Lawndale is a city of less than one-half million population in the western United States. Compared with other western cities, it has a large and growing Negro population; it is also losing its middle-class residents to the suburbs.

The change in population has also begun to threaten the end of Republican rule. In any nonpartisan city it is difficult to talk about political groups, which are usually very fluid. However, we will oversimplify somewhat and consider Lawndale as having three major political factions. Most important is a group we will call main-line Republicans; this is a group of conservative businessmen and professional politicians. The liberal Republicans are less influential; they are centered around another group of businessmen, including some executives in heavy industry. The Democrats in our analysis are a heterogeneous collection; labor leaders, intellectuals, civil rights leaders, and professional politicians. It must be understood that when we say that the school board is made up of main-line Republicans, this does not mean that they were nominated by the Republican party as such, but that they are loosely identified with them.

The school board is the only part of government still in conservative Republican hands. In state and national elections, Lawndale votes Democratic. In 1961 a liberal Republican, Thomas Kelly, defeated a main-line Republican in the election for mayor. Kelly, the son of an Irish policeman, ran a "clean" and "progressive" city government in the eyes of the voters and was re-elected easily.

Interviewing by Thomas M. Landye and James J. Vanecko; first draft by Landye. The superintendent and several members of the school board objected to our analysis in this city. Consequently, we have substituted pseudonyms for the name of the city and the persons involved and have made other changes to maintain the anonymity of the informants.

Lawndale's seven-member school board is in theory elected, but until recently it has been virtually self-perpetuating. Traditionally, whenever a member retired from office, he did so in the middle of his term, so that his successor could be appointed by the other board members. The successor, running as an incumbent, was then elected. Between 1931 and 1958, this formula was used to appoint nineteen new members to the board; in only one case was a new member elected to the board directly. Its present president is a defeated state assemblyman, but another member is a past president of the National Association of School Boards. We might thus think of the board as having had a traditional division between school-oriented members and aspiring or retired politicians; but it is also important to remember that they represented a homogeneous group of white Protestant main-line Republicans. In the last decade, one seat has been held by a Catholic Democratic labor representative, but his labor and Democratic party affiliations are only token. In 1958 a Negro, also a Republican, was appointed.

1956: A SCHOOL FOR THE MIDDLE CLASS

In 1956 the peculiar geography of Lawndale was well suited to high school racial and socioeconomic integration. The low-income and Negro residents were spread along one side of the city. The city had five high schools, arranged in a more or less straight line the length of the city. The northernmost school served a small blue collar area, and this school, Norton, was a predominantly Negro school by 1945. The remaining four schools were "comprehensive" schools, districted so that every school served both rich and poor. Negroes then moved into the low-income areas, with the result that most of Lawndale's Negroes were distributed neatly in predominantly white high schools; every school except Norton was integrated. However, new middle-income housing was being built in "the Woods," on the opposite side of the city from the Negroes. And of course, a growing population meant that more school space was needed. The result was growing community demand for a new school to serve the Woods. The Lawndale school board was responsive to this. (Most of its board lived in the Woods, but in any case the city was conscious of its need to stop the flow of whites into the suburbs.) But a school for the wealthy would disrupt the city's pattern of comprehensive high schools. Two bond issues were defeated partly because of the conflict over the new school. Apparently, the final resolution of the conflict was to build the new school, but also to appease the Norton community by upgrading their school with some of the bond money.

When the bond issue was finally approved, a site for Woodside High School was selected at the very edge of the city boundary. Obviously, this new school would have considerable impact on the racial balance of the other schools, but until it was finished and boundaries set, no one would know how profound this impact would be.

While the school was being built, the board made an additional concession to the Negro community. In 1958 a vacancy appeared on the board, and the board leadership and the Republican party offered the seat to a Negro Republican lawyer who had been one of the spokesmen for Norton, James Clendon. However, presumably because Clendon was Negro, he was not appointed to fill the vacancy. Instead, the vacancy was allowed to remain until the election, and Clendon, with the support of the other board members, was elected to fill the empty seat.

1961: THE SECOND WOODSIDE DISPUTE

In January, 1961, the school board began to discuss setting boundaries for the new school. At the first meeting, it became clear that the board had in mind that Woodside would serve the entire Woods area. This meant that the school would serve an all-white area roughly ten miles long and only one mile wide. Such a school boundary could not be rationalized convincingly. There is no road that runs directly the length of the Woods. Thus students at either end of the district would have to travel through another school district in order to reach the new school. Woodside was a neighborhood school only in the sense that the community it served was of a single racial and economic group. The impact on the other schools in Lawndale would have been considerable, since three high schools which had had relatively small Negro enrollments would now have larger Negro percentages.

The NAACP opposed these boundaries, and they were supported by a prominent civic organization, the Conference on Public

Education (COPE). COPE can be thought of as representing that sector of the civic elite who took a more liberal view than the main-line Republicans. But COPE was also rebuffed.

In March the board approved a ten-mile long district for Woodside. Only Clendon, the Negro, voted against the motion. The school was opened in September. The NAACP apparently took no action in response to this. As we shall see, throughout the Woodside dispute, the civil rights movement was very reluctant to take any action, either in the courts or in the streets.

1962: THE WOODSIDE DISPUTE, PHASE THREE

In May, 1961, two months after the vote on the Woodside boundaries, Dr. William Gordon was elected to the board, defeating a Republican. Gordon is a physician and an active liberal Democrat. He immediately began to criticize the operations of the schools and the quality of Lawndale education. By taking a strong stand on integration he encouraged Clendon to further break with the rest of the board, and they sometimes voted together on non-racial matters.

During the next year the board was engrossed in the problem of replacing retiring Superintendent John Walsh. The issue was whether to bring in another "outsider" like Walsh, or not. (Walsh and the previous superintendent have national reputations.) It seems clear that one of the board's most influential members, Gregory Foote (an ex-state assemblyman) favored a "local" appointment. Finally, on April 27, 1962, the board voted to promote Assistant Superintendent Stephen Jones (Gordon and Clendon voted against the appointment).[1]

Immediately after Jones' election early in 1962, Gordon reopened the Woodside issue. He proposed that the Woodside district be redrawn and that the total enrollment be reduced so that students from outside the district would be able to transfer voluntarily.

At the next board meeting, CORE chairman William Turner, NAACP president James Wadsworth, and a crowd of five hun-

[1]The issue of appointing an "outsider" versus an "insider" was hotly debated, with at one point a majority voting to offer the job to a prominent eastern superintendent. One informant argued that Foote intentionally insulted the candidate in order to persuade him to refuse the offer.

dred of their supporters appeared. The board listened to their statements, and the outgoing superintendent, Walsh, made a statement rejecting all their demands. In some respects, Walsh's statement was unconvincing. For example, he explained that changing school boundaries might cost as much as four million dollars, but he did not explain this statement. He went on to comment that the Lawndale school board was not required by law to eliminate *de facto* segregation. Finally, Walsh stated that the board did not keep racial statistics, and therefore it was impossible to know whether Gordon's proposals would result in increased integration.

Board member Foote picked up the "color blind" theme, stating that it was wrong to consider race in the drawing of school boundaries. Immediately after these statements, the board voted to reaffirm the original boundaries. The other proposal advanced by Turner, that the board appoint a citizens' committee, was supported by a variety of civic groups. Finally, in August, 1962, the board voted to establish a citizens' committee to study the school's finances, building needs, and racial problems.

The citizens' committee was nearly stillborn. In October, the board voted to invite the seven organizations that had asked for the citizens' committee to nominate three members each to serve on it. These included the NAACP, CORE, four religious groups, and a "white liberal" organization. But they then rejected a proposed statement by Clendon which should have put the board on record as wanting to correct *de facto* segregation, and closed the meeting by tabling an open enrollment plan proposed by the new superintendent, Jones.

The NAACP then replied to its invitation to designate three members of the citizens' committee with a flat refusal to cooperate. At the same time, the board continued to strain its relationship with the civil rights groups by appointing as the chairman of the citizens' committee Clarence T. Wilkerson, who had previously served as chairman of the bond issue campaigns and was generally considered to be a conservative on racial matters. However, the board did reverse itself and adopt Clendon's policy statement.

Several efforts were made in the next few months to satisfy the NAACP. During November, another board member, Milton

Clark, presented a resolution stating that since "concentration of minority groups" was unfortunate, the board should counteract this by expanding a program of compensatory education. While compensatory education may have been a useful bargaining tool in 1956, it was no help now.

Jones brought up his open enrollment plan again in December. Basically, the plan permitted voluntary transfers from any school to any other if space was available. However, Woodside had no empty space—in fact, the new boundaries resulted in the school using portable classrooms—so that no one would be able to enter the disputed school as a result of the plan. At the second meeting devoted to the open enrollment plan, Foote argued in favor of placing more portables at Woodside to permit open enrollment. However, he did not put up a strong fight for his amendment and it was defeated. It seems likely that had this motion been adopted, the civil rights movement might have been partly satisfied. A vigorous effort on the part of the school board to get as few as one hundred Negroes into Woodside at this time might have been sufficient to satisfy the movement.

Clendon made one last effort to entice the NAACP back into supporting the citizens' committee. He proposed that the board charge the citizens' committee to make a judgment on whether *de facto* segregation was harmful. Gordon fought to amend the motion, the meeting dragged on, and finally the board voted to adopt the Gordon-Clendon Joint Resolution, which instructed the committee to make "reasonable" recommendations to reduce minority group concentrations. After eight months, the board had agreed that the citizens' committee could prepare an integration plan. Lest the board retreat from its position, Gordon dashed to the TV cameras to make the announcement. With this, the NAACP agreed to cooperate with the committee, and the committee began deliberations.

With establishment of the committee, the third phase of the Woodside dispute came to an end. With the NAACP and CORE both participating in the citizens' committee, the civil rights movement was more or less content to wait for the report to be completed, and the committee did not submit its report until the summer of 1964.

1964: WOODSIDE PHASE FOUR, THE COMMITTEE REPORT

It was generally assumed that the presence of Wilkerson as chairman of the citizens' committee would prevent the committee from proposing any major changes. However, the liberals on the committee, the civil rights leaders, and the liberal Republicans managed to wrest control of the committee away from the chairman and drove through a report which, while moderate on other points, proposed a redrawing of Woodside's boundaries. While the plan would not have districted any Negroes into Woodside, it would have returned some whites to other high schools and prevented these schools from becoming as heavily Negro. In effect, the proposed redistricting would have made Woodside serve only the immediate geographic area. The committee also proposed a redistricting to increase the number of whites in Norton. Finally, the report advocated that the open enrollment program be keyed to the integration issue by setting as its goals the relief of schools with heavy concentrations of minority groups and the improvement of racial balance wherever possible. The open enrollment program adopted by the board was essentially color blind, although it did give preference to students in overcrowded schools.

When the committee report was released, the school system scheduled a series of public hearings on the report. Although it is difficult to be sure what happened here, it would appear that some members of the board approached neighborhood groups in the Woodside area and encouraged them to give testimony on the report. The board scheduled a series of public hearings, during which time the opposition to the report grew steadily. After some five months of community discussion, the board met, and the president (at this time Clark) led a discussion in which the five members of the majority arrived at a consensus that the Woodside boundary change was unimportant from the point of view of integration, and that any serious attempt to stabilize the racial composition of the other schools would require constant redistricting. But they also recognized that it would be good if some sort of concession could be made. Foote consulted Gordon, and they drafted a resolution asking the superintendent to produce a plan to extend open enrollment and to develop a master plan for integration which would include the possibility of phasing out the all-Negro Norton school. Foote was quoted as saying, "I think the support of the whole community would be behind us on that."

This ended the fourth round of the Woodside battle—some eight years after it began. But whereas the St. Louis controversy had merely consolidated the hold of the school board, the aftermath of the Woodside fight was one of the most heated school election campaigns in the city's history. In 1965 Gordon and the most liberal member of the majority bloc, Margaret Willis, resigned from the board. Incumbents Foote and Clark, two of the most influential of the majority bloc, were up for reelection.

The majority bloc of the board had to find two candidates for the vacant seats. It cleared the nominations of Lois Coxe and Harold Smith for Mrs. Willis's and Gordon's seats, respectively. Mrs. Coxe, a defeated candidate for Congress, was identified with the radical right; Smith was a typical Republican candidate for the board. A liberal slate of candidates was informally supported by the Central Labor Council, the Democratic party, the civil rights groups, and a group of Gordon's advisers. The slate included John Schwartz (a Jewish attorney), running for Gordon's seat; a Negro junior college teacher, Rosemary Snow, for Mrs. Willis's seat; and a Negro minister running against Foote. Other candidates were entered with the support of a rival Democratic organization, the ultraconservatives, and the segregationist Woodside property owners, but they were all defeated in the preliminary election. In the runoff election, one of the vacant seats was captured by the liberals (by Schwartz, with 51 per cent of the vote), and Mrs. Coxe's Negro opponent obtained 47 per cent of the vote in losing. The board actually became somewhat more conservative, with the replacement of Mrs. Willis by Mrs. Coxe, but the majority had little cause to rejoice. The liberals were able to consolidate their position by successfully replacing Gordon and came very close to adding a second Negro to the board. Lawndale can expect future elections to be interesting, even though the school board has recently adopted a more extensive integration plan including bussing of Negro elementary school children.

INTERPRETATION

Who were the actors in this decision? We think that the decisions were, in fact, made by the board without outside consultation, although this is not obvious. Since the board majority were associated through the Republican party, it is at least possible that the key decisions were made by party leaders. However, it is not likely that any important discussion of school integration could have taken place in the Republican Central Committee without our hearing of it. A very prominent Republican owns the city newspaper, but it also strikes us as unlikely that he played a direct or consistent role in the issue; certainly no one suggested to us that he did. In fact, we do know that throughout most of the controversy the paper covered the schools with a reporter openly sympathetic to the liberals.

Mayor Kelly has publicly disassociated himself from the school board. It seems likely that his relations with the board are strained. Finally, the liberal sector of the civic elite has attempted to influence the board, but has only been able to do so through the citizens' committee. COPE's earlier attempts to influence the boundaries of Woodside were ignored, even though its chairman was the most prominent industrialist in the city.

Although the Woodside controversy was long and complicated, it is really a simple story. The majority members of the board clung to their original plan—to provide a homogeneously middle-class white school—throughout the debate.[2] Faced with opposition, they attempted to meet it in four ways: First, they adopted, under Foote's leadership, a highly legalistic, color-blind approach, which suggested that the school board's behavior was legitimate if it merely conformed to the *Brown* decision. By claiming a color-blind position, they were able to delay taking a racial census and were able to avoid making open enrollment a policy with direct relationship to integration. Second, they attempted to meet the demands for integration with plans for compensatory education. The action the board took with respect to compensatory education is not discussed in this study simply because it is of little or no political relevance. The civil rights movement did not accept the premise that there was an equation connecting these two goals. Third, the school board seemed to have a conscious strategy of delay, so that each action was put off as long as possible. Fourth,

---

[2]Eventually open enrollment led to the presence of over one hundred Negroes in Woodside, but this took place too late to have an impact on the conflict. There was no objection to the arrival of the Negroes.

when these two approaches did not solve their problems, the board allowed the Woodside community to mobilize to oppose integration.

In response to the board's action, the civil rights movement took virtually no direct action except in the election campaigns. The closest thing to a demonstration was the five hundred spectators in the May, 1962, meeting. Where the civil rights movement has taken action, the board has been responsive; for example, the open enrollment plan was at least partly the result of the NAACP's suit and its refusal to serve on the citizens' committee. It seems likely that had the civil rights movement organized a demonstration, particularly in the fall of 1962, the board might have been more acquiescent. The NAACP did make a halfhearted boycott threat in 1964. A suit against the board had not moved into court at the time of our study.

Why, then, do we find in Lawndale a protracted controversy with no resolution? We can cite the following possible reasons:

1. The board and its critics became hampered by their own ideology. In reading over its struggles with policy statements, one gets the impression that the board has been more willing to support integration in practice than in principle. Similarly, the citizens' committee report represents a position with a heavy ideological tone, in which much attention is paid to a "fair" districting of Woodside which does nothing to eliminate segregation. The civil rights movement also concentrated on the Woodside issue. Attempts to focus attention on segregated elementary schools never got off the ground.

2. The insertion of partisan politics into the issue has the effect of polarizing the community, so that the gulf between Gordon and Foote became unbreachable. For the same reason, the Republican Clendon has little influence on the Democratic Negro community or on the Democratic leadership of the civil rights movement. In addition, the desire to strengthen the Democratic party became a goal that conflicted with the goal of winning the integration battle, and may explain in part the unwillingness of the civil rights groups to indulge in direct action.

3. When we have reviewed the other northern cities, we will see that much of the difference between Lawndale and St. Louis can be explained by differences in their boards. The Lawndale school

board has only one member who might be considered a representative of the business elite of the community; Clark is president of a large retail establishment. But the board's political ties are reflected in the fact that of its seven members in 1965, four were lawyers and another was a defeated candidate for public office.

4

Bay City

Bay City was the first large city in the United States to outlaw school segregation (in 1855). Today it has one of the most highly integrated school systems of any city its size. Unlike St. Louis and Lawndale, the Negro population is relatively small (10 per cent of the population). Students attend school outside of this small ghetto under an open-transfer policy. Less than one-half of Bay City's Negro students attend segregated schools. In addition, the remnants of abolitionist sentiment are still visible in New England politics.

But Bay City, with its integrated schools and its liberal traditions, became involved in what was probably the most bitter school integration battle in the North. The battle involved boycotts, sit-ins, new state legislation, a cutoff of federal funds, a court suit, and two election campaigns. And yet, during the first two years, the controversy revolved around a single point—the school board's refusal to adopt a policy statement acknowledging the existence of *de facto* segregated schools. In contrast to St. Louis and Lawndale, the civil rights movement has not accused the board of intentionally segregating schools.

Stated in this fashion, the controversy seems a bit ridiculous. However, when the public debate is put into context, it is not so implausible. It is not, as we thought for some time, simply a question of semantics.

The Bay City school board is an elected body with the unusual provision that all five members must run for election at the same time every two years. All five are elected at large, a fact which, in a predominantly Irish-Catholic city where ethnic loyalties are unusually strong, naturally excludes Negroes, Jews, Protestants, and even non-Irish Catholics. The elections are strictly nonpartisan

Interviewing by Robert T. Stout and Morton Inger; first draft by Inger. As in the chapter on Lawndale, all names of persons and places are fictitious.

and the candidates run on their own, so that an occasional "outsider" may get elected on the basis of a purely personal following. For example, the only Protestant on the present board is the son of a well-known political figure.

The Bay City school board is viewed by some as a political steppingstone, and one man became governor of the state and then a United States cabinet officer after starting out on the school board. Though his success is atypical, his aspirations are not, for the school committee regularly attracts politically ambitious men and women. Each committee member is given an office in which to conduct school business and money to hire a full-time assistant. Traditionally, these educational advisers have spent much of their energy working on their employer's election campaign.

There have been at least two attempts by reform, good-government groups to slate candidates to the school board. The first, known as the New Bay Committee, had a quick spectacular success, then collapsed and faded from sight. Between 1953 and 1959, the board membership reverted to type, and in 1961 four of its five members were young, ambitious Irish politicians. In 1960 a new group was formed—the Citizens for the Bay City Public Schools. Unlike the New Bay group, the Citizens are exclusively concerned with schools. In 1961 a financial crisis broke before the election, and three of the four incumbents running were defeated. The four vacancies were filled by two Citizens candidates, William Thrall and Thomas Kennedy, and two non-Citizens, Mary O'Connor Smith and John Silverstein. These four, plus the surviving incumbent, Francis P. White, made up the school board during the integration controversy.

THE FIRST BOYCOTT

The issue of *de facto* segregation in the Bay City public schools was first raised publicly in June, 1963, and exploded into a major controversy within one week. Preceding that confrontation was a five-year history of what the NAACP calls "concern," but none of their efforts met with any particular success. Finally, on June 12, 1963, the NAACP obtained a school board hearing on the question of school segregation. At the hearing, Superintendent

Patrick McDonough flatly denied the charges.[1] School officials argued that since the school boundaries were not based on ethnic factors, there was nothing the schools need do. In short, there was no problem for the schools to deal with.

Dissatisfied with this response, Negro leaders called for a boy-cott on June 18 unless the school board agreed to thirteen demands which they presented. To head off this boycott, the five school board members and the superintendent met for seven hours on June 15 with four Negro leaders, representing both the NAACP and the direct-action New England Freedom Movement. The NAACP presented the thirteen demands, and twelve were accepted by the school board. The thirteenth was that the board issue a statement recognizing that the schools were *de facto* segregated. The school board refused to use the phrase, *de facto* segregation, and on this point of semantics the seven-hour meeting broke up.

The question is, Why was the board reluctant to use the phrase, and why were the civil rights leaders so insistent on this point? Let us pause to review the five members of the school board, and the motivation behind each of their positions.

1. Mrs. Mary O'Connor Smith is the daughter of a prominent local politician. Mrs. Smith did not obtain a law degree until she was in her middle thirties and ran for the school board soon after. For her, the school board was a political stepping-stone, and it was generally believed that her position would be entirely based upon political calculus. Her home neighborhood, and political base, was a low-income Irish neighborhood.

2. Francis P. White, the only Protestant and the only holdover from the 1959 school board, has an income from his family's firm which enables him to spend five days each week in his board of-fice, answering queries from parents. Now in his sixties, he has served on the board intermittently since the thirties. His political strength lies in the low-income Irish and Italian wards. The civil rights leaders expected him to be conservative on the race issue, but hoped that he might follow the lead of John Silverstein.

[1]Civil rights leaders commented to our interviewers that McDonough was extremely defensive about their complaints and tended to interpret any criticism of the schools as a personal attack.

3. John Silverstein, a Catholic, ran for the school board in 1959, while still in law school. He ran ahead of all other non-incumbents, and in the reform of 1961 he led the ticket. He was then twenty-four years old. He campaigned well, gained votes in both low and high income wards, and received "reform" votes from Jewish and Yankee wards. He had made no secret of his political ambitions and sought the Democratic nomination for lieutenant governor in 1964. Silverstein was placed in a bind— while he wanted to present a compromise that would bail the school board out of the situation, he wanted to avoid being tagged as an integrationist.

4. Thomas Kennedy, then one of the Citizens candidates, is a college instructor. Although a staunch supporter of reform, he was an equally staunch conservative on the school integration issue. Although his support was primarily in the reform wards, he did well enough in some Irish wards to run second to Silverstein in 1961.

5. William Thrall, the other Citizens candidate, is a broker. His electoral support came largely from the Jewish-Negro-Yankee reform wards. Since coming on the board, he had moved rapidly into a strong integrationist position. He was also an aggressive champion of modernizing the Bay City schools. Throughout most of the civil rights controversies, the board voted four to one against Thrall. Although Thrall was successful in introducing some non-racial legislation, his relationship with the three non-reform candidates was becoming more and more strained.

Mrs. Smith took a position at this point to hold a firm line against any concessions to the NAACP on the integration issue. Kennedy was later to say that he was opposed to discussion of *de facto* segregation because the discussion would be a foot in the door that might eventually lead to massive bussing of students. Francis P. White's position may be in part due to his belief that most of the language associated with race relations, including even the words white and Negro, was misleading. The implication of this is to force him into positions that sometimes appear eccentric.

Apparently the civil rights movement was not completely displeased with the outcome of the negotiations. Some of its leaders felt that, in the long run, the boycott would be of more value than a quick settlement. Prior to the school board meeting, a prominent Negro politician called a meeting where several NAACP leaders urged that the boycott be delayed. It seems clear that the political leader who chaired the meeting was opposed to the boycott. However, the two leaders of the New England Freedom Movement, clung to their position that the boycott would be called unless the board agreed unconditionally to all thirteen demands.

In a last-hour effort to avert the boycott, the state's governor tried desperately to act as mediator and arranged for secret negotiating sessions between the school committee and Negro leaders. This was the only time the Bay City school system came close to a workable compromise on the school segregation issue. It seems clear that the governor wanted the school board to adopt a *de facto* segregation statement, and that he had been in close touch with Negro leaders regarding the statement. Hence, John Silverstein, who undertook the responsibility of drafting the statement, could be confident that it would be acceptable to the NAACP. Knowing the intensity of the struggle, the reader may well be surprised at the blandness of the statement:

While the heading under which these matters have been brought to our attention is that of "*de facto* segregation," any thoughtful person will agree that the fact some of our schools are overwhelmingly Negro is not the result of policies of the city's present nor previous school committee. It is, rather, part of a seamless web of many forms of discrimination in housing, and other areas.

Smith and Kennedy could be expected to vote against the statement, but White accepted it; then Thrall upset the apple cart and rejected it, and the boycott was on. Thrall told the interviewer that Silverstein's statement was designed to avoid a boycott: "I was more concerned with the causes of boycotts." In all our cities, it is one of the few cases when a board member took a more militant position than the civil rights leaders; it is the only case of a vote which was a coalition of both extremes against the middle. There are a number of possible reasons for Thrall's vote against the proposal. Probably he simply thought that since the board was going to reject any specific demands for action later, this was as good a spot to provoke the fight as any. The school boycott went off on schedule, only six days after the first meeting with the board. Three-fifths of the Negro pupils in the upper grades were absent on the day of the boycott.

Partly in response to newspaper criticism of its refusal to acknowledge the existence of segregation, the school board established an advisory commission of fourteen citizens to serve as a medium of communication between the schools and the Negro community. The NAACP angrily refused the three seats it was offered and secretly pressured the other Negroes not to serve on this commission. The argument degenerated even further when the school board announced on July 23 that it would no longer discuss racial issues with the NAACP, stating that it would work only with the biracial commission it had set up. In response to this, the school offices were picketed. The school board election came in the midst of this, with all five members up for reelection.

THE 1963 ELECTION

The NAACP campaign supplied Mrs. Smith with more publicity than she could possibly have obtained on her own. Three days before the election, one newspaper carried banner headlines describing a demonstration led by the NAACP, photographed anti-Smith signs, and quoted NAACP leaders urging Negroes to vote.

A number of our informants, both liberals and conservatives, stated that Mrs. Smith had herself used the race issue to stir up the white wards. Finally, to add to the complications of the election, the board voted shortly before the election to replace the retiring Superintendent McDonough by promoting one of his assistants to the post. Both Thrall and Kennedy urged the school board to search for a superintendent from outside the system. In any case, Mrs. Smith received over 60 per cent of the vote. Lagging behind were the other two non-reform candidates, Silverstein and White. Kennedy ran fourth, and Thrall fell farther behind to fifth place. The Citizens for the Bay City Public Schools had entered two other candidates in addition to Kennedy and Thrall, including a Negro. Although neither won a seat, they ran far ahead of the other three non-incumbents in the race. If Mrs. Smith's good showing and Thrall's poor vote can be attributed to the race issue, Kennedy's fourth place vote is a bit mysterious. Silverstein interpreted it as a repudiation of the reformers' attempt to bring in an outsider as superintendent. This seems on its face to be unlikely, but it is as good an explanation as any.

From November on, the controversy continued to boil. The Freedom Movement set the date for its second boycott for February 27, 1964. In another effort to head off a boycott, the board met in a televised public session not to decide what to do about integration, but to decide whether they were willing to meet with the Negro leaders. Silverstein and Thrall supported the motion to meet with them; Kennedy argued that bussing was the only solution to imbalance, and therefore there was no point in discussing it. (The NAACP had not made any statement requesting bussing.) Mrs. Smith argued they should not acknowledge that any problem existed. White voted for the hearings on the grounds that they heard other petitioners, but added that transferring children out of segregated schools would prevent them from receiving compensatory education. The hearing was approved, three to two.

At the hearing, the NAACP requested that the school committee appoint a panel of school board members and NAACP appointees to consult with experts and determine whether segregated schools are harmful to children. The board eventually decided not to establish the panel, voting down Thrall's motion four to one. Mrs. Smith took the most extreme position at this meeting, with a debating style appropriate to a Senate investigating committee. For example, a professor of education spoke on the correlation between integration and educational achievement, only to have his testimony interrupted by Mrs. Smith:

> Smith: Have you ever visited the Bay City schools?
> Professor: No, I . . .
> Smith: Thank you.

At the end of the board's discussion, Mrs. Smith offered a motion to bring legal action against the two boycott leaders, but the motion was defeated four to one.[2]

---

[2]The boycotters were also threatened with court action by the Negro political leader referred to earlier. (In reply, the boycotters obtained the support of white suburbanites who publicly volunteered to pay the fines!) Indeed, throughout the campaign the civil rights movement had considerable white support. One story is that during one of the boycotts, so many white students turned up at one of the "freedom schools" that some of the Negroes had to be bussed to other locations.

On February 27, 1964, over one-fifth of the city's students stayed out of school. And this boycott had its effects. Twenty-four hours later, the State Board of Education ordered an immediate racial census of the public schools and began to organize a study of the effects of racial imbalance on education. With two "task forces" of educators doing the actual study and with a cast of big names lending prestige to the findings, the State School Board conducted a year-long study. The group included a university president, a major industrialist, the Catholic cardinal, and a banker from Bay City's oldest family. Their report, filed in April, 1965, concluded that racial imbalance (1) does exist in the schools and (2) is harmful to both white and Negro pupils. The major recommendations included (1) the immediate closing of many old, predominantly Negro, school buildings; (2) the transfer of those students to other schools; (3) the expansion of school districts and the construction of larger schools in order to draw from both Negro and white neighborhoods; and (4) an immediate mutual transfer of 5,000 Negro and white students in grades three to six in forty-five schools. "The schools involved in the mutual transfers are relatively close together. . . . No extensive cross-city transportation is involved."

The Advisory Commission noted explicitly that it found no evidence that the school committee was to blame for the racial imbalance. On the other hand, the fourth recommendation went well beyond any integration plan in use in any large city. Of course, the recommendations had no legal force.

Only Thrall supported the report. Smith and Kennedy were outraged. It is interesting to note that virtually all their objections were on the subject of bussing. Mrs. Smith was "appalled" at the suggestion of bussing, and referred to the report as "the pompous proclamations of the uninformed." The proposal, she said, "is undemocratic, un-American, absurdly expensive, unworkable, and diametrically opposed to the wishes of the parents of this city."[3]

[3]Mrs. Smith's political star had already risen considerably as a result of her victory in the 1963 school board race. In 1964 she filed in the Democratic primary for state treasurer. Although she gained a majority in Bay City, she ran last in a field of four in the rest of the state, losing badly in most of the suburbs. Thus her political future seems to be limited to the city proper. During the 1965 school board election, there was some newspaper discussion of her possible candidacy for mayor; she did run and lost in 1967.

But this time Kennedy's comment was more provocative than Mrs. Smith's. Kennedy said, "After forty years in education, twenty-five of which were in the Negro area, I am very certain that moving them around is not going to make them learn any better." White said he was convinced that "white children do not want to be transported into schools with a large proportion of backward pupils from unprospering Negro families who will slow down their education." (The NAACP's president publicly referred to these statements as being as dangerous to the well-being of Bay City as Hitler was to Germany and the world.) Superintendent Joseph Braun expressed "deep disappointment" that a panel of such eminent citizens should have come up with such faulty findings and recommendations.

At the same time, the civil rights groups were experimenting with new weapons. CORE obtained a temporary withholding of federal funds from the schools, and the NAACP filed suit. When school opened in the fall of 1965, several Negro elementary schools were overcrowded. The superintendent requested funds to bus these children to less crowded white schools; this was rejected by the board. Up to that time, the school board had been routinely bussing students to relieve overcrowding; it now voted not to make any further increases in the number of students to be transported. The civil rights movement responded by organizing their own transportation program, "Operation Exodus," and moved approximately three hundred students into white schools. There was a furor over whether the students had a right to transfer, and Bay City again found itself making national headlines. The integration issue reached its zenith just in time to have the maximum effect on the 1965 school board elections. This time the Citizens for the Bay City Public Schools decided not to support Kennedy, obviously because of his votes on the race issue. They attempted to turn public attention away from integration and toward other reform issues, but the damage had been done. All five Citizens candidates survived the preliminary election but lost in the general election, including incumbent William Thrall.

INTERPRETATION

In the racial integration issue, the school board has exercised a great deal of autonomy. The governor and the attorney general were unsuccessful in their efforts to intervene, and during the 1965 bussing battle, the mayor publicly supported the bussing program. The state and federal governments may eventually force the school board to back down, but only by threatening to cut off funds. Nor will demonstrations have much effect. Although the board initially was willing to make some compromises to avoid the first boycott, it seems unlikely that under any condition they would have gone far, and in any case the time for compromise is now past. Nor has the change in superintendents had any effect on the board's action, despite the fact that Braun is noticeably more liberal than his predecessors.

The difference between this school board and those in Lawndale and St. Louis is obvious. The school board's five members include two professional politicians whose career demands frequently conflict with the demands placed on them by the schools' needs. If Mrs. Smith feels that cutting off federal funds is necessary for her to be elected mayor, she will have little choice. If the other three members can be considered loyal to the schools, they express their loyalty in drastically different ways. White is a nineteenth century individualist who tends to depend little upon other board members; Kennedy is a conservative on race, and Thrall a fighting reformer who has little opportunity or willingness to associate himself with White or the board's politicos. (One of the other board members described Thrall with the ambiguous phrase "abominably intelligent.")

Even if there were little public controversy, the board would still be hampered by its natural internal conflict. With the board members competing with each other for votes every two years, and with each struggling to maintain his constituency, they are naturally in conflict.[4] At board meetings, discussion tends to ramble on for hours. As we have noted, the pattern of voting is erratic, and there are no two members who have not disagreed on one of the major issues facing the board. On the five-member board, it is difficult to predict who will be the "swing" member of any

[4]Even routine administrative matters are affected by the school board's style of decision-making. For example, at one meeting it was announced that the post of assistant school custodian was open. The chairman ruled that appointments to this post should be made by the board, and without asking the superintendent for a recommendation, two of the board members nominated persons for the position. After some discussion the matter was referred to the superintendent.

particular vote. In contrast to this, the school board has been faced with a civil rights movement which is united, militant, and has considerable organizational skill. The civil rights movement wasted little time going into the streets, and when they did, they developed considerable support among white suburbanites. Their contacts with state officials seem much closer than do the school board's.

A list of the most important civil rights leaders in the Bay City school controversy would include probably eight persons. Together, they make up one of the youngest, best educated, most articulate (and most militant) leadership cadres that could be constructed. At least three hold degrees from Harvard, and they have studied at Dartmouth, Antioch, Union Theological Seminary, and MIT. At least four are not natives of Bay City, and their median age is only thirty. All are employed as professionals.

The unity of the civil rights movement conceals a serious disagreement over goals. On the one hand, the movement believed that recognition of the evils of *de facto* segregation was a major goal. However, it also felt that a campaign of demonstrations was necessary to overcome the apathy of the Negro community and mobilize public sentiment on a wide scale. Thus the civil rights movement felt that it could benefit from the board's acceptance of a policy statement at the very beginning, but it also knew that its goals would be served if the board chose to take a hard line. Other civil rights movements would have been less interested in demonstrations for their own sake. In addition, the civil rights movement had a third goal, as is indicated by the number of civil rights leaders active in the Citizens for the Bay City Public Schools—general reform of the school board. In the 1959 election, before the Citizens group was organized, its founder, Mrs. Laura Biddle, ran for the school board; even then she ran well in the Negro wards, so that a reform–civil rights coalition was "natural." This has posed a serious dilemma, since the pre-election civil rights demonstrations of 1963 and 1965 seem to have hurt the chances of the reform candidates. (The Negro candidate pulled relatively more votes from white wards in 1961, before the school integration issue came up, than he did in 1963.)

The impressive victories of Mrs. Smith in the school board elections of 1963 and 1965 have been interpreted as evidence of white opposition to school integration. However, the results are not this simple. The marriage of reform and civil rights has done little to help either; but the reformers, whose base never extended beyond the one-fourth of the city that was non-Catholic, were never a potent political force. They probably would not have done well even if the race issue had not come up. More important, the battle in Bay City has not been concerned so much with school integration as it has with deciding a more fundamental issue. The civil rights movement has not made demands for extensive integration. As one civil rights leader commented about one of the negotiating sessions, "If the school committee had done nothing more than say they intended to do something, that would have been enough." But what the civil rights movement has demanded has been something much more valuable. For recognition of the right of Negroes to integrated schools implies a recognition of Negroes as occupying a new social and political position. And more important, reform means granting Jews and Protestants political power as well. It is this issue, we think, that has been put to the test in the school elections.

5

Newark

The remaining five cities in our study have appointed school boards. Of the five, Newark is possibly the most interesting.

There are apparently only a handful of political machines remaining in the big cities today. By "machine" we mean the political organization that maintains itself almost exclusively with patronage and other material rewards. Newark provides us with a textbook example of the machine in operation. Newark has flirted with reform with little effect. In 1954, Newark adopted a mayor-council form of government dropping its obsolete commission structure. At that time, one of the commissioners, Leo Carlin, supported the reform and was elected mayor. In 1962 the present mayor, Hugh Addonizio, was elected with the support of at least part of the Republican organization, some elements of the Democratic party supporting his opponent. (Newark local elections are non partisan.) Thus both of the last two mayors have incorporated limited "reform" elements in their program.

Newark, like Lawndale, could be described either as a suburb— since it is fifteen minutes from Manhattan—or as an industrial central city in its own right. But in Newark the passing tourist would have no difficulty deciding which label better described the city. Newark is primarily a city of heavy industry and working-class housing, though it houses home offices of several major insurance firms, including Prudential. Much of its industry is absentee-owned, and its management lives in "The Oranges"— New Jersey's middle- and upper-income suburbs. Like most older cities, Newark lost much industry after World War II, although new commercial and financial firms have partly offset the loss.

Traditionally, the dominant ethnic group in Newark politics is the Irish-Americans, although the election of Mayor Addonizio

Interviewing by Gerald A. McWorter and James J. Vanecko; first draft by McWorter.

has brought the Italian-American group to a dominant position. Actually, the city was 34 per cent Negro in 1960, and the Negro population is growing rapidly.

Newark, then, has all the conditions necessary for the ideal-typical machine: a heavy concentration of Negroes and ethnic groups, a small and disinterested business elite, a population that is apathetic to local problems and turns its attention toward New York. And the machine has an ideal-typical image; to many of our informants, it is seen as efficient at vote getting and at co-opting its critics, but inept at everything else. We were told a number of stories suggesting that the government was corrupt and tied to organized crime.[1]

The school board's nine members are appointed by the mayor without approval of any other governmental body. The bulk of the board consists of political appointments representing Newark's various ethnic groups. One informant stated that only six of the nine are political appointments who are active in elections. This figure may be correct, but at the time of our study we thought it too low. As one board member said, "I don't know what X is doing on the board; I didn't see *him* in the last campaign!" The board has served as a political stepping-stone. In fact, Mayor Carlin served eight years on the school board before moving to the city council and the mayor's office. Of the present nine members of the board, four are Catholic (two Italians, one Irish, and one Polish), four are Protestants (of whom two are Negro), and one is Jewish. Three of the nine are attorneys, another is the wife of an attorney.

The first Negro was appointed to the Newark school board in 1942. At the time of our interviews, the board president was a Negro (Harold Ashby), and Mayor Addonizio appointed a second Negro to the board. Thus Newark was one of the first cities in the United States to have a Negro board member, and one of the first to have two Negroes on the board. Both are lawyers.

The schools have been the target of much criticism, although, as always, some of the criticism must be dismissed as unfounded. A report by the director of the Newark Human Rights Commis-

[1]We should make it doubly clear that we are talking about the image; we have no way of knowing whether or not these charges are justified. However, the 1965 grand jury raised the issue of organized gambling again.

sion charges that teacher turnover is high and that an abnormally large number of teachers are substitutes. The combined impact of the socioeconomic status of the Newark population and the conditions in the schools result in a system where, at the sixth grade, the median scores on the Stanford Reading Test are below the national norms in a heavy majority of the city's forty-six elementary schools.

1961: THE FIRST SCHOOL DESEGREGATION ISSUE

Prior to 1961, the civil rights movement was concerned with discriminatory practices within the school system, and with the overall quality of education, rather than with school segregation. The first issue raised was the demand that the school system appoint a Negro to an administrative post. Later, an interracial community organization, the Clinton Hills Community Conference, began an attack on Superintendent Edward Kennelly, asking that he be dismissed as incompetent.

A series of factors cooperated to bring the school integration issue to the surface at the same time that the board was defending Kennelly. First, the school system voted to convert a junior high school to high school use in the Vailsburg area. Vailsburg is a peninsula jutting out to the west of the city and is an all-white community of middle- and low-income housing. The boundaries set on the new school would make it all white, and its students would be transferred out of an integrated high school to attend it. Thus the Vailsburg issue is similar to Lawndale's Woodside High School (but without as much circumstantial evidence of gerrymandering). Like the Woodside district, Vailsburg has symbolic significance. It is the home of five of Newark's nine councilmen and of Mayor Carlin.

In the late 1950's the NAACP and Attorney Paul Zuber were active in *de facto* segregation suits in both New Jersey and New York state, and the *New Rochelle* verdict had been handed down only a few weeks before Vailsburg opened. The integrated community adjoining Vailsburg is Clinton Hills, so it is hardly surprising that the NAACP's education director (Stanley Winters, an officer of the Clinton Hills group) picked up the Vailsburg issue and brought in Zuber to file a suit charging that the Newark schools were segregated. As usual, Zuber's presence indicated a split between the national NAACP and the local branch. As seems to be typical of these suits, there was little money. Zuber was simultaneously involved in several other important cases, and the NAACP began looking for an out-of-court settlement. Actually, as in most northern segregation cases, it is difficult to guess how good a case the NAACP had. Winters was clearly the one person most committed to the suit. He produced a report documenting the charges to be leveled in the suit. He was also the only important civil rights leader who was not Negro, and the only member of the branch executive board to oppose an out-of-court settlement. Mayor Carlin, who was then running for reelection against Addonizio, was also interested in settling the case and helped establish contacts between the school board and some of the NAACP officials.

In January, 1962, Zuber and the NAACP branch president met with the school board president, Morris Fuchs, Superintendent Kennelly, and other school officials. They produced an out-of-court settlement that centered around the adoption of a limited open enrollment policy called Optional Pupil Transfer, and the appointment of a Citizens' Advisory Board to advise the board on integration matters. With this minimal victory for the integrationists, the case was withdrawn and Zuber left Newark. It is indicative of the relationship between the actors that when the NAACP was invited to propose candidates for the Citizens' Board, they suggested Ashby, who that same day was appointed to the school board by the incoming Mayor Addonizio.

Under the regulations governing Optional Pupil Transfer, apparently less than two hundred Negro students transferred into predominantly white schools. None of the eight plaintiffs in the original Zuber case received transfers, but the new Negro board member, Ashby, asked the board to pass a motion permitting them to transfer also, and this was done. The Citizens' Board limited itself to watching over the details of the transfer plan and never played a role of importance in the situation. Over a year after it was formed, its president, Ralph M. Caprio, manager of the Newark office of Metropolitan Life Insurance, commented that he "would be the first to admit we've done practically nothing."

While many members of the NAACP executive board seemed

to be satisfied with the outcome of the suit, Winters, who had not been consulted during the bargaining, was not. From this time on, he and the Clinton Hills Council engaged in a guerrilla war with the school board; his testimony about inferior education became a consistent theme of Newark school board meetings. However, he was never able to mobilize a sufficient protest movement to force any action.

1963: THE ISSUE REAPPEARS

The segregation issue reappeared in another community a year later. In the spring of 1963, the school board rearranged the boundaries between Peshine and Hawthorne elementary schools, just south of the Clinton Hills area. In an effort to balance overcrowding in these two schools, the school board transferred 161 students, some of whom were white, from Hawthorne (74 per cent Negro) to Peshine (96 per cent Negro). Hawthorne was a middle-income area in racial transition, while Peshine was a working-class Negro area. The parents protested the transfer, partly because both white and Negro parents objected to their children's attending nearly all-Negro schools, and partly because they felt the quality of education to be lower at Peshine. While the parents received some advice from the Clinton Hills Council and from one of the Negro board members, and had the support of civil rights groups, this was primarily a neighborhood protest, which used the tactics of the civil rights movement without really attempting to identify the issue as a civil rights issue. At first the school board paid little attention to the protest.

On September 9, the first day of school, 111 of the transferees boycotted. Five days later the board rejected the request of the parents that their children be allowed to transfer to other schools. The parents had submitted a list of white schools that were less crowded than Peshine. When the board rejected their request, they organized a picket and sit-in at one of the schools to which they had requested transfer. In addition, the parents organized a "freedom school," using volunteer teachers in a private home. Immediately after the sit-in, Mayor Addonizio met with the parents. After the meeting, the mayor announced that the board would consider their cases on an individual basis. Ashby, who also participated in the negotiations, added that the board would reconsider the entire matter. On September 24, the board met and entertained a motion to give the 161 Peshine transferees top priority over the other students in the Optional Pupils Transfer waiting list. Although some board members protested that this was discrimination in favor of the protesters, and against the other applicants, the board adopted the motion by a six to three vote. This meeting was held on September 24, exactly two weeks and one day after school opened.

INTERPRETATION

The characteristics of the political machine, as an "ideal type," are: (1) The members are disciplined by material rewards, such as patronage, graft, or appointments to public positions. In addition, potential critics are co-opted by the party by these appointments. Consequently, there is no internal dissension, and external criticism is muted. (2) Ideology is secondary to organizational maintenance. The machine takes whatever policy is considered necessary to get the votes. (3) The machine deals with individual voters rather than adopting general legalistic universals; it "makes deals" on an individual basis.

When the machine actually operates in this manner (many do not), the resulting government has some advantages. It tends in general to be a good "broker" of the conflicting demands upon it, and it can move quickly and decisively to avert conflict. This is basically what happened in Newark. In Bay City, a school board member used the racial issue for personal political gain. This did not, and could not, happen in Newark. In Lawndale, the controversy became pitched on an ideological level, and became a virtual holy war. In fact, the board members in Newark are more conservative than those in Lawndale,[2] but they took the necessary minimum action to avert controversy. A school superintendent in Kennelly's position could have easily become involved in an ideological war with the liberals, especially since they had already attacked him. But Kennelly's public behavior showed commendable restraint. Again this is consistent with the Newark political "style." In St. Louis the school board agreed to a program to increase integration. Newark did not do as much because few persons in the political machine are as liberal as those on the St.

[2]See Chapter 11 for the questionnaire data on this point.

Louis board, and because it was not necessary for the maintenance of political power. Newark does have a policy of bussing students from overcrowded schools, and this has resulted in integration of several white schools. This bussing program has never been the subject of controversy; white parents have not protested, and civil rights leaders (to our knowledge) have not asked for expansion. The highly pragmatic behavior of Mayor Addonizio suggests that had the civil rights movement pressed harder on the schools, they might have gotten much more from the system.

Of course, it is impossible to know what would have happened if the movement had made more demands. Presumably, Mayor Addonizio would eventually have refused demands in order to avoid alienating white voters, but we do not know at what point this would have occurred. However, machine cities characteristically seem to have weak civil rights movements. Any NAACP branch is in danger of falling into the hands of those Negro lawyers and others who have political ambitions; this is especially true in a machine city that can use patronage to win political support and can extend other favors to non-lawyers.

The Newark NAACP has always had a group of young turks and white liberals like Winters. They have remained in a minority on most issues, and in 1965 their candidate for branch president was defeated. They did play a major role in the Zuber suit, as reflected by the presence as legal advisor of Clyde Ferguson (then on the Rutgers faculty and later chief counsel of the Civil Rights Commission).

The militant civil rights group is CORE, and it has generally avoided taking a major role in the school issue and has worked on employment problems. Employment discrimination is handled by a non-governmental biracial group, the Business and Industry Coordinating Council. It has been fairly effective, and it is perhaps an accurate reflection on Newark that it has operated completely independent from the government. Indeed, Newark's use of private enterprise for public purposes is impressive. In another case when a major industry attempted to cooperate with the public schools in establishing a training program, it took over many of the public schools' functions, apparently on the assumption that it would be simpler to do the work itself.

It seems clear that the Newark school board has little autonomy.

The two mayors participated in the crucial negotiations in both the Vailsburg and Peshine issues, and in both cases the school board wound up reversing its position.[3] It is understandably difficult to assess what the school board might have done had it acted on its own. Apparently it was not planning to make concessions to the Peshine transfer students, although it might have done so later. The board members vary considerably in their attitudes toward race issues. Ashby, despite his school board position, is respected by Negroes and apparently exerted a liberalizing influence behind the scenes. But this is characteristic of the ideal machine—it does not require conformity on ideological grounds, as long as the boat is not rocked unnecessarily. In Newark the mayor goes against the trend of keeping politics out of the schools by publicly handling controversial issues. As a result, if the city does not resolve the school desegregation issue to the satisfaction of the committed civil rights leadership, it at least handles potential controversy with impressive speed and efficiency.

[3]One critic of the school system has argued that the serious financial problems of the Newark schools could be partly alleviated if the schools had a politically independent board with its own taxing powers.

6

Buffalo

Like Newark, Buffalo is an undeveloped democracy; but unlike Newark, and more like Bay City, this is reflected in a political system that borders on chaos. The effect of this is to produce a city government that has been incapable of supplying much more than the minimum of amenities to the city.

Buffalo, like most northern industrial cities, delivers a consistent Democratic majority in presidential elections, and its local elections are partisan. Under these conditions, we might expect a stable Democratic political machine to exist. In fact, mayors usually serve only one term, and two of the last four mayors have been Republican. In the last two mayoralty elections, there were competitive primaries in both parties, and a major third-party candidate in the general election. Since a plurality and not a majority is required for election, the result is highly unpredictable. In 1957, the Democratic candidate, Frank Sedita, was elected by sixty votes over the Republican, with another Democrat running on the Independent Citizens ticket running a close third. Four years later Sedita was defeated in a primary fight and ran as an independent in the general election. He ran ahead of the Democratic candidate, but the split in the Democratic ranks helped to elect the Republican, Chester Kowal.

At this time Buffalo was split into four factions—two in each party. The Democrats are permanently split, not by personality, but by ethnicity. The major bloc of votes is Polish: the city is said to be 35 per cent Polish-American (Dawidowicz and Goldstein, 1963). The Poles are opposed by the Italian and Irish ward organizations. The absence of party discipline is reflected not only in the third-party candidates for mayor, but also in the fact that the Democratic party seriously considered slating a Republican councilman as their candidate for U.S. congressman in 1964. The

Interviewing by Robert T. Stout and Morton Inger; first draft by Inger.

59

existence of both the Liberal and Conservative parties complicates the picture further. Just as it is not clear which party will win the mayoralty, it is also not clear which ethnic group will be victorious. Of the last four mayors, three had Polish names, but Sedita is Italian.

The Negro voters do not have a home in any of these factions, and in the 1957 and 1961 mayoral races, the Negro vote was divided three ways. There is only one Negro elected official, an alderman (councilman in Buffalo) elected from the Negro ward, and he has been quiet on the school issue.

During the past decade, politics has tended to be scandal ridden, and the city government has had few accomplishments to its credit. For example, Buffalo's urban renewal program led to the clearance of 160 acres of slum land in 1952; thirteen years later, the land still stood vacant. In 1964, all federal and state aid for new housing programs was cut off because the city did not have a housing code. A code was adopted about one year later. The present mayor, Kowal, and his corporation counsel are under indictment for taking unlawful fees, having an interest in the disposal of city property, and perjury. After this was written, Mayor Kowal, who did not stand for re-election, was replaced by Sedita, who had served as mayor from 1957 to 1961.

In this political climate the school system has had a checkered career. In the 1940's, a fierce battle raged over the schools because the superintendent, Robert J. Bapst, was a devout Catholic who was accused of making the public schools into a stepchild of the parochial school system. He did lend some of the public school teachers to the Catholic schools, and he urged his administrators to hold down spending because of the burden which operating two school systems placed on the citizens of Buffalo. He was supported by a school board consisting of four Catholics and one Jew. When the Protestants launched an attack on Bapst, two of the Catholics on the board were replaced by Protestants. Bapst resigned after this (and was ordained as a priest a short time later). In the 1950's, Mayor Sedita departed from the practice of appointing two Protestants. He appointed what are called "public school Catholics," but pressure from Protestants, Negroes, and organized labor eventually forced the enlargement of the board from five to seven members to give broader representation.

The Catholic-Protestant issue is still visible. In his 1965–66 budget message, Mayor Kowal said:

I am well aware that the allocation of $37,700,000 for the Board of Education falls short of their request [$43,089,905] but the fact remains that to provide additional funds would require a substantial increase in the tax rate and thereby add to the burden of many thousands of our property owners who are presently supporting two school systems.

The city council's budget cutting, plus the limited tax base in Buffalo, make the school system the most poorly financed one in the state. The average expenditure per pupil is $200 per year less than the average in the five other large cities in the state; on some measures of expenditure, Buffalo ranks last among the 107 school districts in western New York.

In 1964, the seven members of the board included two Italians, two Poles, one Greek, one Jew, and one Negro; the two Italians and the two Poles are Catholic, and the other three are Jewish, Protestant, and Greek Orthodox. The composition of the board is unstable in both its ethnic and religious makeup; for example, there are no Irish members, although there were a few years earlier, and in 1965 one of the Italians was replaced by a "Yankee." There was, briefly, a tradition of bipartisanship in appointments, but Mayor Kowal broke this by appointing only Republicans. (He also did not reappoint any incumbents.) Five of the seven present members were either friends or supporters of the mayors who appointed them. It is important to understand the type of people who make up the Buffalo board. Nine different persons served on the board between 1963 and 1965; we shall describe six of them.

Paschal Rubino, a funeral director in an Italian neighborhood, retired from the board in 1965 after a record fifteen years of service. He is now only forty-eight. In general, he has taken the position that the board should rule the schools and the school superintendent. (If he has sometimes been very rude to the superintendent, other board members have shown the same trait.) Rubino is a dynamic and outspoken man and shows some of the qualities of the effective politician.

Peter Gust Economou first joined the board in 1956. A Republican, he was appointed and reappointed by Democratic mayors

Pankow and Sedita. He owns and manages the huge Park Lane Hotel and Restaurant, and is a respected member of the Republican party. He has worked hard to improve the schools in his special area of competence—the efficient handling of food and the teaching of food preparation in the vocational schools—and is a member of the State Education Department's Advisory Committee on School Lunch Programs.

The board's Jewish member, Sam Markel, was appointed in 1961 by his close friend Mayor Sedita (he had also served for eight years in the 1940's). Although an active Democrat, he is not politically ambitious. He was forced to go to work at the age of fourteen, and he is now a successful businessman. He was very conscious of the prestige of being a school board member, and was one of the superintendent's staunchest supporters. In 1965 Mayor Kowal replaced Markel with a Republican dentist, Dr. Bernard Rosenblatt.

When the board was expanded to seven members in 1962, Kowal appointed Dr. Lydia Wright, a pediatrician and the first Negro to serve on the board. Kowal originally intended to appoint another Negro to the position, but Wright waged a highly effective campaign to attract support. She is generally considered a militant fighter for civil rights, and has also fought to obtain more money for schools. Although she is respected by most of the other board members, her aggressive manner has at times limited her effectiveness.

Carmelo Parlato was appointed in 1963, after working for Mayor Kowal in the primary. He is a young attorney, a militant anti-Communist, and politically ambitious. He considers the superintendent of schools to be an integrationist who must be carefully checked by the board, to prevent "racial ideas from predominating over educational values."

Another recent appointment to the board is Anthony Nitkowski, who holds the Labor seat. Kowal had originally nominated another union leader who was unable to accept the appointment. Nitkowski then proposed his own name to the mayor. Nitkowski is a supporter of the superintendent and has a strong commitment to the schools. He is a liberal on racial issues.

Buffalo, like St. Louis, Lawndale, and Bay City, has a superintendent who has risen through the ranks within the school systems.

The superintendent of schools, Joseph Manch, has over the years demonstrated a personal commitment to integration which is unusual among school superintendents. Manch has been vice-president of the Urban League, active in the NAACP and the Anti-Defamation League, and has received awards from the National Conference of Christians and Jews and many other groups. Manch's background is also unusual for a school superintendent. He is one of the very few Jews who are superintendents, and was very active in the teachers' union during his years in the Buffalo system.

The general situation in Buffalo is made worse by the fact that the city has had a strong radical right organization, which has, for example, made the unlisted telephone popular among liberals and even unknown University of Buffalo faculty members. The far right's preoccupation with communism has blocked needed innovations. One story will give an example of this and also indicate a little about the school board policy-making style. Buffalo has been financially unable to embark on a strong compensatory education program for slum schools, and a predominantly white group, the Citizens Council on Human Relations (CCHR), organized an after-school remedial education program staffed by volunteers, most of whom were city school teachers. However, when CCHR became involved in the school integration issue, two board members virtually accused them of having Communists in their membership. Although a majority of the board voted to uphold CCHR, the two board members conducted a public campaign that caused CCHR to cancel the program for fear of jeopardizing the careers of their volunteer teachers.

THE SCHOOL INTEGRATION CONTROVERSY, 1963–65

During the two-year period from 1963 to 1965, the school board changed considerably in its decision-making style. During 1963, the board suffered from considerable internal dissension and alienated the civil rights movement by its decision to open the new Woodlawn Junior High School as all-Negro over the initial objection of Manch. However, in the following year, the internal structure of the board changed so that in 1965 a liberal majority dominated the board and voted as a cohesive bloc in adopting an integration plan proposed by the superintendent. We will look first at the Woodlawn decision, then at the adoption of the integration plan in 1965, and in our interpretation try to understand the factors that caused this change.

The Woodlawn Junior High School Decision

In the late 1950's, Manch proposed, and the board adopted, boundary changes that led to the integration of three high schools; later, the system integrated several elementary schools. In addition, the board repeatedly went on record as favoring integration and endorsing it as a major goal.

In the spring of 1964, the board was forced to face the segregation issue and establish boundaries for the new Woodlawn Junior High School. The board was under considerable pressure to make Woodlawn an integrated school, from both the NAACP and the State Department of Education.

The racial ecology of Buffalo gave the board an opportunity to integrate Woodlawn. The Negro ghetto is a narrow peninsula, and Woodlawn School was located just inside the ghetto. However, the Negro peninsula is bounded on one side by a Polish area and on the other side by an Italian community. Both communities are working class and at one time or another have expressed considerable anti-Negro sentiment. If Woodlawn Junior High School were to be integrated, it would require feeding some of the all-white schools from the west, or Italian, area into it. In the Civil Rights Report written a few months before the final decision, Manch is quoted as saying that Woodlawn would be integrated: "The Zone will cross Main Street if I have anything to say about it."

When the board brought up the Woodlawn boundaries question, only six board members were in the city. They proposed four competing plans. Only Parlato proposed that Woodlawn be made entirely Negro. Economou and another board member drafted a plan that would include two all-white elementary schools and would make Woodlawn 76 per cent Negro.[1] Parlato said that he would be willing to compromise and vote for this plan. Nitkowski and Rubino supported a plan that differed slightly from Economou's, lowering the proportion Negro to 69 per cent.

[1]These and the other percentages are those given by the *Buffalo Evening News*.

Manch endorsed their version. Finally, Dr. Wright proposed that students from three other white schools be sent to Woodlawn, resulting in a school that would be 38 per cent Negro. At this point, Manch's prediction that Woodlawn would be integrated seemed to be coming true; upon Markel's return, it seemed likely that the superintendent and five members of the board would find themselves supporting some variant of the Economou or Rubino-Nitkowski plan. But in the following month, pressure from integrationists and segregationists was stepped up. The white neighborhoods threatened by the plan circulated a petition, obtained 12,811 signatures, and protested long and loudly at a public meeting held by the board. We were told that one of the members on the board was threatened by a local politician that he would be bankrupted if he did not support Parlato's plan. At the same time, the NAACP and other civil rights groups were endorsing the integrationist proposals and threatening a school boycott. At the next board meeting, Parlato moved that the board ask the corporation counsel whether it might consider race in establishing boundaries. When Manch pointed out that the State Education Department's legal counsel had said that "the question is no longer whether to integrate but how," Rubino attacked Manch for "his unfortunate and supine concern with these unclear statements emanating from the state." Kowal's corporation counsel supported Parlato's view that race could not be considered a factor, but based this opinion on a decision by the state's lowest appellate court which was shortly to be appealed and reversed.

At the next board meeting, the board capitulated to the segregationist opposition, and Parlato's plan was adopted. Manch made it clear that he was surrendering to the white opposition, first stating that Parlato's plan was "as good a plan for a district which will be organized on the basis of the immediate neighborhood as any other," leaving open the question whether the plan was as good as one that was organized on the basis of some other definition of the neighborhood. He then went on to say "It is not feasible . . . to draw the district lines for Woodlawn as to achieve a racial balance that would be *meaningful* or *stable*" (italics added). Thus he made it clear that he felt it would be impossible to maintain Woodlawn as integrated given the extent of white opposition. He bemoaned the fact that Woodlawn had become the "test of the board's and the superintendent's intention in this total matter of racial balance" and cited the previous cases when they had redrawn lines to integrate schools. Markel and Nitkowski cast reluctant votes in favor. Nitkowski made it clear he was influenced by Manch's change of opinion. Only Wright voted against the Parlato plan.

This total retreat of the board and the superintendent from their previous position spurred the civil rights movement to mobilize for the first time. On the day of the board's decision, the NAACP staged a poorly attended march in the rain to Niagara Square. Within two months, however, the threatened boycott was held and was rather successful. The following fall (1964), when Wood-lawn was opened, the civil rights movement was torn by the national NAACP policy that no demonstrations be held until after the Johnson-Goldwater election. One group, called the Mothers' Alliance, attempted an opening day boycott of Woodlawn which was an almost total failure. It is indicative of the weakness of the boycotters that they were very critical of Dr. Wright for refusing to ride the streets in a sound truck.

It was after this debacle that the NAACP began preparing a petition for State Commissioner of Education James E. Allen. The University of Buffalo faculty provided the legal advice. (Of course, the Citizens Council on Human Relations had many contacts among the Buffalo faculty, so it was easy for the movement to obtain help from this source.)

Manch had been attempting for over a year to persuade the board to adopt an open enrollment plan expressly designed to further racial balance. Under this plan, only students from schools that were designated as imbalanced would be qualified for transfer to predominantly white or integrated schools. The board had earlier adopted the conventional "color-blind" version of the plan, but had declined to tie it expressly to integration. In May, the board voted down the amendment four to two, with Dr. Wright and Nitkowski in the minority and Dr. Rosenblatt abstaining. However, in September, 1964, the board adopted a stronger policy statement, committing the board to achieving integration in nearly any way short of a wholesale transportation program. Only Parlato and one other conservative on the board voted against the proposal. In December the board again rejected the amendment of the open-enrollment plan. The Buffalo newspaper, which had consistently been highly critical of the school board, took this opportunity to chastise the schools again.

Allen acted on the NAACP petition in February, 1965, rebuking the board and requesting an integration plan by May 1, 1965. Manch immediately asked the board to take action and the board responded, first, by accepting the color-conscious restrictions on the open-enrollment plan (which it had rejected again a few days earlier) and, on April 28, by approving the superintendent's eleven-point plan, which involved the closing of one segregated school and the redrawing of boundaries in other areas. In this vote, the two liberals were joined by the moderate board members (Rubino, Economou, and Rosenblatt); only the two conservatives voted against the plan. One of the liberal members, Nitkowski, expressed slight misgivings that the plan did not go farther, but voted in favor of it. Dr. Wright also voted for it but publicly expressed her disapproval. Manch's continued pressure on the board and Allen's request for a plan had enabled the board to develop a moderately liberal consensus. In May, President Rubino retired from the board, and Mayor Kowal named as his successor George F. Goodyear. Goodyear's appointment is important for two reasons. Not only was his appointment non-political, he was moreover an Anglo-Saxon Protestant member of the Buffalo civic elite. In addition, he was known to be a liberal on racial issues, since he had been very active in the Urban League. When Goodyear joined the board, the board elected Nitkowski as board president. Nitkowski, who had been only a year earlier a member of a liberal minority, was now the leader of a five-member majority that would support Manch's recommendations.[2]

The 1965 Integration Plan

In the fall of 1965 the first steps in the implementation of the new integration program were taken; Negro students were transferred to several white schools, and plans were drawn to close another antiquated school building. By this time, the anti-

[2]In a political situation as unstable as Buffalo's, it is difficult to guess whether this is the first step toward reform. One of our informants calls to our attention the formation of Citizens for Better Education. Our informant adds that it is "doing a fairly good job of rousing public support for increased school budgets and better methods of choosing the board."

integration opposition had organized formally, with the open support of the two conservative board members. A suit was filed contesting the legality of the new integration plan. (The suit lost in the local courts and may be appealed.)

In the fall of 1965, the board and the staff had another opportunity to demonstrate their commitment to integration. One of the Negro elementary schools in the Woodlawn Junior High School district was partially disabled by a Sunday night fire. The staff immediately prepared a plan to reassign some of the students into two adjoining all-Negro schools and a nearby integrated school. The parents from the burned school protested the transfer to all-Negro schools and Manch met with a large group Monday night. At the meeting he agreed to try to develop a new plan. The plan was prepared the next day and involved dispersing the students into eight integrated or all-white schools. The plan was approved by the "normal" five to two vote and the students were back in class on Friday.

INTERPRETATION

The outstanding characteristic of the Woodlawn decision was the inability of the board to operate as a cohesive group to produce a single plan. Although five of the six board members (one was out of town) favored integrating Woodlawn, they wound up producing four different plans. Then, in the face of the petition campaign, they all retreated. Throughout 1963, the school board's decision-making process was nearly as chaotic as Bay City's. This is somewhat surprising, given the fact that this board was appointive. However, it may be that the disorder of the appointment process, which boiled down to rewarding the faithful, with little regard to maintaining any particular ethnic, religious, or political composition, explains the situation. Of our cities, Buffalo is the only appointed board where members could not expect to be automatically reappointed. Thus there was considerable pressure on board members to play roles that would gain them political followings. In addition, two members waged campaigns to be appointed initially. In this way, the board had pressures on it that made it resemble an elected board. In Newark, the machine, with its devotion to political discipline, serves to keep board members "in line," but the multi-factional politics of Buffalo reward dissidence, especially under a lame duck mayor. Finally, we should note that in a city like Bay City or Buffalo, where ethnic rivalries find their way into the political arena, racism is a more politically rewarding position.

The presence of many new appointments on the board, coupled with criticisms of Manch by several board members, created an air of tension around the board's decision-making process. The board refused to be led by the superintendent, but on the other hand, there was no board member whom they recognized as a leader. The result was that no one was quite sure what the board should be doing, or who should be doing it. It was extremely difficult to single out any members of the board as being key members, and the pattern of votes was somewhat unpredictable. What is most interesting is the heavy emotional investment made by the board members. Insults were thrown, not only at Manch, but at other board members; board meetings included hours of speechmaking, and several board members wept publicly at one time or another.

The presence of a single person who chooses to harass the superintendent and the other board members by taking campaigns to the public can almost immobilize the board. The collapse of the volunteer compensatory education program indicates that such tactics can succeed even over the opposition of a majority of the board. Regrettably, there was more than one outspoken board member, and the three members who made up the center of the board—Nitkowski, Markel, and Economou—were less aggressive.

In the case of Lawndale, we noted that the civil rights movement's weakness might explain why the school board did not take any action to increase integration. In Buffalo, where the movement is somewhat more militant but organizationally very weak, it is interesting to speculate whether a stronger movement would have had more success in the Woodlawn case. The civil rights movement is very weak in Buffalo. CORE is essentially a one-man organization, and the NAACP, which carried the brunt of the school issue, is not much larger. The NAACP is unusual in that it does not seem to represent the Negro elite as one might expect. Its education chairman during most of the Woodlawn controversy, Raphael Dubard, is not the usual lawyer, but is a toll collector for the New York Department of Highways. Its present president is a steelworker. The organization does not even have a paid receptionist. The "white liberal" group, the Citizens Council for Human Relations, sees itself as viewed with outright hostility by the white citizenry. But how much difference would it have made if demonstrations like those in St. Louis could have been staged? With a couple of board members ready to ride on a "white backlash," the demonstrations might have simply stiffened the board's resistance to integration.

In Lawndale, the demonstrations by white neighborhood groups came only after the board had committed itself to rejecting the integrationist demands. Thus the Woodlawn Junior High School incident is the only case that we have yet seen in which the demonstration of opposition to integration had a direct effect on the board. Why was the demonstration so effective? One reason is that the board made it clear to the community that it was open to influence. Rather than simply uniting about a plan drawn by the administration, the board presented four different plans of its own. Thus the community did not see the situation as an accomplished fact. Rather than trying to defeat the board's plan, it was trying to persuade the board to adopt Parlato's recommendation. The board and the superintendent had made it clear that there were no overriding considerations which required that the boundaries be at any certain place. The board could not fall back on any computer mythology and say, "We know best." In addition, it seems to be generally true that effective demonstrations can be mobilized more easily by the parents from a sending school as opposed to a receiving school. The whites were defending the status quo; they were being required to send their children into a Negro neighborhood (admittedly only a short distance into it), which is psychologically akin to "reverse bussing." In contrast, Manch had been successful every time he had proposed sending Negro students into white areas to school.

Finally, the school board did not feel a strong moral compulsion to integrate Woodlawn. The civil rights movement did not argue that the segregation of Woodlawn would be an illegal gerrymander. If they had, the board might have reacted differently. Rather, the movement took the position that the board had a moral obligation to integrate schools whenever possible. This is a vague position. It is not a universally accepted principle, and it does not have the support of law. Moreover, the meaning of "whenever possible" is not clear. The board had integrated other schools; couldn't they dodge the issue this one time? Economou reflected this legal and moral confusion when, as he voted to support the segregation of Woodlawn, he read a short statement pleading for a decision from the Supreme Court to establish the guidelines for decisions like this one. To some extent, providing this moral guideline was the important function of Allen's intervention. Even a clear moral perspective would have been of little value if the board had remained as badly disorganized as it was in 1964. But by 1965, Superintendent Manch had a clear majority supporting him.

In 1965 the stable five-to-two split on the board (one newspaper story referred to a unanimous vote as "a rare moment of unanimity" and called the five-to-two vote "normal") still meant that conflict was quite high, and board meetings were still likely to turn into shouting matches lasting long into the night. But the level of cohesion among the majority meant that public controversy could be controlled and attempts to make decisions were not bogged down in confusion. Individual board members were now able to act with more security because of the presence of a consensual group. In many ways, this seems to be as important a factor as Allen's intervention.

7

Baltimore

In every city we have examined so far, the school desegregation issue has been accompanied by demonstrations, court suits, and considerable controversy. Baltimore, during the summer of 1963, was faced with a series of complaints; by the end of the summer major action had been taken to meet the demands made, and yet there had been no demonstrations of importance and hardly any public statements that suggested conflict. For this reason, Baltimore may provide us with an important case history.

The Baltimore school system desegregated immediately after the *Brown* decision in 1954. Like many eastern cities, Baltimore had traditionally been permissive in its student transfer policy. Desegregation was accomplished by simply opening most schools to both Negro and white students. However, schools that were overcrowded or in danger of becoming overcrowded were "districted," meaning that students from outside the school's "district" were not allowed to enter. Prior to 1963, Baltimore experienced a rapid growth in its Negro population, and many of Baltimore's schools became overcrowded and went on double shift. As this happened, more schools were "districted." In addition, the schools began bussing as many as two thousand students annually to relieve overcrowding. From 1954 to 1963, civil rights groups had made sporadic criticisms of this policy, charging that it was administered in a discriminatory fashion.

In 1961, the wife of a Johns Hopkins faculty member, Mrs. Shirley Bramhall, led her community group downtown to complain about the local school. Although the neighborhood was an integrated one, the public school was entirely Negro. The school system was transporting Negro students from more overcrowded schools in one door, while resident whites had organized transpor-

Interviewing by Robert T. Stout and James J. Vanecko; first draft by Vanecko.

tation to take their own children out the other. Mrs. Bramhall's group specifically complained that the transfer program was likely to drive whites out of the area.

The following year another white mother, Mrs. Dorothy Sykes, was notified that her child would be put on part-time attendance because of overcrowding. Mrs. Sykes carried her complaint about this to her principal, to assistant superintendents, and finally to the superintendent of schools, George Brain. While she was doing this, she also contacted the Civil Rights Commission in Washington and the staff of the Office of Education. Mrs. Sykes' daughter was not put on double shift, but this did not deter her from her campaign. In her search for a lawyer, she contacted Baltimore Neighborhoods, Inc., an organization financed by Baltimore industrialists which has as its mission promoting racial stability in the central city. Its director, Edward Holmgren, put her in touch with Mrs. Bramhall, and an informal committee of parents was organized. Over the next year, the Sykes-Bramhall group began to see their own community problems as part of a general city-wide issue and decided to attack the general question of segregation and overcrowding in the whole school system.

We can get an idea of the group's relationship to the school staff from one of the interviews between Mrs. Sykes and Superintendent Brain.[1] Although the tone of the interview was friendly, a clear disagreement between the parties appears in Brain's insistence that Mrs. Sykes was asking the schools to become an "instrument of social policy, to force integration through racial balancing." Nevertheless, Brain continued to give the Sykes group access to large amounts of school system data. The parents' group prepared a report on their findings. They also contacted Melvin Sykes (not related to Dorothy), who agreed to serve as legal counsel to the group. Some members wanted to make the report public. After some debate, Melvin Sykes and Mrs. Sykes persuaded the committee to make a private presentation of the report to Brain and the Board of School Commissioners. (Apparently, they felt that making the report public would place the board in an uncom-

[1]Mrs. Sykes prepared a written summary of the interview and submitted it to Brain, who approved the document. It was later incorporated into reports of both the school system and the parents' group. Thus we have an "official" insider's view of this interview.

fortable position and possibly engender controversy.) They also obtained a resolution of support from Baltimore Neighborhoods.

Holmgren and Melvin Sykes presented the report to Brain and to the board president, Eli Frank, in February, 1963. At this meeting it was agreed that the school administration would be given an opportunity to reply to the report, and Frank asked for additional copies for all board members. This is apparently the first time that the Sykes-Bramhall group had made any contact with Frank. The protesters were promised action by April, and in late February Frank appointed an ad hoc board committee to prepare a statement on the report.

The report, which was simply called *Seven Years of Desegregation in the Baltimore Public Schools: A Report,* was strong and accusing in tone. It charged the school system with intentionally segregating schools and overcrowding Negro schools by (a) not building enough schools in the inner city; (b) "districting" white schools to keep Negroes out; and (c) refusing to issue transfers to Negroes to permit them to attend predominantly white schools. The report is striking in the skill with which a great deal of statistical data was presented and analyzed.

Throughout April and May, there were meetings of the board's new ad hoc committee with both the administration and the protest group. The school staff prepared a response to the *Seven Years* report. It broke statements of the report into what it called 120 different "concerns" and rebutted many of them by asking that the terms used be defined. Thus a point was "rebutted" by a demand for a definition: What is a "predominantly Negro" school? At another point, an error was corrected—the response noted only that there was an omission in a listing of schools that "fit the definition of 'predominantly Negro.' " The theme running through the reply is that the report was not clear enough to be commented on, that it showed no valid evidence of discrimination, and that its recommendations that the school system adopt a policy of "forcing" integration would be of questionable legality. This response was dismissed as meaningless by the protest group and criticized by at least one board member. A second reply, with the same title, was prepared by the school administration.

By the beginning of May, the protest group had become impatient, and Melvin Sykes wrote Frank that unless they could reach an agreement with the ad hoc committee within the month they would make a public presentation of their grievances at the June 6 board meeting. Sykes was granted a hearing at the June 6 meeting, but on May 22 the administration submitted to the board and the Sykes-Bramhall group the new reply to the *Seven Years* report. Although not nearly as condescending in tone as the earlier reply, the new statement was a categorical denial of all 120 concerns, accompanied by an occasional misrepresentation of the protesters' positions and an insistence that a school could not be considered segregated if it had both Negroes and whites, regardless of proportion. (The *Seven Years* report used 10 per cent as its criterion.) Meanwhile, the protest group had not succeeded in reaching agreement with the ad hoc committee. Thus it began to seem that the June 6 board meeting would consist of the presentation of the *Seven Years* report, followed by the presentation of the school administration's rebuttal, and the board's adoption of the ad hoc committee's recommendation. At this point, Melvin Sykes and the parents' group announced that they were preparing a revision of their report, which they managed to complete by working night and day between May 22 and June 6. The new report was titled *Eight Years of Desegregation in the Baltimore Public Schools: Fact and Law*. It was studded with legal citations, and was affectionately referred to as "The Brief." It charged discrimination in the transfer and bussing policies, in "districting," and in the location of new school building, all these factors leading to unnecessary and hence illegal double-shift schooling for Negroes. At the same meeting, the NAACP's June Shagaloff and the equally militant representative of the local branch appeared and gave testimony supporting the parents' group. It was now clear that the ad hoc committee report would not go far enough, although it had recommended the complete abolition of "districting." The board unanimously adopted the ad hoc committee report and the meeting was quickly adjourned.

At this point, the issue could have exploded. It seems clear that the school staff regarded the charges made as unfounded, while the parents felt that none of their statements had been rebutted. Strategically, the Sykes-Bramhall group had by now made it clear that they were prepared to go to court; furthermore, it was assumed by everyone that the militant Baltimore NAACP was waiting in the background, ready to begin demonstrations any time the original protest group failed in its tactics. Meanwhile, one of the Negro board members issued a statement urging the board to take action to meet the demands. At the end of July, the NAACP did stage a small demonstration, but generally they were trying to stay in the background to avoid jeopardizing the negotiations. The suit was never filed. Instead, a series of private meetings were held which included at various times board members, the superintendent, Melvin Sykes, and members of the parents' group. At the same time, Frank kept in touch with the board and built a consensus in favor of action to meet the demands. By the end of the summer, the school system had purchased enough school buses to transfer five thousand students and completely eliminate double shifts. In addition, the transfer policies were liberalized and all districting was eliminated, which also introduced Negroes into several previously all-white schools. Then the board adopted, by a six-to-two vote, a new policy statement which committed the board to drop "color-blindedness" and to establish a policy of integration. (The new statement had been submitted to the protest group for approval.) The sudden integration of previously all-white schools met with short-lived opposition.

INTERPRETATION

This is the first case we have examined in which the civil rights movement achieved something close to a total victory. Was this because the Baltimore parents' group was more skilled and used superior tactics? This may be part of the story, but it is not the major part. It is true that the parents' group, and especially Melvin Sykes, were determined not to publicly embarrass the board, to make their charges as specific as possible, and to maintain a good atmosphere for negotiation. It seems likely that their ability to make a rather convincing case that school policy was being administered in a discriminatory fashion may have made it easier for the board to act. Although ideological issues were involved, they were not prominent. And of course the demonstration in the *Eight Years* report that they were able to prepare a court suit helped strengthen their position. In addition, the Baltimore NAACP, which is sometimes accused of being rabble-rousing and difficult to work with, was a model of cooperative behavior, staying in the background during almost the entire period of negotiation.

But this in itself is not a convincing explanation. First, there is no evidence that if they had taken the case to court, the court would have ordered the complete elimination of double shift, the complete elimination of districting, or the new policy statement. Second, there is no evidence in our other cities that discreet negotiations are more successful than demonstrations.

While the tactics used may have been best for this situation, they succeeded primarily because the Baltimore Board of School Commissioners was made up of men who took very liberal positions on race relations. As we turn to examining the structure of the leadership of Baltimore, we see that this would almost necessarily be the case.

One might argue that the protest group had an advantage in presenting its case because of its informal ties to the school board; its attorney, Melvin Sykes, was on close personal terms with the board president, Frank. (During May of 1963, while he was threatening to make a public statement at the June 6 meeting, Sykes went to the Maryland Bar Association meeting in Atlantic City. Frank was also at the meeting, as chairman of a committee on judicial selection. Sykes also spoke in favor of the committee report, and Sykes and Frank worked together on this issue.) It was no mere accident that Frank and Sykes should be able to work together like this, but neither was it a shrewd tactic on the part of the parents' group to select Sykes for this reason; rather it was a consequence of community structure.

To understand this, we must start, literally, at the top. The industrial and financial elites of Baltimore are organized into the Greater Baltimore Committee (GBC). The Committee is limited to one hundred men. Each member must be the president of a large corporation, and minimum membership fee is $1,000 per year. The GBC has committed itself to rebuilding Baltimore and has been heavily involved in developing urban renewal projects and attracting new construction and new industry to the city. But it has also gone beyond these goals, which are the common denominator of civil elites across the country, to a commitment to saving the central city through what might be called social urban renewal. In this way they have committed themselves to improving race relations and getting benefits to Baltimore's large Negro population. This commitment is reflected in the personality of its leadership. One of the top influentials in GBC is James Rouse; he is nationally known as a builder of "new towns" with a flair for using social scientific ideas in the process. In addition, his biography in *Who's Who* mentions that he is a past president of the Maryland Chapter of United World Federalists. The executive director of GBC is William Boucher; he previously was employed as state director of Americans for Democratic Action, and was president of the local American Civil Liberties Union.

Baltimore Neighborhoods, Incorporated, was set up by the GBC to deal with the problems of stabilizing integrated neighborhoods. They employed Edward Holmgren, previously with the Chicago Urban League, as director and have worked closely with the parent GBC. It was Baltimore Neighborhoods that put Dorothy Sykes in touch with Shirley Bramhall, and its seems likely that Holmgren (who was one of the signers of the *Seven Years* and *Eight Years* reports) participated in the recruitment of Melvin Sykes.

At the same time, the Baltimore civic elite have played a role in the selection of school board members for many years. In 1954, when Baltimore planned to desegregate its schools, one of Baltimore's most prominent men, Walter Sondheim, became president of the board. After desegregation went off without incident, he resigned to head the Baltimore Urban Renewal Commission, which was about to embark on a series of major projects. Thus it was not completely an accident that the president of the Board of School Commissioners and the attorney for the plaintiff should both be prominent Baltimore attorneys.

In addition to its usual role of representing religious and racial groups, the Baltimore board has one other "ticket-balancing" device; each of Baltimore's three major schools—the University of Maryland, Johns Hopkins, and Morgan State—must be represented. The University of Maryland's board member is William Stone, dean of the medical school. He is one of the two board members who voted against the second policy statement. William McElroy is the distinguished young chairman of the biochemistry department at Johns Hopkins. A committed liberal, McElroy chaired the ad hoc committee set up by the board at the beginning of the controversy. J. Percy Bond is vice-president and director of admissions at Morgan State; a liberal and a Negro, he has not, however, been active in civil rights issues.

There are six remaining members of the board. Eli Frank, Jr., the only Jew, is a corporation lawyer and comes from an old and prominent Baltimore family. IIis father served on the board and also founded a private school. John Sweeney is a young Catholic lawyer who is a partner in a substantial law firm. He has been active in civil rights issues, and showed potential as a civic leader before being appointed. As chairman of the board's building committee, he is possibly the third most influential member of the board (behind Frank and McElroy). Mrs. Elizabeth Murphy Moss, the board's other Negro, is the daughter of Carl Murphy, publisher of the *Afro-American,* and considered by many to be the most influential Negro in the city. She is a columnist with the paper and is an outspoken militant on civil rights issues. During the controversy, she issued one major statement urging the board to take action. Sidney H. Tinley heads a large mortgage banking firm. (Tinley was not present when the policy statement was adopted.) John Sherwood, the senior member of the board, is from an old and wealthy Baltimore family. He introduced the policy statement. The last member, Mrs. M. Richmond Farring, is the board member most closely identified with local politics. She is a neighborhood clubwoman who is close to the regular Democratic organization in her area. She voted with Stone against the final policy statement.

This board is quite different from any we have seen so far in this report. Not only Frank, but several other board members, are liberals on racial issues who seem to have had little difficulty mastering the complexities and ambiguities of the school integration issue.

For a brief time during the controversy, the liberalism of the Baltimore board was almost offset by the more conservative school staff, which in its general position was as conservative as any administrators we have observed in other cities. However, it had little difficulty controlling the school administration; this may be because of the high level of education of several board members. In addition, the authority of the school board is implicit in the fact that it traditionally does not give its superintendent a contract; he is employed on a day-to-day basis.

The Baltimore staff did take one important action during the summer which probably helped the preparations for the new policy statement. Brain planned and held a conference of school superintendents on issues of racial integration. Superintendents from several cities that had successfully handled the integration issue were present. Not only does a conference such as this permit exchange of specific tactical ideas, it also enables big city superintendents to develop ways of relating the integration issue to the educational ideology that they share. In the case of Baltimore, our informants felt that the conference had an important effect on local public opinion.

It is perhaps curious that our most liberal boards so far have appeared in the two border cities, Baltimore and St. Louis. In fact, there are many parallels between the two cities. But in St. Louis there is not the clear impression that the elite of the community are committed to civil rights (although St. Louis did pass a series of civil rights bills in the city council); this may explain why Schlafly moved somewhat more slowly than Frank. (More likely, it was simply because Schlafly was restricted by serving on an elected board.) The other difference is in the support that schools receive from the voters. Whereas St. Louis, like most cities, must always worry a bit about bond issue referenda, the voters support the Baltimore bonds by overwhelming votes.

Thus we see that the Baltimore story is simple and brief, but it stops short of being a complete explanation. Is it really true that Baltimore has a more liberal "political culture" than that in our other cities? We are really ill-equipped to examine the possibility in this study. It may be true. If it is, we do not have a good explanation for it.

8

San Francisco

In the other cities we have seen how concern over a particular school can escalate into a full-scale assault on *de facto* segregation (Baltimore and Newark are examples). In both these cases, the rejection of the specific demands led to increased pressure for more general solutions. In San Francisco we see an unusual reversal of this pattern; a specific demand was made and it was more or less met by the school board without reducing any of the pressure for a more general solution. San Francisco is in some ways our most important case, for it points out better than any other city that there is no necessary relation between the actual number of students in integrated schools, or the school's willingness to take concrete steps to integrate schools, and the ability of the school system to avoid conflict.

From the beginning, the San Francisco schools and the civil rights leaders were poles apart in ideology. Like the Bay City movement, San Francisco's civil rights leaders wanted to talk about *de facto* segregation in the abstract; the school administration would have no part of such a discussion.

At the January, 1962, school board meeting, two white liberals, Mrs. Beverly Axelrod, representing CORE, and Frank Quinn of the Council of Civic Unity, an interracial human relations organization, presented statements. CORE asked for a racial census; the Council added a request that a board-appointed citizens' committee and the superintendent each prepare a report on *de facto* segregation.

The board asked Superintendent Harold Spears to reply, and his report, presented on June 19, was a complete disappointment to the civil rights groups. Spears began by saying, "Although the question of racial interaction in any area of civic affairs has its

Interviewing by James J. Vanecko and Thomas M. Landye; first draft by Landye.

emotional overtones, the subject can lend itself to rational and deliberate treatment. The point of departure in this investigation has been the educational implications, since the function of the American public school is the effective instruction of the pupils therein. . . ." He then went on to discuss in detail the changing racial composition of the city and the way in which attendance boundaries are set, and reviewed the census data (for non-whites including Orientals, rather than Negroes) for different parts of the city. Although the superintendent noted that bussing to relieve overcrowding sometimes resulted in integration, he added that he did not (and by implication, should not) consider racial integration as even a secondary goal of the transportation of pupils to relieve overcrowding. He also stressed that bussing weakened the home-school tie, and noted that bussing was inconvenient to Chinese children who were in a hurry to reach after-school classes in Chinese culture.

He then stated the school system's philosophy on the issue of the racial census of pupils:

We are now faced with the movement to emphasize differences in the color and race of pupils, with teacher, parent, and child. In some Eastern school systems, such records are now prepared annually. One asks for what purposes do we so label a child, and in turn, post a sign on his school, indicating the racial make-up of the student body at the moment?

If we were preparing to ship these children to various schools, in predetermined racial allotments, then such brands would serve the purpose they have been put to in handling livestock. But until somebody comes up with an educationally sound plan for such integration, then this racial accounting serves nothing but the dangers of putting it to ill use. . . .

It is quite apparent that as more courts face the technicalities of the issue, we should expect the injection of the question of the purpose of the American public school, a matter that has been somewhat ignored up to this point.

Without a doubt, state school codes do not speak of social adjustment as a purpose in the establishment of public schools. Instead, they speak specifically of subjects to be taught. . . .

It is true that any school or any classroom provides a social situation, for when two pupils or more are grouped for instruction the element of human relationships enters the picture. But this social situation has never been stated in law as a purpose of a school. Rather it is a condition that arises because efficiency of school operation demands that children be grouped for instructional purpose, rather than to be tutored individually. The teacher naturally takes advantage of the group situation to teach beyond the subjects which constitute the curriculum, but nobody has ever justified through public expenditure the organization of schools primarily for the social purpose.

The school is an instrument through which society both preserves the culture and brings out social change. The school is actually an instrument of social change, but as such an instrument, the children are not to be used as the tools. . . .

The *Brown* case in 1954 and the *Taylor* case in 1961 were both concerned with the civil rights of individuals. As there is an attempt to push broader interpretations in the court cases ahead, then the child's educational rights must be brought out in relationship to his civil rights, lest there be possible conflict. Certainly such refinement of issue will demand the opinion of the educational profession as well as that of the legal profession.

. . . .

Returning to the specific case at hand, I have no educationally sound program to suggest to the Board to eliminate the schools in which the children are predominantly of one race, as has been suggested to the Board by the Congress of Racial Equality. If such schools are educationally unsound, as has been charged by the Bay Area Human Relations Council, then certainly any program to improve the situation would need to be educationally sound if established by official Board action.

CENTRAL JUNIOR HIGH SCHOOL

At the same time, the Central Junior High School issue came to life. Central Junior High was a new name for the old building originally used by the elite Lowell High School. The area around the proposed Central Junior High School had experienced a steady increase in Negro population from approximately 8 per cent in 1950 to 35 per cent in 1960, resulting in overcrowding in Franklin Junior High School, an overwhelmingly Negro school. With the opening of the new school, several predominantly Negro elementary schools could be redistricted to relieve this overcrowding. Although we have no racial data on the schools for that time, it appears that Central Junior High School would have been approximately 60 per cent Negro when it opened. The new boundaries also included two predominantly white schools which would be

transferred from a white middle-income junior high school. One
was Gratten, serving a predominantly white area adjacent to the
University of California Medical School. The community included
moderate and high-income whites and Negroes and a number of
local civil rights leaders. By May, the Gratten Parents and Friends
Committee has been organized to protest that their children were
being transferred into a racially imbalanced school and that panic-
peddlers were already ringing doorbells through the Gratten area.
Spears had incurred the wrath of one of San Francisco's most
articulate and outspoken neighborhoods. Since Mrs. Axelrod was
one of the Gratten group, CORE was quick to back them. The
Gratten group was not, however, completely trusted by the
NAACP. Gratten, after all, had a choice: they could simply try
to get out of the predominantly Negro school themselves or they
could choose to stay in Central but press for a redrawing of boundaries to increase the number of whites in the school. They chose
the latter tack and thus established themselves as integrationist,
rather than merely anti-Negro.

The Gratten group asked for and received a hearing at the June
board meeting. More than three hundred persons were in the audience. The board listened with some sympathy to the Gratten
parents. However, they also noted that this was their last meeting
before adjourning for their July vacation. At first they proposed
to postpone the matter until they had developed a general policy
in September. This would, of course, be after school opened. Then
the board decided to hand the responsibility for a decision over to
Spears and instructed him to meet with the Gratten parents within
ten days; they further instructed Spears that he should feel free to
take any action he wished on the matter. The board themselves
had not gone on record whether they favored or disapproved of taking race into consideration in setting school boundaries. Granted,
the school board did have a policy of general support for neighborhood schools, but within these rather vague bounds, they were in
effect empowering Spears to make policy on this matter while the
board was on vacation. Spears was reluctant to accept this carte
blanche position.

At this meeting with them, Spears apparently managed to
conciliate some of the parents by promising to keep the school

under review during the first semester it was open. But there was also a good deal of misunderstanding. Apparently an agreement was reached with the Gratten parents which collapsed the next day. In any case, by the end of July, an impressive array of statements and threats had been made. The *San Francisco Chronicle* called for elimination of every predominantly Negro school and strongly backed the Gratten parents. Terry François of the NAACP spoke to the Gratten parents and urged them to consider filing suit, picketing, and boycotting the school. CORE began a sit-in. The Gratten parents won the support of Mayor Christopher, the San Francisco Labor Council, and the Teachers' Union. In August, the *Examiner* joined the *Chronicle* in urging that the racial imbalance of Central be improved.[1] That same day the NAACP announced that it would boycott the school and would arrange for volunteer teachers to maintain a private school for the Central students. On August 14, Spears announced that Central Junior High School was a temporary expedient. This is the first public hint that the school system was considering not opening the school at all. But as Spears was making this statement, the Gratten parents announced that they would participate in the NAACP boycott. The next day they filed suit against the schools. The suit was hurriedly drafted and was not taken very seriously by any of the participants; however, it did provide the mechanism for negotiations. When the Gratten attorneys appeared before Judge Alfonso D. Zirpoli, Zirpoli refused to set a date for the hearing, but instead urged the board to meet with the plaintiffs. The parties agreed to try to settle out of court. School board attorney Breyer had originally asked that hearings be put off until after the special September 18 meeting of the board, but Judge Zirpoli merely postponed the hearing until after the regular August 21 board meeting. Although no agreement was made at this meeting with Judge Zirpoli, the Gratten representatives did mention that they would be satisfied if the Central plan was scrapped completely.[2]

[1]The *Examiner* called for the addition of three all-white schools to the Central district. The result was to add impetus to the organization of a segregationist group in that area.

[2]Judge Zirpoli was in a strong position to chair the negotiating session. As a liberal Democrat on the Board of Supervisors, he had had previous experience dealing with the school board and the civil rights leaders.

Board president Ladar stated he was willing to meet with the Gratten group, and a meeting was set for three days later. Meanwhile, the noise level increased steadily. An anti-integrationist group, the Citizens Committee for Neighborhood Schools, was organized and released a series of statements. This group, which drew much of its strength from the all-white areas just beyond Gratten, was arguing that any move to redistrict Central to improve racial balance would be illegal discrimination against whites. If Central were to be balanced, their children would be likely candidates for transfer into it.[3] In the midst of this, Ladar met with the Gratten group's attorney (who had a few days earlier been quoted as advocating a campaign of harrassing board members with phone calls at home). He later said that the meeting had been friendly and helpful.

The August 21 board meeting, like the preceding two, was held in the school system's auditorium. This time there were 1,200 persons in the audience. At the meeting, Spears informed the board that community pressures had made it impossible to maintain an educationally sound program at Central, and he recommended that plans for opening the school be dropped. Ladar stated that this represented no victory for anyone but would settle the issue, and the board voted unanimously to leave Central vacant.

Everyone expressed a little bit of dissatisfaction with the situation. Spears had stuck to his position that the schools were only concerned with education by giving an "educational" reason for changing policy on the school. The NAACP expressed concern that many of the Negro pupils would be in a less balanced school than Central if they were returned to Franklin. And the Citizens for Neighborhood Schools accused the board of giving in to anarchy. The board, and particularly Ladar, had continued to maintain a good image with the civil rights groups, but Spears remained

[3]It should be noted that the congruence of neighborhood of residence and civil rights ideology was by no means perfect. As seems to be the usual case, those persons who were faced with problems of retaining whites in an integrated neighborhood were supporting integration, and those groups who had not yet had Negroes move in were segregationists. But this does not mean that every member of the Gratten group was a loyal civil rights activist; the chairman of the Citizens Committee for Neighborhood Schools—Leon Markel—was the ex-treasurer of the integrationist Council for Civic Unity and a well-known supporter of a state FEPC law.

very much a target now. In any other city the solution of the Central School issue would have been viewed as a radical integrationist act, for many of the students were reassigned into white junior high schools, including one in the heartland of the Citizens for Neighborhood Schools. However, the civil rights groups were still on record as opposing bussing.

THE *DE FACTO* SEGREGATION ISSUE CONTINUES

The school segregation issue was still very much alive. Spears told a teachers group that they could expect the civil rights movement to pick out more schools for attack. At the September 18 meeting, demands were made that the board call for a racial census, adopt a statement endorsing "maximum" integration as a goal, and appoint a citizens' committee. The board took no action on the first two demands, but appointed a board committee composed of Mrs. Claire Matzger, James E. Stratton (the board's Negro member), and Joseph Moore to make a report. The following month the NAACP filed suit, asking the court to order the school system to present a plan to eliminate *de facto* segregation.

The board's committee reported six months later, in April, 1963. The committee endorsed the idea that race be considered when new school sites were selected, and advocated redrawing of school boundaries to reduce segregation. It also advocated the open enrollment of all high schools and the appointment of an assistant superintendent for racial problems. The report went on to reject the possibility of bussing as a solution to racial imbalance. (At that time the schools were still transporting to relieve overcrowding, moving three thousand students, many of whom were Negroes attending white schools.) The NAACP endorsed the report as a "delightful surprise." The board discussed the recommendations, and only one board member, Adolfo De Urioste, was critical of it. He joined the rest of the board in an unanimous vote adopting it.

During the next two years, the school desegregation issue moved along in a slow-paced fashion. The NAACP suit was pursued unenthusiastically, since its legal position was ambiguous. Meanwhile, the civil rights movement was busy demonstrating on the employment front. The school system implemented its high school open enrollment plan in the fall of 1963. A minor explosion occurred in 1964 when the board voted four to three to take no position on the referendum to repeal the state fair housing ordinance, and a board meeting was picketed shortly thereafter.

In the spring of 1964, only a few days before the deadline for submitting propositions for the November election, Spears presented the board with plans for a bond issue for new school construction. The board and the community reacted with surprise and some confusion. Since the plan called for a high school in a location which would result in it "being properly integrated," Spears commented that he expected the civil rights groups to "go along with it." In fact, the movement at this point was in no mood to go along with anything. The NAACP finally decided to oppose the bond issue. Bond issues require a two-thirds vote, so the NAACP opposition would be a serious threat to passage. In addition, the Central Labor Council announced that it would oppose the bonds unless the NAACP agreed to support them. Spears met in a pair of meetings with the NAACP. The agreement reached was a strange one, for the meeting found Spears opposed to building permanent schools in the ghetto and the NAACP in favor. The result was that Spears modified the plan to include construction of schools that Spears said he "would have never dreamed of asking for."

In the summer of 1965, after another round of picketing, Spears agreed to meet one of the demands presented in January, 1962, and took a racial census of the schools. The census found that the eight high schools ranged in their Negro populations from 4 to 34 per cent. The fifteen junior high schools ranged from 2 to 90 per cent, but only two were more than 50 per cent Negro. Of the ninety-five elementary schools, all had some white students. Using the 10 per cent point as a threshold, nine of the elementary schools would be classified as segregated Negro, compared with eighty-five where Negroes attended school with whites. One school of the ninety-five had no Negro students at all. Seventy-six per cent of all San Francisco Negro pupils were in integrated elementary schools. (For St. Louis and Baltimore, the figures are 14 per cent and 20 per cent.)

INTERPRETATION

The civil rights movement's unfriendly critics sometimes accuse it of provoking conflict for no apparent reason. The San Francisco story helps us to understand why school integration conflicts sometimes appear this way. As the conflict escalated, it became easier and easier for new demonstrations to break out. It also became harder and harder to understand what the fights were about. On two occasions Spears told his board that they could expect the civil rights movement to support a particular proposal. In the first case he was planning to reduce overcrowding in a school by transferring students into a new integrated school nearby. That was Central Junior High School. In the second case, he was planning the construction of a new, integrated high school. That was the 1964 bond issue. Spears can be forgiven for not understanding the civil rights movement. On the other hand, there is a steady underlying theme of the conflict that does make sense. It would be difficult for any civil rights movement to be at peace with the San Francisco schools.

At the most concrete level, Central Junior High School and the 1964 bond issue were not primarily civil rights issues. The Gratten neighborhood saw the threat of engulfment by the ghetto and asked for, and received, relief. As in Baltimore and Newark, it was easy for a liberal and militant integrated neighborhood to incorporate its demands into the policy of the civil rights movement, and thus it was easy for the movement to support them in turn. As we have now seen in four cities, the people who feel they have the most to lose from segregation are whites who are forced into predominantly Negro schools. But the Gratten demands were met. In the bond issue, the NAACP took a stance apparently in rejection of integration, and demanded ghetto schools.

But in the abstract, the demands of the civil rights movement were fairly consistent, and these demands were never agreed to. It is important to recognize that the civil rights leadership is not, and does not attempt to be, the general leadership of the Negro community. Whereas the general leader must work toward a variety of goals to meet the many needs of a neighborhood or a community, the civil rights movement has a much more restricted task. To oversimplify considerably, their aim is to eliminate racial discrimination and to create the symbols of racial non-discrimination—in other words, to establish racial equality in both the concrete and the abstract. The San Francisco movement recognized from the beginning that there would be little if any actual discrimination against Negro pupils in school districting. They therefore focused on asking the school board to recognize that racial integration was a positive value, by drawing up a plan to intentionally integrate schools. Like the other northern movements, they did did not feel it necessary to actually achieve anything resembling total integration. At the minimum, they wanted a statement of policy endorsing integration as a positive value, and some evidence that this statement was being implemented in good faith. In fact, the movement waited from January, 1962, until April, 1963, when the board subcommittee reported for the policy statement that merely committed the board to consider integration as a goal in new school construction and redistricting. Even after that, they complained that Superintendent Spears was not enforcing the new policy. At this level, it is understandable why the issue exploded as it did.

If this interpretation is correct, then we see why in San Francisco, as in other cities, compensatory education cannot be considered a substitute for integration. Compensatory education may be good for Negroes, but it does not help to meet the specific goals of the civil rights movement. Thus compensatory education is more or less irrelevant. But this line of reasoning leads us to another question. Why did the civil rights movement oppose the bond issue and demand ghetto schools? One tentative explanation is that the NAACP, like the Urban League, is not single-mindedly concerned with civil rights. The Urban League was originally developed as a social welfare agency and has only recently become an accepted member of the civil rights community. The NAACP is in many cities a well-established organization with a large membership which is the spokesman for the Negro community on many issues.[4] Thus it tends to supply general leadership rather than civil rights leadership. In addition, the NAACP concentrates on legal action, and thus becomes the natural home of Negro lawyers—some of whom expect to become holders of political office. But political leaders are by definition general leaders. Throughout our story, the San Francisco NAACP was badly split

[4]Lewis M. Killian (1965) has said that it is "... a peculiar product of the minority community. If it must be compared to any institution of the white community, it has corresponded most closely to government."

between the militants and moderates. The militants may have been reluctant to support anything the school board did, but after having taken the leap into opposing the bond issue, needed to think of some compromise which would enable them to support it. A campaign against the bonds would have been a serious drain on organization resources. With the NAACP board evenly divided between militants and moderates, some compromise device was in order—the construction of new schools was an obvious candidate, and it was attainable. Of course, schools must sometimes be built in racial ghettos; if François, as supervisor, had asked for this, no one would have been surpised; what is surprising is that the NAACP elected to play François' role.

This switch from "status" to "welfare" goals is only one of the ways in which the San Francisco civil rights movement was unstable. It was also in a state of organizational flux: Spears was forced to deal with at least nine different civil rights groups.[5]

From this viewpoint, Spears' 1962 report, from which we quoted, is very important. In the report, he refused to set racial integration as a goal of the schools and dismissed it as irrelevant. In addition, he accused the civil rights leadership of having illegitimate values—of wanting to stigmatize children by conducting a racial census.[6] Thus in this speech he managed to reject entirely the basic goal of the movement—to establish the symbols of racial equality. Despite this, we have no reason to think that he was in any way anti-Negro. Spears had apparently no hesitation at all about sending Negro children into all-white schools, including schools in recognizably anti-Negro areas. But he insisted that this was by accident; he simply did not believe that he, as an educator, should do anything to increase integration. Spears has articulately presented a point of view which seems to be shared by many

[5]In addition, the *San Francisco Chronicle* was responsible for much of the confusion about bussing. Its editorial, during the Central Junior High School controversy, called for total integration—meaning the same white-Negro ratio in every school. In its way, the *Chronicle* is as flamboyant as any blood-and-gore tabloid, except that the *Chronicle* gets its headlines from (sometimes ridiculous) civic crusades. It may be that the *Chronicle* is a prototype of the future American newspaper, in which civic affairs, rather than sex, becomes amusement for the masses.

[6]More practically, Spears was also concerned that white parents might start running from schools where the head count showed a high Negro enrollment.

school administrators—that the details of school operation are matters which laymen are ill equipped to consider. The civil rights leadership was simply not qualified to make sound decisions on questions of school organization. Or as Spears told a teachers group, "We are the ones who know about teaching and about the best way to group children for learning."

Spears' aggressive response is reflected in two public comments that the school system could expect more difficulty with the civil rights movement. In the speech just referred to, given during the moratorium on direct action which was in force during the Johnson-Goldwater campaign, he told the teachers to expect a boycott. Earlier, at the end of the Central Junior High School issue, he had predicted that the movement would not be content, but would go looking for another school to make into an issue.

If Spears was a political martyr, he was martyred as much by his school board as by the movement, for the school board was surprisingly conservative for cosmopolitan San Francisco, and, more important, it seemed to be consistently reluctant to take action. It was Spears who conducted the actual negotiations over the bond issue. The board instructed Spears to take whatever action he wished in the Central issue and then dawdled through the summer until the issue nearly exploded. Spears was not insulated by his board from the civil rights issue; he made many of the major decisions. It is fashionable now for critics of the schools to accuse professional schoolmen of arrogance. But as Joseph Pois suggests in his intelligent study of Chicago (1964), the superintendent-dominated system is often the result, not of an arrogant superintendent, but of a weak board.

The reason for the relative impotence of the board lies in its complex, semi-political recruitment structure. Between 1962 and 1965, the board included four Republicans and three Democrats; three Protestants, two Catholics, and two Jews; two women and five men; one Negro, one labor leader, and at least two members who were active in Republican party politics. With a seven-member board, it is not easy to construct such an arrangement and still guarantee the presence of enough skilled and energetic persons to make up a leadership core. Since we did not trace the history of the board, we do not know how rigid this appointment formula was.

It may have been partly a consequence of the fact that Mayor George Christopher, who appointed this board, was planning to run in the Republican primary for governor. But it is traditional in San Francisco to appoint a religiously balanced board that contains some civic leaders but that is, politically, as much bipartisan as it is nonpartisan. Before the appointment of the board's first Negro, Stratton, there were three white Protestant Republicans. In order to maintain the same religious and political composition, the Negro would have to replace one of these.[7] In addition, Christopher needed Negro support in his forthcoming attempt at the governorship, and Stratton was going to campaign for him. It is easy to find a Negro Protestant, but harder to find one who is active in Republican politics.

Assuming that we are correct in describing the rules for balancing the board, such an appointment formula would be tight enough to make it difficult for the mayor to select a board with a strong core or leadership. The appointment formula would also naturally result in a very heterogeneous board. Four members (the two white Protestants and the two Jews) are unusually wealthy— probably wealthier than any of the board members in the preceding six cities. The other three members are a social worker, a small businessman, and a union official.

Bipartisanship also results in a board that is heterogeneous on ideological lines. The result is that the board has at times had difficulty agreeing on policy. The racial issue has tended to divide the board on ethnic lines; for example, the board voted against opposing the Constitutional amendment prohibiting fair-housing legislation by a four-to-three vote, with the two white Protestants and the two Catholics outvoting the two Jews and the Negro.[8]

Finally, several of the board members are politically active, although none of them can be considered to be purely political appointees. One of the board members is a member of the Republican

---

[7]We are told that Negro leaders were invited to ask the Jewish leadership to surrender a seat. This may have been a facetious statement.

[8]The San Francisco school board was strongly criticized for taking this position. In California, governmental agencies take positions on referenda frequently. In addition, the civil rights movement argued that since the board had blamed *de facto* segregation on housing patterns, it was incumbent upon it to lend its support to any movement to break down housing discrimination.

National Committee; others apparently have participated in political club or fund-raising activities. Although four board members are wealthy, only two can be considered active members of the "civic elite" who are involved in community "projects." In neither of the two western cities studied is there a clear line separating the political activists from the civic elite. Thus, although this is not the usual "political" board, it cannot be considered "nonpolitical," either. This is an intriguing point to which we shall return in Chapter 13.

Again we see that a principal factor in deciding the course of the school integration issue is the composition of the board. In San Francisco, an inarticulate board passed a good deal of responsibility on to the superintendent. He took an extremely "professional" stance, which in turn resulted in his being accused of arrogance. However, his ideological position is really not much different from that of other superintendents who are protected by their boards.

The San Francisco board is above average in its degree of acquiescence to civil rights demands. If we look only at action, not words, the San Francisco board and Superintendent Spears have probably gone as far as any of our cities in integrating their school system. Had they not been confronted by a very militant civil rights movement, they would have had less difficulty. But San Francisco did make a serious mistake in not realizing that while action may speak louder than words, words speak also.

9
Pittsburgh

The school integration issue appeared some time between 1959 and 1963 in all seven of the cities we have examined so far. But in Pittsburgh the schools experienced a unique history of racial peace up to 1965, and when the *de facto* segregation issue was raised in 1965, it was done with relatively little controversy. Pittsburgh has not yet seen any large-scale demonstrations aimed at the schools.

Since the school integration issue arose in earnest only after we had completed interviewing in Pittsburgh, we will not describe the action in great detail, but an overview of the debate, coupled with the history of race relations prior to 1965, will be sufficient to permit analysis.

In most cities we could locate a period of smoldering opposition to the school system which led to the eruption of conflict. However, this is not the case in Pittsburgh. The *de facto* segregation issue was raised by the Urban League at one closed-door meeting of a school board committee in the early 1960's. Reports by the Urban League and the Pittsburgh Commission on Human Relations also raised the issue, but all of this hardly adds up to a concerted campaign.

The school system has effectively headed off demonstrations by doing three things: First, it has taken only limited action to increase integration, but more important, it has not waited for the demonstration before taking action; instead it has acted in anticipation of protests. Second, it has pioneered in compensatory education. Third, it has developed a pattern of close, and indeed constant, communication with the civil rights leadership. It is an essentially simple formula.

And even when we look in detail at what the schools have done, we do not uncover a complex story. For example, when a group of

Interviewing by Robert T. Stout and Morton Inger; first draft by Inger.

parents met with the board and asked for some action to relieve overcrowding in their schools, the board's senior Negro member, Richard Jones, spoke up at the next meeting and suggested that the board discuss the situation. Almost immediately, an open-enrollment plan was adopted. Students were permitted to transfer (paying their own bus fare) to any underutilized school in the city. Some 450 students took advantage of the transfer plan the first year. (The number is now 900.) Although this is less than one-half of 1 per cent of the Negro enrollment, it did result in the integration of at least two all-white elementary schools. Since that time, the school board has continued to take racial censuses, has redrawn at least one school boundary to improve racial balance, and has experimented with bussing to relieve overcrowding.

Pittsburgh has been a leader in developing compensatory education. The schools received Ford Foundation funds to develop a team-teaching program, which has now been expanded to include over one-half of the city elementary schools. The school system has also promoted Negroes to administrative positions, has increased integration of faculties, and has pioneered among big cities in crusading against what school superintendent Sidney Marland called "lily white" school texts.

The civil rights leadership reacted to this with mixed emotions. They generally saw the board as well intentioned, but resented the fact that very little had actually been done to increase integration. The board had no immediate plan for integration; it was setting its hopes on a long-range plan to establish educational parks—high schools of as many as five thousand students, surrounded by feeder schools in educational parks. Even when this was only in the planning stage, the educational park program had already attracted national attention.

But the civil rights movement was generally restrained. There are probably two reasons for this. First, the civil rights leadership respects the school board and the superintendent. As one leader puts it, "It is a good school system, and we would hate to do anything to get it into trouble." Second, the civil rights movement may have some trouble getting far enough away from the school system to attack it. The school board and the superintendent have as a matter of policy held regular informal meetings with many civil rights leaders. The board has worked closely with the Urban League, and Marland and one of the two Negro board members, Mrs. Gladys McNairy, are on the Urban League board. Marland, who was previously a suburban superintendent, has made excellent use of Frank Bolden, a Negro ex-newspaperman now on his staff, to strengthen his contacts and help him to develop a sophistication in dealing with civil rights groups.

The school board also has good contact with the civil rights leadership through the Negro board members. In the 1940's Richard Jones and Homer Brown were two of the leading civil rights attorneys. Together they brought suit to force the schools to hire Negro teachers in 1937. In 1950 Jones (then NAACP president) obtained an injunction against the city requiring it to provide police protection to Negroes swimming in integrated swimming pools. Brown was appointed to the school board, then left to accept an appointment to the County Court. Jones was later appointed to the board and has moved into an influential position on the board. At the same time, Jones has retained his contacts with the civil rights movement.

The school integration issue appeared in 1965 primarily as an outgrowth of concerns about overcrowding at Westinghouse High School. The NAACP, the Urban League, and the City Commission on Human Relations made statements critical of the school system's inactivity. The board responded by bussing 140 Negro students out of an overcrowded elementary school, but took no action at the high school level. Civil rights groups picketed in August. The board responded to these actions in three ways: First, it recruited a group of consultants to make recommendations to increase integration. Second, it devoted its annual report to "The Quest for Racial Equality." While the report did not list any short-run plans for integration, it did commit the board to integration and upgrading Negro education in strong terms. (We shall return to the annual report later.) Third, in direct response to the Westinghouse protest, the board adopted a plan to pay the transportation of students transferring out of overcrowded schools. The transfer plan was adopted in November, 1965.

As we have seen in other cities, the style of communication, and the ideological position implied by the communication, are important factors in the board's relationship with the civil rights movement. For this reason, we will take a closer look at the Pittsburgh school board's annual report. In its actual recommendations, the report could be considered moderate. While it commits the board in no uncertain terms to pursuing integration, it announces no new specific plans and promises not to adopt integration proposals which are "forced, unnatural, or irrational." Thus it seems to promise that no large-scale bussing program will be adopted. The report does place high hopes in the construction of the educational parks (but this is admittedly distant) and offers to use any reasonable integration plan in the short run. It goes on to emphasize the importance of compensatory education, integration of faculties and hiring of Negroes in non-professional positions, and the importance of using texts that present racial issues fairly. All this is not too unusual. What is unique is the amount of information, the candid way in which it is presented, and the overall tone of the document. The report contains twenty-two tables presenting such information as the percentage of Negro teachers in the system over the past ten years; the percentage of Negroes among non-professional employees hired last year; the number of scholarships awarded to graduates of predominantly Negro schools for each of the last four years; racial composition of the faculties of various schools; the number of segregated schools and the extent to which segregation has increased over the past decade; and the median achievement scores of white as opposed to Negro schools. These data are well-guarded secrets in most cities.

The tone of the report is reflected in the letter of transmittal:

This report is addressed to all the people of Pittsburgh. It seeks to declare the position of the Board of Education on the subject of racial equality in the schools. It is a statement, as starkly honest as we can make it, of the progress so far and of the large unfulfilled hopes that we in the Board of Public Education have for Negro boys and girls in the Pittsburgh Public Schools. It is a statement of the frustrations and contradictions confronting the Board on this immensely difficult subject. The report is intended neither to pacify Negro citizens, nor to console or reassure white citizens. . . .

We will disappoint the civil rights advocates who look for sudden integration but who give little help in concrete counsel toward solutions. We will startle the white citizens who seek to live in white isolation. We will disturb those, both Negro and white, who think that the social revolution of 1965 will pass over soon and that we will return to the old ways. We will not return to the old ways, and your Board of Education is determined that every possible resource of the schools shall be invested in the education of every Negro child for his ultimate, genuine integration by his own choice and by his own worth. We and our faculty declare ourselves in this report prepared to take every reasonable and rational means at our disposal to achieve this goal.

We believe that a lifetime of work remains to be done.

The letter of transmittal and the rest of the report talk about the Negro revolution, not in pedestrian legal or educational terminology, but in the language of the civil rights movement. Other cities have shied away from this, probably because it implies acceptance of the goals of the civil rights movement, or because the school system feels that Negroes would be offended. The report itself notes this:

Any report such as this, which deals with the facts of a major social revolution, risks the use of words which have acquired emotional overtones. We have not tried to avoid these words. We speak of "deprived neighborhoods" as those sections of the city where social, economic, intellectual, and residential conditions are low. While not all Negroes by any means are deprived, nor is deprivation confined to Negroes, the fact remains that most of our deprived neighborhoods are occupied primarily by Negroes, and most of our Negro families and children are deprived in one way or another. Many other terms in our current vocabulary stir emotional reactions from Negro or white. . . . We use these terms without apology or undue explanation. They are meaningful terms, contemporary to contemporary problems.

The commitment of the board to integration is made in no uncertain terms. For example, it expresses "pity" for those white children whose parents have taken them to the suburbs to avoid integration. The *Christian Science Monitor,* commenting on the report, said, "This is strong stuff. One hesitates to use the word unique, but if any other board of education has seen fit to make as equally strong a statement in an annual report sent to the public, we do not know of it."[1]

[1]Newspaper reactions to the report were varied, and a study of the reactions would itself be interesting. For example, the *Wall Street Journal* concluded that the main point of the report is that it expressed the board opposition to "reassigning students to relieve racial unbalance" and that it took "a relatively 'hard' line on forced integration." The *Journal* article implied that Pittsburgh had done less than other cities to integrate faculties; the *Monitor,* that it had done more.

But the report is also determined to avoid a self-congratulatory attitude; thus a section of the discussion of racial integration is headed "A Losing Battle." At another point, referring to the number of students using the new free-transfer provisions, it comments, "A record of 900 transfers out of a total of 18,000 Negro students enrolled in schools with predominantly Negro enrollment gives no great cause with satisfaction." (Actually, this seems to be a quite high number in comparison with other cities.) The general theme of the report is one of pessimism. It notes with candor some of the dilemmas facing it:

This report in many ways has been a recitation of forces working at cross purposes, one against the other. We have not attempted to please anyone in declaring the hard facts we face. *We have stated without qualification that we believe in integrated schools.* This works at cross purposes with those who seek to preserve all-white neighborhoods. . . .

Compensatory education means just what it says. As long as there are marked deficiencies in the educational achievement of children in schools in our deprived neighborhoods, those children must have a larger share of the limited tax dollars. So long as there is not enough money to do all the things for all the children of the city that we feel we should do, we must make the bitter choice to do more for the deprived, even at the expense of those not deprived, if necessary.

But the note of pessimism is tempered with great aspirations. It refers to a long-range goal of rebuilding the school system into educational parks as the most promising of the board's "feverish efforts to bring about improved integration." In rejecting a demand by the Urban League to appoint an assistant superintendent for integration, it even includes this comment, which could be read as a satirical reference to the way in which other cities have used the appointment of a Negro "superintendent of integration:"

We do not contemplate the establishment of a staff position such as that of "Director of Human Relations." The struggle for equality of opportunity and the rejection of discriminatory practices are the responsibility of every employee of these schools, starting with the Superintendent. In fact, the Superintendent of Schools spends approximately half his time working with matters of racial equality. . . .

INTERPRETATION

The whole approach of the school board to the issue of integration reflects a carefully thought-out position, a position that emphasizes understanding and anticipating the demands of the movement and taking action in advance, and that stresses the importance of communicating with and supporting the "responsible" leadership. Or, as one of the staff said, "This is what keeps the Larry Landry's out of Pittsburgh."[2] The board's position also involves an emotional commitment, reflected in the language of the annual report quoted above.

Several school board members commented that after Calvin Gross resigned to accept the New York superintendency, prospective candidates were interviewed extensively about their attitude toward racial issues. At that time, race was not a salient issue to the rest of the community, and this again demonstrates the fact that the school board's actions are part of a long-range "strategy."

A "strategy" consisting only of fine pronouncements and no action would be disastrous in the long run. Hence, we should reemphasize that Pittsburgh has taken action, and it has taken some action without waiting for demonstrations. This is really not true in any other city, except possibly in Buffalo before the Woodlawn issue broke out.

Since the board has had at least two superintendents during the period when the strategy was in effect, it seems fair to conclude that this policy was set by the board and not by the administration. In addition, the school board has shown its capabilities in other areas—for example, the board has been able to attract as superintendents "promising young men" who have received national recognition while at Pittsburgh. Sidney Marland is one of these; his predecessor was Calvin Gross.

What kind of school board does Pittsburgh have? Before the reform of 1911, Pittsburgh schools were governed by two separate central boards and sixty-one local district boards—all politically controlled and graft ridden. The reform of 1911, coming at a time when progressivism was strong and when the chief Pittsburgh industrialists—Carnegie, Mellon, and others—were very active in

[2]Landry was the militant leader of the two Chicago school boycotts in October of 1963 and February of 1964.

the city, established a strong elitist tradition in school board appointments. The board has fifteen members, who are appointed by the Court of Common Pleas. With a board of this size, it is relatively easy to "balance the ticket" with the appointment of a labor representative, two Negroes, two Jews, Catholics, and persons to represent the less prestigious west side of the city. But the board also has a number of prominent attorneys and industrialists. The large board relies in its decision making on a core group that includes predominantly high status persons, but that also has included Negroes and retired teachers. (One of the two Negroes on the board, Mrs. Francis McNairy, is the wife of a steelworker.) Thus the board, while predominantly high status, does effectively cross status levels. The continuity of the board is partly maintained by the board members, who locate prospective candidates for vacancies and recommend them to the judges. With the possible exception of the two Negro appointments, the ticket balancing seems to us to be only a token gesture. Pittsburgh, sometimes called the birthplace of Czechoslovakia, does not have a single East European Catholic on the board. And of all the board · members, only Richard Jones can be said to have any strong ties to the ruling Democratic party. The appointment of the second Negro, Mrs. McNairy, might be seen as an attempt to increase Negro representation. At the time of her appointment, influential Democratic party leaders were urging an appointment from the CIO (the present union representative, John A. Feigel, is a typographer; William Hart, a steelworker, also served on the board with him until a few years ago). However, the judges rejected this advice. Mrs. McNairy, like Richard Jones, is not just a Negro— she was city-wide president of the PTA at the time of her appointment. The inability of the Democratic party to influence appointments (or its unwillingness to do so) is reflected in the large number of Republicans on the board. In addition, the judges of the Court of Common Pleas represent both parties; this also tends to minimize the number of political appointments.

As in Baltimore and St. Louis, the presence of members of the civic elite on the Pittsburgh board is associated with the existence of a powerful organization of the elite. The Pittsburgh equivalent of St. Louis' Civic Progress or the Greater Baltimore Committee is the Allegheny Conference. The post–World War II renaissance of Pittsburgh, which culminated in the anti-air pollution campaign and the redevelopment of the Golden Triangle, was the work of men like R. K. Mellon, H. J. Heinz, Benjamin Fairless, department store owner Edgar Kaufmann, and Alcoa's Roy Hunt, to name only a few. It is interesting to note that few of these men would stand to gain economically from rebuilding the city—their businesses are tied to national markets. Our informants explained this by saying that these men were concerned about Pittsburgh not as an economic center, but as a place to live.[3]

In the area of our research—race relations—we can say that the Pittsburgh schools have received the support of the community. At first glance, the Pittsburgh annual report would seem to be an invitation to attack from the white conservative voter. Furthermore, if the ethnic blocs are the strong opponents of integration, they will not hesitate to assault a school board dominated by Anglo-Saxons, Jews, and Negroes. Yet it seems unlikely that such an attack will ever come. On the other hand, those cities that consciously attempted to represent the citizenry are the ones most torn by conflict. This is one of the dilemmas that this report seeks to analyze.

[3]Williams and Adrian (1963) refer to this political style as being "oriented toward providing amenities."

Part II

An Analysis of School Policy-Making

10

Definition and Overview

In the preceding chapters we have examined school integration in eight cities. There is a great deal of range, from the repeated demonstrations of Bay City to the half-hearted civil rights activity of Lawndale, from the quick agreement reached in St. Louis to the protracted fighting in San Francisco. In this chapter, we will try to sort out the common threads in these stories. First, we will look at the civil rights groups involved and the demands made by them; then we will turn to the other actors—the school superintendents, the school boards, and the white voters—to see if we can find the recurrent factors in their responses.

THE CIVIL RIGHTS GROUP AND WHAT THEY WANT

Perhaps we should pause here to point out the obvious—that in none of the eight school systems did the civil rights movement succeed in integrating a particularly large number of schools. In no city did the proportion of Negro students who were attending integrated schools increase by more than 5 per cent as a result of the raising of the integration issue. Given this, it seems fair to ask why the civil rights movements in three of these eight cities have dropped the issue. Don't they want integration?

Table 10.1 points out that there is no relationship between the number of Negroes in integrated schools and the extent to which the movement is satisfied. The data suggest that integration is not the "real" issue, and there is some truth to this. If we review the eight cases again, we see that the issue is further complicated by the fact that many of the protesting groups were not really civil rights organizations. In four cities, interracial neighborhood groups and white liberals were in the forefront of the protest.

Therefore, we must begin by separating out the various types
of organizations that made demands on the schools and by looking
at the goals of each. It is perhaps surprising that the integrated
community group appeared so frequently. In St. Louis, Baltimore,
Newark, and San Francisco, the protest originated from a community that was integrated but in danger of becoming all Negro.
In all four cases the community group wanted to maintain a sufficiently high percentage of whites (or a sufficiently low percentage of Negroes) to prevent whites from moving out. Stated
in this way, their position sounds closer to the "keep the Negroes
out" demands of segregationist white communities than to those
of a civil rights group. However, in three of the cities the neighborhood group was clearly identified as pro-integration. In all
three cases, the community group believed that the school system
was favoring all-white schools at the expense of integrated or all-
Negro schools. They argued that preventing Negroes from attending all-white schools caused Negroes to overload integrated
schools, and hence they pressed for a city-wide program of
integration.

In St. Louis the West Side Community Conference argued that
the schools were allowing whites to transfer out of neighborhood
schools. In Baltimore the parents charged that the board was
bussing Negroes into schools in integrated neighborhoods in order
to avoid sending them to all-white schools. In Newark they
charged that construction of an all-white school near them would

Table 10.1 Percentage of Negro Students Who Are in Integrated
Schools and Amount of Civil Rights Activity

City	Percentage of Negroes in Integrated Schools	Level of Civil Rights Activity[a]
San Francisco	70	High
Bay City	57	Very high
Pittsburgh	48	Very low
Lawndale	37	Moderate
Newark	28	Low
Buffalo	20	High
Baltimore	17	Very low
St. Louis	14	Moderate

[a] This ranking will be discussed and justified in Chapter 11.

pull whites out of the presently integrated schools. In each case the relief requested involved either keeping whites in the integrated schools or sending Negroes into all-white schools, or both. In San Francisco the goals of the Gratten group were not as clearly in agreement with the civil rights movement. Basically, the Gratten group wanted their junior high school to have a minority of Negroes and opposed the opening of Central Junior High School because it would have been 60 per cent Negro. However, in terms of integration, Central was an improvement over the existing situation, for some of the Negroes scheduled to attend Central were in a virtually all-Negro school. The Gratten parents solved the dilemma by arguing, not that Negroes should be excluded from Central, but that racial balance should be a city-wide goal, with no school having a majority of Negro students. When they were denied this goal, the community accepted, as a compromise, the closing of Central and the return of the students to their respective schools. Thus, although the organization was committed to integration, it accepted a compromise which actually retarded integration. In all four cases the integrated community groups adopted a universalistic approach to the issue—they could not support school integration in their own area without advocating it in the the whole city as well. Thus we see that one of the major forces operating to integrate schools is the need to maintain racially stable neighborhoods.

We were surprised at how frequently the integrated neighborhood group appeared as a proponent of school integration; we were also surprised at how seldom the Negro "community leader" appeared in this role. The distinction between civil rights leaders and Negro community leaders was made in the interpretation of the data on San Francisco. In the North, community leaders might be elected officials, members of the Negro civic elite, or leaders of neighborhood groups, while only leaders of full-time civil rights groups like the NAACP or CORE would qualify as civil rights leaders. Community leaders are concerned with the complete range of needs of the Negro community they attempt to represent. Civil rights leaders are concerned only with preventing discrimination or promoting the equality of the races. In the Deep South, community leaders might well be considered civil rights leaders, since nearly anything the Negro community wants may require overcoming the prejudices of whites before it can be obtained. Thus, if a group in a northern city were to protest the absence of a library in an elementary school, this might be treated as a community action with no racial significance. In the South, however, that same protest could easily be a demand by Negroes for equal educational facilities, and the leaders of the protest would be fighting to overcome racial discrimination. For this reason, one often cannot distinguish between community leaders and civil rights leaders in the Deep South; the local Negro business elite or the most prominent Negro political leaders may also double as leaders in the NAACP or even SCLC and CORE. In the North, however, we usually have no difficulty distinguishing between civil rights and more general leaders.

Except for the interracial neighborhood groups, school integration demands were usually pressed by civil rights leaders. In only two cases can we find Negro community leaders in the forefront of the school desegregation protests, and even these cases are ambiguous. The only Negro political leader who was active as a proponent of school integration was Alderman Clay in St. Louis, but he is one of the new breed of civil rights–oriented politicians. Most of our Negro school board members behave like community leaders. They are not anti–civil rights; they just do not specialize in it. Of course, when a civil rights issue acquires overriding importance in the community, Negro board members, like other Negro community leaders, tend to concentrate on civil rights.

The three types of actors—white liberals, community leaders, and civil rights leaders—seem to differ in the goals toward which they are oriented. James Q. Wilson distinguishes between "welfare" and "status" goals among Negro leaders. He defines "welfare" ends as "those which look to the tangible improvement of the community or some individuals in it through the provision of better services, living conditions, or positions." "Status" ends are "those which seek the integration of the Negro into all phases of the community on the principles of equality—all Negroes will be granted the opportunity to obtain the services, positions, or material benefits of the community on the basis of principles other than race" (Wilson, 1965, p. 185). When an integrated community struggles to maintain itself, it is primarily concerned with protecting the life-style of its residents from the evils of the ghetto. Hence we put this goal toward the welfare end of the continuum. The integrated neighborhood groups are frequently led by white liberals, and we hypothesize that, compared with Negro civil rights leaders, white liberals are welfare-oriented in other ways as well.

For example, the Buffalo Citizens Committee for Human Relations was involved in operating a compensatory education program. The white education chairman of the Newark NAACP stressed inadequate educational opportunity in Negro schools. Both are clearly welfare goals. Even when the white leadership asked for integration, the approach often seemed to be welfare-oriented. Thus the demand for integration in Baltimore resulted in the complete elimination of double-shift schooling for Negroes. Among the white liberals, there is often the implicit or explicit assumption that integration is a positive educational value for the child in the integrated school, and that every Negro child in a segregated school is a victim of inferior education. Thus, we argue that white liberals, with their lack of concern for symbolic victories, are most determined to achieve total integration and are dissatisfied with anything less. (Of the eight cities, the civil rights leader who expressed most dissatisfaction to our interviewers was white in five cases. It may also be that white leaders have a stronger sense of efficacy than Negroes and thus are less satisfied with, or accustomed to, taking "no" for an answer.)

There is another seeming contradiction here: How can a utopian goal such as total integration go hand in hand with a welfare orientation? The contradiction is not a logical one. There is nothing in the notion of welfare orientation that requires that it be accompanied by limited goals. Wilson (1965) argued that Negro welfare leaders tend to be more conservative. We are merely saying that in our biracial sample we have found a somewhat different pattern. [1]

[1] The relationship between "status" goals and limited goals has probably changed in the past few years; SNCC's and CORE's southern shock troops may be more welfare-oriented than the NAACP leaders who were the militants of a decade ago. However these new groups do not appear in our study.

The Negro community leader must almost of necessity hold welfare goals, and thus he is like the white liberal in this respect. However, the traditional Negro civil rights leaders—the NAACP officers, for example—are much more status-oriented. The typical civil rights leader's main goal can be put simply. Stated negatively, it is to eliminate racial discrimination and all the symbols of it. Stated positively, the goal is to persuade society to accept the concept of racial equality. This approach is stated most clearly in the Pittsburgh Urban League's report on school segregation in that city: "We regard a community as integrated when opportunities for the achievement of respect and the distribution of material welfare are not limited by race." We will call these goals "symbolic" ones; our definition is close to Wilson's definition of "status" ends. This definition, deceptively simple, seems to explain the pattern of demands made by the movement in almost all our cities. In particular, it clarifies the Bay City and San Francisco situations.

In Bay City and San Francisco, most of the focus was upon the demand for a statement of policy committing the school system to integrate the schools. Here we see excellent examples of the *de facto* segregation issue. These two school systems are statistically the most integrated in our sample. In neither case was it assumed that the school system was trying to prevent schools from being integrated. Rather, the board was asked to recognize and to express regret over schools that were segregated as a result of housing patterns. In neither Bay City nor San Francisco did the demands go much beyond this point. The great concern over the importance of policy statements about *de facto* segregation fits with the hypothesis that the goal of the civil rights movement is to obtain public commitment to the principle of racial equality.

In none of the eight cities was there any real pressure to desegregate a large number of schools. The most significant action, in terms of number of students, occurred in Baltimore, where white liberals handled the negotiation. This brings us to our second hypothesis: if the goals of the movement are oriented toward symbolic equality, then limited integration is sufficient to meet the demands. A commitment toward integration, and the demonstration that the commitment was made in good faith, are enough.

The phrase "symbolic goals" has a somewhat negative con-
notation, and it may be important to clarify our meaning at this
point. In a sense, most arguments in favor of integration are
symbolic. The social science literature referred to in the *Brown*
decision's Footnote 11 argues that the Negro child is unable to
develop an adequate sense of self-worth in the segregated school,
since the school is a symbol of the unwillingness of whites to
permit interracial contact. Thus, there are two arguments in
favor of integration of schools. The first, stemming from *Brown*,
is that the segregated classroom is a barrier to the child's learning.
Since this argument assumes a direct link between integration
and the improvement of education for each individual child, we
have called this a welfare orientation. The other approach sees
the integrated classroom as a symbol of racial equality that the
entire city will see. Integration may not benefit the individual
child, but it will benefit Negroes as a whole by helping to break
down the traditional beliefs in social inequality. We have called
this the more symbolic orientation, but really both arguments see
integration as a valuable symbol. The only argument that sees
integration in non-symbolic terms is the statement that the school
system will provide better education to a classroom that has some
white students in it. ("Sitting next to a white child is no guarantee that my child will learn, but it does guarantee that he will be
taught.")

From this viewpoint, the battle over Lawndale's Woodside
High School makes much more sense. Recall that Woodside was
built to serve high income families. After the school was completed,
there was no reasonable way to district the school so as to enroll
more than a handful of Negroes in it. Nevertheless, there was
considerable pressure to redistrict the school "fairly." The board
voted not to redistrict, stating that no redistricting could integrate
the school. What was the point of the argument? In our terms of
reference, the construction of the school, with its gerrymandered
boundary, and the removal of these students from the older integrated schools, was perceived as an act of favoritism toward
these students. But the goal of the movement is to eliminate any
symbols of favoritism, and to prevent any action which would indicate that white students are "more important" to the board than

Negroes. Thus integration was not the relevant issue; the symbol of racial favoritism was. This same parallel appears in southern desegregation; even when only a handful of Negroes are involved, a school board is seen as more liberal if it spreads the Negroes through several schools rather than only "contaminating" one group of white students. The success of an integration plan is measured by the number of whites affected. *Southern School News* and this report both measure integration in terms of the number of Negro students in white schools—presumably on the assumption that this is the number of students benefiting from integration. From the point of view of the civil rights movement, it might be better to measure the number of white students in integrated schools.

Compensatory education is another good example of how the civil rights leader sets priorities. From the viewpoints of one concerned with eliminating discrimination and establishing the symbols of desegregation, actual educational techniques are more or less irrelevant. And this is the attitude of the "ideal" civil rights leader toward compensatory education—it is irrelevant to his goals. It may take on some relevance if the school board chooses to state that compensatory education is designed to compensate for the deprivations which Negroes have been and are being subjected to. Unfortunately, the typical school board makes it clear by its use of the phrase "culturally deprived" and by its extension of compensatory education to poor whites that compensatory education is not designed for this purpose but only to overcome inadequate home and neighborhood environments. In some cases the civil rights leaders will object to this failure to recognize the special case of the Negro. However, the common reaction is to express support for compensatory education but to consider it no substitute for integration.

We are now able to understand why the school integration movement can so easily become a personal attack upon individual school board members or school superintendents. If the overriding need of the Negro community is recognition as racial equals, and if the demands of the civil rights movement to achieve this end are rejected, then it might seem to follow (although this is poor logic) that the demands were rejected because the school board or the superintendent rejects the concept of racial equality. Just as procedures like school gerrymandering are symbols of racial inequality that must be eliminated, so the individual who opposes the civil rights movement is also a symbol of racial inequality who must be removed from office.

The distinction between welfare and symbolic goals applies to other civil rights issues as well. The major goals of the civil rights movement—fair employment, open housing, integrated schools, equal use of public accommodations—all fit our definition of symbolic demands, in that the emphasis is upon removing barriers to Negro mobility, rather than actually trying to move Negroes into these newly opened opportunities. For example, the NAACP may negotiate with an employer to hire Negroes, but once the employer has agreed, the NAACP ordinarily will not feel that it is its function to recruit applicants.

Of course, no civil rights organization is purely symbol-oriented. This is especially true of the Urban League, which has a strong social welfare orientation, the "white liberal" civil rights groups, and the NAACP, which often includes some major community leaders and young political leadership. It is this conglomeration of symbol- and welfare-oriented goals that makes the movement somewhat unpredictable. We discussed this earlier in analyzing the San Francisco NAACP's insistence upon construction of new schools. Ordinarily, school construction is irrelevant to the civil rights movement's symbolic goals. When a northern NAACP begins pressing for school construction, the shift of goals may baffle the school system. Similarly, the frequent combination of welfare and symbolic demands may lead to internal contradiction—for example, the demand that good teachers be kept in Negro schools and the demand that Negro teachers be allowed to teach in white schools.

Much of the criticism of the movement—that it personalizes the conflicts, that it is not really interested in the improvement of Negro education, or that it pays excessive attention to the words and not the deeds of the schools—can be seen as a misunderstanding of the symbolic goals of the movement.

In another respect, these criticisms serve to stress the tension between the civil rights movement and the Negro community as a whole. The movement is a specialized interest group, with highly restricted goals. As we have pointed out, there is some contradiction between these goals and the more welfare-oriented goals of the "man in the street." This is best reflected by the fact that before the St. Louis civil rights movement began supporting bussing, there had been community opposition to it; conversely, after the new schools in the West End were opened, the most militant of the movement picketed the construction of these "ghetto schools." The problem is complicated by the fact that it is not clear how the civil rights leadership is responsive to the will of the Negro community. They are not elected as political leaders are. How, then, can we know that they represent Negroes?[2] This problem exists on paper more than it does in reality. For one thing, the movement receives votes of confidence in the form of participation in massive demonstrations. If the movement becomes too extreme, its support from Negro general leaders and from the Negro masses will fall off, boycotts will flop, and the competition among civil rights groups will influence the leaders to find a more popular issue. This is the sort of social control advocated by Carl Sandburg: "Maybe some day they'll give a war and nobody will come."

The other reason why this tension is not troublesome is that the civil rights leaders have been recognized as the heroes of Negro culture. And this in turn is evidence that Negroes endorse the values of the civil rights movement. In the 1940's it was common practice for the NAACP to listen to a complaint about schools in some southern community, then transform the community's grievance into a demand for integration. Similar tactics have been used in northern schools in the past few years. That the tactics are successful indicates that the Negro community is willing to accept the values, and the leadership, of the civil rights movement.

THE RESPONSE OF THE SCHOOL SUPERINTENDENT

One barrier to the civil rights movement is the school superintendent. During the civil rights controversies, ten different superintendents served in our eight cities. Seven can be said to

[2]NAACP officers are elected by vote of the full membership. This occasionally results in the replacement of civil rights leaders by community leaders. One striking example is Chicago, where in the early 1950's the precinct workers associated with the Democratic party voted as a bloc to elect a candidate supported by Negro political leaders.

have acted autonomously, without board instruction, in rejecting demands of the civil rights movement; in contrast, only three stand out as having urged their board to take a liberal position.

In studying the statements made by these superintendents, three themes recur very regularly. The most common is the insistence on a "color-blind" policy of ignoring racial distinctions. Thus superintendents have opposed referring to schools as segregated or integrated and have argued that taking racial censuses of either pupils or teachers would be illegal or at least embarrasing to both students and staff. Plans that require the schools to attempt to obtain integration have been accused of being discriminatory. One Buffalo board member's statement, that integrating Wood-lawn Junior High School would discriminate against Negro students by limiting their numbers in the new school to make room for whites and that these students "should not be sacrificed on the altar of racial balance" reappears, in less colorful language, in the statements of several superintendents. All eight cities in our sample have some sort of open enrollment policy; in several cases it was adopted as a result of demands for school integration. Yet in only two cases is the plan actually keyed to a racial criterion. Everywhere else, transfers are allowed only on the basis of overcrowding and available space, and in most cases the school system does not attempt to determine whether such plans increase or reduce integration. The exceptions are Buffalo and Newark, where students transferring from predominantly Negro schools are given priority.

Although seven of the eight cities use busses to transport students out of crowded schools, and in each case the result is to increase integration, yet in none of the cities is the racial composition of either the sending or receiving school considered officially as a criterion in arranging such transfers. Compensatory education programs for the culturally deprived are also officially color blind. Very frequently, pointed reference is made to poor whites or other non-Negro minorities in order to advertise the fact that the program is not for Negroes per se. (This is why the Pittsburgh annual report's statement on compensatory education is so unusual.) In extreme cases, school superintendents have sometimes managed to speak at length about integration or civil rights issues without ever using the word Negro.

Coupled with this attention to color blindness is the stress placed on a narrow definition of the function of the school as "educational," rather than "social." This is most clearly expressed in Spears' statement that the bringing of students together in the classroom is a necessity of teaching, but the effects of the resulting interaction between students are not within the purview of the educational system. The school administrator expresses great reluctance to "expand the function of the schools" as demanded by color-conscious plans.

The third theme which recurs in the statements of school superintendents, although not as often as the first two, is an extreme defensiveness about the schools, coupled with an intolerance of "lay" criticism. Thus some school administration reports seem to delight in pointing out errors made by their critics. Frequent references are made, not always with justification, to the inability of lay persons to make decisions on problems requiring educational expertise. Finally, the defensiveness of some school staffs is reflected in their unwillingness or inability to engage in coherent dialogue—criticisms are frequently answered with either flat disagreement or vague, off-the-point replies, or replies with vast quantities of irrelevant detail. The two most striking exceptions are Pittsburgh's Marland, who has regularly engaged in long conversations with civil rights leaders and supplied highly specific and clear information on racial issues, and Buffalo's Manch, who openly admitted that there was no particular computer mythology involved in the selection of a school boundary for the Woodlawn school.

On the basis of our interviews and the documents collected, we propose that these three themes taken together represent one sort of ideal type of superintendent behavior. Obviously, no superintendent behaves in this way at all times, and some school administrators do not fit the ideal at all. If we try to capture all three of these themes in a single phrase, we could say that they represent components of a narrow and defensive definition of their occupational role. What are some possible explanations for this ideology?

We should consider the possibility that the ideology is just a device to conceal anti-Negro sentiment. This strikes us as unlikely, however. The private attitudes of the superintendents, as expressed on our questionnaires, are not particularly conservative on racial issues. Further, the men who are more liberal on race are just as likely to express the values we have discussed here as are the more conservative men; there does not seem to be much correlation between the racial attitudes and the ideological position we have defined here.

A much more reasonable hypothesis is that the superintendents feel insecure in their positions and react accordingly. This could easily be the result of their social backgrounds. The only channel into the school superintendency is through the ranks of teaching. This means majoring in education in college, usually teaching school for several years, and then rising through administrative posts. This restricts the number of persons eligible for the post dramatically. First, they must be male in almost every case. Education is a woman's field, and male students who major in education tend to be of low socioeconomic status. Any school superintendent will, then, be highly mobile socially, and he may bear strains associated with his position in an unprestigious and feminine occupation. It is hard to imagine that the big city school superintendent anticipated becoming a highly paid executive when he entered teachers college. We know of no relevant data on the occupational attitudes of men who are highly mobile, but it seems reasonable that they might have difficulty accepting the responsibilities of their position and might feel insecure about their ability to stay in office.

There are other important reasons why an administrator might develop a defensive ideology. As a teacher, he is solely responsible for the success or failure of his students, and unlike the college instructor, he must deal directly with their parents. Other occupational roles, such as doctors, lawyers, and ministers, require direct confrontation with clients, but usually their professional competence cannot be so easily questioned. The teacher, however, is not obviously doing anything that the parent is incapable of doing. Furthermore, he has few or no criteria by which to determine whether he is doing a good job. He is also subject to a second criticism—not only is he not teaching Johnnie well enough, he may be teaching him the wrong way. For in at least some cases, he is the harbinger of foreign values—classical learning or middle-class behavior patterns, for example. Fortunately for the contemporary teacher, these "foreign values" now seem widely diffused through the society. Parents want their children to go to college, and if they must learn certain subjects to get into college, the parent is agreeable. But the present generation of superintendents began teaching in the 1920's, when this problem may have been much more serious. The problem is complicated by the fact that the teacher must resist parental intrusions in the classroom while at the same time urging the parents to "take an interest in their child's education."

Thus the teacher must develop values to protect himself from being required to justify the material he teaches and the grades he gives. The professional ideology of the teacher does this—by insisting on certification, on methods courses, on rejecting the use of lay persons in teaching roles, and, in extreme cases, in the theories that preschool education by parents may retard the child.[3] Whatever the legitimacy of such a position, it enables a teacher to resist the criticisms of parents and of citizens' groups. In addition, the use of educational testing may help the teacher to justify his actions; if his students don't learn as much as the parents expect, it is because of their low I.Q.'s.

When a teacher becomes a superintendent, he again finds himself in conflict with the community, this time as represented by a school board, which he sees, often correctly, as conservative and traditionalist.[4] The simple dichotomy between policy and administration is a false one; the superintendent finds himself spending part of his time trying to persuade the board to adopt his policy ideas, and more time trying to protect himself from board interference in ongoing administration.

[3]Harper Lee satirizes this in *To Kill a Mockingbird;* her treatment of the teacher who forbids the child's father to teach her to read reflects a disrespect for the teaching profession which is common in twentieth-century writing.

[4]Vidich and Bensman (1958) paint a portrait of a local school administrator as an innovator constantly straining to get his conservative board to support some new step. One study of school board members in Illinois found that 28 per cent of the board members stated that one factor in the board's rejection of a candidate for school superintendent was the candidate's "unsound educational views." In addition, the study notes, "It was particularly noticeable during interviews with board members that they were especially conscious of the need for the candidate's having a background which would fit the community. Most boards expressed the quality desired in these terms: 'We wanted someone who would fit into the community and become a part of it—someone who would be happy here.' " (See Baker, 1952, pp. 69–71.)

If a profession is made up of men who share common needs for a defensive ideology, the profession will develop such an ideology. In addition, the profession as a whole may need such defenses. The public school system has had to deal with a variety of encroachments. It has had to contend with corruption in politically sponsored systems. It has fought with the public on Deweyism, on the teaching of reading, on vocational education, on the teaching of German during World War I, on communism in textbooks, and a host of other issues. Keeping politics out of schools has now become a watchword.

The educational profession and many individual superintendents have responded to these conflicts in three ways: (1) by narrowing their frame of reference so that they can silence critics by refusing responsibility for increasing juvenile delinquency, moral decline, and the lack of patriotism of its graduates; (2) by trading low priority values, about the rights of labor or of Negroes, for higher priority values such as freedom of curriculum reform; and (3) by developing the claim that expertise is required to make school decisions, so that critics can be ignored.

The pattern of a defensive profession made up of low status men who have had to resist public demands throughout their careers is present in big city school systems, but it was even clearer in the small town America of the 1920's and 1930's. The foreignness of education, the demands of parents on teachers, the absence of academic freedom, and the conservatism of elected school board members—all the factors we have listed—were exaggerated in the dense social network of the small town. For the teacher, *Stadt luft macht man frei*. And, curiously enough, the recruitment pattern for big city school superintendencies tends to attract men from small town and farming backgrounds. First, the rural or small town high school student, presumably because of his more limited occupational horizons, is more likely to go into teaching. In addition, if he begins teaching in a small town (where he is one of the few male teachers), he can more quickly rise to a principalship and become a superintendent at a young age. Thus the small town teacher gains administrative experience while his big city colleague is still in the classroom. Big cities want experienced men as superintendents, but experienced men can only be found in the small cities; the men who become superintendents in small cities tend to be teachers in smaller cities, and the men who teach in such cities tend to be born there.[5]

This argument is supported by an analysis of college seniors choosing educational administration in 1961 (Davis and Bradburn, 1961). Only a tiny fraction of college freshmen (0.2 per cent) chose educational administration as a career. This number increased through the four years of college very rapidly, but even as seniors, barely enough students selected educational administration to fill the demand. Only 5 per cent of all persons going into public education specified educational administration; this would imply a ratio of one administrator to twenty teachers, which is probably too low. The population was too small to make accurate estimates possible, but we do find the following statistically significant differences: Students who chose educational administration were from poorer families, and from families where both parents have low educational attainments. Of thirty occupational careers, educational administration students were lowest in father's education; even students choosing nursing and agriculture were higher. They were also overwhelmingly rural; students from farm areas were twice as likely to choose educational administration as were students from metropolitan areas. Students oriented toward educational administration saw themselves as religious, conventional, and not intellectual. A majority intended to put off graduate training until after they had taught for at least a year.

We can also document this pattern by examining the biographies of the men who direct the schools that participate in the "Great Cities" research program (Table 10.2). The eleven superintendents listed in the 1964 edition of *Who's Who* can be divided into two groups—the "locals" and the "mobiles." The three "locals" all grew up in large cities and began their teaching in the

[5]Baker (1952) notes that even boards of education in very small communities place high value on previous experience in considering candidates for superintendent; in fact, 53 per cent of the superintendents in systems employing ten to nineteen teachers had been superintendents prior to coming to their present job. Baker writes, "This emphasis [on having experience as a superintendent] seems somewhat unrealistic in terms of recruiting young men." And later he notes, "There is little question that boards are seeking young men as superintendents." Thus we see that the small town teacher is probably the only one who can climb the ladder fast enough to be both young and experienced, as these boards wish.

Table 10.2 Careers of Prominent School Superintendents

City	Name	Place of Birth	Undergraduate College	First Teaching Position	Number of Years As Teacher or Principal	Age at Advanced Degree	First Administrative Post	Age (1963)
Locals:								
Los Angeles	Jack P. Crowther	Salt Lake City	Univ. Utah	Los Angeles	8	M.A.—46	Asst. supt., Los Angeles	54
Buffalo	Joseph Manch	(In Poland)	Univ. Buffalo	Buffalo	12	Ed.D.—45	Staff, Buffalo	53
Philadelphia	Allen Wetter	Philadelphia	Temple Univ.	Philadelphia	22		Dist. supt., Philadelphia	63
Mobiles:								
Washington	Carl Hansen	Wolbach, Nebraska	Univ. Nebraska	(In Nebraska)	20	Ed.D.—38	Asst. to supt., Washington, D.C.	57
San Francisco	Harold Spears	Snayzee, Indiana	Wabash College	Evansville, Indiana	No data	Ed.D.—37	Supt., Highland Park, Illinois	61
Baltimore	George Brain	Thorpe, Washington	Central Washington State	(In Washington State)	6	Ed.D.—39	Asst. supt., Bellevue, Washington	—
Milwaukee	Harold Vincent	Knox, Indiana	Greenville College, Illinois	Asst. principal, Washington Springs, South Dakota	11	LL.D.—54	Asst. supt., Canton, Ohio	66
Chicago	Benjamin Willis	Baltimore	George Washington Univ.	Henderson, Maryland	12	Ed.D.—49	Supt., Denton, Maryland	62
Deviants:								
Detroit	Sam Brownell	Peru, Nebraska	Univ. Nebraska	Principal, Peru, Nebraska	2	Ph.D.—26	Supt., Grosse Pointe, Michigan	63
New York	Calvin Gross	Los Angeles	UCLA	Los Angeles	4	Ed.D.—36	Supt., Weston, Massachusetts	44
Pittsburgh	Sidney Marland	Danielson, Conn.	Univ. Connecticut	West Hartford, Connecticut	3	Ph.D.—41	Supt., Darien, Connecticut	49

city where they are now superintendents. Of the remaining eight, six were born in small towns, only two went to urban universities, and seven began teaching in small cities. They spent a median time of eight years at the rank of teacher or principal. Notice that three of these men deviate from this pattern conspicuously. Calvin Gross is a mobile urbanite, the only superintendent who began teaching in one big city and then wound up as superintendent in another. Samuel Brownell also differs from the other mobiles, since he went on immediately for a doctorate without pausing to teach. He is possibly the only man in this list who could have had a clear picture of his future career at the time he took his bachelor's degree. Sidney Marland's career resembles Gross's and Brownell's in that he also took less than the usual eight years to move into central administration. The presence of these three deviant cases actually tends to support our general thesis, since these three men are highly respected by the critics of the "eduational establishment." We have one final bit of data to bolster our argument. Five school superintendents gave us background data that included their father's occupation and the educational attainment of their parents. Of the five, two were the sons of farmers, one of a small town merchant, and two of blue collar workers. None of the five had fathers who attended college, although three had mothers who had at least finished junior college.

Thus we see that the interaction between civil rights leaders and school superintendents has the preconditions for conflict. They literally do not speak the same language. In addition, both live in a world hostile to them and are unlikely to be very patient in dealing with each other. In six of the eight cities, school integration quickly became a conflict between the movement and the superintendent. In St. Louis and Baltimore, the superintendent wrote rebuttals to the charges of the civil rights leadership which were received angrily by the protesters. In Newark, demands that the superintendent be dismissed were made even before the first school integration incident occurred. In Lawndale and San Francisco, the superintendents flatly refused the first demands made upon them. Finally, in Bay City, the superintendent, McDonough, was criticized by the movement, although his successor has taken a more liberal position than his board and has not been criticized as much. Only two superintendents, Manch and Marland, have held the respect of the civil rights leadership (and Manch fell out of their favor after Woodlawn).

THE SCHOOL BOARD AND THE WHITE VOTER

But the school superintendent, in almost every one of our cases, has found that racial policy was taken from his hands by the school board. In six of our cities we can mark a point when the major decision which most influenced the outcome of the school integration issue was made not by the superintendent, but by the board. In some cities it is easy to locate such a point—in Baltimore, for example, when the school board assumed responsibility for negotiation with the civil rights leadership, or in Newark on the two occasions when the board members and the mayor met with the civil rights leadership to reach a compromise. In San Francisco the board's ad hoc committee presented a report which was, according to one NAACP leader, a "pleasant surprise" after Spears' earlier speech. In Bay City the superintendent's recommendations were disregarded. In Buffalo, while it is true that the school superintendent supported the final plan to segregate the Woodlawn school, it seems likely that he would not have done so if the board had not made its own position clear. In St. Louis, it is harder to trace out the relationship between the board and the superintendent, but the board, not the superintendent, appointed the citizens' committee which made the recommendations on which the compromise was reached, and we have other evidence to indicate that the superintendent was advised by the board to take action to meet the demands. In the remaining two cities, Lawndale and Pittsburgh, there has been no evidence of any disagreement between the board and the administration, but in both cities the administration stays in close touch with the school board and seems to be responsive to its will. Both these cities changed superintendents without changing policy on civil rights.

We cannot easily characterize the "typical" school board in the way we have the "typical" superintendent and the two types of civil rights leaders. As we have seen, board members vary considerably in their backgrounds, motivations, and attitudes toward school integration. Further, board members are in an ambiguous situation, where there are few clear guidelines to permit them to reach a decision easily. There are several reasons why there are no convenient guidelines.

The typical school board is not closely knit. It ordinarily meets to handle the legal paperwork of the schools; at irregular intervals it makes specific decisions about a particular school or on a particular policy. But it can be thought of as making school policy only in a firefighting fashion. If an issue comes up, it acts; otherwise, it does not. It may not take a position at all on some of the most fundamental issues of school policy, simply because those particular policies have not been made salient by community discussion. The result is that the school board members do not, either as individuals or as a group, have a highly articulated educational policy. Almost every time they oppose the superintendent, or the superintendent comes to them for guidance, the board has some difficulty making a decision. Every issue is different and every decision can take a good deal of time. The school integration issue is a good example of this.

The typical school board avoids issues that are not important, if for no other reason than to save time for issues that are. The result is that in virtually every city the initial complaints of the civil rights movement are ignored. Even Pittsburgh did not take action on integration until the second time the issue was brought up. Of course, the board then appears to be defending the status quo. By the time the civil rights movement begins to make noise, they can rightly claim that the school board has been ignoring the problem, and the school board begins to discuss the issue with one strike against it.

The second step the school board may take to avoid lengthy discussion of an issue is to refer it to the superintendent. As we have already pointed out, the superintendent and the civil rights leadership do not make a good partnership, and in none of our eight cities was the issue resolved at this level. In the typical case, the civil rights movement interprets the superintendent's remark as a flat rejection of their request, or even as an insult. Thus, by the time the board realizes that it must itself handle the issue, tempers are already frayed on all sides.

When the board does begin to consider the issue, it must first develop ground rules for its decision-making process and a frame of reference for its decision. This is difficult, principally because the issue is different from most that the board faces: it involves the total community, it has strong emotional overtones, and it is general, rather than specific. If the board adopts the standard tactic of holding public hearings in an effort to determine what the citizens want, it may not receive much help. Two school systems used an outside committee of citizens at this point. St. Louis appointed such a committee only a few days after the issue opened. In Lawndale the Citizens Committee was appointed at the request of the civil rights movement.

In other cases, the board or a special committee of board members may attempt to formulate policy without the help of outsiders. In such cases, if the committee members attempt to serve as a fact-finding body, they may be overwhelmed by the reports of the administration, and become mere spokesmen for the administration position. (For example, the report of the board subcommittee in Baltimore was considerably more cautious than the board's behavior only a few months later; this despite the fact that the subcommittee members were quite liberal in outlook.) If, however, the board attempts to develop a position independent of the administration, it will soon be in relatively uncharted waters. Left to its own devices, the board must develop a philosophical position on the school integration issue.

One might argue that the board's situation is not so ambiguous; that the board realizes that the white parents will not tolerate school integration; and that it therefore has the simple, if not easy, job of trying to squelch the civil rights movement. Actually, this does not seem to be the case. First of all, we know that some elements of the white community supported the civil rights movement in most of our cities. In addition, we know from several national surveys that northern whites express support for integration. For example, an NORC poll taken in 1963 found 75 per cent of northern whites saying "same schools" to the question, "Do you think white and Negro students should go to the same schools or to separate schools?" More to the point, another poll found only 7 per cent of northern whites saying they would object to sending their child to a school with a few Negro students, and only 34 per cent would object if the school were half Negro (Erskine, 1962; Hyman and Sheatsley, 1964). We can also see from our eight case studies that segregationist opposition was not an overriding factor. In Baltimore and St. Louis, the opposition to school integration appeared principally after the school integration decision had been made; in both cases the opposition was short-lived. Since these are our most southern cities, we would expect the opposition in other cities to be even weaker. The opposition to school integration in Bay City and Lawndale appeared only after the board had made it clear that it would not integrate the schools in question; in these cases the segregationists played the role of supporting the school board rather than opposing them. (When one of the leaders of the Woodside homeowners' association in Lawndale ran against a school board member in the election, he was eliminated before the runoff election.) In Buffalo the petitions opposing the integration of the Woodlawn school were submitted before the board took a final decision on the matter, but they were in support of board member Parlato's proposal. In all three cases the white parents' groups appeared only after their point of view had been taken by either the school board or some members of the board. They did not initiate the opposition. In effect, the school board recruited their support in two cases.

When the anti-integrationists are in opposition to the school board, they can be squelched fairly easily. San Francisco is perhaps the most striking case. The Committee for Neighborhood Schools protested plans to increase the number of whites in Central Junior High School and also opposed bussing of Negro students, but the school system did bus Negroes into the junior high school where the Committee was strongest, and there was no public opposition. Obviously, these anti-integration movements are weak; they are not self-initiating except in the border cities and usually do not survive their first defeat. (Contrast this with the reaction of the typical civil rights movement to rejection of demands.) We might even go so far as to advance this hypothesis, which the data in all our cases seem to fit: that the school board can mobilize community support for its position, *regardless of whether that position is segregationist or integrationist!*

If the incidents described in the eight cities are representative, we can hypothesize that, generally, white parents will not protest integration as long as (1) the school their children are to attend is not predominantly Negro; (2) white students are not tranferred out of their present schools; (3) white students are not forced to attend schools located in the ghetto; and (4) neighborhood racial stability is not threatened. To this we might tentatively add one qualifying statement—whites may protest if they feel that the school integration program is too obviously a surrender to Negro political power. This statement is still somewhat oversimplified; we do not mean to suggest that this is a hard and fast formula. But this "formula" might explain why in at least seven of our eight cities, Negroes are traveling into all-white neighborhoods to attend previously all-white schools without community objection.[6]

Thus we see that the board is free to take action within broad limits. It will not be under much pressure from segregationist groups while it is making its decision. At the same time, the civil rights movement is not exerting much pressure either. At least it is difficult to argue that the demonstrations and other tactics of civil rights groups are particularly frightening to the school board. In most cities court suits were filed, but they were either dropped or settled out of court in every case. In both Bay City and Buffalo the state government was brought in, and in the case of Buffalo this seems to have forced the board to act. (In both cities state action came after our interviewing, so we have only newspaper reports of the action.) But in at least five cities the board was in little danger of being overruled by higher political authority. Picketings, sit-ins, and street demonstrations are embarrassing to the school board only if the school board chooses to be embarrassed. (In St. Louis the rush-hour march was a minor public inconvenience.) The ultimate weapon in the civil rights arsenal is nothing more impressive than a one-day school boycott. In contrast, when the school board deals with a teachers union, it is often threatened with a strike of indefinite duration; the National Education Association can even take action to discourage new teachers from entering the system.

Finally, the school boards in most of these cities operate inde-

[6]The eighth city, Lawndale, began bussing in 1966.

pendently of other community leaders. Only in Newark did the mayor take an active role in negotiating a settlement. In Lawndale, Bay City, and San Francisco the mayor expressed some dissatisfaction with the way the schools were handling the issue, with little effect. Lawndale and Bay City have independently elected boards, so that the mayor has very little power. In San Francisco, Mayor Christopher's letter in support of integration was presented to the school board, but it is difficult to know how much effect this had on the board. In Baltimore the city council threatened to call the school board down for having been negligent enough to have to use widespread bussing to solve its overcrowding problems. However, the mayor managed to squelch this issue. In general, we do not think that any of these boards were greatly influenced by other city officials. Thus the school board is free to act within a very broad range of options.

We have suggested that the typical board has no clearly articulated philosophy of education. In fact, school boards seem to behave in a highly pragmatic fashion. They move from one issue to another as issues become urgent. But the first question raised by the civil rights movement is a philosophic one: Should school boards intentionally attempt to integrate schools, or should they continue to operate in a color-blind fashion? In all eight cities the school boards have been asked to go on record to (1) recognize the existence of segregated schools, and (2) promise to do something about it. Such a statement meets some of the more symbolic goals of the civil rights movement; it puts a governmental body on record as opposed to discrimination, not only in the schools but in effect in housing as well, and commits it to making a demonstration of its belief in racial equality.

No clear educational arguments can be made either for or against such a policy statement. Until the publication of Coleman (1966), there were very few data indicating that Negro children learn more or derive other psychological benefits from being in integrated schools. On the other hand, no educational argument suggests that the integration of schools is a bad policy. The school board thus makes its decision without any particular rationale. An obviously important question is, "Does the board trust the motives of the civil rights movement?" They may feel that the movement is "really" asking for immediate integration of all schools, or something like that. The roots of these differences in perception lie in the view the board members have of the civil rights movement, and these roots appear in the tone with which the board carries out the negotiation and in the wording of the statement that they finally issue.

Normally, the board is next faced with a concrete issue—a particular school or policy becomes the issue. There are fewer elements of ambiguity, but there is also more pressure on the board to try to anticipate the reaction of whites. At this point, the board is likely to look first for tactics to establish firm ground rules for the negotiation by defining the issue in either "legal" or "educational" terms. One school board chose to file suit to determine the legality of the existing policies. Other boards have not actually filed suit, but have stressed legal interpretations of their action. For example, the board might charge that a proposal for integrating schools is unconstitutional. The school board may also attempt to redefine the issue in the terms of the educational profession by developing a plan for compensatory education.

The action taken by the board will tend to be a compromise; frequently it is a compromise that gives the substance of integration without the form. The board may, for example, choose to integrate a particular school, explaining carefully that this was not done to increase integration, but only to relieve overcrowding. (This was the standard Pittsburgh approach.)

Whether the board meets the demands of the civil rights movement depends again to a considerable extent on the perception the board has of the movement. If it decides that the movement does not have the support of the Negro community, or that it is shortsighted and unreasonable, then the board may feel there is at least a good possibility that its proposals are unsound, and ignore or attempt to refute them. Or the board may feel that it has been insulted by the movement and take steps to defend itself.

Thus the board, operating without any clear guidelines or educational policy, hunts for a pragmatic solution, one that will keep the schools functioning and satisfy the various complainants. In doing so, it reacts more than anything else according to its general attitude about the Negro revolution. And it is this feeling which sets the "tone" of the action and determines the response of the movement.

THE EFFECTIVENESS OF DIFFERENT TACTICS

Since the amount of civil rights activity does not seem to have much effect on the outcome, we do not expect different types of tactics to be important. However, we can draw a few conclusions about the effectiveness of different strategies on the part of the civil rights movement.

Specificity

One of the differences between civil rights movements is the specificity of the demands made. In Bay City a very general demand for the recognition of *de facto* segregation led to a complete escalation of conflict and a severe defeat for the civil rights movement. In the two cities where the phrase "*de facto* segregation" was widely used, the controversy became very intense. In addition, the subtle demands, such as the redistricting of Woodside in Lawndale, also caused difficulty. On the other hand, the highly specific demands—don't open Central Junior High School, stop segregating bussed children, don't transfer students to Peshine School, etc.—were more likely to be met. However, the pattern is not very strong; the redistricting of Vailsburg High School in Newark was a specific demand which lost. It may be that one reason why specific demands are more often met is that the board lacks a frame of reference for dealing with highly abstract or subtle issues.

The Effectiveness of Neighborhood Groups

One rather intriguing finding is that the traditional civil rights groups (in most cases, the NAACP chapters) are less successful in achieving their goals than are neighborhood groups. In Table 10.3 we have listed the twelve major organizations involved in the eight cities. In the left-hand column we have listed traditional civil rights groups and noted whether their demands were rejected, partly accepted, or accepted. On the right we have done the same with the other groups involved.

This very striking difference is not easy to explain. Part of this is due to the fact that the neighborhood organizations usually had much more specific demands, and part of it is because they are sometimes willing to settle for less. But, intuitively, this does not seem to be the total explanation. It does not seem likely that any NAACP could have extracted as many concessions from the Baltimore board as the Sykes-Bramhall group did, and it is hard to believe that any community group would have been rebuffed as thoroughly as the Bay City NAACP. What are some other explanations? One factor is that the board is accustomed to dealing with parents' groups. They have a favorable "response set" which leads them to almost automatically try to meet the demands. To pick up a slightly different shade of this statement, the parents' groups appear somewhat more "legitimate" in that they are obviously self-interested. (One might argue that the altruistic NAACP, which is concerned with all Negro children, should be considered more legitimate, but this is obviously not the case. Their altruism is often viewed with suspicion.)

Second, possibly because of its deeper commitment or because of this sense of legitimacy, the neighborhood group is more willing

Table 10.3 Effectiveness of Civil Rights Groups and Other Organizations

| City | Traditional Group | | Other Group | |
	Name	Outcome: Demand Was	Name	Outcome: Demand Was
Pittsburgh			Community group	Accepted
Baltimore			Parents' organization	Accepted
St. Louis	NAACP	Accepted	West End Community	Accepted
San Francisco	NAACP-CORE	Partly accepted	Gratten parents	Accepted
Newark	NAACP	Partly accepted	Clinton Hills	Rejected
			Hawthorne parents	Accepted
Buffalo	NAACP	Rejected		
Lawndale	NAACP-CORE	Rejected		
Bay City	NAACP-NEFM	Rejected		
Percentage "accepted"		17%		83%
N		6		6

to take drastic action. The Bay City NAACP called two one-day boycotts, but the Gratten and Hawthorne parents were willing to go on indefinite strike. This, we think, is one of the more interesting aspects of the civil rights movement that has been overlooked in other discussions. In general, civil rights groups seem to be quite conservative in the types of actions they are willing to take. Consider just two examples of other groups. Labor unions, including teachers unions, have called indefinite strikes. White parents protesting integration have boycotted schools for long periods of time, not only recently in the South, but fifteen years ago in cities like Gary and Chicago as well (Tipton, 1953).

The third reason that community groups are more effective is that they represent, in several cases, white as well as Negro parents, and the simple fact is that regardless of how liberal a school board is, it treats white people with more respect than it does Negroes.

The Effectiveness of Court Suits

Here we have few data of value since none of the eight cities saw a suit carried all the way into court. Six suits were filed in five cities, but two of them (Newark and San Francisco) were settled out of court and the other four (San Francisco, St. Louis, Lawndale, and Bay City) never came to a hearing. These suits seem to have died for different reasons. The one in St. Louis became moot when the school system abolished bussing in contained units. The San Francisco suit was apparently considered to have doubtful legal merit. The Lawndale suit seemed to have somewhat better chances, however, and we have no explanation for the NAACP's refusal to pursue this one. It is difficult to see what the civil rights movement has gained from these suits. The open enrollment plan adopted in Newark can hardly be considered a major victory, and it probably could have been obtained more easily by direct action. It is true that the suit provides a vehicle for communication between the opposing parties. This was especially true in San Francisco, where Judge Zirpoli was able to prod the parties into negotiations. The main problem, of course, is that the courts have not taken a clear position on *de facto* segregation. The filing of suit works to the disadvantage of the civil rights movement and to the advantage of the school board, since it tends to discourage other action. Either party can claim to be waiting for the outcome of the suit. In several cities the filing of the suit brought other demonstrations to a halt. The petition to the state department of education serves the same sort of function as a court suit, although state departments vary in their legal authority. In Buffalo, the petition to Commissioner Allen brought very quick results for the civil rights movement.

The School Boycott

The school boycott is the heaviest artillery in the civil rights movement's arsenal. We should distinguish again between the strike, which is of indefinite duration, and the boycott. The strike is a very powerful and very effective weapon. In the two cases where it was either threatened (Central Junior High School) or used (the Hawthorne-Peshine transfer), it seemed to be very effective. The school boycott is a different sort of tactic. The boycott, like any other demonstration, is merely an attempt to embarrass the board, and to demonstrate the support within the community for the civil rights movement. People are "voting with their feet." We noted earlier that one reason why the civil rights organization is not as effective as the community group is that its base of support is not as obvious. By holding a successful boycott, the movement makes the entire Negro community the protagonist in its fight. In terms of bargaining, however, the disadvantage of using the boycott is that it is the heaviest artillery. Once the school board has survived it, it knows that it has nothing worse to fear. Another disadvantage of the school boycott is that it is difficult for the Negro school board members to support it. If they do, they can be criticized for condoning truancy.

SEGREGATIONIST ACTIVITY

As we noted earlier, none of the school boards had difficulty suppressing segregationist opposition after an integration program had been adopted. The two cities confronted with this problem (Baltimore and St. Louis) handled this opposition in essentially the same way—by mobilizing the support of the community elites, acting with as much unanimity as possible, and pressing the integration program through at a fairly rapid rate. In 1954, when Baltimore was faced with the problem of integrating its schools, the mayor appointed one of the city's most influential citizens to the school board presidency. When the board adopted its new policy statement in September, 1963, the resolution was presented, not by a Negro, or a college professor, or a Jew, but by the board's only Protestant businessman. In this way the board was able to indicate that the policy had the support of the mainstream of the white community. In both Baltimore and St. Louis, the affected communities were given opportunity to protest, but in both cases the decision was taken late in the summer so that the issue was nearly a fait accompli by the time these hearings were held. The effect of all this was to make the segregationists feel that they were a minority among whites.

SUMMARY

In this chapter we have described the school integration issue. To summarize the discussion very briefly, we have advanced the following series of hypotheses.

1. The demand for school integration comes either from the NAACP (or other civil rights groups) or from the residents of integrated neighborhoods. Demands tend not to come from all-Negro neighborhood groups or from the Negro political or civic elites.

2. If the demand comes from the NAACP, it will tend to be general in tone. If the demand for integration comes from an integrated neighborhood, it will grow out of the community's concern for maintaining integrated schools in order to prevent the flight of whites.

3. The goals of the civil rights leadership can be seen as either "welfare" goals or "symbolic" goals. White liberals and Negro community leaders tend to hold welfare goals, while Negro civil rights leaders tend to hold symbolic goals. Persons who hold welfare goals are concerned with the education of individual Negro children; thus they support compensatory education. They favor integration because they believe it beneficial to the student; thus they hold to the long-range goal of completely eliminating segregated schools. Leaders with symbolic goals are concerned with elimination of racial discrimination and with establishing racial equality as a major community value. Thus these leaders are not so concerned with compensatory education and tend to evaluate an integration program not merely on the basis of the number of students involved but according to whether the school

system has demonstrated its acceptance of the principle of racial equality. These leaders may be more conservative in their use of demonstration than are welfare-oriented leaders.

4. Since traditional civil rights groups tend to have symbolic goals, while the Negro community as a whole must hold both symbolic and welfare-oriented goals, the civil rights movement can best be understood, not as the representative of the Negro community but as a special interest group which is concerned with a limited range of social problems. While this occasionally leads to conflict between community interests and civil rights concerns, the civil rights movement can usually depend upon the Negro community for support.

5. The response of the school superintendent to the civil rights movement frequently contains three elements: (a) an insistence that the only morally correct position is strict non-discrimination (color-blindness) and that efforts to intentionally integrate schools are improper for this reasons; (b) an insistence on a narrow definition of the function of the school which stresses "educational" rather than "social" values and hence sees integration as outside the school's province; and (c) an unwillingness to engage in serious discussion of the issue with lay persons, and an extreme defensiveness in the face of criticism.

6. The school superintendent's narrow and defensive ideology may have its roots in the need of the educator to protect himself from the criticism and the interference of the community and also in the fact that big city school superintendents tend to be from very low status (and frequently rural) backgrounds.

7. In the northern cities studied, segregationist groups had difficulty organizing and were usually short lived. The strongest segregationist groups came into being when the school board was also opposed to integration. In general, the school board is able to muster community support for its position, regardless of whether its stand is pro- or anti-integration.

8. In seven of the eight cities, the school board, rather than the superintendent or the mayor, made the major decisions on the school integration issue.

9. The school board makes its decisions about integration in the absence of any guiding frame of reference or general educational philosophy. The decision is a difficult one for other reasons: The issue is highly symbolic and hence vague, the civil rights movement does not state clearly what it wants, and there is a heavy moral tone which suggests the possibility of bitter conflict. This tension and ambiguity mean that the board's decision is heavily influenced by the subjective attitudes of the board members toward the civil rights issue in general.

10. There is one interesting exception to the general principle that the tactics used by the civil rights movement have little effect on what the board does. We find a general pattern that the board will be more likely to act if it is confronted by a neighborhood group than if it is dealing with civil rights organizations.

11

School System Acquiescence

THE STAGES OF THE DECISION PROCESS

In the preceding chapter we presented a description of the school integration issue. In this chapter we shall use a comparative analysis of the eight cities to demonstrate two facts: first, that the behavior of the school board is largely independent of the extent of civil rights activity; second, that the outcome of the school integration issue is very largely dependent upon the character of the school board.

We are now in a position to construct the profile of the typical northern school integration controversy. The issue seems to divide itself into six stages. We can describe the controversies in all eight cities in terms of these stages.

Stage 1: Appearance of the Issue

The desegregation issue does not arise in a vacuum. In each of our cities civil rights groups had previously made occasional statements, and in some cases there was a full-scale discussion of some issue. Usually these events were of minor importance or were far enough in the past to have little effect on the present negotiations. Some time after 1961, the issue was raised again. This time, however, the groups who presented the request were armed with the tactics developed by the southern civil rights movement and the legal precedent of the *New Rochelle* case. The demands may vary from concrete (opposing boundaries around Vailsburg High School at that particular place) to procedural (demanding the preparation of a report on *de facto* segregation) to highly symbolic (demanding the adoption of a policy statement).

Stage 2: The Rejection of the Demands

In most cases this initial complaint was rejected, and in several cases the civil rights movement interpreted this as an insult. In St. Louis and Baltimore, the board appointed committees to prepare reports on the question; in both cases the school administration released a report first which denied every charge made. In Bay City the board refused to make the requested policy statement. In Lawndale and San Francisco the superintendent issued statements rejecting the demands. In Newark the board refused to reconsider the Vailsburg school situation. Only in Buffalo and Pittsburgh did the board take a particularly sympathetic position to these first demands, and only the Pittsburgh board actually did anything—they adopted an open enrollment plan at the next meeting. Following the argument developed in the preceding chapter, these initial rejections of demands are the result of three different factors: the delegation of authority to the superintendents, who are opposed to expanding the school's value system to include integration as a goal; the reluctance of the school board to deal with an issue which has not yet become very salient; and the school board's distrust or disapproval of the civil rights movement.

Stage 3: The First Civil Rights Action

The civil rights leadership next proceeds to call the issue to the board's attention more forcibly. In most cases this means threatening demonstrations. In Baltimore, it meant preparing the report, threatening to release it to the press, and then threatening to bring suit. In Bay City the first school boycott was held. In Newark suit was filed. The effect of these first demonstrations was to make it clear that the issue would not be a transient one, and that the board would soon be forced to take a clear public position on the issue.

Stage 4: The Key Response

At this point, the school board makes a response which we call the key response simply because it sets the tone for almost all the later actions. In most cases, the body which makes this decision (except in Newark, the school board) makes all later ones as well.

The actions taken at this point tended to be more favorable to the civil rights movement than anything the board did previously. In St. Louis the Maher report was more favorable than the earlier administration report; similarly, the Baltimore board began to look like it would not support Superintendent Brain's position. Newark adopted open enrollment in order to settle the suit out of court. In San Francisco the board agreed to close the proposed Central Junior High School. In Buffalo and Lawndale, however, the board rejected the demands of the civil rights movement. Since the negotiations are still going on at this writing, we will not use Pittsburgh as an example in our discussion of stages of the process.

Stage 5: Escalation and Resolution

By its action, the board has taken a position, and in the eyes of the civil rights movement "has shown its true colors." If the board has begun to acquiesce to the demands made of it, continued demonstrations will be accompanied by negotiations until additional concessions are made. Three things can happen: the civil rights leadership will be satisfied and drop the issue; the school board can publicize certain concessions that will tend to satisfy the general Negro community leaders or the Negro community as a whole, thus cutting off the movement's grass roots support; or the civil rights movement will remain dissatisfied, but will be unable to find a particular issue to focus on. In this last case, the issue will remain dormant for a period of time, only to spring up again later. Baltimore is the best example of the first case; St. Louis is a good example of the second case; and San Francisco and Newark are cases where the issue was resolved, but only temporarily.

In the remaining cities the issue was not resolved. Here demonstrations in protest of the board's position increased in intensity. In some cases they were not directed so much to bringing about negotiations, but were efforts to embarrass and therefore punish the board for its failure. Since the position of the civil rights leadership tends to be directed toward bringing the board members to a position supporting racial equality, it defines those board members who do not respond as immoral; since they are immoral, they should be punished. The board may reply in similar language, attempting to define the protesters as themselves lacking in moral qualities; they may for example, emphasize that the movement is made up of beatniks, Communists, or just "trouble-makers." At this point the issue has escalated beyond a point of resolution, and in principle this state of affairs could continue indefinitely.

It is interesting to note that the comparison of the case studies suggests that demonstrations, once they have succeeded in raising the issue, have little effect on the board's behavior. The board has committed itself in what we have called the "key" response and continues on this line thereafter. If the key response was favorable to the movement, then continued low-pressure demonstrations will be sufficient to extract the additional concessions which the movement wants. But if the initial response was not favorable, more intensified demonstrations will do little to change the public attitude of the board. Additional concessions will be given grudgingly if at all. However, the increased pressure may have the important effect of bringing other actors onto the scene. The second boycott in Bay City resulted in state intervention, for example. Similarly, it was rumored that large-scale demonstrations in Buffalo would have caused State Commissioner Allen to intervene. (The demonstrations flopped, but the commissioner did take action when the Buffalo NAACP petitioned his office formally.)

Stage 6: Introduction of New Actors

If the state commissioner or some other new actor enters the picture, the issue is drastically redefined. The board is no longer negotiating with the civil rights movement, but with a figure of authority. Thus the board is provided with a new frame of reference. If integration is necessary in order to conform to state law, then few school boards will oppose integration. The entry of the state (or federal) authority is also gratifying to the civil rights movement. The school board has taken an immoral stand; the state has therefore rebuked them. Higher authority has recognized the principle of racial equality. Because it clarifies the issue so well, it may be to the school board's advantage to encourage state or federal intervention. The school board will sacrifice some freedom, but it is not obvious that they will regret the loss.

ACQUIESCENCE

In order to capture the element of "tone" in the response of school boards, we will define a special variable called acquiescence. Acquiescence can be thought of as the extent to which the school board acted to bring the civil rights movement closer to its goals, both welfare and symbolic. Thus acquiescence must consist of two elements—actions taken to further integration or upgrade education for Negroes, and actions that recognize the value of racial equality and the legitimacy of the civil rights movement. Acquiescence can be defined for any particular period of time, but throughout most of the study we will define it for the entire period from the first raising of the issue to the time of our interviewing.[1] This rank ordering, like most of those to be presented in this report, is subjective. In this case it was developed by first having the interviewers fill out a questionnaire summarizing the actions taken by the school system. Armed with these questionnaires, the staff met several times to clarify the definition of acquiescence and agree upon a rank ordering. We cannot demonstrate with "hard" numerical data that this is the correct rank ordering; instead, we will describe in detail the basis for this ranking of the cities.[2]

[1]This time period does not include the 1965 controversy in Pittsburgh, nor the integration plan adopted by Buffalo that year.

[2]Since this use of "subjective" ratings of the cities on variables may properly be considered suspect, we should perhaps point out how it differs from more conventional techniques of analysis. In any analysis we are concerned with the correlation between two variables, which we shall call *A* and *B*. Ordinarily, we measure *A* and *B* with "indicators." Indicators are usually measures taken from a questionnaire or from some other "hard" source of data, so that there is little opportunity for bias to enter the analysis. However, the indicator is very frequently not an exact measure of the variable with which we are concerned. Furthermore, it is usually impossible to know what the true relationship between the indicator and the variable is. And bias does enter, in an important way, in the choice of indicator. Once the indicators which connect the two variables are agreed upon, routine statistical analysis can be used from this point on. Schematically, the result is shown in the accompanying figure.

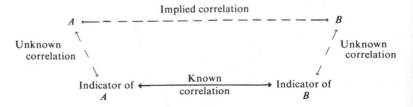

First, let us consider our ranking of cities based only upon the specific actions taken. We were unable to arrive at a complete rank ordering and were forced to permit some ties. In particular, it was difficult to distinguish between the two cities which seemed to have done the most to meet the specific demands of the civil rights movement, and the two cities which have done the least. Our ranking is as follows; for each city we have listed the factors that seem most important in locating the city on the scale.

1-2   *Baltimore and St. Louis* are tied for most acquiescent. Baltimore's large-scale increases in bussing, its total elimination of double shift, and its expansion of open enrollment qualify it for first place; St. Louis' integration of the bussing program greatly increased the amount of integration. In addition St. Louis increased teacher integration, adopted open enrollment, and has a widely publicized and apparently successful compensatory education project.

3   *Pittsburgh,* which began limited bussing, adopted open enrollment and has a highly regarded compensatory education program. We rank Pittsburgh below Baltimore and St. Louis because the number of students affected by desegregation is not as large as in the other two cities.

4   *San Francisco* met the specific demands of the movement by closing Central Junior High School and building schools as requested. However, it did not adopt any general program which increased integration as the first three cities did.

The existence of a correlation between A and B can be assumed only if there is a correlation between the two indicators, there is a high correlation between the two indicators and the two variables which they are assumed to measure and if A and B are unbiased indicators. There is relatively little opportunity for the investigator's bias to enter, but there is a good deal of opportunity for unknown bias and error. The result is that it is usually very difficult to make any statement about the size of the true correlation between A and B; even if the correlation between A and B is high, we can expect the use of the two indicators to give us a much lower measured correlation; on the other hand, a low measured correlation could be the result of bias or some other error, without a real correlation between A and B.

We have chosen to approach this problem in a different way. We have not used indicators, but have instead measured subjectively the magnitude of the real variables and performed our analysis with these subjective measures. This procedure should increase the amount of bias but decrease the other kinds of errors. In our judgment the technique we have used is preferable for this particular problem, but of course we cannot prove that this is a better procedure.

5 *Newark*, which adopted open enrollment and met the specified demands to reassign the students from the Hawthorne school, has done little else to further integration. Like San Francisco, its program of bussing to relieve overcrowding has not figured directly in the integration issue. It also has not met various criticisms of the education in Negro schools.

6,7,8 It is difficult to distinguish among the last three cities, all of which have refused some demands made but have also made other concessions. *Buffalo* refused to integrate the Woodlawn school, but did integrate other elementary and high schools. (It adopted open enrollment after our interviewing was completed.) *Lawndale* refused to adjust the boundaries of Woodside or permit transfers into it, but it did adopt an open enrollment plan. *Bay City* publicly refused all demands, but in fact was bussing Negroes into integrated schools to relieve overcrowding. Of the three, we rank Buffalo highest, leaving Lawndale and Bay City tied for seventh place.

We next attempted to rank the cities according to the tone of the board's behavior. Tone is mostly dependent upon the public and private statements of the board members or other decision makers to the civil rights leadership.

1-2 Both *Pittsburgh* and *Baltimore* reacted to the movement in highly positive ways. However, we considered that Pittsburgh took some action without being prodded, and that Baltimore's administration was hostile during the first days of the negotiations. Therefore, we placed Pittsburgh ahead of Baltimore.

3-4 We found it difficult to distinguish between *St. Louis* and *San Francisco*, both of whom took a generally pro-integration stance, but were also publicly critical of the civil rights movement. However, we felt that San Francisco's refusal to oppose Proposition 14 was sufficient to place it below St. Louis.

5,6,7 *Newark's* board was generally unfriendly to the civil rights movement, but not in a very agressive way. It remained graciously silent most of the time. *Buffalo*, on the other hand, alternated between some strong anti–civil rights statements from some of the board members and strong pro-integration statements from the superintendent. *Lawndale* took a firm anti–civil rights position, but was not critical of the civil rights leadership. We found it impossible to distinguish among the three cities and left them tied.

8   A review of the case study indicated clearly that *Bay City* qualified for this position.

Our final ranking of acquiescence is simply the average of these two rankings. There is a strong correlation between the two. Whether this was caused by our inability to separate the two factors or by the natural correlation between public attitude and public behavior is difficult to say. The most acquiescent cities are simply those with the lowest ranking on both scales as shown in Table 11.1. After considerable discussion, we were unable to agree upon the ranking of the first two cities, and left them tied in the ranking.

CIVIL RIGHTS ACTIVITY AND THE KEY RESPONSE

Now let us look at some of the relationships among the stages of the decision process as we have described it. First, let us define the key response in each city and look at the effect of civil rights action on the key response and on final acquiescence. The key response is defined as the first response made by the school board after civil rights has been defined as an issue of importance. In keeping with this, we chose the following incidents; they are listed from most to least acquiescent.

1   *Pittsburgh:* adoption of open enrollment after hearing parents' testimony
2   *Baltimore:* decision by ad hoc committee to eliminate districting (June, 1963)

Table 11.1   Ranking of Cities on Acquiescence Scale[a]

Ranking	Name of City
1–2	Pittsburgh, Baltimore
3	St. Louis
4	San Francisco
5	Newark
6	Buffalo
7	Lawndale
8	Bay City

[a]Ranking is from 1 (most acquiescent) to 8 (least acquiescent).

3 *San Francisco:* decision to close Central Junior High School (August, 1962)
4 *Newark:* adoption of open enrollment to settle suit (January, 1962)
5 *St. Louis:* receipt and adoption in general terms of Maher committee report (June, 1963)
6 *Lawndale:* refusal to change Woodside boundaries (January, 1961)
7 *Bay City:* fruitless discussion of *de facto* segregation prior to the first boycott (June, 1963)
8 *Buffalo:* designation of Woodlawn School boundaries (March, 1963)

It should be noted that in most cases the action taken in the key response plays only a partial role in determining the final level of acquiescence for the city.

We noted earlier that the key response seems to depend upon the civil rights movement's acting forcefully enough to make it clear that the issue will have to be resolved, but that otherwise the response is relatively independent of the level of civil rights demonstrations. We ranked the eight cities on the level of civil rights activity preceding the key response.[3]

When we compare this ranking to the key response, we see that there is virtually no correlation between the two rankings. Spearman's rank-order correlation coefficient is $-.15$, indicating a negligible tendency for cities with less civil rights activity to be more acquiescent in their key response; the coefficient is far below statistical significance, however. One reason why there is no significant relationship is evident if we contrast Pittsburgh and Newark. Both adopted open enrollment. In the one case the action was criticized; in the other it was accepted. In Newark it seemed clear that open enrollment was accomplished only because of the court suit. The fact that it took a suit to get it left a bitter taste in the mouths of some of the NAACP leadership. On the

[3] The ranking is as follows, from highest to lowest:

1 *St. Louis:* street demonstrations, partial boycott
2 *Newark:* suit filed
3 *San Francisco:* threats of suits and boycotts
4–5 *Bay City* and *Buffalo:* threat of boycotts
6 *Baltimore:* threat of public release of *Seven Years* report
7 *Lawndale:* testimony of NAACP
8 *Pittsburgh:* testimony of parents' group

other hand, the decision in Pittsburgh was unanticipated, and therefore doubly pleasant. Given our definition of the symbolic goals of the movement, this is as it should be. That demonstrations are required is evidence of the school board's unwillingness to endorse integration. Therefore, the more one demonstrates, the more likely it is that the school board will capitulate, but the less value their capitulation will have in paying homage to racial equality as a community value. Demonstrations both encourage and prevent acquiescence. Actually, this is only a minor part of the story. In general there is simply no correlation between the level of civil rights activity and action taken by the board. San Francisco agreed to close Central Junior High School under considerable public pressure; under much less pressure the Baltimore board did more. Presumably neither of these cities would have acted without some pressure from the movement, but how much pressure seems irrelevant.

Let us now move to the next phase, which we have called the period of escalation and resolution. What effect does the key response have on this period? In Figure 11.1 we have plotted the acquiescence of the key response against the level of the civil rights

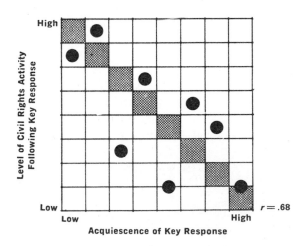

Figure 11.1 Influence of Board's Key Response on Subsequent Civil Rights Activity

activity following the response.[4] The correlation, as one might expect, is negative and of considerable magnitude. The cities that were acquiescent thereby earned themselves a period of grace; those that refused to take action were punished accordingly. Two cities are deviant cases in that there was considerably less civil rights activity than one would expect, so that they are located below the diagonal in Figure 11.1. They are Lawndale and Newark.

On the basis of this finding, we might expect the school desegregation issue to behave in a cyclic manner in these cities. The cities that initially acquiesce avoid further demonstrations and hence can avoid further concessions, while the initially unresponsive cities are subjected to more demonstrations. Later these cities respond to the demonstrations by becoming more acquiescent, and the demonstrations shift back to the cities which have rested on their laurels. In the long run, all cities become targets for demonstrations, and all cities acquiesce. This is in part true, in the sense that there is not quite as wide a divergence between the most and least acquiescent cities at this time as there once was. But this is a minor part of the story; in general, cities which are acquiescent at the beginning remain most acquiescent.

In Figure 11.2 we have plotted the acquiescence of the key response against the final acquiescence scale developed in detail earlier. The correlation between the two ratings is very high. Two deviant cases lie above the diagonal (meaning that their later actions were more acquiescent than one would guess from the key response), while the rest are very near it. The deviant cities are St. Louis and Buffalo. St. Louis lies above the line because at the time of the key response, it was still unclear whether the board intended to take action or not. In retrospect, it seems likely that

---

[4]Our ranking of level of civil rights activity in the period immediately following the key response is as follows, from highest to lowest:

1   *Bay City:* two boycotts, sit-ins, etc.
2   *Buffalo:* demonstrations, a boycott, and a petition to the state department of education
3   *St. Louis:* some picketing, threat of boycott
4   *San Francisco:* testimony, threat of pursuing suit
5   *Baltimore:* threaten suit
6   *Lawndale:* testimony
7–8   *Pittsburgh and Newark:* no action

action would have been taken under almost any condition; that Trafford Maher had been asked to head the citizens' committee should have been a tip-off to this. The other case, Buffalo, is simply unstable because of the delicate balance of power between the liberal superintendent and the more conservative school board, and because of changes in the composition of the board.

Thus we see that the acquiescence of the school board is determined almost at the very beginning of the decision process. It follows as a corollary that the extent of civil rights activity has relatively little influence on the degree to which the school system meets the demands made. Rather, the extent of acquiescence determines the level of activity, as we have seen. In Table 11.2 we have summarized the total civil rights activity over the entire period of the decision,[5] and in Figure 11.3 we have plotted this against the level of acquiescence. Civil rights activity includes various types of demonstrations, testimony, and threats of demonstrations, and court suits and petitions to other authorities.

[5]It is difficult to arrive at this ranking of cities in total level of civil rights activity, simply because we must necessarily compare apples and oranges in the process. (How many boycotts are equal to a court suit?)

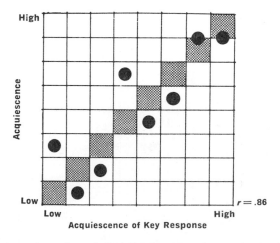

Figure 11.2 Relationship of Board's Key Response to Its Final Level of Acquiescence

We see that the general negative correlation persists; non-acquiescent cities are faced with the most activity. The correlation is not especially high. More important, there is no single deviant case that can be singled out as lowering the correlation. Through-

Table 11.2 Ranking of Cities on Total Amount of Civil Rights Activity[a]

Ranking	Name of City	Amount of Civil Rights Activity
1	Bay City	Sit-ins, vigils, street marches, two boycotts, election activity
2	San Francisco	Two suits (one settled, one dropped), intense but sporadic demonstrations
3	Buffalo	No suit, but petition to state commissioner of education, one boycott and one threat of a boycott, limited other demonstrations
4–5	St. Louis and Lawndale	St. Louis threatened a suit, held a limited boycott, threatened a general boycott, and held a street demonstration Lawndale did not engage in very much direct action but did file a suit and conducted a well-organized election campaign
6	Newark	Settled suit out of court, and in one neighborhood boycotted a school
7	Baltimore	Threatened a suit, prepared reports
8	Pittsburgh	Prepared reports, testified

[a]Ranking is from 1 (most activity) to 8 (least activity).

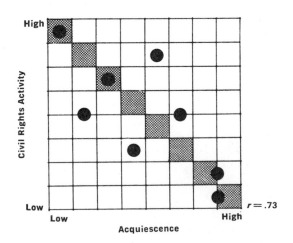

Figure 11.3 Relationship between Acquiescence and Amount of Civil Rights Activity

out the middle range of the figure, there is considerable free variation. Apparently the civil rights activity is not wholly determined
by the behavior of the board. (In Chapter 18 we will return to this
table and try to locate the factors that cause the unexplained
variation.)

That civil rights activity tends to be caused by level of acquiescence, rather than the other way around supports our thesis that
the civil rights movement is concerned with symbols of interracial
morality; we might think of the demonstrations as attempts to
punish the board for its "sinful" behavior. This may in part
explain why the later stages of the decision process in some non-
acquiescent cities take on the character of a war, in which punish-
ing the enemy becomes more important than anything else.

Of course, we are neglecting the effect of demonstrations in
one city on the national climate of opinion, which in turn affects
other cities. Certainly, cities like Pittsburgh seem to have been
affected by their desire to avoid the rancorous situations in Chicago,
Cleveland, and a dozen other places.

We can summarize the data shown thus far in two statements:

1. The acquiescence of the school system is determined to a
large extent at the beginning of the decision process. It is not
greatly affected by the amount of civil rights activity that takes
place.

2. The amount of civil rights activity is, however, partly caused
by the board response—the less the school system acquiesces, the
greater the civil rights activity in retaliation.

THE ACQUIESCENT SCHOOL BOARD

We are now ready to begin tracing out the causes of the differences between our cities. We shall approach this problem with
a conceptual scheme that can be summarized as follows: In the
final analysis, a decision is made by the group of men who have
the legal authority to make it. They make the decision in the way
they do because of the kind of men they are and the kind of pressures operating on them.

In this case the final authority for the decision lies with the
school board. They must determine what the issue is, assemble
needed information, decide upon their range of alternatives,
evaluate the pressures operating on them, and make a decision.

Our task is to sort out those factors influencing their decision and decide which ones make important differences. All this is conceptually a simple process. The problems arise from the large number of components, all interacting simultaneously. We have sketched the main components in Figure 11.4.

The solid lines in the figure represent communication between the incumbents in the various positions and also perceptions of attitudes between actors who are unable to communicate. The dashed lines represent the recruitment of actors to fill the positions. For example, in the top of the figure, we admit to the possibility that the local economic elite can influence the decision two ways— by directly communicating its desires and by having its unspoken desires anticipated (this is the meaning of the solid line); or by participating in the selection of the board members (the dashed line). Let us look first at the solid lines, which represent channels of possible influence. The most important influence on the school board comes from the civil rights movement. While the civil rights movement is trying to influence the board to acquiesce to their demands, the board is also trying to influence the movement to cease demonstrations. Thus we should have a continuous negotiation process between these two actors. But the board is limited in its possible range of action by influences from the political and economic leaders, by the influence of the superintendent of schools, and by its perception of what the Negro and white voters in the community will accept. The kinds of influence which these actors will exert on the board depend upon a host of factors: the importance to the community of racial peace, the history of previous racial negotiations in other areas of the community, and the balance of political power, to cite three. We can then trace the chain of causation back one more step, by observing that the kinds of pressure exerted (the solid lines) will depend upon the kinds of economic elites, politicians, and voters who are present in the city. This is presumably a function of the background characteristics of the city—the kind of industry, the character of the population, and the formal rules for electing political leaders.

Given this conception of the political process, the background characteristics of the city—its industrial structure, population composition, and its formal rules for electing city officials—

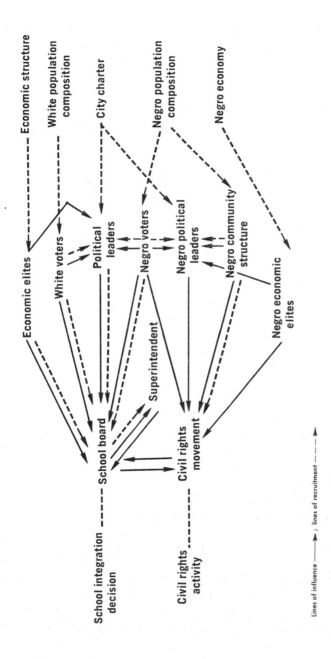

Lines of influence ⎯⎯⎯▶ ; lines of recruitment ⎯ ⎯ ⎯▶

Figure 11.4 Flow Chart of Recruitment of Decision Makers in School Integration Decision and Channels of Influence Operating on Them

affect the behavior of the school board in three different ways. First, they determine the types of economic elites, voters, and politicians the city will have, and hence the way in which these groups will attempt to influence the school board. Second, by influencing the types of actors in these roles, they in turn influence the recruitment process for the school board, and hence the kind of board members the city has. Third, these background factors influence the relationship between the economic elites, voters, and politicians and hence set a pattern for the amount of influence exerted by each group on both the recruitment process for the school board and the actual school integration decision. For example, a city with a high status population will presumably be more liberal in racial matters, but in addition, a high status city will have a public opinion which will not permit political appointments to the school board. Or, to cite a different causal factor, a city with nonpartisan elections and a strong civil service might have weaker political parties; hence the school board might be more susceptible to influence by the mass of voters.

If we attempt to trace out the ways in which the character of the city might affect the behavior of the civil rights movement, we complete the flow chart of Figure 11.4. Ultimately, the behavior of the civil rights movement and the school board can be traced to a final cause (for our purposes) in the economy, population, and governmental charter of the city. But the flow chart, with its thirty-five lines of direct influence and indirect influence through recruitment, indicates that there may be as many as one hundred ways in which these factors affect the behavior of the school board. And of course the chart is not complete. There are other structural relationships. For example, the influence of the white economic elites on their Negro counterparts is not shown. There are also factors that cannot easily be represented in the flow chart, such as the influence of recent history on the actors. The model pictured is that of an influence system in equilibrium, where the influences balance each other out in such a way that there is no change. If there were change, we would have to allow for actors who are being influenced by the way things used to be.

We have painted a picture of a hopelessly complex process. Fortunately, the bulk of these possible chains of causation are of no importance. In the first part of this chapter we discussed the goals of the civil rights movement, and from this discussion developed a definition of the key variable—acquiescence. We then found that the tactics of the civil rights movement had relatively little effect on the rank ordering of the cities by acquiescence, and in particular the amount of civil rights activity had no discernible effect. We also accumulated some evidence to show that usually the superintendent had little effect on the final acquiescence score and observed that we could find little evidence of any direct and effective influence on the school board from the political or economic elites. If we are right, the solid lines in Figure 11.4 can be largely dropped from consideration. Most important, we can avoid any complex analysis of the school board–civil rights movement negotiation process and partition the flow chart into two separate figures—one showing the factors that influence the board and the other showing the factors that influence the civil rights movement.

We shall next attempt to demonstrate that such a partitioning can be made. First, we shall show that some of the factors which could be expected to correlate with acquiescence if certain influences were operating do not in fact correlate, or do not correlate well. Then we will show that a factor which is not directly related to the kinds of influence the board is subjected to does explain most of the variation.

If the school board were directly influenced by the power of the civil rights movement, then we would assume that the ultimate currency in political influence—the vote—would play a role. Presumably the school board will be most strongly influenced if the civil rights movement is backed by a large bloc of Negro votes. In Figure 11.5 we have correlated acquiescence with a ranking of the cities by percentage of Negroes living in each city. There is a correlation: the cities with the largest Negro populations are most likely to have acquiescent school boards. The correlation is not very good, however. Four of the cities lie on the main diagonal, but four lie some distance away from it. The correlation is actually a little worse than it looks, for the only sharp break in the percentage Negro comes between the cities which rank fourth and fifth in percentage Negro—Pittsburgh (17 per cent Negro) and Lawndale (28 per cent Negro). But Pittsburgh is very high on the acquiescence scale, and Lawndale very low. (It may be that Lawndale is in a state of political instability, and the present non-acquiescent board will be replaced by a more acquiescent one in the future.) The size of the Negro population does have an effect, but it is not a very large one.

Possibly one reason why percentage Negro does not correlate so well is that the cities with the largest Negro populations have more anti-Negro sentiment among whites. We cannot test this hypothesis directly, but we can look at it indirectly in two ways. The hypothesis is that the pressure from a large Negro population is offset by the stronger anti-Negro sentiment among whites which results from having a larger Negro population. We have no direct measure of the attitudes of whites in each city, but the indirect evidence indicates that the school system is not affected by the attitudes of the white population. Suppose, for example, that we consider the region of the country that each city is located in, in hopes that cities in the far West will be most acquiescent, while those in the border states, with more conservative white voters, will be least so. But when we do this, the result makes no sense. School systems in the liberal West and Northeast are least acquiescent; those in the border states are most acquiescent.

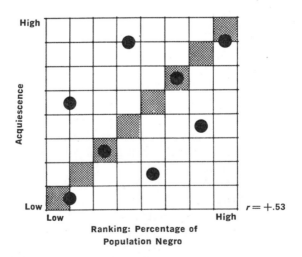

Figure 11.5 Percentage of Population Negro and Acquiescence

We can also look at the socioeconomic level of the cities. High status persons are less prejudiced, so that boards in high status cities should be most acquiescent. The data do not support this, either. Figure 11.6, which plots the percentage of the white population who are high school graduates against acquiescence, shows a weak correlation in the opposite direction; high status cities are least acquiescent. (We shall present an explanation of this in Chapter 13.)

So apparently we are correct in arguing, as we did in the preceding chapter, that the board operated independently of the attitudes of the white population. This is reasonable, of course, since they have no easy way to determine what those attitudes are.

CIVIL RIGHTS LIBERALISM

On the basis of these three figures, this approach of searching for community factors which might influence the board does not seem very efficient. Let us instead work backwards, beginning with the characteristics of the board and exploring their cause. The most obvious characteristic is the liberalism of the board members on racial issues: their attitudes toward Negroes, civil

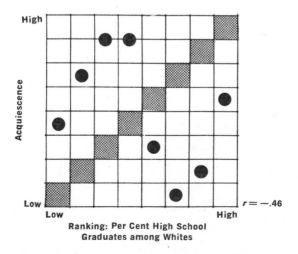

Figure 11.6   Education of White Population and Acquiescence

rights, and the civil rights movement. We administered a questionnaire containing five agree-disagree questions dealing with attitudes toward race relations and other issues, and found that the questions (listed in Table 11.3) produced a useful scale. Of the five questions, only the first deals with a simple question of civil rights. Obviously, these school board members believe that whites do not have a "right" to segregated neighborhoods. They also reveal themselves to be much more liberal than the population at large. When a similar question was addressed to a national sample in 1963, only 43 per cent gave the liberal response. Questions 18, 26, and 27 all measure perceptions of the civil rights movement. The respondent is asked, in effect, whether the civil rights movement asks too much, demonstrates too often, or is uncompromising. Of course, there is no obviously right or wrong answer to these questions, but that does not concern us. We only want to know whether one person respects the civil rights movement more than another.

The five questions do seem to measure the same basic factor. People who give liberal responses to the "hard" questions—such as whether Negro leaders are willing to make reasonable compromises—are almost certain to give liberal responses to the other,

Table 11.3 Questions Used To Measure Attitudes toward Civil Rights

Question	Per Cent Saying "Disagree" or "Tend To Disagree"	N
7. White people have a right to keep Negroes out of their neighborhoods if they want to, and Negroes should respect that right	91	45
18. There is a problem with the civil rights movement because many Negroes are demanding privileges which whites do not have	68	44
17. There is no reason to think Negroes will learn more in integrated schools (not used in scale)	61	44
26. Most demonstrations have hurt the Negroes' cause more than they have helped	57	42
27. In many cases, Negro leaders have not been willing to make reasonable compromises on civil rights issues	43	21

"easier" questions as well. This is indicated in Table 11.4, where the association between each pair of questions is indicated by a matrix of Yule's Q's.[6] The fact that all the Q's are high indicates that all the questions tend to tap the same basic attitude.

One might also criticize the questions by arguing that civil rights movements vary from city to city. A school board member in a city with a militant civil rights movement might give a different answer from one in a more peaceful town, without necessarily being more conservative. However, this does not seem to be the case. Most of the questions are worded so vaguely as to be nearly meaningless, and consequently it is very difficult to give an objective answer. In any case, this would not explain the fact that there is a high correlation between the answer to these three questions and the other two, which presumably have nothing to do with local conditions. In constructing the final liberalism scale, we dropped Question 17, which deals specifically with schools, in order to avoid contaminating the data with the actual experience a board member has had. (If he has helped to integrate schools, we might expect him to justify his action by saying that this is educationally beneficial.) This question also has the lowest correlations with the others. The remaining four questions, which

[6]Q is a measure of the association which ranges from -1 to $+1$. It will be 0 if there is no relationship between the answers to one question and the answers to another. If it is $+1$, as it is in four places in the table, this means that everyone who gave a conservative response to the question numbered in the row (the "easy" question) gave a conservative response to the one numbered in the column (the "hard" question) and everyone who gave a liberal response to the "hard" question gave a liberal response to the "easy" one.

Table 11.4 Association between Items of Civil Rights Liberalism Scale (Yule's Q)

Item	Item				
	7	18	17	26	27
7	–	1.00	.72	1.00	1.00[a]
18		–	.76	.82	.87[a]
17			–	.57	1.00[a]
26				–	.95[a]
27					–

Note: Item 17 was deleted from the final scale.

[a]These Q's are based on nineteen or twenty cases. All other cells have forty-one or forty-two cases.

have nothing to do with education directly, were then combined into a simple score for each respondent. He was given three points for each "disagree" response, two points each time he said "tend to disagree," one point if he only "tended to agree," and zero if he "agreed." With four questions, this gave us a scale ranging from 0 to 12, 12 being the most liberal response possible. (If a person did not answer one question, his score was developed by extrapolating from the other persons who answered the other three questions the same way he did.) We shall simply refer to the scale as "civil rights liberalism."

We intend to examine the relationship between the average "civil rights liberalism" of the board and its level of acquiescence. To do this, however, we must first take into consideration the twenty-eight board members who for one reason or another did not fill out this questionnaire. We were able to solve this problem by independently estimating the scale score of everyone in the entire sample, without looking at the data. We found that we could do this rather easily, from other interview data and the person's voting record. The agreement between our estimate and the actual score for the forty-three board members who did respond is shown in Table 11.5.

The amount of agreement is extremely high ($Q = +.93$), which means that we can estimate with considerable accuracy the position of other board members relative to those who filled out the questionnaire. We then used our estimated scores to locate the median person on each board—the person who fell in the center of the board and hence could be considered the swing vote to make up a liberal or a conservative majority. On the scale from 0 to 12, the medians varied from 9.0 for the most liberal board down to a low of 5.5.

Table 11.5 Actual Civil Rights Liberalism Scores and Interviewer Estimates of Liberalism

Interviewer Estimate	Actual Score			
	12–15	9–11	5–8	0–4
Liberal	8	11	3	0
Conservative	0	4	10	7

In Figure 11.7 we have plotted median civil rights liberalism against the acquiescence of the school board. At first glance, the correlation (.65) is disappointingly low. However, a second glance reveals an intriguing pattern. The three cities which fall below the line, being less acquiescent than we would expect from the liberalism score, are all elected boards; the other five are all appointed. The correlation of liberalism with acquiescence is perfect among the three elected boards and the five appointed boards taken separately.

With only eight cases, we must proceed cautiously in our analysis. If we can assume that the elected boards are, because they are elected, less acquiescent, then we can conclude that the median liberalism score of the board explains most if not all of the variations in acquiescence. Can we make this assumption about the effect of elections? It has a certain amount of plausibility. Certainly, if our analysis of Bay City is correct, the refusal of the board members to acquiesce is largely due to the fact that they are in a competition for the votes mobilized by Mrs. Smith. And in Lawndale, race was very much an issue in the school board elections.

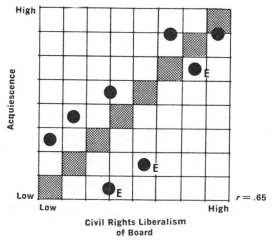

Note: **E** indicates an elected board; *r*, among appointed board = .97; *r*, among elected board = 1.00.

Figure 11.7   Civil Rights Liberalism of Board and Acquiescence

In all three elected boards there was considerable internal friction—even in the elite-controlled St. Louis board. In our analysis of Lawndale we suggested that this conflict within the board seriously hampered the negotiation process. In St. Louis the wide differences in opinion, and the slightly different political bases of different board members, may have slowed the decision process so that the liberal actions taken did not have the tremendous impact on the civil rights movement that they did in Baltimore or Pittsburgh. And in all three cities we believe that there was more thorough newspaper coverage, and hence a higher level of community interest. This also should have the effect of immobilizing the board, at least until an election like Bay City's could clarify the vote-getting appeal of the participants.

When we add to this picture the fact that the boards that were acquiescent—Baltimore and Pittsburgh—seem to be least concerned with representing the community, or with public opinion, we see that we have reason to believe that the same school board will take more acquiescent action if it is freed from having to participate in general elections. In the next section of this chapter we shall present more evidence for this point of view.

If we accept the premise that the correlation between election of the board and acquiescence is a true and causal relationship, then we can conclude that the civil rights liberalism of the board is by far the dominant factor in explaining acquiescence. This may seem altogether reasonable, but this finding does raise some disturbing questions. We would like to believe that the school board is somehow more than the sum of its parts, that the interaction of board members in the solution of school problems should cause a group consensus to develop which would play down the importance of the subjective attitudes of the board members. We would also like to believe that the negotiation process itself affects what the board does—that there are some ways of influencing the board which are more effective than others. Instead we are continuing to find the school integration outcomes virtually predetermined before the negotiation process begins.

COHESION

We can support our argument that the correlation between board appointment (rather than election) and acquiescence is real in another way. We suggested two possible reasons: first, that the elected board is more conservative because it must face an election campaign. There is nothing we can do to prove or disprove this with our data. However, we also suggested that the elected board has more difficulty in taking innovative action because of the higher level of internal disagreement. If this is true, then appointed boards which have high internal disagreement should also have difficulty taking acquiescent action. Certainly, there seems to be considerable difference between boards in their decision-making style. Some seem to handle an issue quietly and smoothly; others seem to be constantly involved in some difficult or tense situation. Several efforts were made to define a variable which would capture this difference. The final choice was "cohesion."

Cohesion (as used by Festinger, Schachter, and Back, 1950, for example) refers to the average level of positive feelings between the members of the group. It might be operationalized by asking each board member to give a numerical score to every other board member according to the extent of agreement (or friendliness) between them, and then averaging these values across every pair of board members. Thus a board would be lowest in cohesion if every board member disagreed with or disliked every other; it would be higher if the board were divided into two factions, with members on each side who support each other, but argue with the members of the other faction; it would be fairly high if the board members agreed with each other with the exception of a single deviant whom all others disliked; it would, of course, be highest if all the board members were friendly with one another. With this criterion in mind, we were able to arrive at a rank ordering. There is a great deal of variation on this variable. At one extreme, we estimated that if two members were selected at random from one particular board, the chances would be two to one that they would disapprove of each other! Several boards are divided into a majority and minority faction, and three boards seem to have very little internal dissension.

The cities were ranked on cohesion using several pieces of data. School board members had been asked to name the board members they agreed with and disagreed with. They were also asked to evaluate the level of agreement. In addition, for each board we collected many public statements, some private statements of opinion about other board members, and records of votes on various issues.

There is a definite correlation between cohesion and acquiescence, as indicated by Figure 11.8. The least acquiescent elected board, Bay City, is the least cohesive; and the least acquiescent appointed board, Buffalo, is the least cohesive of its group. Conversely, the boards which are most acquiescent seem to have the least internal conflict. Thus this figure supports our argument that elected boards are less acquiescent because they are less cohesive.

Are there any grounds for supposing that there is in fact a causal relationship between cohesion and acquiescence? There are only two obvious incidents which were the result of dissension and clearly prevented acquiescence. One was Buffalo's handling of the Woodlawn situation, where the board members prepared four different plans and submitted them to the public, rather than agreeing privately on a single plan. The result was the building of sentiment for the Parlato recommendation. The other case was the inability of the Bay City board to vote for the policy statement

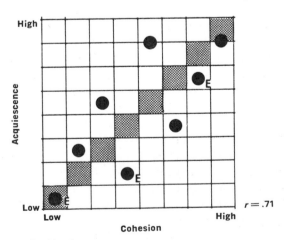

Note: E indicates an elected board.

Figure 11.8 Cohesion and Acquiescence

drafted by Silverstein, despite the fact that three of the five board members favored it. Both these incidents were important, and they came in the two boards with the lowest level of consensus. There is also a suggestion in San Francisco that the relatively low level of consensus there kept the board from acting decisively. In San Francisco a board which frequently had difficulty taking action dragged its feet in responding to the civil rights movement. It seems plausible that this inability to act is partly a consequence of lack of consensus.

From these first three cities, we can present three hypotheses:

1. The uncohesive board will be less acquiescent because it will be unable to prevent the issue from becoming a matter of public controversy. Each board member will attempt to win public support of his point of view; but the public statements will invite public reaction. Under conditions of controversy, the most extreme positions in the community will be articulated first. The liberals are already organized in the civil rights movements; hence public discussion will next lead to organization of the segregationist extreme. In the ensuing controversy the board will be unable to evaluate public opinion, yet hesitant to act in the face of public opposition; further, it will be unable to determine the extent of opposition. The result parallels a finding from a study of fluoridation controversies. Public debate tends to prevent adoption of fluoridation even though repeated surveys have indicated that it has public support (see Crain, Katz, and Rosenthal, in press).

2. Whereas the cohesive board may be able to put up a "united front," each dissenting board member will air his public position. This means that the most conservative board member will become a symbolic leader for the segregationists, whose position will gain legitimacy from the support of a public official. Thus the segregationists not only have more opportunity to organize, they also have a more legitimate position to organize around.

3. Even if the board does not have to contend with segregationist public opinion, the demands of the civil rights movement require change on the part of the school board. There is an inertia in any public body which tends to maintain the status quo, and any innovative action requires discussion and agreement on the part of the board members. However, discussion will be inhibited in the

non-cohesive board, and the remnants of previous arguments will plague efforts to obtain agreement on any new issue.

These seem to be plausible arguments for assuming that the correlation between cohesion and acquiescence is a causal relationship. This means that we have three variables—civil rights liberalism, election versus appointment, and cohesion—which are sufficient to predict level of acquiescence. If we combine the variables by adding each city's ranks on each variable, we can (depending upon the amount of weight we assign to each variable) arrive at correlations with acquiescence which range as high as +.96. Of course, with only eight cities, such techniques are not very helpful, and we have almost no grounds for drawing any conclusions about the relative importance of each variable.

The task of explaining acquiescence is greatly simplified by these findings, of course. In the next chapter we will try to determine what characteristics of the school board explain the differences in liberalism and cohesion; we will then, in Chapter 13, try to relate this to differences in the structure of the cities which these boards represent.

SUMMARY

The main task of this chapter has been to demonstrate that the principal dimension of the outcome of the school integration issue—the extent to which the board acquiesced to the demands of the civil rights movement—can be largely explained by differences in the structure and composition of the school board. We have attempted to demonstrate this in three ways. First, by separating the decision process into stages, we have shown that the behavior of the school board can be predicted from the action it takes early in the campaign, before the negotiations with the civil rights groups have reached their peak, and that rather than higher levels of civil rights activity causing the board to take action, the board's actions determine the extent of demonstrations.

Second, we considered such factors as the region in which the board is located, the socioeconomic status of the white population (which should indicate the extent of white opposition to integration), and the size of the Negro population (which should reflect the power of the civil rights movement) and found that these factors

were not very helpful. (Only the size of the Negro population correlated with acquiescence; R = + .53.) Apparently a line of analysis based on these factors is unpromising.

Third, when we turned to examine the characteristics of the
school board, we found three factors which do explain acquiescence—the liberalism of the attitudes of individual board members, the cohesiveness of the board, and whether it is an elected or
appointed body. The correlation of race liberalism with acquiescence is only +.65, but the correlation is perfect among the elected
or appointed boards considered separately. The correlation of cohesion with acquiescence is +.71.

We are now ready to pursue this aspect of the school integration
issue one more step back in the chain of causation, by asking what
factors cause certain boards to have liberal, rather than conservative members, and why some boards are cohesive and others not.

12

The School Board

It is a truism that liberals are different from conservatives. In the case of American race relations, we know that middle-class whites are more liberal than working-class whites, for example. However, these statements apply to American whites as a whole, and we have no reason to believe that any statements made about the national population will apply to the rather special collection of people who govern the schools in the eight cities in our sample. In this chapter we will examine the attitudes of the school board members to determine what factors distinguish liberal board members from their conservative peers. (Perhaps we had better say clearly here at the beginning that liberal and conservative are relative terms and that the most conservative board members are still a good deal more liberal on civil rights than many whites.) It will not come as any surprise, of course, that liberals and conservatives tend to be recruited from different sectors of the community; hence whether a board is liberal or conservative is determined in large measure by the procedures used to recruit school board members. We shall also see that the way in which board members are recruited has a good deal to do with whether the board members function as a cohesive group.

BOARD MEMBER ATTITUDES

Each school board member was given a thirty-item questionnaire designed to measure his attitudes toward a variety of issues. We shall now look at those responses to determine how attitudes toward race relate to other attitudes—in other words, to find out what the civil rights liberalism scale means. Slightly more than two-thirds of the fifty-nine white board members filled out the questionnaire. A few of the others refused to be interviewed, but most non-respondents are either from St. Louis (where no attempt was made to interview many board members), were out of the city or otherwise unavailable, or were judged to be relatively inactive on the board. The sample will tend to overrepresent the most active board members and, to a lesser extent, the more liberal board members.

Ten questions were combined into four scales, which we shall call "economic liberalism," "constituency orientation," "attitude toward the radical right," and "sense of civic duty." Three items were used to measure economic liberalism. The intercorrelations as measured by Yule's Q are high, suggesting that we have succeeded in measuring a single factor. The pattern of responses is somewhat surprising. Although 50 per cent of the sample agree that, "Business enterprise can continue to give our high standard of living only if it remains free from government regulations," which sounds like a conservative platitude, nearly half of the sample agree that, "It would probably be a good idea if the U.S. Government set up a national health service to provide low-cost medical care to persons of all ages."[1]

"Constituency orientation" is a scale based upon agreement with two statements: "A politician's first duty is to represent the view of his constituency," and "A school administrator's job is to give the community the kind of school system which the public wants." The correlation between the two responses is only .63, however. Fifty-three per cent of the sample agreed with each statement.

[1]Fifty per cent of the population agreed with this statement, but this is based on only twenty-two responses, since the question was introduced after some interviewing was already completed. (The other questions have usually forty-one or forty-two responses.) Sixty-one per cent agreed with the third statement in the scale, "The government has the responsibility to see to it that all people, poor or rich, have adequate housing, medical care, and protection from unemployment." The intercorrelations are given below:

Question	Question		
	11	6	5
11. Business enterprise can continue.. . .	–	+.81	+.83
6. . . . a national health service . . .		–	+.91
5. The government has the responsibility . . .			–

Three other questionnaire items measure a more effective component of liberalism, reaction against right-wing radicalism, and again the results seem somewhat surprising. While 65 per cent of the sample disagree that, "The radical right is not a serious threat compared to the U.S. Communist party," only 47 per cent of the sample are willing to say, "Organizations such as the John Birch Society harm the U.S." Finally, only 32 per cent of the sample endorse the statement, "My first thought when President Kennedy was assassinated was that it was done by a radical right winger." It is impossible to tell whether these responses stem from a lack of disapproval of the radical right, or simply an unwillingness to take it seriously.

When we look at the relationship between these questions and the economic liberalism series, we find that none of the economic conservatives consider the right wing a problem, and only a bare majority of economic liberals do. The persons who score high on this scale tend to be associated with subcommunities that have a special concern with the right wing: of the twelve, eight are either Negroes or Jews and two of the remaining four are union officials. The items seem to scale; one low Q occurs in a case where the distribution of responses makes the calculation extremely unreliable.[2]

The last scale deals with the extent to which the respondent sees civic activity as a duty. Thirty-five per cent disagree with the statement, "If a businessman who is involved in a civic issue finds that it hurts his business, he is justified in withdrawing." Seventy-one per cent do agree that, "Once a man has attained an important position in business life, civic leadership becomes more important

[2]The intercorrelations are:

Question	Question		
	22	12	30
22. The radical right is not a serious threat . . .	–	+.63	–.03
12. Organizations such as the John Birch Society . . .		–	+.75
30. My first thought when President Kennedy was assassinated . . .			–

than his business. Yule's Q between the items is $+.77$. To us, both items seem to show a strong service orientation.

CORRELATIONS WITH CIVIL RIGHTS LIBERALISM

Among the white school board members, the three dimensions which might be called "liberalism"—attitudes toward economic issues, the radical right, and race—fit together rather loosely. Economic liberalism correlates only moderately with attitudes toward civil rights; 37 per cent of the economic conservatives are liberals on the civil rights series, compared with 53 per cent of the economic liberals. The radical right scale is a slightly better predictor of liberalism; 35 per cent of those who discount the dangers of the radical right are liberals, compared with 57 per cent of those who score high on this scale.

The two scales that do not have obvious liberal-conservative aspects are actually as good or better predictors of liberalism. Persons who stress the importance of civic duty are more liberal on race than those who do not (53 per cent versus 33 per cent). But by far the best correlation of all the scales is between civil rights liberalism and rejection of constituency orientation. The finding is complicated by the fact that it holds true only in boards which do not experience competitive elections. In Bay City and Lawndale, almost all board members are not constituency-oriented; this probably only means that they are trying to persuade us (or themselves) that they are willing to oppose their electorate. If, however, Bay City and Lawndale are dropped, we find that the race conservatives are almost universally constituency-oriented ($Q = .84$). There could be some sort of tautology operating here, since the second question in the constituency-orientation scale specifically mentions the school administration. But if we look only at the other question—"A politician's first duty is to represent the views of his constituency"—we find an even stronger pattern (despite the very small number of cases) shown in Table 12.1.

If we search the remaining questions that were administered to the school board members, we find two more correlations of interest. The questionnaire attempted to tap a militant identification with the working-class whites with the statement, "Most students in expensive private schools don't learn any more than they would if they had gone to the public schools." Those who agree with this statement are more conservative on race ($Q = .33$), but the correlation is low again. The second best predictor of civil rights liberalism, next to constituency orientation, is the response to, "If people really understood the issues, there would be no disagreement over school policy." People who agree with this are considerably more conservative than are those who disagree (25 per cent versus 54 per cent, $Q = .56$). However, the two predictors of civil rights liberalism are not correlated with each other ($Q = .16$), so that taken together they make a rather powerful predictor of liberalism (Table 12.2).

Despite what should be insignificant case bases, the correlation is very strong. All seven of the persons who attached low priority to following the wishes of their constituency and who felt that disagreement would always be present in school affairs are liberals.

Table 12.1 Civil Rights Liberalism and Response to "A Politician's First Duty Is To Represent the View of His Constituency" (Bay City and Lawndale Excluded)

Response To	Per Cent Liberal	N
Agree politician should be constituency-oriented	8	13
Disagree politician should be constituency-oriented	69	16

Table 12.2 Constituency Orientation, Attitudes toward Disagreement, and Civil Rights Liberalism of School Board Members (Bay City and Lawndale Excluded) (Per Cent Liberal on Civil Rights Liberalism Scale)

Constituency Orientation	If People Really Understood the Issues, There Would Be No Disagreement about School Policy	
	Disagree	Agree
Low	$100_{(7)}$ [a]	$50_{(4)}$
Medium	$50_{(6)}$	$0_{(2)}$ [b]
High	$0_{(4)}$ [b]	$20_{(5)}$ [b]

[a] Conflict-tolerant cell.
[b] Conflict-resistant cell.

At the other corner, three cells are made up entirely of conservatives, with one exception. It may not be too surprising that the interviewer had pointed out at the time of the interview that this one liberal respondent seemed less than candid. So, with only twenty-nine respondents, we have something very close to a perfect pattern. Why? For simplicity, we will reduce the six categories shown in Table 12.2 to only three, by combining the three cells toward the lower right (those high on constituency orientation, whether they accept disagreement or not, and those who reject disagreement and are medium on constituency orientation) into a single category, called conflict-resistant, and then combining the two intermediate cells (those medium on constituency orientation and who accept disagreement with those who reject disagreement but are low on constituency orientation) and leaving the upper left hand cell as a separate category, conflict-tolerant. When this is done, γ (a generalized version of Q) is .94.

One very real possibility is that the respondents, having taken a position on civil rights, develop a framework of attitudes consistent with this. Certainly, if one is a liberal on civil rights, he may recognize that there will always be people who disagree, and if he is not following the wishes of his white constituency, how can he expect other leaders to do so? Conversely, the conservative on civil rights may rationalize his position by arguing that he, and hence others, should follow the wishes of the people. This argument is plausible, but an equally plausible interpretation could be offered for the precisely opposite finding. If liberals were constituency-oriented, we would say that this is because of their desire to argue that they are only following changing public opinion. Certainly, we would not be surprised if in the face of current events the conservatives were the ones who claimed that there would always be disagreement, while the liberals argued that if other people would only understand, integration would be accepted by everyone.[3]

[3]Since the case base for this study of attitudes is small, we should point out that we found parallel findings in a survey of thirty-three southern school board members conducted in connection with our study of New Orleans. Southerners who are conflict-tolerant are more liberal (78 per cent liberal compared with 40 per cent in the intermediate group and 22 per cent of the conflict-resistant). We have excluded the one southern appointed board and compared only the six elected boards. N's are conflict-tolerant, 9; intermediate, 15; conflict-resistant, 9.

Let us rephrase the question, then, and ask what it is that makes these three attitudes consistent with each other. The one phrase which seems to sum up all three attitudes is that they are part of a "search for simplicity." Anyone who thinks that there are only two kinds of people—those who agree with them and those who misunderstand the issues—and who further believes that the task of a public official is simply to poll the public and vote as directed by the results, has an extremely simplistic view of life. Most people believe that what they do is consistent with their attitudes about what they should do. And most people believe they are right when they take a stand. If they believe disagreement is only a matter of misunderstanding, then they are in effect saying that they are right, and anyone who understands the issue will agree with them. If, in addition, they believe they are carrying out the wishes of the majority, then they are also saying that most people agree with them, and that the others not only misunderstand but are in a minority. This suggests more than simply a closed mind. It implies that "all is right with the world."

These attitudes also reflect an intolerance of the difficult decision, of the ambiguous issue, of the irreconcilable difference of opinion, of the possibility of being wrong. It is in effect a rejection of politics, where compromises must be hammered out and difficult decisions must be made. The questions in the civil rights liberalism scale are not primarily concerned with the legal rights of Negroes. It can be taken for granted that the vast majority of board members would disapprove of illegal discrimination against Negroes, at least in a questionnaire like this one. The questions are concerned with the legitimacy of the civil rights movement— whether Negroes are asking for too much, offending people with their demonstrations, and being generally unreasonable. Thus one interpretation is that the conservatives are not responding merely out of prejudice, but out of a deep-seated resentment of controversy (or possibly they resent Negroes because their presence is controversial). Some other data lend support to this point of view. Recall that one question dealt with whether "expensive private schools" were better than public ones. The conflict-tolerant respondents all agree that they are, while one-half of the other respondents believe that they are not. Again, one interpretation is that the conflict-tolerant men are willing to admit that this is not the best of all possible worlds, and the public schools they are operating are not ideal.

Another question is interesting. We asked if the respondent agreed that, "Perhaps the most important qualification a school superintendent needs to have is professional qualification in school administration." Eighty-three per cent of the conflict-tolerant respondents rejected this statement, compared with 37 per cent of the others. This seems to support our notion that the conflict-resistant respondents are looking for simple solutions— if the school problems could be solved by getting a man with the right credentials, life would be simple indeed. Finally, one other pattern appears in the data. The most conflict-resistant men are almost uniformly not the influential board members.[4] This would seem to be in evidence in favor of the interpretation that the "conflict-resistant" do in fact resist becoming involved in difficult decision-making roles. These last three findings are summarized in Table 12.3.[5]

[4]The interviewers rated each board member in terms of his influence and involvement in board activity.

[5]The southern school board members were not rated on influence. The response to professionalism of school superintendents is not correlated with conflict orientation in the South, but conflict-tolerant southerners, like the northerners, think private schools are better (67 per cent of the tolerants versus 33 per cent of the intermediates and 0 per cent of the conflict-resistant persons).

Table 12.3 Conflict Orientation and Attitudes toward Professionalism of School Superintendent, Quality of Private Schools, and Importance of School Board

Conflict Orientation and Attitude	Conflict-Tolerant	Intermediate	Conflict-Resistant
Per cent who think expensive private schools better than public schools	100(6)	44(9)	45(11)
Per cent who think professional qualifications are not most important for school superintendent	83(6)	37(8)	36(11)
Interviewer rating of respondent's role on school board:			
Very important	3	6	1
Important	2	3	5
Less important	2	1	5
Total	7	10	11

Earlier we referred to the conflict-resistant group as people who in effect reject politics. Certainly it is hard to imagine anyone surviving in the world of local politics while believing that disagreements are only matters of misunderstanding or that decisions should be made on the basis of public opinion polls. Rather we see the politician as a skilled broker of conflicting interests who is constantly confronted with difficult decisions and frequently forced to create public support for an unpopular decision. We would also expect the political leader to be more tolerant of such protest groups as the civil rights organizations. We would expect his experience with such organizations to lead him to perceive them as effective in reaching their goals and as no more unreasonable than other political actors. In other words, his experience should lead him to tend to score as liberal on civil rights attitudes. We can test these two hypotheses. It is not difficult to divide our sample into those who are political professionals and those who are political amateurs. In general, there are only three ways to become a school board member: having achieved status in civic leadership, being active in political party work, or being nominated to represent a special interest group such as organized labor. The interviewers coded each school board member into these categories.

Table 12.4 shows the number of conflict-tolerant and conflict-resistant respondents whom we identified as having been appointed because of activity in political party work. The result is again a very strong correlation, but it is exactly the opposite of the one described above. The political amateurs are conflict-tolerant.

Table 12.4 Political Activity and Conflict Tolerance (Bay City and Lawndale Excluded)

Conflict Tolerance	Background of School Board Member	
	Politically Active	Politically Inactive
Per cent conflict-tolerant	0	41
Per cent intermediate	28	41
Per cent resistant	72	18
Total	100	100
	(11)	(17)

It is the political professionals who reject politics. In Table 12.5 we show the parallel correlation, that the political activists are racial conservatives.

Why should the politically experienced board member be constituency-oriented? It is almost taken for granted that a practicing politician in an American city will be constituency-oriented, but why is this? Even if he represents a particular ward in the city council, there is considerable pressure on him to put the welfare of the entire community uppermost. If he holds a city-wide post, such as mayor or school board member, the notion of a constituency becomes somewhat meaningless. On many issues the community will divide, making it impossible for the decision maker to merely "give the community the kind of school system the public wants," to quote one of the questions which make up this scale.

It is even more difficult to understand why the politically active school board members should feel that, "If people really understood the issues, there would be no disagreement over school policy." One rather tentative explanation is that those political leaders receive their first experience, and are "socialized," in ward-based organizations. Strong neighborhood and ethnic ties may produce consensus within the neighborhood, and this apparent consensus may be heightened because actual decisions are not made at this level, but on a city-wide basis. Thus the politician does not initially gain experience in the actual negotiation of conflict. The ward-based organization teaches the young politician not that decisions are difficult, but that the world is divided into "we" and "they" (and "they" are wrong). There are few posts in government and the party that involve city-wide reconciliation of

Table 12.5 Political Activity and Civil Rights Liberalism

Civil Rights Liberalism	Background of School Board Member	
	Politically \Active\	Politically Inactive
Per cent race liberals	23	55
N	(13)	(29)

differences, and the typical political school board member has not served in any of these.

Another possibility is that the political school board member is less secure about his status than the non-political board member. Most non-political board members hold high status in other spheres of the community—they have distinguished themselves in business or in other civic activity. For many of the politically sponsored board members, however, appointment to the school board may be their first honor. They are not in a position to take risks with their newly won prestige.

If we may continue speculating on this point, we should observe that in the typical big city political organization the primary motivation for participation is not ideological commitment. The goal of the practicing politician is to become a vote-getter— someone with personal popularity. Thus pressure not to offend is very great. There is a serious internal contradiction in the demands made on political leaders. On the one hand, they are required to develop personal popularity; on the other, they are asked to be leaders. If they make decisions, they are considered too controversial; if they do not, they are ineffective. The non-political school board member, who has never had to look to public opinion for his prestige, can more easily avoid this dilemma. It is usually assumed that the politician is popularity-oriented during the early stages of his career, and when he reaches high office he spends this political capital. A few of the political board members are still on their way up (or think they are). For them, it is important to avoid the controversial decision. But even those school board members who have reached the peak of their careers may have difficulty unlearning the popularity orientation which they have developed. Thus there are two reasons why these men are conflict-resistant. To put it simply, they dislike conflict because conflict threatens to destroy their popularity. Or if their motivation is more complex, they want simultaneously to do that which is right and that which is popular and therefore wish to believe that they can do this—that everything which is popular is also right, and that there is no reason for disagreement except misunderstanding. Thus there is great pressure on the politician to search for simplicity.

Wilson (1962) points out that one of the dangers of the reform clubs in New York City, Chicago, California, and elsewhere is that by injecting ideology into electoral contests, they force the politician to follow more closely the wishes of his constituency. This is reasonable as far as it goes, but we are suggesting here that the unreformed city administration is also plagued with a constituency orientation. There is no contradiction between Wilson's argument and the one presented here. According to Wilson, the grass roots, issue-oriented amateurs force candidates to take clear positions on issues. This often means that a candidate will only be elected if his views represent the constituency; once in office, he is bound by his campaign pledges to carry out the action the public wants. On the other hand, the issueless election make it possible for the candidate to avoid committing himself and hence leaves him free to bargain, to innovate, or simply to change his mind. However, the reformers offset this to some extent, we think, by recruiting amateurs who have not been socialized in ward politics and who are less constituency-oriented. So the two factors tend to balance each other out.

SOCIOECONOMIC STATUS AND LIBERALISM

The other personal characteristic that correlates well with race liberalism is socioeconomic status. Of course, nearly all the board members are managers, owners, or professionals, so the range of socioeconomic status is limited. In Table 12.6 the occupations of the board members have been coded into nine categories. They are listed roughly in order of prestige. Business executives have been divided into three categories: very large business includes either owners or top managers of large firms who report personal incomes of over $50,000; small business refers to low-level executives or owners of neighborhood businesses; large business is the category between these two extremes. Lawyers are divided by separating those who are members of firms specializing in corporation law and other high status legal work from all others. We have grouped persons in government service with those who are employed by not-for-profit organizations (unions, social welfare agencies). The professionals in the sample are primarily physicians, dentists, or university faculty. High school teachers are considered in the residual category, along with white collar and blue collar workers. Wives are ordinarily assigned their husbands' occupations. In the second column is the percentage of each occupational group who are liberals on civil rights. Categories have been combined where possible in percentaging.

Despite the usual small number of cases, the percentages show a consistent pattern. If we combine the three highest categories, we find that 69 per cent of these persons are liberal, compared with 29 per cent of the remainder.[6] The high status persons are also more likely to deny that disagreement is merely a result of misunderstanding, supporting our hypothesis that this question reflects one's sense of security in dealing with controversial issues.

It is impossible to sort out the various factors which are operating in the sample of school board members. We have suggested some reasons why politically active board members should be more conservative, but it is also true that the political men in the

[6]For the South, these percentages are 53 and 43 per cent, based on fifteen and twenty-three cases.

Table 12.6 Occupation of School Board Members and Civil Rights Liberalism

Occupation	Number	Per Cent Civil Rights Liberals	Per Cent Politically Active
Very large business Large business	4 } 10 }	67(9)	25(12)
Corporation law	10	71(7)	10(10)
Professional	14	33(6)	44(9)
Small business	9	0(5)	62(8)
Lawyers	12	40(5)	75(8)
Not-for-profit employees White collar, etc. Retired	5 } 4 } 1 }	38(8)	25(8)
Total	69		

Note: N's for percentages (in parentheses) exclude Negroes and non-respondents.

sample are of lower social status, and this could be the main factor influencing their attitudes. The pattern is especially clear if we look at the social origins of the school board members. Nearly all the non-political board members are from middle-class families, while the bulk of the political board members are upwardly mobile. Father's occupation is nearly as good a predictor of racial attitudes as is present occupation. Table 12.7 indicates that persons from low status backgrounds are more likely to be conservatives and more likely to be politically active.[7]

Thus we see that there are two mechanisms operating here which might explain the conservatism of professional politicians on school boards. On the one hand, they are drawn from low status origins and have lower status occupations. On the other, they experience pressures that make them intolerant of conflict and might cause them to define the civil rights movement as illegitimate. The choice between the two explanations depends in part upon one's conception of the psychology of prejudice. If, following the work of psychologists like Adorno, we believe race prejudice to be deeply imbedded and very resistant to change, the first explanation is the most plausible—politicos are prejudiced, and that's that. If, on the other hand, we assume that racial attitudes are not deeply imbedded and are subject to change (such a point of view appears in the work of R. M. Williams, 1964, and

[7]For the South, 52 per cent of the sons of businessmen and professionals are liberals, compared with 38 per cent of the others. The association is stronger if we use father's education as one measure of socioeconomic status: seven of the nine men whose fathers attended college are liberals, compared with only 41 per cent of the twenty-seven others.

Table 12.7 Political Activity, Civil Rights Liberalism, and Father's Occupation of School Board Members

Political Activity and Civil Rights Liberalism	Business or Professional	Small Business, Farm, or White Collar	Blue Collar
Per cent politically active	20	31	60
Per cent liberal on race	60	46	20
N	(15)	(13)	(10)

Note: For three respondents, the civil rights liberalism score was estimated from interviewer ratings.

Hyman and Sheatsley, 1964) we might lean toward the second explanation—that social pressures operating on politically active board members make it difficult for them to handle conflict, and they retreat from it by becoming conservatives. Our own guess, and it is little more than a guess, is that these two alternatives are both correct, but with the second more important than the first.

SCHOOL BOARD RECRUITMENT AND SCHOOL BOARD ACQUIESCENCE

We have said that there are two basic means of recruitment to the school board. The politically sponsored candidate, who has earned his board appointment through work for the party, is likely to be upwardly mobile, a small businessman or neighborhood lawyer. If he is not himself active in a ward organization, he may be a close personal friend of the mayor or another leading politician. The bulk of the non-political appointees are businessmen who have developed reputations as civic leaders or at least have been spotted by the civil leadership as men with potential. These men are usually corporation lawyers, owners of middle-sized businesses, or second-rank executives, but in some cases owners of large corporations (or their wives) may show up on school boards. These two groups together account for over four-fifths of the white school board members. The remainder are selected by formulas which require representation of specific interest groups. In five cities a labor representative serves on the board. In Baltimore the three universities must be represented, and in several cities a woman, often active in the PTA or the League of Women Voters, serves on the board. In general, these formula appointees are relatively inactive members, although there are exceptions. Some professions are surprisingly underrepresented. There is only one white minister on a school board. Baltimore is the only city which has a college professor on the board. And the bulk of the dentists and physicians are political appointees. One reason why these occupations are underrepresented is that these persons are not known to either the civic elites or the political leadership, who are the unofficial appointing bodies.

In the preceding chapter we developed a complex flow chart pointing out the ways in which community characteristics can influence board action. We are now ready to simplify that flow chart in two ways: First, we can discard the bottom half of the chart dealing with the civil rights movement, since we have seen that the actual negotiation process has relatively little effect on acquiescence. In addition, the original chart distinguished between channels of recruitment of the decision makers and channels of direct influence; but we can now ignore actual influence, for the bulk of the explanation lies in character of the school board. Hence the new chart, Figure 12.1, contains only four key elements—the four dotted lines which feed into school board liberalism and which symbolize the process of recruiting board members. We have also assumed that the Negro business and political elite and the Negro community structure will ordinarily have little effect on the recruitment procedures for the school board.

Figure 12.2 correlates the median civil rights liberalism of the board with the percentage of board members who have been active in local political parties. The school board falls into three main groups: (1) Pittsburgh, Baltimore, and St. Louis, where the number of political appointments is insignificant; (2) Newark and Buffalo, where an overwhelming majority of the board are politically active; and (3) Bay City, Lawndale, and San Francisco, where the boards are evenly divided between political and non-political members. In the next chapter we will try to determine why these cities have these recruitment procedures; for now we will only concern ourselves with their effect. The correlation between these three groups is perfect: the two political boards are least liberal, the three non-political boards most liberal, and the other three fall in between.[8]

The correlation of the proportion of political board appointments with liberalism, and hence with acquiescence, is so high

[8]It is worth the time to point out that the political party allegiance of these boards is not relevant. Many board members chose to keep their political party identifications confidential; we can therefore only estimate the differences between boards and have divided the boards into four groups: Democratic, leaning Democratic, leaning Republican, and Republican (one board was not rated on this variable due to lack of information). There is only a low correlation (.27) between these categories and the board's civil rights liberalism. (Democratic boards are slightly more liberal.) However, we probably have not misclassified the cities badly since there is a good correlation (.78) between party affiliation and median economic liberalism.

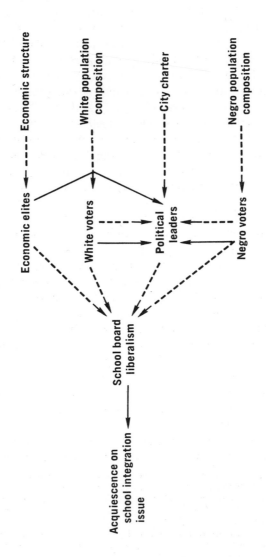

Figure 12.1 Revised Flow Chart for Predicting Acquiescence

that there is no systematic way to bring in other variables. We have explained nearly all the variation, so other variables cannot be expected to help. However, there are other explanations which must be considered. One is that political appointments are conservative only because they are low status, and not because of their political involvement. The rank-order correlation of socioeconomic status with liberalism, shown in Figure 12.3, is lower than the correlation of political activity with liberalism, but it is still high enough to keep the situation ambiguous. There are three deviant cases; the most important is San Francisco, which is tied with Pittsburgh for highest status but ranks fifth in liberalism.

COHESION AND BOARD RECRUITMENT PATTERNS

The other major factor which seems to determine the level of acquiescense is the cohesiveness of the school board. Not surprisingly, one factor which keeps a board from being cohesive is the heterogeneity of the backgrounds of its members. In particular, there is a good deal of tension between the political and nonpolitical members of the board.

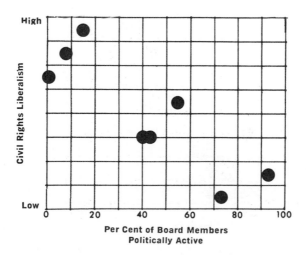

Figure 12.2 Political Activity of Board Members and Civil Rights Liberalism

As Figure 12.4 indicates, the least cohesive boards tend to be those which are neither purely political nor purely non-political in makeup. The closer the board is to being exactly 50 per cent political, the lower the level of cohesion. (If we ranked the cities by their distance from the 50 per cent point, the correlation with cohesion would be an impressive +.81.)

In Bay City, low cohesion is a result of a sharp disagreement between politicos and reformers. But this is only one of the ways in which a "mixed" board has difficulty. In Lawndale, San Francisco, and Buffalo the selection procedure is a compromise between appointing "qualified" board members and paying political debts. But in every case the attempt at this compromise contains the seeds of dissension. In San Francisco there is considerable internal conflict between high and low status board members. In Buffalo there is conflict in a board which is ethnically diverse without any overriding loyalties to a political party. And in Lawndale, there is some tension among even the members of the majority coalition, at least in comparison with the other cities in the sample. The mixed appointment process also leads to dissension by restricting the number of highly skilled persons who can assume leadership roles.

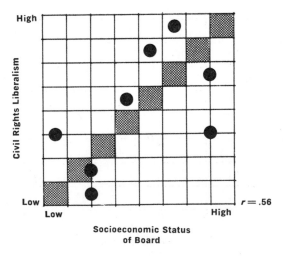

Figure 12.3 School Board Socioeconomic Status and Civil Rights Liberalism

There are some interesting parallels between San Francisco and a city not in our sample, Chicago, which also has a mixed appointment process. In both cities there is sharp disagreement which tends to divide the higher status non-political appointments from the politicos. In both cases the result has been that the board has difficulty developing a consistent style of action. No one member is universally respected and hence there is no clear leadership. With the boards both split near the middle, votes are often close, and therefore every action tends to be preceded by long discussion as the "swing votes" take their position. And in both cities the superintendent gradually took over many of the board's functions and was accused of being autocratic. The school board has the capacity to at least partly control the kind of relationship it has with the administration, and Pois (1964) has pointed out in his case study of the Chicago school board some of the reasons why the Chicago board has had difficulty dealing with its superintendent. (Pois had served on the board before writing the monograph.) In both Chicago and San Francisco the presence of a mixed board results from the city's being in a state of political transition. Chicago is undergoing a gradual reform, and the presence of the high status appointments on the board is the result. However, the reforms were not completely successful, so that

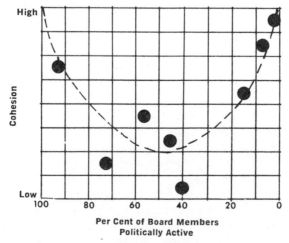

Figure 12.4 Political Activity of Board Members and Cohesion of Board

some of the board members are political appointees. San Francisco, on the other hand, seems to be in a state of transition toward working-class politics, which may result in more political appointments in the future.

BOARD ORGANIZATION AND COHESION

The boards which are most cohesive are also the ones with the most pronounced hierarchical patterns. For example, one highly cohesive board, Pittsburgh, has a clear inner core of influential board members. This core leads discussion in private session in such a way that nearly all votes are unanimous. In this case, the hierarchy seems to develop naturally according to the interest or ability shown by the various board members. In contrast, the St. Louis board members are almost forced into an informal hierarchical structure because of the election campaigns. As long as the founder of the citizens' committee which slated the members for election serves on the board (and serves as chief political adviser in the committee's electoral campaign) the board members are almost forced to pay attention to him. For the same reason, the senior Negro member of the board must be respected, since he is instrumental in obtaining the support of Negro voters. The result is that despite considerable heterogeneity in background and in attitudes, the board functions as a tightly knit unit on many issues. In Newark the hierarchy is also present, but here it is deference to the political party (and the mayor) which reduces tension.

Hierarchy does not explain the cohesiveness of the Baltimore board, but in this case it may be that the majority members of the board are quite homogeneous in attitudes and background (they are two university men, two prominent lawyers, and a prominent newspaperwoman—all quite liberal in their racial and economic attitudes.)

At the other extreme, the two most egalitarian boards seem to be Buffalo and Bay City, and these are also the least cohesive. In both cities this egalitarianism is in part caused by the competition for the spotlight among politically ambitious members; no one is willing to take a back seat. Each issue requires that an ad hoc leader put together a winning coalition, and it is conceivable that each coalition could be different. In Bay City every board member has publicly disagreed with each of the others on at least one issue.

THE EFFECT OF SIZE OF BOARD

A rather surprising pattern appears if we look at the number of members on each board. The most cohesive (and the most acquiescent) board, Pittsburgh, is also the largest. The least cohesive (and the least acquiescent), Bay City, is the smallest. The full rank ordering of cities by cohesion is given below:

Ranking by Cohesion	Number of Members
Pittsburgh (High)	15
Newark	9
St. Louis	12
Baltimore	9
Lawndale	7
San Francisco	7
Buffalo	7
Bay City (Low)	5

$$R = +.93$$

The correlation is of impressive magnitude. If the reader has the urge to dismiss the correlation as a statistical freak, we should add that in our parallel study of seven southern school boards, the two smallest boards had five members; these two were the least acquiescent boards and most torn by community controversy.

Regrettably, there is a trivial argument which might explain this finding. One way in which a school board is reformed is by adding new members. This has happened to three of the seven southern boards and to one of the northern boards (Buffalo) in the past decade; there may be other cases which we do not know of. Thus reform boards should be larger than political ones.

Nevertheless, there may well be a relationship between size and cohesion independent of this. The school board is in effect a non-partisan legislative body. Suppose that an issue came up which would normally divide a school board very closely. Suppose that across a number of school systems, 55 per cent of all school board members voted yes and 45 per cent voted no on this issue. If we then constitute a five-member board by selecting persons randomly from the population of school board members, we would find that 61 per cent of the time the board would split 3–2 on this issue, while a fifteen-member board would split 8–7 only 36 per cent of the time. Or to put it another way—if one member were absent (again chosen randomly), the chance of a tie vote in the five-member board would be .37, but only .19 in the larger board. (The absence of two members would reverse the outcome of the vote one-fifth of the time in the small board, and only one-tenth of the time in the larger board.) On issues which ordinarily do not divide the board this closely, the differences are even greater. For example, if we took an issue on which board members normally split 65–35 per cent, the chance of a single absence creating a tie in a fifteen-member board is 11 per cent; in a five-member board it is 31 per cent.

Under these conditions, it is much more difficult for the small board to develop a hierarchical structure. An uninterested board member cannot simply stay away from meetings. If he does, he will be pressured by the two board members who need his vote. This also forces everyone to vote cautiously. His vote is often crucial. With more intense concern attached to each vote, stable voting factions are liable to break down. This, coupled with the intimacy of the small board, makes an opportunity for bad feeling to emerge.

The other characteristic of a small board is that it has a smaller pool of leadership to draw upon. This means that it may be difficult to develop specialists in various fields and may make it difficult for the board to select a president who is respected by other members.

ELECTION VERSUS APPOINTMENT OF BOARD MEMBERS

There is an old saw that the best method of electing school board members is the one you don't have right now. Like many popular sayings, this one does not seem to hold true. The majority of the school board members interviewed preferred the method by which they were selected. Only two of fifteen elected board members think appointed boards do a better job and only seven of twenty-eight appointed board members prefer elected boards (six of the seven are in either Newark or Buffalo; we suspect that some of these are persons who aspire to holding elective office).

It seems obvious that there is no simple answer to this question. It is very likely that research will show that appointed boards do certain kinds of things, elected boards others, and the choice between the two will depend upon the values of the observer. In studying integration we have collected data on only one aspect of board behavior. We should first note that only one city, Bay City, has a history of contested elections for school board. Lawndale and St. Louis have at one time or another seen board members nominated who ran without opposition. In particular, we must consider St. Louis as having an appointed board during the time period of our study since the last two elections were virtually uncontested. These leave us only two elected boards, unfortunately.[9] However, the following similarities between these two elected boards are striking: they are the two least acquiescent boards in the sample. In both, racial integration became an election issue. Both have low levels of consensus. And both have politically active members. These are all factors which are associated with low acquiescence and extended debate. A rereading will also indicate that these two cities probably had the highest level of controversy.

There are several obvious reasons why this should be so. The elected board rewards the politically ambitious with exposure and inhibits the high status candidate for the same reason. Once in office, the elected board member must be willing to risk a segregationist candidate running against him, as happened in both Bay City and Lawndale. The election campaigns maintain a higher level of public interest in board activity and reduce the social distance from the public which insulates boards like Pittsburgh and enables them to take unpopular steps. The Bay City (and St. Louis) system is particularly cruel; the board members run at large and those getting the largest vote are elected. This means that the incumbents are running against each other, although they must work together both before and (hopefully) after the election.

On the other hand, we can point out that some of the appointed boards are low in cohesion and acquiescence, so that an appointed

[9]Our sample is unrepresentative in this respect; most northern big city boards are elected.

board is no guarantee of racial peace. Finally, what can we say about St. Louis? Here is an elected board which has high cohesion and was able to acquiesce in the civil rights movement. This may be evidence that an elected board can handle civil rights issues just as an appointed board can. However, it must be remembered that the St. Louis board would have been reformed earlier than it was if Mayor Tucker had had the power of appointment when he was first elected. Second, the reformed school board has only been in office less than five years. It is difficult to predict what will happen in the future when the spirit of reform has died and the voters get bored, if they do, with uncontested elections. Finally, we should note that the St. Louis board operates as it does only because the civic elite of the city invested considerable amounts of money in winning the two crucial elections.

METHODS OF BOARD APPOINTMENT

The remaining five boards are all appointed—four of the five by the mayor and the fifth, Pittsburgh, by the judges of the Court of Common Pleas. In Newark and Buffalo the mayor is able to re-cruit most of the board members from the ranks of his active supporters and friends. The school board positions are highly de-sirable, so that there is considerable competition for these ap-pointments. In both cities a pattern of ethnic assignment of seats reduces the competition for each post somewhat, since, for example, only Jews need harangue the mayor when a Jewish seat comes up. In three cases that we know of, the candidate in effect waged a campaign to get the appointment. In at least two other cases the appointment was made to a close personal friend or rela-tive of the mayor or another top leader in the party. The ap-pointees tend to be young. Of the eight persons whose ages we know in these two cities, the median age at appointment was only forty-four. In contrast, Pittsburgh now has a median age of sixty. It is unlikely that any were younger than forty-three when first appointed.

In San Francisco and Baltimore the same formal procedure of appointments by the mayor results in quite different groups of board members. In Baltimore there is no uniform technique for recruitment. Three of the Baltimore board members must be representatives of the three universities; apparently two of these three board members were recruited by elites who serve on the boards of trustees. Two key members of the present board were recruited by other board members, so that there is a pattern of continuity, at least among the high status appointments. Two of the key board members were recruited by a board president. Since the board presidents tend to be members of the Baltimore civic elite, we can conclude that the elite exert an important influence on board recruitment.

In San Francisco, several board members stated that they had helped to locate candidates for the board. Some of the appointments came from key members of the civic elite. Others came from close advisors of the mayor. The result produced the most heterogeneous board in our sample.

The Pittsburgh technique of having board members selected by a panel of judges should operate somewhat differently from the mayor-appointment system. Since judges serve for life, changes in the mayor's office will have no appreciable effect on the appointment process—the newly elected mayor cannot punish his enemies or reward his friends until he has control over the judges. In addition, the judges will be less sensitive to pressure than the mayor, since there are fewer people who can perform important favors for a tenured judge. This does not guarantee that the board will be non-political, of course. If all the judges are members of the local political party and the party is well disciplined, then the judges might choose to appoint only candidates recommended by the party. Or the judges might engage in logrolling, with each faction of judges having the right to make a certain fraction of the appointments. However, this requires close communication and negotiation among the judges. In the event of disagreement, the judges might easily succumb to pressure from the civic elite to name high status persons.

In practice, the judges consult with incumbent board members for recommendations so that at least a part of the board can be considered to be self-perpetuating. Those appointees who have earned the respect of other board members are able to recommend other board appointments. The result is that Pittsburgh, like Baltimore, has a self-screening process which tends to select new board members by the same criterion which board members use to evaluate each other. Thus both boards should be quite stable in political style.

It is clear from this discussion that the formal appointment procedures in these five cities do not vary enough to explain the great difference in the informal recruitment process and the composition of the boards. Similarly, the three elected cities do not differ very much in the electoral apparatus. The explanation for the differences in the school boards must now be traced back one more step into the political, economic, and social structure of the city. This is the task we will attempt in the next chapter.

SUMMARY

The behavior of school boards in handling school integration is largely dependent upon the process of recruitment to the board. Among the eight cities studied, we have found that the procedure for selection of board members operates in two important ways to determine the degree of acquiescence to school integration demands. The recruitment processes vary considerably, above all, in their tendency to recruit either political professionals or higher status political amateurs, often loosely associated with the civic elite.

Political professionals have more conservative attitudes on race than political amateurs. This may be because of their social backgrounds, but in addition, their disapproval of the civil rights movement seems to fit with a constellation of values which indicate that the professional politician on the school board is less willing to participate in decision making under conditions of conflict.

The proportion of politically appointed board members is a good predictor of the liberalism of the school board, as measured by attitude questionnaires administered to school board members. Liberalism, in turn, is correlated with the level of acquiescence of the school system.

The other factor which seems to be independently correlated with acquiescence is the degree of cohesion of the school board members as a social group, cohesive boards being more acquiescent. Highly cohesive boards tend to be made up entirely of political professionals or entirely of non-political members, to have a hierarchical internal structure, and to be large in size.

13

Community Characteristics and School Board Recruitment

In the preceding chapter we isolated three factors which seem to explain the acquiescence of the school board to the civil rights movement's demands. These are the number of political professionals on the board, the socioeconomic status of the school board members, and the cohesion of the board. All seem to be a function of the procedure used to recruit school board members. By this we do not mean the formal procedure, although electing rather than appointing the school board has an important effect. But mainly we will focus upon the informal influence exerted by different sectors of the community on the recruitment process.

Interest groups and others can influence board appointments by proposing candidates or by screening potential candidates before they are nominated (or appointed). But the process of influencing board selection is not, and need not be, even this formal. Rather, we think that the appointing or nominating body develops over the years a mental picture of what a school board appointment should be like. In one city it may be considered "only fair" that a prospective candidate should demonstrate political loyalty; in another any such an appointment might be considered "tainted."

In some cities this image of the ideal board member is clear; in others it is fuzzy. In Newark, Baltimore, St. Louis, and Pittsburgh, almost all the board members might fit a single set of criteria: "proper ethnic and political association" in Newark; "intellectualism" in Baltimore; "dedication and ability" in St. Louis and Pittsburgh. In the other four cities the picture is not so simple. The Lawndale board contains political leaders, civic leaders, per-

First draft by James J. Vanecko.

sons active in voluntary organizations, and reformers. Certainly no single image will fit board members DeUrioste and Ladar in San Francisco, or Goodyear and Parlato in Buffalo. And the complex set of reasons that motivate residents of Bay City to run for the board, or to vote for particular candidates, almost def·′ description. The result of these unclear or contradictory "job descriptions" is to produce boards that are heterogeneous; this in turn leads to lower cohesion and thus makes the board less acquiescent.

But let us ignore for the moment the clarity of the "recruitment image" and concentrate on how the image differs from city to city. There is a strong negative rank-order correlation between the number of high status appointments to the board and the number of political appointees (−.70). The basic difference between cities is a single dimension: either the board is made up of politicos, or it is made up of persons representing the civic elite. The nominee to the school board must have some sort of qualifying credentials, and the most common are achievement in politics or achievement in civic affairs—service on citizens' committees and in the fundraising campaigns that Peter Rossi called "non-destructive potlatches." There are other kinds of credentials—personal wealth, special skills (in education, real estate, financing, architecture), achievement in grass-roots organizations like the PTA, or the ability to represent major interest groups, such as labor unions. But these types of appointments are in the minority. The main choice is between civic and political activity.

This suggests that the appropriate model for studying school board recruitment is one of conflict between the two most powerful groups in the city—the political party and the civic leadership. This is not usually a visible conflict, and we doubt that very many people in these cities recognize it as conflict; but in fact this is simply a continuation of the pressures which divided these two groups over fifty years ago, when the industrial cities of the North developed professional politicians who could use ethnic and class conflict as a resource to compete with Yankee money.

In Figure 13.1 we have located cities on this dimension by comparing for each board the number of board members who are political appointees with the number who have high occupational status—businessmen from large firms, corporation lawyers, or other professionals. Since even the most elite board will reserve some seats for PTA or union representatives and the like, and the most political board may have members who hold these occupations, we cannot expect any board to be made up entirely of high status or entirely of low status persons. For this reason we have drawn a dashed line indicating the possible range, from 85 per cent high status down to only 20 per cent, as we move from completely non-political boards to completely political ones.[1]

Reading from upper left to lower right in Figure 13.1, we have a ranking of cities according to the power of the civic elite over appointments, relative to the power held by the political organizations. In this ranking we have tied the first two cities (Baltimore and Pittsburgh). We shall call this new ranking simply "reform orientation."

It is our impression that this ranking of the power of the civic elite relative to the political leadership in school board nominations is very nearly the same ranking that one would produce considering all other areas of civic decision-making as well. In the three top cities—Pittsburgh, Baltimore, and St. Louis—there are formal organizations in which the business elite are active, take stands on various issues, and do actual promotional work for various programs. All three organizations have been quite involved in urban renewal programs in the downtown areas of their

---

[1]The exact shape of this line is hard to determine. We assume a slight negative curvature on the basis of two assumptions: (1) There is a floor of 20 per cent high status appointments which no board will fall below. (2) There is a "take-off" effect, in that once a board is completely controlled by non-political persons, it will be easier to recruit persons of very high status. There is also a ceiling effect—no board can be 100 per cent high status because of the need to represent PTA or union officials.

We might also assume a simple double-saturation curve of this form:

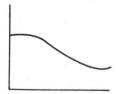

Our ranking of cities would be the same, however.

cities. The Greater Baltimore Association has promoted the expansion of the local airport for use by jets, has given support to the art museum and the opera, has supported open occupancy legislation, and is in the process of organizing a broad program of compensatory education. (The reader will recall that the Greater Baltimore Association supports Baltimore Neighborhoods, Inc., whose executive director was one of the plaintiffs in the school integration issue.) The civic elite in this city participate as members of boards and commissions of the city government. An illuminating comment was made by a leading businessman who was also a major actor in education. When asked, as all our respondents were, how often he talked to the mayor, he responded, "Very rarely more than once a day." There was not such a close relationship between the mayor and the business elite in any other

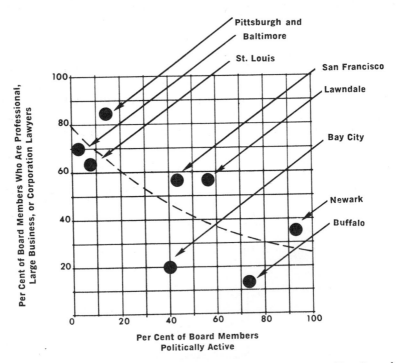

Figure 13.1 Per Cent of Board Members of High Social Status and Per Cent of Board Members Politically Active

city we studied. In Pittsburgh the formal organization was consciously committed to problems on at least a metropolitan scale and probably even larger, but the organization was also quite effective locally, especially in the urban renewal program.

In San Francisco and Lawndale (ranked 4 and 5 in Table 13.1) the economic elite were quite active in civic affairs. In San Francisco there were a number of formal organizations such as those in Pittsburgh, Baltimore, and St. Louis, but not one of these organizations could claim to speak for the majority of the business elite. On some issues, these organizations took different sides and opposed one another. The business elite in these cities are also quite active as individuals apart from the organizations; in fact, individual participation may be more important than organized participation. These are the only cities in our sample where it is not at all unusual for a quite prosperous and prominent businessman to run for local office. In Lawndale, the business elite is active in three distinct factions. One group is quite conservative in ideology and works for the maintenance of conservative control over the local Republican party. (This is the group that was closest to the school board.) The interests represented by this group are those of a number of local industries with regional markets, including warehousing, small manufacturing, food processing, and the local newspaper. A second group is one which is identified with a major national corporation which has the executive offices of all its branches in Lawndale. Besides the executives from this company, there are many younger professional people involved. Politically these people are involved in both the liberal wing of the Republi-

Table 13.1 Suburbanization of Economic Elite

City	Per Cent of Population in City	Per Cent of Elites in City	Suburbanization of Elites
Newark	23	4	5.9
Bay City	26	8	3.2
St. Louis	36	14	2.6
Lawndale	14	10	1.4
Buffalo	41	31	1.3
San Francisco	26	21	1.2
Baltimore	54	49	1.1
Pittsburgh	24	29	0.83

can party and in the Democratic party. The third grouping is composed of the hotel, motel, bank, and financial interests and is mainly concerned with booster activities to promote the city. They become involved with projects such as bringing professional football and baseball teams to the city, promoting the airport, and developing local transportation. This group cuts across the other two. While the participation of the economic elite in these two cities is quite high, the conflict and competition within the economic elite itself often curtails their influence.

Newark, Buffalo, and Bay City all represent similar patterns. The economic elite are only slightly involved with civic affairs. In Newark there is minimal involvement in response to demands of civil rights groups.[2] The other two cities show almost no signs of involvement of the business elite in civic affairs.

These different types of participation of the economic elites in these cities were quite clear. But participation is not necessarily influence, and it is harder to say how much influence they wielded. We must speak only of fairly open influence, not of secret contributions to campaigns and attached promises, not of particularistic intervention for special treatment, not of quiet threats to leave the community and disrupt the economy. This type of influence was not uncovered in any of the studies which we have reviewed, though, and there is room for broad doubt whether such conspiratorial activity is of major importance. The way we have devised the rankings of the cities on the influence of the economic elite contains a certain bias. We have started from specific issues (reported to be the most important issues in the city in the past few years), and looked to see who were influential in the decisions involved. In doing this we probably have encountered a bias toward new programs which have gotten underway and thus toward people who have been influential in bringing about change. We may be missing the business elite who are influential in maintaining the status quo. It is then possible that this ranking is not one which shows the economic elite who are most influential at the top but rather one which shows the least influential civic elite resistant to change at the top. Given the near total representation of the major business institutions in Pittsburgh, Baltimore, and St.

[2]The Newark Urban Renewal Program operated in a virtual power vacuum for years before the businessmen became involved (see Kaplan, 1963).

Louis, this seems a highly improbable interpretation of these findings.

In summary, we would rank the cities in terms of general participation of the civic elite in community decision making in approximately the same order that they are ranked with regard to school board recruitment, except that we do not believe the leaders in San Francisco to be as active as those in Lawndale. Thus we think that two characteristics of the acquiescent board—having high status members and being "out of politics"—result from the presence of a powerful civic elite.

The third factor which correlates with the acquiescence of the school board is the level of cohesion of the board. In Figure 13.2 we have plotted reform orientation against the cohesion of the board. (The plot is of course similar to the plot of cohesion against political activity in Chapter 12.) In the figure, we seem to have developed a map that places similar boards near each other. The three boards in the upper left are the three in which we found powerful civic elites, and which have the fewest political professionals—Pittsburgh, Baltimore, and St. Louis. The two West Coast boards—San Francisco and Lawndale—tend to fall

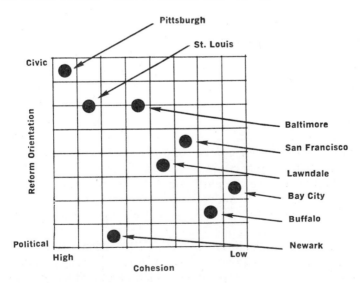

Figure 13.2   Reform Orientation and Cohesion

toward the upper right. It is hard to imagine a school board in the extreme upper right. This would require that it be made up of very high status persons who strongly disliked each other. In the lower right we have Bay City and Buffalo. It is hard to say whether these two cities should be considered similar or not. The Bay City board is elected, and it is hard to guess what sort of school board the city would have if it were appointed. However, the two cities do have similarly chaotic political systems, which suggests that under the same system of board selection their boards might not differ too much. Finally, in the lower right we have Newark, resembling Buffalo in its politicalness, but similar to Pittsburgh in its cohesion.

One can find these same similarities in Figure 13.1 (which correlates status and political activity), with San Francisco and Lawndale near each other, Buffalo lying between Newark and Bay City, and the three high status reform boards lying near each other. Thus the eight school boards in this study seem to fall into four distinct categories. In order to make clear the relationship between Figures 13.1 and 13.2, we will present the map shown in Figure 13.2 as a four-cell typology in Figure 13.3. The two dimensions of the figure are level of elite involvement and level of organization of the recruitment process. Cell A, the cities dominated by civic elite recruitment style and with high levels of cohesion, are the cities we refer to as "balance-of-power" cities. In this case, the balance of power is between the political parties, which are tightly structured and wield considerable influence in the day-to-day politics of the city, and the civic elite, who are organized and possess enough countervailing power to capture the school board, to play a major role in city decision-making, and, on occasion, to elect a mayor. While we have chosen to look at this as a conflict situation, another observer might say that a division of labor has been agreed upon between the parties and the elites in these cities. The three cities, St. Louis, Baltimore, and Pittsburgh, are the three high status non-political boards in Figure 13.1, and they are the three cohesive reform boards in Figure 13.2.

Reading down the first column, Cell C is the machine city. Newark clearly falls in this cell, and during certain periods Buffalo might fall here as well. In the machine city, the school board is controlled by the working-class and ethnic-based political party.

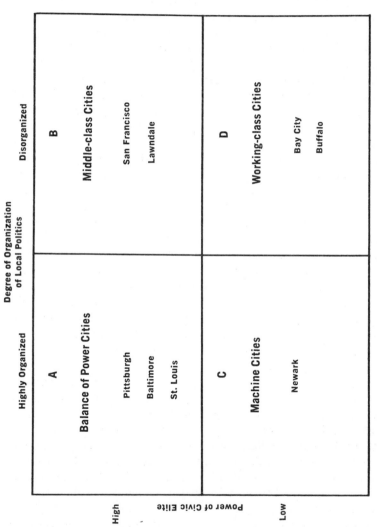

Figure 13.3 A Typology of School Board Recruitment

Here there is also a conflict between the elites and the party, except that the elites are too weak to compete with the party; the elites have withdrawn from city decision-making. In Figure 13.1, the board is located at the lower right, being made up almost entirely of low status political appointees; if the political party in fact functions as a machine, there should be a high level of cohesion.

The right-hand column contains the cities where power is more diffuse. In Cell D the civic elite has withdrawn from municipal decision-making; but in addition, the political parties are very weak. The result is that politics is dominated by class and ethnic considerations, just as in the machine city, but politics are highly disorganized. Thus both cities have unclear images of the "proper" type of board member. With neither strong parties nor a strong elite dominating the selection of school board members, there is no clear criterion for board selection. The result is that these boards appear in Figure 13.1 toward the lower center of the chart; some of the board members are political, but some are not; and even the non-political members tend to have low status. One does not need clearance from the elite or the party to serve on the board, and the result is that in principle almost any resident of the city would have a reasonable chance of selection. There are probably very few places in the country where important political offices are "up for grabs" in quite this way. It is hardly surprising that these boards should have low cohesion.

Cell B in Figure 13.3 remains—middle-class cities. Both are western cities, are younger, and have larger Protestant populations. The result is that neither city has a sharp bifurcation between the civic and political spheres. In both cities we find high status Protestants campaigning for elective office. Both cities grew up in a reform era, so that nonpartisanship resulted in the weakening of political parties. Since individual members of the business elite are directly involved in politics, it is possible—indeed necessary—for them to take ideological positions which prevent the elites from pulling together to form a unified interest group. Liberal businessmen are active in this organization, conservative businessmen in another. The result is that while high status persons tend to dominate city decision-making and fill a number of positions on the school board, board members are recruited in different ways, and the board remains heterogeneous and not a co-hesive group. In Figure 13.1 both these cities appear in the upper center of the graph; while one-half of the board members are political appointees, the board contains a large number of high status appointments. These two cities are probably representative of a large number of American cities, particularly small cities and cities in the South, where there is no clear distinction between the politician and the civic leader.[3]

In summary, we see that the only way a school board can be cohesive is for appointments to be made with a consistent and clear image of the ideal board member in mind, and this can only occur if the school board is dominated by a strong political party or by a strong civic elite. If these groups are weak, the result will be that the board can be either high or low status, but it will be heterogeneous and will have high internal conflict. Buffalo is the most problematic city in the typology. It probably varies, from one time period to another, between being disorganized working class and being a machine city.

There are several assumptions implicit in the fact that these two typologies work out this way. We shall discover some of these as we begin to investigate the factors which cause cities to fall into different cells.

REFORM ORIENTATION

What are the conditions that enable the civic elite to retain (or recover) their influence in city decision-making? There are two general possibilities. One is that the city has a population that is sympathetic to good government. The obvious test of this is to examine the socioeconomic status of the population. Six indicators of socioeconomic status—median income, percentage of families earning under $5,000 per year, percentage earning over $10,000 per year, median education, percentage of adults with at least some college, and percentage in white collar employment—were used to rank the cities, and the rankings were averaged. The resulting correlation with the reform orientation of the board was −.11, indicating a very slight tendency for the low status cities to

[3]In fact, these two cities resemble in some ways the two small southern cities described by Agger, Goldrich, and Swanson (1964).

have civic boards. The correlation is in the wrong direction and of trivial magnitude.

Another possibility is that the cities with large manufacturing plants would develop a more powerful civic elite and thus be better able to control the school board appointments. The assumption is that the concentration of economic power into large units, as in large manufacturing plants, concentrates considerable resources in a small number of men, who can then use these resources to build an organization of civic elites and make demands on the political system. On the other hand, if economic resources are diffusely headed by many owners of small plants, or service industries, such a concentration and organization of economic power will be less likely. Mills and Ulmer (1946) make essentially this assumption when they argue that cities with large manufacturing plants provide a low level of services to their residents. They assume that this concentration of power will be used for selfish purposes by the manufacturers. Their finding is disputed by Fowler (1958), who argues that this concentration of power will be used unselfishly and that cities with large industry in fact provide higher levels of services.

With these arguments in mind, we constructed a centralization index by combining the percentage of the labor force in manufacturing with the average size of manufacturing firm. (This is essentially the procedure used by Mills and Ulmer and by Fowler.) This index places the heavy industry cities—Buffalo, Newark, St. Louis, and Pittsburgh—above the less industrial cities—Baltimore, Lawndale, San Francisco, and Bay City. However, this correlation with recruitment source is also in the wrong direction and of insignificant magnitude. Centralized (i.e., industrial) cities are slightly less likely to have "civic" boards ($R = -.26$).

Our respondents spoke a good deal about the problems created by the flight of the civic elite to the suburbs. This turns out to be a very good predictor of elite control. The index we have used to measure the suburbanization of the civic elite is taken from census data: it is the percentage of the total metropolitan population living in the city divided by the percentage of the metropolitan area's families earning over $25,000 who live in the city. The index would be below 1.00 if all income units of over $25,000 were in the central city; it would be 1.00 if high income families were no more or less suburbanized than the total population; and it would go to infinity if none lived in the city. There are two reasons why this measure recommends itself. First, it is not affected by the total suburbanization of the city. Thus it isolates elite suburbanization from general suburbanization. (This also means that we can compare our two satellite cities to the six central cities. Elite suburbanization will be high if high income families avoid these satellites.) Second, the index is independent of the size of the elite population, thus separating suburbanization from this factor. The suburbanization scores of the eight cities were given in Table 13.1.

As Figure 13.4 indicates, there is a correlation of $-.75$ between suburbanization of the economic elite and reform orientation. The cities with the longest tradition of high status appointments to the school board are the ones where the economic elite are least suburbanized. There are two exceptions to the rank ordering—St. Louis, which has a more civic board than would be expected, and Buffalo, where the board is more political than one would predict.

It could be argued that suburbanization is caused by loss of power, rather than the other way around. High income families

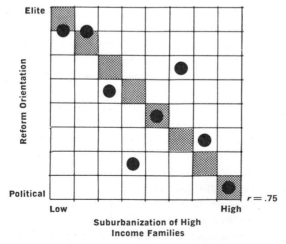

Figure 13.4 Suburbanization of Economic Elites and Reform Orientation of Board

stay in the city if they have a paternalistic attachment to it. They move out if they lose this power. The argument is not particularly plausible on its face. In addition, a glance at Table 13.1 suggests that there are more reasonable explanations. The cities which have retained their economic elites tend to fall into two groups—those which are not heavily suburbanized in general (Baltimore and Buffalo compared to Bay City and St. Louis) and those where special problems of geography make living out of the central city more inconvenient (Pittsburgh and San Francisco). There is also a tendency for cities which have retained their elites to have the lowest population density in persons per square mile. (Although the young satellite city, Lawndale, is lowest on the scale, Pittsburgh and Baltimore are second and third, respectively.)

If suburbanization is the best predictor of the influence of the civic elite, we must reconceptualize this whole question of elite influence. The bulk of the literature, including Mills and Ulmer (1946), Fowler (1958), and Hunter (1953) and his disciples, has been concerned with the existence of community power structure. A power structure implies a somewhat rigid set of relationships between persons, with some sort of hierarchy. Hunter's conclusion is that the top elites of Atlanta are the persons who hold the greatest economic resources, and that they in turn assign specific tasks to their underlings. There are problems in reconciling this picture with our data. For example, how can we explain the apparently autonomous power wielded by Daniel Schlafly, who owns a relatively small business in St. Louis? And how can we explain the fact that we found no evidence in any city that key school decisions were checked out with economic higher-ups?

Even more disturbing from this point of view is the finding of Sternlieb (1961) that executives who live in the suburbs are much more likely to be active in the civic affairs of the suburb, rather than the central city. We cannot reconcile this with the structure model which implies that civic activity on the part of businessmen is based upon the economic resources of their corporations, something entirely unaffected by the man's place of residence.

We think the civic elite can be more accurately described, not as a structure of power, but as a collection of individuals, each of whom has some resources and some contacts with other elites, who participate as individuals, but who constitute a diffuse class (by Marx's definition) in that they have a common set of values.

Much has been written about the withdrawal of business elites from local parties, but little has been said about their re-entry in decision-making. Certainly the American city of the 1960's seems much more dependent upon the elite who are serving on school boards, urban renewal commissions, Urban League boards, and so forth, than it did three decades ago.

The original withdrawal of the civic elite from city decision-making was probably a result of two factors: the growth of the ethnic vote, which disqualified all but the most unusual Protestant from office in the northern cities, and the rapid urban growth of the late nineteenth century, which brought considerable disorder to the structure of the city.

By the turn of the century, the business elite were no longer able to elect one of their own to the mayoralty of either New Haven or Chicago (Bradley and Zald, 1965; Dahl, 1961). The disorder of the business community resulting from the tremendous urbanization and economic development of the 1880's and 1890's (Chicago's population was growing at an annual rate of 10 per cent at this time), and the frequent scandals resulting from the participation of individual businessmen in buying utility franchises and city contracts, had already made city politics disreputable. Businessmen never completely withdrew from politics, however, but remained on the fringes, organizing reform tickets and lobbying for state laws to prevent this and that bit of corruption.

Finally, as ethnic rivalries began to fade out and middle-class political values became more widely diffused, the reformers like Clark in Philadelphia and Tucker in St. Louis began to win elections. Dahl refers to Lee of New Haven as an example of a new breed of mayors who are not working-class political bosses, but men who combine administrative skill with the ability to muster support from the growing bloc of middle-class voters. Even in cities which have not moved this far from working-class politics, the change is present. It is in this environment that the civic elite has become reactivated.

But this is not a return to the patterns of the nineteenth century. The business elite have accepted the notion of a bifurcation between themselves and the political professionals—holding high status in the business community is worth little in an election campaign. In addition, the growth of national corporations selling to national markets, the shutoff in population growth of the central city, and reform of city purchasing practices mean that few members of the business elite will reap any direct personal benefits from participation in politics. Thus, with no basis for competition between elites, a common ideology and an agreement among goals have developed that permits the civic elite to behave as a class. The key elements in this common set of goals are:

1. General economic development: Any action that furthers economic development will benefit most of the elites.

2. Reform: While in a sense this is a carry-over from the original ideological wars that displaced the elite from power, it is a widely accepted value now.

3. Improvements in public welfare: Charitable giving, and charitable action on the part of government.

4. Maintenance of social stability: "Peace-keeping" is as honorable a mission in the city as it is in the United Nations.

These four goals—peace, prosperity, charity, and reform—constitute a common denominator around which the civic elite can agree. If the businessman moves beyond this framework, he may find that he has become involved in controversy, but within this framework he can expect the other members of the elite to give their endorsement to his action.

Within this framework the businessman participates, not so much on behalf of his company, but as an individual. The direct financial return to his company for the time he invests is minimal, and while the corporation may earn some prestige from his participation, most of his motivation stems from personal reasons.[4] The participation differs in degree, but not in kind, from the participation of his wife (or anyone else's wife) in PTA work or the League of Women Voters. He participates because the work is entertaining and because it brings him prestige. But beyond that, his participation furthers his class interests; he is helping to change the city into the kind of community which the members of his class—the civic elite—want.

[4]Of course, certain firms, such as downtown department stores, reap more benefits from this participation.

We now see that if this argument is correct we do not need to postulate the existence of a power structure. Rather, the civic elite can remain merely a loose association of men who meet in the downtown clubs. If one of their members is invited to serve on the board of the Urban League, he knows that his luncheon companions will generally approve. If he uses this position to begin some program of action, he will have the tacit support of the other members of the elite (unless, of course, he commits some blunder or wanders outside the common denominator of goals). In fact, his participation may quickly brand him as the specialist in this area, the man to see for advice.

By participating, the businessman receives status in the eyes of his colleagues. In addition, the participation of the elites makes for a common bond between men who otherwise would have little cause for interaction.

All this makes the negative correlation of suburbanization with elite control of the school board more plausible. If in fact the civic elite is only a loose association of men who meet at lunch and on committees, then a sort of compositional effect can occur. If most of the men around the luncheon table are city residents, city problems are more likely to be the topic of conversation, and each man more likely to become active. Conversely, if most of them are suburbanites, the conversation will stray to other subjects, and even the city residents will feel little incentive to be active. In addition, many activities originate from one's place of residence, not from the place of work. Contributions to political parties, school activities, participation in residential conservation programs, voting, contributions to charities, are all examples of activities which might result from having one's doorbell rung at night.

Another implication of this model is that the resource that a member of the civic elite has that makes him valuable in civic affairs is probably not the control over economic resources in his business. Rather, his personal skill, personal wealth, and willingness to work, coupled with the status he holds as a businessman, make his participation desirable.

At the same time we cannot overlook the fact that his participation depends upon his ability to earn the respect of other members of the elite. Thus he participates primarily in issues on which other elites agree, and in many cases he can be said to be consciously furthering class interests. Thus the effect is not so different from what it would be if the civic elite were a tightly organized interest group, but the conditions under which civic activity takes place might be quite different.

DEVIANT CASES

Although suburbanization is a reasonably good predictor of elite influence, there are no doubt other factors that remain undiscovered. Our two most deviant cases are St. Louis and Buffalo. As we saw in our case study of St. Louis, Banfield (1965) also noted that it does not seem to have the necessary population composition to maintain a reform government. One idea which we advance rather tentatively is that the reform vote in St. Louis does not come from the usual "silk stocking wards," but also includes the bloc of Germans in the city. These voters remained in the Republican party, and the Republicans remained competitive with the Democrats until after World War II. Today these voters appear as Tucker supporters in the Democratic primaries. This brings us to the possibility that the civic elite have more influence in cities which have a stable, competitive two-party system, where they constitute an important swing vote. Alternatively, it may be a consequence of the presence of German voters, who have also demonstrated a sophistication in local elections in Milwaukee and Cincinnati; both those cities have strong reform traditions.

One possible explanation for the weakness of the civic elite in Buffalo is that the bulk of local industry seems to be absentee-owned. Absentee ownership is often discussed, but as far as we know its effect has not been empirically evaluated. In addition, the civic elite's access to municipal decision-making may be hampered by the presence of unstable and factional political parties, whose leaders must conduct repeated mass campaigns to obtain a majority in each election.[5] Somewhat the same theory is advanced to explain why mayors in nonpartisan or weak party systems are less likely to support fluoridation (see Crain, Katz, and Rosenthal, in press). It may seem surprising that the strength or level of organi-

---

[5]In Buffalo, Mayor Kowal needed every bit of patronage he could find to be a viable candidate for reelection, and hence went farther than most mayors would in replacing school board members with his supporters.

zation of political parties should play a role in the behavior of the civic elite, and hence in the school board, for both these groups are very far removed from everyday partisan politics in the reformed cities. But when we turn to our other major variable, cohesion, we will see that political parties do seem to play a role in determining the structure of even non-political decision-making groups.

THE CAUSES OF BOARD COHESION

We have seen that the eight school boards include boards which are high and low on cohesion, regardless of whether the recruitment source is the civic elite or the political professional. We have argued that the root of this cohesion lies in the clarity and stability of the criteria used to select board members—or the image of the ideal board member. In Table 13.2 we have tried to state what these images are and at the same time to rank the cities by consistency and clarity of the image. This ranking cannot be very precise, of course, and we have only divided the boards into four categories.

In general, the most cohesive cities are at the top of this list. If Bay City and Buffalo had fallen into the very mixed category, the four groups would be ordered perfectly—the clearer the image, the

Table 13.2 Criteria Used To Select Board Members

Clarity Ranking	City	Criterion
1. Most clear	Pittsburgh	High status, and/or demonstrated leadership ability
1. Most clear	Newark	Loyal to party; ethnic representation
1. Most clear	St. Louis	High status if possible; commitment to reform
2. Moderately clear	Baltimore	Most seats to high status persons, but must represent schools, ethnic groups
2. Moderately clear	Buffalo	Loyal to mayor, ethnically diverse, but also represent special groups and good government
3. Mixed	Lawndale	Drawn from business leadership, or those interested in education, but represent interest groups and give preference to politicians
3. Mixed	Bay City	Must generally be Irish, but reformers are acceptable; selection based on either personal attractiveness, on campaign promises to improve schools, or on anti-integration appeals
4. Very mixed	San Francisco	Either high status, with demonstrated leadership ability, or politically loyal; must be ethnically representative

greater the cohesion. Of course, the ranking is based on impressionistic data, so that the correlation is probably exaggerated. We will not try to be more specific than to say that the main component of cohesion seems to be the clarity and stability of the criteria used. There may be other factors of less importance.

The ranking of clarity of image shows a perfect correlation with the socioeconomic status of the community. San Francisco, with the least clear criterion, is highest in status, whether measured by educational attainment, income, or white collar employment. Lawndale and Bay City, in the next group, are second and third, and so forth. The higher the socioeconomic status, the less clear and stable the recruitment procedures seem to be. The result is that, as Figure 13.5 indicates, socioeconomic status is a good correlate of the cohesion of the board.

The finding is not exactly unexpected. For example, a study of fluoridation decisions (Crain, Katz, and Rosenthal, in press), which found that cities with higher levels of education had more difficulty with fluoridation although well-educated people were more favorable to it, concluded that high status cities have two

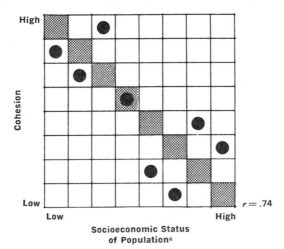

$r = .74$

"Average of six measures of population status: median income, per cent under $5,000, per cent over $10,000, per cent white collar, median years schooling, and per cent with some college education.

Figure 13.5 Socioeconomic Status of the Population and Cohesion of School Board

characteristics that cause the decision-making process to be more unstable, and these factors presumably would produce an unclear or unstable recruitment pattern for school boards:

1. High status communities are less apathetic. This means that in general more people will participate in the making of any decision. Newspapers will play a more important role; it will be easier to mobilize sectors of the population. This means that the mayor or the appointing or nominating body is more often under pressure to change the recruitment system. More important, having a clear recruitment criterion means that the majority of the candidates will be excluded, and hence there will always be objection. Just as a higher level of public participation in Newark would cause a great deal of pressure to put "reform" candidates on the board, it is probably also true that a higher status population would exert pressure on the Court of Common Pleas to represent some of the ethnic groups in Pittsburgh. After the board is appointed, the presence of a high status population continues to lower consensus, since it tends to keep a public spotlight on the board and gives each board member more opportunity to mobilize public support for his position.

2. High status cities have weak political parties. Among our eight cities, the higher the status, the weaker the political parties ($R = -.77$). The ranking is again subjective; while it is not too difficult to distinguish among the weaker parties, we did not have sufficient data to distinguish among the three cities with the strongest parties and have tied them in rank.[6]

The four low status cities all have stronger parties than the four higher status cities. This is a well-known relationship and is hardly surprising, given the independence, issue orientation, and reform orientation of higher status voters. What may be more surprising is the very strong relationship between strength of parties and cohesion of the board. While a more objective and more precise measure of party strength might lower the correlation somewhat

[6]The ranking is as follows: Pittsburgh, Newark, and St. Louis are judged to have the strongest parties. Baltimore is ranked fourth, primarily because it was able to elect a Republican mayor in an overwhelmingly Democratic city. Fifth is San Francisco, which has parties, but only within the general context of California nonpartisanship. Lawndale, sixth, is nonpartisan but has stable factions. Buffalo, seventh, is partisan, but has a highly unstable pattern of factional conflict. Bay City, eighth, has neither parties nor stable factions.

from its present value of .90, it is obvious that we have a close relationship; strong parties breed board cohesion.

This relationship is to be expected among the three political boards. The high cohesion of Newark seems to be a direct result of the power of the political party, and the chaotic election procedure of Bay City seems to be a function of nonpartisanship as it is practiced in that city. However, the same pattern holds among the five civic boards as well. Partly this is because the mayor (who is the appointing officer in two of these cities, and who made certain key appointments in St. Louis as well) will be restricted in his range of appointments if they must be cleared by the political party (that is, he cannot appoint a personal friend if the party refuses to go along with it). More important, the presence of clear party or factional alignments insulates the appointing official from public opinion. At the same time, the civil rights conservatism of the political party rank and file does not seem to have much effect on the appointment process. Eldersveld's research on the parties of Detroit leads him to talk about the party as a stratarchy in which power is diffused through several strata, each with considerable autonomy (1964, p. 9). He also argues that the party must be viewed as a coalition of conflicting groups who are kept together by downgrading the importance of ideological differences. "As a power-aspiring group, 'greedy' for new followers, the party does not settle conflict; it defers the resolution of conflict" (Eldersveld, 1964, p. 7). It is possible for the party to tolerate ideological differences because the party members serve for non-ideological reasons—even in Detroit, where there is relatively little patronage.[7]

As a result, there is little ideological communication either up or down the party hierarchy. This has two implications for our study. First, it means that the party does not serve to articulate mass opinion up to the party leadership, but instead as a barrier to prevent the leadership from being heavily influenced by public opinion. Since party workers are loyal in large part for non-ideological reasons, the mayor knows that whether they work or not will not depend much upon his position on issues. On the

[7]Eldersveld (1964, p. 200) finds the ideological differences between party workers actually to be greater than the differences between the districts they "work."

other hand, this absence of ideological communication means that party workers will not be socialized by party activity into taking a particular view.

This means that the mayor is free to appoint people to the school board who are more liberal than the voters as a whole; and if he appoints civic leaders, this is what he will get. But if he recruits board members from within the party, he will get appointees who are not more liberal. The result is that the four cities with strong parties tend to have school boards that are extreme, either liberal or conservative, while the four cities with weak parties tend to fall toward the center of the distribution on civil rights liberalism.

There is another way in which the presence of strong political parties might affect the appointment process. In the three cities that have civic boards and strong political parties, the civic elite are organized formally and seem to exert effective influence as a result of this organization. We have already mentioned two reasons why this should be the case. First, the nearly complete separation of the civic elite from the everyday workings of the political parties prevents party differences or ideological issues from dividing the elite. Second, the presence of strong parties tends to make reform an issue which unites the elites. In addition, the presence of a working-class political organization restricts direct communication between individual party leaders and individual elites. This condition, which earlier led to the withdrawal of civic elites from policy-making, now tends to organize the communication through a limited number of channels. If the only public official who will listen is the mayor, the elite are under more pressure to organize themselves so as to speak with a single voice.

We have now isolated the community variables that seem to provide the explanation for school board behavior on school integration. In the process, we have developed a tentative typology of northern cities which might be useful for other issues. The typology is presented in Table 13.3.

There are a number of hypotheses implicit in the typology. Of these, possibly the most interesting is this: The civic elite will only participate in political decision-making in northern large cities in a highly organized fashion if they have been prevented by

Table 13.3 Typology of Cities and School Boards

Variable	Type of City			
	Balance of Power	Middle Class	Machine	Working Class
Socioeconomic status	low	medium–high	low	low–medium
Elite suburbanization	low	low	high	high
Parties	strong	weak	strong	weak
Political style	Civic elites organized and active in policy-making but not in party politics	Civic elites active in small groups and as individuals in policy-making and politics. Elections are contests between individuals, with weak parties or factions	Civic elite inactive. Elections are contests between strong and stable parties or factions	Civic elite inactive; politics highly personalized; strong ethnic voting patterns
School board recruitment criteria	High status, demonstrated interest in civic affairs; non-political	Varies: high status or politically active or both; some ethnic or intergroup representation	Political activists: party workers, some ethnic and inter-group representation	Varies: persons loyal to mayor, or who have personal contacts or support; or persons active in organizations or with ties to civic elite
Board socioeconomic status	high	medium–high	low	low–medium
Per cent political appointments	low	medium	high	medium–high
Cohesion	high	medium	high	low–medium
Liberalism	high	varies	low	low–medium
Acquiescence	high	medium–low	medium	low

ethnic or class factors from direct participation in political parties.

The hypothesis cannot be considered proven by this analysis of only eight cities. Furthermore, the hypothesis will need to be more specific, in order to account for the possibility of an amateur's being elected mayor in a strong-party city (such as Raymond Tucker in St. Louis).

As a check on our argument, let us consider how well we can predict acquiescence from two "hard" variables—elite suburbanization and city socioeconomic status, both measured from census data. While multivariate analysis with only eight cities is somewhat pretentious, the result is still worth reporting. Our argument states that middle-class cities with suburbanized elites will be least acquiescent, and blue collar cities with elites living in the central city will be most acquiescent, and the combined ranking of these two factors correlates +.89 with acquiescence. The two deviant cases are San Francisco, which is more acquiescent than expected, and Buffalo, which is not as acquiescent as the model predicts. Thus, the argument of this chapter could be summarized by saying that the least acquiescent cities are those which have no upper class; the most acquiescent, those which have an upper class and a working class but no middle class.[8]

SUMMARY

The findings of this chapter are summarized in the flow chart shown in Figure 13.6. The arrows indicate the location and presumed direction of correlations. The chart is indefinite in that we cannot determine the intervening variables that link high socioeconomic status to heterogeneity of school board appointments. Our best hunch is that strength of political party is most important, but factors such as the presence of heavy industry in low status cities and the general impact of political apathy are also relevant. Of course, the flow chart does not reveal all the complexities of the typology shown in Table 13.3.

With many more cities, we would be able to separate out the effect of more specific variables, such as size of board, appointment versus election of board members, or the size of the Negro popu-

[8]A similar analysis is presented in Banfield and Wilson (1963).

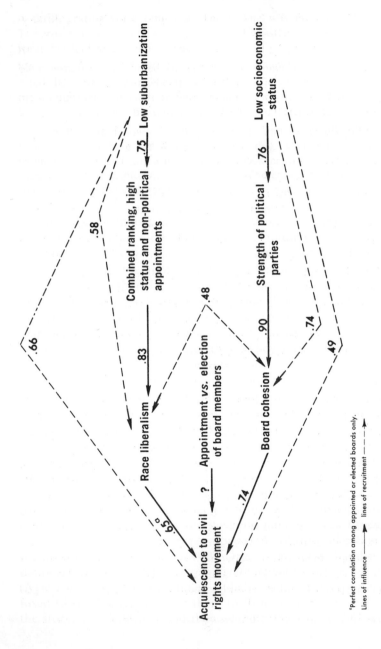

^aPerfect correlation among appointed or elected boards only.

Lines of influence ⟶ lines of recruitment – – – ⟶

Figure 13.6 Rank-order Correlations between Variables Linked to Acquiescence

lation. Each of these factors probably plays a role, but it is difficult to say how important each is.

The presence of elites in the city, the presence of strong political parties, and the presence of a low status population are all relevant to the way the school board is recruited and the way the school integration issue is handled. This means that for the purposes of this one issue, large northern cities with ethnic groups can be divided into four groups: (1) the blue collar city with active civic elites; (2) the blue collar city with inactive civic elites; (3) the unbifurcated, or middle-class city; and (4) the blue collar city with inactive civic elites and weak political parties. Presumably, for other issues other factors would appear and this typology would have to be expanded to include more categories.

The typology cannot itself be considered final. With limited data from only eight cities, we have pushed our analysis to reveal what seems to be the most plausible pattern of correlations. However, several of our rank-order correlations are high; although part of this is no doubt due to our own bias, it nevertheless seems to us that our data are overexplained—we can produce a rank-order correlation of .89 with acquiescence using only two variables. The result is that we have removed all the variance, but have some independent variables left over. This is no doubt more satisfying than exhausting all variables and having variance left, but it is an unpleasant problem, nevertheless. The only answer is to replicate the study using the largest possible population of cities.

Part III

Desegregation in New Orleans

Although it was not recognized in the original design of this study, there is very little similarity between the school desegregation issue in the North and in the South. Thus, although the same research techniques used in the North were also used in our study of seven cities in the Deep South—Miami and Jacksonville in Florida, Atlanta and Columbus in Georgia, New Orleans and Baton Rouge in Louisiana, and Montgomery in Alabama—it is necessary to present the findings of the southern study separately. In the North, we were interested in understanding why certain cities desegregated while others did not. This is not a relevant question to ask in the South, for no southern city refused to desegregate under court order, and very few desegregated before they had to. And at the time of our study, few southern cities had progressed past the most limited degree of token integration. However, in studying the response of these seven cities to the federal courts, our attention was attracted to one striking difference. In each of these cities, the school board approached desegregation warily, wondering whether they would find themselves embroiled in a furious community conflict that would bring violence in the streets, a boycott of the schools, or the state government's closing the schools altogether. And generally speaking, disaster was avoided in six of the seven cities. In New Orleans, however, desegregation brought on an intense conflict which lasted the entire school year.

Relatively little is known about the way social control is maintained in the face of community opposition to governmental action, and almost as little is known about the reasons why this control sometimes breaks down. We grew so fascinated by the difference between New Orleans and the other cities in our study (particularly Atlanta, which desegregated a year later with no difficulty) that after the initial survey (by Morton Inger and Robert Stout), we arranged for Inger to return to New Orleans and spend an additional ten days interviewing participants in the school crisis there. In all, forty-one people were interviewed (forty in person and one by long-distance telephone). The interviews ranged from fifteen minutes to five hours in length, averaging one hour and twenty minutes.

We must emphasize that this research is not simply a case study of New Orleans. We also prepared analyses of the other six cities (based on a total of 120 interviews), although we do not report them here. The material from these analyses has afforded the research staff a comparative context for the analysis of New Orleans. Thus, our report is as much a study of why social control prevailed in the other cities as it is a study of why control failed in New Orleans.

Chapter 14 is an overview of the ways in which school desegregation was resisted (or not resisted) in the South between 1954 and 1964. It provides the reader with an understanding of the alternatives which southerners perceived when faced with court-ordered desegregation. Chapter 15 is the longest chapter and is a detailed study of the school crisis in New Orleans. Chapters 16 and 17 are devoted to analyzing the data provided in Chapter 15, first by examining the evidence for and against several possible explanations for the New Orleans crisis and then (in Chapter 17) by making some comparisons, both subjective and statistical, among the seven cities in the study.

The principal conclusion our analysis has drawn is twofold: first, it was not a matter of chance that there was much conflict in New Orleans and so little in Atlanta, and second, the roots of the conflict lay in the social structure of the city. At the heart of such an analysis is the study of the men who hold positions of high prestige in the city—the civic elite, as we have called them. In a sense, this study gives support to both sides of the argument concerning whether there is a power structure in American communities. On the one hand, the absence of social control in New Orleans can be attributed largely to the failure of the civic elite to become involved in the issue. By avoiding the most important decision in recent New Orleans history, the elite almost disqualifies itself from consideration as a power structure, in the sense in which that term is sometimes used. On the other hand, the fact that the withdrawal of the elite so heavily influenced the community's behavior in the issue indicates that the composition and structure of the civic elite was an important factor in shaping the decision-making processes of the cities studied here. Hence we consider the civic elite an important object of study to the social scientist interested in the American city.

14

Overview

On "Black Monday"—May 17, 1954—the Supreme Court of the United States presented its decision in the case of *Brown et al. v. the Board of Education of Topeka.* The decision ushered in a decade in which the desegregation of southern schools remained the dominant issue in each fall's newspaper headlines; a decade in which Thurgood Marshall and Earl Warren became heroic figures; a decade of violence and the beginnings of a revolution in American racial relations. A great deal has been written about this story, and we have no reason to summarize it here.[1] The task of this chapter is to describe the issue facing the southern school boards we have studied.

Over the ten years from 1954 to 1964, the school desegregation issue was constantly changing, since the perceived choices available to a school board differed depending upon where the school board stood in the pattern of diffusion of desegregation. We can oversimplify a bit and say that the desegregation issue moved south from the Mason-Dixon line in four stages.

Immediately after the *Brown* decision, there was a period of relative quiet which, as it turned out, preceded a storm. A separate suit, heard at the same time as *Brown,* resulted in desegregating the public schools of Washington, D.C. There was a flurry of picketing, a slight jump in the number of whites withdrawing from the public schools, and the crisis there was over. Although the *Brown* decision did not order immediate desegregation anywhere, three large border cities (Baltimore, Louisville, and St. Louis) chose to desegregate immediately.[2] Cincinnati had desegregated a few years earlier, and Topeka, the city in the title of the Supreme

[1]The most complete history is by Muse (1964). Of course, the day-to-day chronicle appears in the *Southern School News* from 1954 to 1965, whose staff produced a volume on the period edited by Shoemaker (1957).

[2]Louisville's desegregation is described by Carmichael and James (1957). St. Louis is described in a report of the Civil Rights Commission (W. H. Davis, 1962), and one useful source on Washington is Hansen (1957).

Court decision, had adopted a desegregation plan eight months before the decision.[3] In response to the Supreme Court decision, most southern editors and political leaders rode the fence; the *Times-Picayune* of New Orleans foresaw strife, but other papers were more optimistic. In the reaction of the politicians there was no evidence of a solid South. Senator Allen Ellender of Louisiana commented, "I don't want to criticize the Supreme Court. . . . [The decision] is bound to have a very great effect until we adjust to it." Virginia's Attorney General, J. Lindsey Almond, who would be elected to the governor's office on a platform of upholding massive resistance to school integration (but who as governor would see that massive resistance collapse) said, "Virginia will approach the question realistically and endeavor to work out some rational adjustment." But other southern leaders, such as Senator James O. Eastland of Mississippi and Governor Herman Talmadge of Georgia, were ready to throw down the gauntlet. Said Eastland, "The South will not abide by, or obey, this legislative decision by a political court."[4]

Soon the Deep South would rally around the Eastlands and the Talmadges. Meanwhile, the border states continued to desegregate schools. In 1954, 1955, and 1956, the border states of Texas, Oklahoma, Kentucky, West Virginia, Maryland, and Delaware experienced considerable desegregation. There were scattered demonstrations of opposition in 1954 and 1955, and in 1956 there were three demonstrations of considerable importance. In Sturgis, Kentucky, the local high school students went on strike. At first the school board agreed to put off desegregation for a year; then the governor called in the National Guard and a serious effort was made to break the strike. But a few weeks later the Attorney General ruled that, since neither Sturgis nor Clay (an adjoining county) had adopted desegregation plans, the enrollment of the Negroes was illegal, and desegregation was put off for a year. In Clinton, Tennessee, a near-riot was broken up by state police, but desegregation was accomplished. In Mansfield, Texas, however, where another mob formed, Governor Allen Shivers chose to intercede for the segregationists, and the Mansfield schools re-

[3]For accounts of several pre-1954 desegregation decisions, see Williams and Ryan (1955).
[4]All quotes from Muse (1964, Chap. 2).

mained segregated until after much of the rest of Texas had integrated. Clinton and Mansfield each represented innovations. Clinton was the first community aroused by a professional racist agitator—in this case, John Casper, whose travels through the South were later cut short by a jail sentence. Mansfield, on the other hand, represented the first intervention on the part of the state to prevent local desegregation, and such intervention was to become the pattern throughout the South.[5] By the beginning of the 1956–57 school year the South was divided neatly into two regions: the border states, where considerable integration had already taken place, and the Deep South, where nearly all schools would remain segregated for the next few years.

In 1957, two different and contradictory examples were set, and these two examples were to serve as precedent for two opposing theories of desegregation. One of the examples was, of course, Little Rock. The Little Rock story is long and a good deal has been written about it.[6] Governor Orval Faubus of Arkansas repeatedly argued that there would be violence if the Little Rock schools were desegregated. Then, in order to prevent violence, he marched the National Guard into Little Rock, and the Negro students were turned back. After ten days of negotiation, the Department of Justice obtained an injunction to permit the Negro students to cross the National Guard lines. Faubus replied by removing the guard and again prophesied that there would be violence. When school opened, a mob of about one thousand persons succeeded in driving the Negro students away from the school. Then federal troops descended upon the city with fixed bayonets, and Little Rock's Central High became virtually a military outpost. This did not end the Little Rock crisis. The troops remained at the school during the rest of the 1957–58 school year; then in the fall of 1958 the state legislature passed a bill giving the governor the authority to close the public schools, and Faubus did so. During 1958–59 most of the white students attended private schools, and many Negro students went to school outside the city. Also during 1958 the segregationists attempted to

[5]Mansfield, Sturgis, and Clinton are all reported in pamphlets prepared by the Anti-Defamation League. For Mansfield, see Griffin and Freedman (n.d.); for Sturgis, see Giffin (n.d.); and for Clinton, see Holden, Valien, and Valien (n.d.).

[6]There are several books on Little Rock; in particular, see Hays (1958), Blossom (1959), and Record and Record (1960).

•

recall the Little Rock school board, and the board obligingly re-signed to permit new elections. Two rival slates—one segregation-ist, one moderate—entered candidates, and each took three seats on the six-member board. Conditions remained rancorous, grad-ually building to a new climax, and recall petitions were again circulated—one recalling the moderates and one recalling the seg-regationists. Both recall questions were put on the same ballot, and the segregationists were recalled. (Thanks to the small number of voters who voted to recall both groups, the ballot came close to eliminating the entire board, but the moderates managed to stay in by a few votes.)

When the 1958–59 school year ended, Little Rock's private schools were on the verge of bankruptcy, and a federal court order requiring the reopening of public schools brought the issue gracefully to a close. Over the course of the crisis, a school super-intendent, one and one-half school boards, and a congressman had been turned out of office, and, according to one widely cir-culated estimate, Little Rock had attracted absolutely no new in-dustry during the crisis. Faubus had demonstrated, for any southern official who wanted to learn, how to offer total resistance to desegregation. Unfortunately, he had also demonstrated what lay in store for the school system that tried it. Two important precedents had been set: First, federal troops had been used to prevent disobedience of court orders. Second, when the Little Rock school board had asked for a delay in desegregation (until after Faubus' term as governor had expired), the Supreme Court, meeting in special session in which each member signed the "stern and sweeping" decision, had made it clear that violence was not a justification for delaying desegregation.[7] Eventually, Governor Faubus was to retreat from his inflammatory segregationist posi-tion. In the entire Little Rock situation, there was only one person who clearly seemed to profit from the conflict. Dale Alford, the only segregationist on the original school board, had managed to win a seat in the House of Representatives.

[7]Muse (1964) calls this decision (*Cooper* v. *Aaron*) "The most important pro-nouncement of the [Supreme Court] on public-school desegregation next to the *Brown* rulings of 1954 and 1955." Peltason (1961, p. 190), in his account of the ambiguities facing the judges who enforced the *Brown* decision, describes the court's opinion as "blunt, forceful, and powerfully written." He then adds, "Many civil rights advocates wished that the Court had been as forceful in 1954."

Earlier we commented that there were two precedents set in 1957. The second involved a group of three cities in North Carolina that desegregated together that year. Under the leadership of Governor Luther H. Hodges, North Carolina adopted a pupil-placement law giving local boards authority to assign pupils to schools according to various criteria. In order to demonstrate that the law was not simply a device to prevent any desegregation, a call was made for cities to volunteer to desegregate their schools. The three largest cities in the state—Charlotte, Winston-Salem, and Greensboro—agreed. None of the three cities was under court order to desegregate, but preliminary legal action was taking place in all three. The three cities stayed in constant communication, made their public announcement simultaneously, and desegregated the same day. Only twelve Negroes entered white schools in the three cities, but this was an important crack in the wall of southern resistance.

In Charlotte, white students badgered one Negro girl into withdrawing, but this incident was eclipsed by Little Rock, and North Carolina congratulated itself. So here was the alternative example: a city could accept school desegregation as inevitable, take whatever action was necessary to keep it limited to token integration, and define as the enemy the segregationist demonstrators, rather than the NAACP or the Supreme Court.

During 1958, the South watched Little Rock, and school integration was at a standstill. Virginia experimented with closing public schools in Warren County, Charlottesville, and Norfolk.[8] School-closing was unpopular in Norfolk and Charlottesville, and the "massive resistance" laws were ruled invalid in time for school to open for the second semester in both cities. Only Warren County managed to maintain a private school organization: there, whites did not reenter public schools until September, 1959, and the private schools continued to draw off white students even then. For the segregationists, Warren County was an ideal battleground. The major industry was absentee-owned and determined to keep silent. The result was that the local labor union was able to rule the situation unopposed and supply the leadership for the private school movement. But this combination of a weak busi-

[8]For a discussion of the general situation in Virginia, see Muse (1961). For the Norfolk case, see Campbell, Bowerman, and Price (1960).

ness elite, a strong working-class organization, a disorganized middle class, and an absence of institutions promoting political pluralism is a rare one.[9] In Norfolk, for example, a powerful public school movement organized very quickly.

By 1959, local school officials throughout the South were aware of the dangers that accompanied massive resistance, and people began trying to learn from Little Rock and from North Carolina. The phase of "massive resistance" really ended at this point. From then on, school systems continued to stall on desegregation but spent most of their energies trying to avoid interference from segregationist governors and the citizens' councils.

Between 1959 and 1963, the largest cities in each of the southern states desegregated their schools: Miami in 1959; Houston and New Orleans in 1960; Atlanta, Dallas, and Memphis in 1961; Birmingham and Charleston in 1963. At the state level, the war was over. The victory was not without bloodshed, however. First, a white boycott made New Orleans "another Little Rock," as network television showed the near-hysterical "cheerleaders" screaming at the Negro children who walked each day into two nearly empty desegregated schools. Then, on September 15, 1963, in Birmingham, five Negroes (four children and one teenager) were murdered—four by the bombing of a Negro church.

The year 1963 was more or less the last of this third period of school desegregation, when local school systems were looking for ways to permit token desegregation without violence and without closing the schools. After this, the battle against the *Brown* decision became a rout. In 1963, as many as 126 school systems desegregated without waiting for court orders;[10] and in 1963 and 1964, the Defense Department, the Department of Health, Education, and Welfare, and the Department of Justice began teaming up to deal with cities in "impacted areas"—areas having high concentrations of military and other government personnel, where federal funds were supplied to local systems to educate their children. In 1964, over three hundred districts were desegregated without being under court order. Then, in 1965, Title VI of the new Civil Rights Act, requiring the government to withhold federal aid from any segregated district, went into effect, and 94 per cent of the

[9]For this case study, see Levy (1961).
[10]All statistics from *Southern School News.*

remaining districts agreed to desegregate that year. The only remaining pocket of resistance was a part of Mississippi and Louisiana.

Thus there were four distinct climates in which initial desegregation could take place: the climate of border-state voluntarism, the climate of massive resistance, that of the post–massive resistance era (from 1959 to 1963), and that of the period after the collapse of resistance at the state level. The statistical data for each period are given in Table 14.1. Of course, after initial desegregation, southern school systems soon found themselves under pressure to go beyond tokenism. For example, some of the larger southern cities have agreed to speed up desegregation. We can view this as a fifth period or climate in which desegregation must be faced.

In a sense, school desegregation is a different issue in each of these eras, since the perceived alternatives available to the school system are different and the different aspects of the problem change in their relative magnitude. In 1957, the major problem facing a southern school board was deciding what the courts would do if the school system tried this or that device. As Peltason has pointed out, the Supreme Court's decisions were ambiguous, and the individual federal judges in the South had no handy way of resolving the cross-pressures they were under. One judge might demand immediate desegregation, another might accept a very gradual plan. But by 1959, a pattern of court decisions had made it clear that token desegregation would be acceptable and that it could not be put off much longer. Similarly, before Faubus, local school boards did not know what possible action they might expect from the governor; afterward they knew enough to expect considerable difficulty from the statehouse.

All seven of the cities we studied desegregated in the third, or post–massive resistance, climate. In many ways their task was simpler than that faced by cities that acted earlier. But it was probably also more frightening. It seems safe to say that any large southern city which desegregated in the late fifties or early sixties did so in fear and trembling. These school boards could take it for granted that they were going to desegregate; the board that did not know this could be accused of extreme naivete. Their first and least difficult problem was to find ways to put off desegregation

Table 14.1 Percentage of School Districts Desegregated Each Year

School Districts	Border Voluntarism (Compliance)			Massive Resistance (Little Rock)			Post–Massive Resistance (Post–Little Rock)			Resistance Collapses (Compliance)	
	1954	1955	1956	1957	1958	1959	1960	1961	1962	1963	1964
West Virginia	68ᵃ	80	95	100	100	100	100	100	100	100	100
Maryland	4	48	87	91	100	100	100	100	100	100	100
Missouri	47	47	79	86	86	93	93	95	95	95	95
Kentucky	0	21	61	64	70	73	83	83	89	99	100
Oklahoma	0	33	76	80	75	75	79	81	81	81	66ᵇ
Delaware	17	19	21	29	33	37	47	100	100	100	100
Texas	0	10	12	17	17	17	18	17	19	29	52
Virginia	0	0	0	0	3	5	9	16	25	43	64
North Carolina	0	0	0	2	2	4	6	6	10	23	51
Tennessee	0	1	1	2	2	3	5	13	19	32	45
Arkansas	1	1	2	4	4	4	4	4	5	6	11
Florida	0	0	0	0	0	2	2	7	15	24	33
Louisiana	0	0	0	0	0	0	2	2	2	3	4
Georgia	0	0	0	0	0	0	0	0.5	0.5	2	7
South Carolina	0	0	0	0	0	0	0	0	0	1	17
Alabama	0	0	0	0	0	0	0	0	0	4	8
Mississippi	0	0	0	0	0	0	0	0	0	0	3

Source: Southern School News Statistical Summary, 1965–66.

ᵃItalicized figures represent an increase of 7 per cent or more from previous year.

ᵇSlight decreases in percentages are the result of combining school districts. The number of school districts was generally decreasing during this period.

as long as possible. The best solution was simply to find the most capable lawyer and let him use all the legal tricks he could borrow or invent. The second problem was to mobilize whatever resources were necessary to develop a favorable climate for desegregation and to minimize demonstrations, violence, or bad publicity. Third, the school board members had to decide whether they were willing to be labeled integrationists; if they were not, they had to decide how they could protect themselves by expressing public disapproval of integration and at the same time not give aid and comfort to the citizens' councils and the potential trouble-makers. Finally, the school board had to decide how to prevent the intervention of the state legislature or the governor. Throughout this time, every school board's motto was, "Don't let Little Rock happen here."

Of course local conditions varied, so that as we look at our seven cities we can see how different elements in the formula became more or less important and how different cities took advantage of local resources. The seven cities in our sample are Miami, Jacksonville, Atlanta, Columbus, Montgomery, New Orleans, and Baton Rouge.

Miami, which was the first in this group to desegregate, did so in large part at the urging of Florida's moderate governor, LeRoy Collins. A desegregation suit had been brought against the Miami school board, but the court had not taken action at the time the board voted to desegregate. In this case, several board members made no attempt to conceal their willingness to accept integration.

In Atlanta, the school board and the city had to proceed with some caution, since it was not clear what the Georgia state legislature would do. However, several forces combined to protect Atlanta. The federal judge ruled that any attempt to close Atlanta's schools would require closing schools in the rest of the state. The governor agreed to appoint a commission, headed by Atlanta banker John A. Sibley, which held hearings in all parts of the state and then recommended a local option law. The mayor of Atlanta, William B. Hartsfield, also exerted influence. The school board asked for and received a year's delay in the integration plan so they might have ample time to get the state legislature to agree to stay away from Atlanta. Then a massive educational campaign was carried out to prepare the community for integration. As a result of all this, Atlanta desegregated peacefully and made itself a reputation as a leader in the "New South."

New Orleans, at the other extreme, exploded. The difference between New Orleans and Atlanta provides the most intriguing question of this report: Why was one city peaceful and the other not? The answer does not lie in the fact that one city is in Georgia while the other is in Louisiana. To make one comparison between the two states, the University of Georgia had desegregated in January of 1961 by admitting two students in a welter of confusion and court injunctions.[11] Governor Jimmie Davis was vowing never to permit a Negro in a white school in Louisiana, but in fact Louisiana State University had been integrated long before he took office, and in 1960 there were 634 Negro students in the state's previously white colleges.

The second city in each state was obviously in less danger of direct state intervention, but the danger was still there. In the case of Baton Rouge, Governor Davis signed legislation enlarging the school board and then packed it with arch-segregationists. The city's moderate leadership responded by organizing an election campaign that succeeded in defeating three of the governor's men, and the school system then was able to prepare for desegregation gracefully.

Montgomery, Alabama—the capital of the Confederacy, the capital of Alabama, and the birthplace of the Southern Christian Leadership Conference—faced desegregation in 1964. Montgomery's answer was to establish a public biracial commission, which included top economic leaders and all three of the city commissioners. When the schools were desegregated, tight police control prevented any demonstrations, and newsmen were given little more than a quick peek at the schools involved.

Columbus, Georgia, is the service city for Fort Benning. As an impacted area, it was quietly ordered to desegregate or lose the students from the military base and the federal funds they brought. At the same time, a suit began making its way through the courts. When after three months Columbus agreed to desegregate, the city's leaders and elected officials committed themselves to maintaining law and order, and, as in Montgomery, desegregation took place peacefully.

[11]For the University of Georgia story, see Trillin (1964*a*).

With each succeeding desegregation in a state, the chance of violence decreases. Nevertheless, preparation of the community remains necessary. Duval County, in which Jacksonville, the final city in our sample, is located, has the second largest school system in the state. But it waited until nine other cities had desegregated. Then the county made only minimal preparation for peaceful desegregation. One Negro mother applied to send her child to a "cracker" elementary school; the school system attempted to dissuade her and offered to send the child into a middle-class white school; she refused and her house was later demolished by a bomb.

There is little in the way of interesting or explainable difference in the way this group of seven cities dealt with the decision to desegregate. None wanted to desegregate (except possibly Miami), and all did so anyway. What is interesting is that desegregation was peaceful in most of these cities, but it created intense conflict in New Orleans and some trouble in Jacksonville. In both cases, our research indicates that the cities simply did not mobilize community support for peaceful desegregation. No one wanted violence—at least no one in a responsible position—but it was impossible to prevent it. We will approach the question of why these cities had violence in three steps. First, we shall present a detailed case study of the New Orleans crisis and, while doing so, point out elements which are unique to New Orleans—or, ideally, which appear in New Orleans and Jacksonville but not in the other cities. After the case study, we will try to test our hypotheses, first by making statistical comparisons and then by examining the structure of school decision-making in the cities that escaped catastrophe.

15

New Orleans: The Failure of an Elite

INTRODUCTION

When four Negro first-graders entered two previously all-white schools in New Orleans on November 14, 1960, the reaction of extremists was so intense and went unchecked for so long that the city suffered a near catastrophe. Mobs of whites numbering in the thousands rampaged through the downtown business district hurling bricks and bottles. White children boycotted the two schools for a whole year, and for months an unruly crowd stood before the national network television cameras and cursed, shoved, stoned, and spat upon the few white children who continued to attend one of the schools. The school board members who had desegregated the schools under federal court orders were ostracized by their friends, harassed and threatened, and addressed out of office by the state legislature. Many teachers and other school personnel went unpaid for months at a time, while the legislature held up the school funds and local banks refused to cash paychecks drawn on school funds held on deposit. Hotels and department stores reported their worst business slump since the Depression. It was one of the nation's most chaotic and violent school desegregations. All this, not in some landlocked Bible-belt country town, but in the nation's second largest port, home of liberal French Catholicism, and one of America's most cosmopolitan cities, thronged with tourists and businessmen from all over the world—cultured, civilized, heterogeneous New Orleans.

In February, 1959, about eighteen months before the New Orleans school crisis of 1960, Helen Fuller (1959, pp. 14–17) wrote

This chapter was written by Morton Inger. Interviewing by Inger and Robert T. Stout.

in the *New Republic* that the South had good reason to fear New Orleans "as a chink in the wall of 'states' rights' defiance of the Supreme Court." For many reasons—the long history of racial mixture in the city, the absence of tight residential segregation, the Catholic rather than Protestant culture—New Orleans could be expected to be a leader in the peaceful integration of the South. But looking at New Orleans in February of 1959, Miss Fuller found a surprising "stillness." No leadership for moderation had emerged.

There is no organized effort—as in Atlanta—to encourage people to think in advance of what the loss of the public schools would mean to them and to make their views known. . . . There is no organized defense of the schools by Protestant clergy or professional men and women, and most Negro leaders in New Orleans seem more interested in their personal political organizations than in matters of principle. The press— an anemic force in New Orleans life—gives its readers no hint that there is cause for concern about the future of the schools.

Miss Fuller nevertheless saw hope for New Orleans. Her hope— and the hope of New Orleans moderates—was pinned to the "enlightened self-interest" of the power structure of the city.

Only the "power structure" of New Orleans business and finance appears to be beyond reach of the [White Citizens Councils]. They have no congregations or clients to consult or fear, and their main preoccupation is to keep New Orleans the flourishing center of a growing state. The forward-looking "reform" mayor, deLesseps S. Morrison, whom they have kept in office for 13 years, looks coldly on anything that might sully the image of the modern progressive city he has helped create. The mayor, the chief of police, and the superintendent of schools are determined that there will be no mob rule in New Orleans. (The police have been professionalized under Mayor Morrison: the assistant chief says in cases of violence his force is trained to crack skulls, no matter what color.) And past experience indicates that coordination between city officials and the judiciary is such that they will succeed in keeping the peace—when and if desegregation of the schools is ordered.

Miss Fuller's analysis is quoted here because it expresses the conviction of most thoughtful observers of New Orleans in the

1950's. Mayor deLesseps ("Chep") Morrison, had built an image of New Orleans as a progressive city, gradually improving the condition of the Negro while consolidating the gains of the prosperous and conservative businessmen. Most observers felt that these business and financial leaders could be expected to prevent any disruption of the flourishing business of the city.

But as desegregation day drew near, the mayor and the business leaders did nothing. In May of 1960, four months before desegregation, an editorial by television station WDSU in New Orleans (*New York Times*, 1960*a*) stated, "It seems as if most community leaders are trying to look the other way. Few people want to talk about it. Newspapers play it down. . . . It seems to us that New Orleans is drifting in an atmosphere of unreality toward a catastrophe, which if it occurs, could seriously hurt the city." Regrettably, this prophecy was accurate—neither Morrison nor the business elite acted, and the result was catastrophe.

THE BACKGROUND: REFORM POLITICS

Because of Louisiana's state constitution, New Orleans has long been vulnerable to depredations by the governor and the legislature. As a consequence, the political leaders of New Orleans constantly try to protect themselves by forging alliances with the governor, and local affairs are always being dragged into state politics. When it has suited the convenience of the governor, he has formed his own New Orleans organization, as Governor Huey Long did in 1930. He formed the Louisiana Democratic Association, with Robert Maestri, who had saved Long from impeachment in 1929, as its local boss. At first the Association worked with the regular organization, the Choctaws, but by 1934 the alliance was over and Huey had declared war on the Choctaws and the city administration. "War" is the correct word.

In 1935, Governor Allen—Huey's man in office[1]—sent the National Guard into New Orleans and seized the offices of the city's voter registrar. After safely getting Long's state candidates elected, the Guard retired from the city. Next, the legislature enacted laws designed to bankrupt New Orleans and bring it to heel. City license fees were kept by the state, and New Orleans

---

[1] In Louisiana the governor cannot succeed himself in office.

was prevented from borrowing in anticipation of its 1935 taxes. In 1935, the state took over supervisory control of the city's finances, and the city was pushed to the brink of bankruptcy.

In the winter of 1935–36, Longite Governor-elect Richard Leche let it be known he would like to grant New Orleans the right to govern itself, but not if it meant strengthening the hands of the Choctaws and Mayor Walmsley. In March, 1936, Walmsley, taking the hint, announced that if he were the obstacle, he would resign, but only if local government would be restored to the city and the choice of his successor would be put to a vote of the people. Two days later, Maestri, Governor Leche, and the president of the New Orleans dock board (appointed by the governor) met in Hot Springs, Arkansas, to decide who should succeed Walmsley.

They chose Maestri. No one dared, or wanted, to oppose him, and on August 17, 1936, Maestri was declared mayor without the formality of an election. In return for this favor, state aid was returned, and a spurious form of self-government was entrusted to New Orleans. Control over local taxes, license fees, and city departments was formally returned to the city council (and hence to the Choctaws), but the legislature revamped the city's charter without submitting the revisions to the electorate, giving Maestri almost absolute authority over the city government and patronage. This control was so extensive that Maestri took over the Choctaw organization. To complete the conquest of the city, Leche's legislature enacted a constitutional amendment eliminating the New Orleans mayoralty election for 1938. Thus Maestri would not have to stand for election until 1942.

The enemy now controlled the city. And the obvious question to ask is what the business leaders—the natural enemies of the Long faction—were doing and saying about all this. The conservative *New Orleans Times-Picayune* put Walmsley's promise to resign on the front page but made no editorial comment. The editorial cartoon for that day dealt with a proposal to build a memorial to the Battle of New Orleans and Old Hickory. The next day's cartoon welcomed a surgeons' convention to the city. The day after the three men met in Arkansas to select the city's next mayor there was still no editorial, and the cartoon showed a man and wife giving old clothes to the needy. At the end of June, Walmsley resigned, and the *Times-Picayune* and the *Item* praised his wise self-sacrifice, attacked the Choctaws (the traditional spokesmen for the conservative businessmen), and glowed over Leche's friendly gesture in promising to restore self-government to the city. There was no outcry or organized activity by the city's economic leadership.

Maestri ran a corrupt administration and kept a tight grip on the city, even to the point of turning out a majority vote for Earl Long in New Orleans in 1940 while Long campaigned against the city. Maestri's power sprang from three sources: exclusive control of patronage, support from the state-wide Long faction, and the support of organized gambling. The first source got out the vote, the second provided the supportive and protective legislation, and the third provided the muscle and the money.

Maestri won easily in 1942, and in 1946 he was again considered a certain victor. But the ten years of his corruption had aroused the anger of many middle-class voters. In 1945 they cast about for a candidate and chose a professional politician named J. O. Fernandez, but only six weeks before the primary, Fernandez announced that he was supporting Maestri. The independents asked Colonel deLesseps Morrison, still in his army uniform, to run, and he agreed. (He was not a first choice; a dozen other men had refused.) Morrison was only thirty-four but had a good war record, was handsome, Catholic, and had served two terms as an anti-Long state representative before the war. Though he was the scion of a 150-year-old Creole family and came from the uptown silk-stocking section, Morrison had somewhat of a playboy reputation. No one expected him to beat Maestri.

But no one knew what the women of New Orleans could accomplish. A group of women worked so hard for Chep Morrison—with door-to-door canvassing and their famous march down Canal Street with brooms "sweeping out corruption"—that Morrison surprised everyone and upset Maestri. Maestri told reporters, "Them widder women beat me."

Encouraged by their success, the women (known by then as "the Girls") turned their reformist zeal to the public schools. There, a politically influenced school board had let a weak school system deteriorate. The school board had become little more than a job disbursement agency for Maestri: all jobs, from principals to janitors, were distributed as patronage. In 1948, there was one maintenance worker for every 439 students in the New Orleans schools. In Baltimore, the ratio was 1 to 1,760; and in New York, 1 to 3,950. Despite the huge maintenance force, many school buildings were in such a state of disrepair that they were condemned by the state fire marshal, and an independent study in 1948 rated 37 per cent of the white and 84 per cent of the Negro elementary schools unfit for use.

The Girls decided to reform the schools by "taking the school board out of politics." New Orleans is a city of clubs, from purely social clubs to the city-wide, civic-interest organizations. In the Morrison campaign of 1946, virtually all the women's clubs participated, and afterward the leaders of that campaign organized and called themselves the Independent Women's Organization (IWO). The most politically astute of the women became leaders in IWO and were able to command rather large followings, especially on an issue so appealing to women as reforming the schools.

In 1948, the Girls could not find a man willing to run for the single opening on the school board.[2] The economic leaders said— as they said in the thirties and as they were to say again in 1960— that their businesses were too sensitive to allow them to take part in controversial issues. So one of the Girls, Mrs. Jacqueline Leonhard, made the race. She was a most atypical New Orleans citizen. Not a native of New Orleans, she was part Indian, divorced, pro-labor, and pro-Negro. Her liberalism made her an anomaly among the Girls. As is typical of reform groups, the Girls are more interested in the structure of government—eliminating corruption, instituting civil service, finding well-qualified candidates, and "removing the school board from politics"—than in the content of the government's policy. The Girls are not a liberal bloc; they represent a range of political opinions, including many who were for Goldwater in 1964. But New Orleans women do not ordinarily run for political office. Only an unorthodox woman would have done so in 1948. Mrs. Leonhard did and won, and the reform of the school board had begun.

[2]The board is composed of five members serving staggered six-year terms. Every two years, either one or two board members are elected, depending on whether the terms of one member or two members expire at that time.

Two years later, the Girls induced two men to run for the board. Making an estimated 60,000 phone calls during that campaign, the Girls were again successful. With a three-to-two majority, the reformers immediately elected Mrs. Leonhard president of the board. Two years later, in 1952, they captured the remaining two seats by running what they called "young independents," Theodore Shepard and Emile Wagner. By 1954, Mrs. Leonhard's unorthodoxy had made too many enemies, and she was defeated by Matthew Sutherland, a man supported by many of the Girls. The sloughing-off of Mrs. Leonhard indicated that the reform movement had "gone respectable." In 1956, the Girls elected Louis Riecke and Lloyd Rittiner. Shepard, Wagner, Sutherland, Riecke, and Rittiner—young, honest, non-political businessmen, but not members of the economic elite—were the school board members who had to cope with the desegregation crisis of 1960.

The mayor during the 1960 crisis was still the man elected in 1946—Chep Morrison. Morrison took office pledging to give New Orleans an honest reputation and to have his city outstrip Miami as the "gateway to Latin America." During his first year in office he made three sales trips to Latin America and visited twenty countries. Civic and business leaders formed a group called Greater New Orleans, Inc., and launched an advertising campaign to attract industry to the city. In 1947 one of Morrison's favorite projects came about: a twenty-acre Foreign Trade Zone, a free port. Argentina immediately announced that it would spend $200 million in New Orleans on processing and storage plants. In 1948, businessmen gave $100,000—and the Pan-American Life Insurance Company loaned the city $750,000—to build the Pan-American Mart, another attraction for the city's port users.

These moves seemed to pay off. The port, which ranked sixteenth in the country in dollar volume of imports and exports after World War I, became the nation's second busiest port by 1948. In 1951 more than $200 million worth of new industry moved into the area.

Morrison lived up to the expectations of the reformers and achieved some structural changes in the government. He selected a nonpartisan commission of civic leaders to prepare a new charter for the city. Their efforts won for the city a home rule charter which replaced the mayor-commission form of government with the mayor-council form, although it did not provide much protection from state legislative control. The charter also contained provisions which would achieve efficiency and economy and provided for two (out of seven) at-large members of the city council.

All this seems to indicate that New Orleans was by 1960 a typical reformed city. But this is not quite true. First, the political power had not moved into the hands of the major business leaders. The Girls were never able to interest influential businessmen in running for the school board, and the Girls remained only an autonomous political movement with an extensive precinct organization. In addition, Morrison built a personal organization, the Crescent City Democratic Association, and tarnished his reform image by making a run for the governor's office in 1956. Reform never became institutionalized, so that when Morrison did leave office in 1961, the city council was able to appoint a regular Democrat, who in turn was able to defeat the reform candidate in 1962.

The economic development of New Orleans also stalled in the late 1950's. The port was still thriving, but major corporations were moving out of the city. The major association promoting economic growth, Greater New Orleans, Inc., declined in influence. International House, which was built in the late 1940's to bring the shippers together and facilitate the operation of the port, became nothing more than a social club for third-generation wealth. During 1958, 1959, and 1960, not one major industry moved into New Orleans.

THE INTEGRATION ORDER

Legal efforts to desegregate the New Orleans public schools began when the NAACP filed suit against the Orleans Parish[3] school board in September, 1952, but the suit lay dormant until after the second ("all deliberate speed") decision in the school desegregation cases (*Brown* v. *Board of Education of Topeka,* 1955). In February, 1956, in the first of the many decisions in the

---

[3]The parish in Louisiana is the geopolitical area known as the county in most other states. Geographically, Orleans Parish and the city of New Orleans are identical. Historically, the two units had different political functions, and though the two were consolidated in 1870, some functions are still distinct. For example, the school board is a parish board responsible directly to the state, not to the mayor of the city.

case (it reached the U.S. Supreme Court six times), a three-judge United States District Court in New Orleans held that segregation of the races in public schools was invalid under the *Brown* decision. On that day Federal District Judge J. Skelly Wright, one of the most famous of the liberals in the southern district courts, directed the board to "make arrangements for admission of children . . . on a racially non-discriminatory basis with all deliberate speed . . ." (*Bush* v. *Orleans Parish School Board,* 1956).

The school board's response to this order was a determination to use "every legal and honorable means" to maintain segregation. One member, Dr. Clarence Scheps, Tulane University's comptroller, was asked if the board was making plans for eventual integration in case the Supreme Court upheld Wright's decree. Dr. Scheps replied, "Absolutely not. We will not integrate. We couldn't integrate even if we wanted to" (Dolcher, 1956).

At this point, the school board's attorney, Sam Rosenberg, told the board members that the law was clearly against them. Since the school board seemed determined to fight integration, Mr. Rosenberg asked the board to relieve him of the task of arguing the case. Accordingly, the board retained Rosenberg as its general counsel but hired Gerard Rault, a former assistant attorney general for the state, to handle the desegregation case at a yearly salary of $25,000 ($10,000 of which was paid by the state of Louisiana). Rault was an apt choice for this job, for he was the attorney for a downtown savings and loan association whose president, Emile Wagner, Jr., was a school board member and one of the most fervent segregationists in the city. Rault and Wagner were also close personal friends.

A series of appeals by Rault kept the case in the courts for the next few years. Finally, the plaintiffs (who had not been particularly aggressive in the case throughout these appeals) asked Judge Wright to direct the board to draw up a desegregation plan. On July 15, 1959—more than three years after he had first ordered desegregation—Wright directed the board to file a desegregation plan by March 1, 1960 (see *Race Relations Law Reporter,* 1959).

1959–60: THE WASTED YEAR

The school board did not prepare a plan as they had been ordered to. Indeed, between July 15, 1959, and March 1, 1960, nothing happened to suggest that anyone believed the New Orleans schools would ever be desegregated. The entire state government—Governor Davis, the attorney general, the state commissioner of education, and the state legislature—had made it clear that they would do their utmost to preserve segregation, even if the only way was to close the Orleans Parish schools. Previous state administrations had provided them with some potent weapons.

In 1954 the state had adopted a constitutional amendment requiring segregation in the schools. In 1956 the legislature provided for the removal of principals and superintendents who aided desegregation, lifted the requirement of compulsory attendance at desegregated schools, provided for the dismissal of school bus drivers at integrated schools, and provided for the dismissal of any state employees, including teachers, who advocated integration. In 1958 the legislature authorized the closing of desegregated schools and the transfer of property of such schools to private, non-sectarian schools.

The five members of the school board were thus caught neatly between the federal courts and the state government. In this dilemma, only Emile Wagner and attorney Rault had an easy decision: they would continue working against Wright's order. Wagner, an organizer of the New Orleans White Citizens Council, fed information he thought might be useful to the Council and drafted some of the laws which the legislature would use in their effort to take over control of the New Orleans school board. Rault continued to work in the courts alongside the state attorney general. But for the other members of the school board the choice was not so clear. Four men—Matthew Sutherland, Louis Riecke, Theodore Shepard, and Lloyd Rittiner, the president of the board—had disapproved of integration, and Rittiner had briefly been a member of a White Citizens Council. Yet these were respectable middle-class businessmen who, along with Wagner, had been recruited by the reform faction. They wanted to do what was "right." It was now clear that the alternative to integration was the closing of the schools. Not one of these four men ever contemplated closing the schools, but two of them did seriously contemplate escaping the dilemma by resigning.

Mayor Morrison said nothing publicly. Privately, he indicated

he would have nothing to do with the school desegregation controversy. He had nearly been elected governor in 1960 and wanted
to run again in 1964. To do so, he would need the votes of many
segregationists. The most influential businessmen—all natives of
New Orleans who strongly believed in segregation—were likewise
silent. Television station WDSU was a voice in the wilderness,
but the dominant paper, the *Times-Picayune,* provided editorials
like this as late as six weeks before school was to open (*Times-
Picayune,* 1960*b*):

Public education, unquestionably, is a foundation of democracy, but
whether public education can survive the forced integration of schools in
a community like ours, with a large Negro population and ingrained
customs, remains to be seen. Forced integration . . . is a tragedy, just as
closing of the schools would be a tragedy.

Admitting that the choices facing the community were, unfortunately, either token integration or no schools at all, the *Times-
Picayune* (1960*b*) refused to take a stand:

The choice as to whether closed schools are to be preferred to integrated
schools is one which the people themselves must make. We would not
presume to make it for them.

The school board had also considered the idea of letting the
parents decide whether they wanted to retain public schools. The
president of the board, Lloyd Rittiner, believed the board's job
would be made easier if it could be shown that a majority of New
Orleans parents would rather have token integration than have no
schools at all. If this could be shown (and he was certain it could),
it would be easier to draw Mayor Morrison into support of the
board. With this in mind, Rittiner persuaded the rest of the board
and the superintendent to conduct a poll of the parents and received from Judge Wright a delay, until May 16, in the deadline
for submitting a plan. On April 22, a letter was sent to the parent
or guardian of every pupil asking them to check their preference
between the following alternatives:

1. I would like to see the schools kept open even though a small
amount of integration is necessary.

2. I would like to see the schools closed rather than be integrated even in small amounts.

The emphasis on the "small amount" of integration and the use of the phrase, "I would *like to see* the schools closed," were attempts to load the questions in favor of the first alternative, but apparently the silence in the city made desegregation seem like something in the distant and unforseeable future. Within two weeks of the mailout, almost 64 per cent of the white parents responded. To everyone's astonishment, almost 82 per cent of the white parents voted to close the schools. The results were announced on May 8, just eight days before the board was due to present a plan to Judge Wright. Rittiner, who had said before the tabulation that the poll would "wake up the people to the problem they face," was so stunned by the results that he now said he would disregard the Negroes' ballots (which were overwhelmingly in favor of keeping the schools open) and "abide by the wishes of the white people because they are the people who support the school system and elect us to the School Board" (*New York Times,* 1960*b*).

With the white parents seemingly eager to close down the schools, and with the mayor and the business elite offering the board no support, the beleaguered board members found themselves even more stranded when the expected moral example of the Catholic Church never materialized. Everyone had expected the Church to pave the way for community acceptance of desegregation, and indeed, the New Orleans hierarchy gave early signs of providing the necessary leadership. New Orleans, approximately two-thirds of whose population is Catholic, has by far the largest Catholic diocese in the South; in fact, half the total number of Catholics in the entire South live in the archdiocese of New Orleans. The diocese had the reputation of being one of the most liberal on race relations, a reputation that was due largely to the statements and actions of its archbishop, Joseph Francis Rummel. As early as 1949, Rummel had canceled a Holy Hour service because the religious procession would be segregated. That same year, he had ordered the "white" and "colored" signs removed from pews in the churches. In a pastoral letter in 1953, the archbishop had written, "Let there be no further discrimination or segregation in the pews, at the Communion rail, at the confessional and in parish meetings, just as there will be no segregation in the kingdom of heaven . . ." (Peters, 1959, p. 106). None of these early steps aroused any significant opposition.

Then, on the Sunday following Judge Wright's February 15, 1956, ruling that the Orleans Parish public schools would have to be integrated, Archbishop Rummel announced in a pastoral letter to the 525,000 Catholics of his diocese, "Racial segregation is morally wrong and sinful because it is a denial of the unity and solidarity of the human race as conceived by God in the creation of man in Adam and Eve." This time, there was considerable opposition. Some priests refused to read this pastoral letter, and that night a cross was burned on the lawn of Rummel's residence. Several legislators, some of them Catholic, spoke of giving the state police power to keep the parochial schools segregated. When on July 31, 1956, Rummel announced that racial integration of the parochial schools on a grade-per-year basis would begin in September, 1957, the reaction from his parishoners was swift and overwhelming. Rummel's rectory was picketed, contributions to the Church declined seriously, and pledges for capital projects were not honored. A group that called itself the Association of Catholic Laymen, led by Emile Wagner of the school board, appealed on August 8, 1957, directly to Pope Pius XII to overrule Rummel's pronouncement on segregation. (The group received a stern rebuke from a high Church authority in the Vatican newspaper for its "doctrinal error" and its "breach of discipline.") Despite the support from above, the pressures from below proved too much, for when September of 1957 arrived, the parochial schools remained segregated and the archbishop was silent. In fact, from July 31, 1956, until July, 1959, Rummel made no further public statements on the subject of segregation. According to one unverified account, Rummel's long silence was in part due to his advisers' having persuaded him that his pronouncements had gone beyond the demands of the Negroes. As evidence, his advisers are said to have pointed to the silence of the Negro community in New Orleans and to the lack of initiative by the Negro attorneys in the *Bush* case.

Finally, in July of 1959, Rummel, still retreating but trying to find some place to draw the line, announced rather lamely that the parochial schools would be integrated "at the earliest possible opportunity and definitely not later than when the public schools are integrated." But when the date for public school desegregation arrived, the parochial schools had once again put off desegregation. On October 9, 1960, eighty-three year old Rummel fell and broke an arm and a leg, and a triumvirate acting in his absence had no stomach for a fight against the segregationists. The parochial schools were not integrated until 1962, two years after the public schools.

In 1959 Msgr. Henry C. Bezou, superintendent of the parochial school system, said, "Segregation in the parochial schools can be ended with the stroke of a pen. The Archbishop of San Antonio did it [in 1954]. . . . And it will happen here." The Bishop of Raleigh, North Carolina, also did it in 1954, before the Supreme Court decision and despite virulent protests. Raleigh showed that it could be done "with a stroke of a pen" if the hierarchy was willing to fight it out.

Eight years had elapsed since the initial filing of the suit by the Negro plaintiffs, four years since Judge Wright directed the school board to begin making arrangements for desegregating the schools, and nine months since Judge Wright ordered the board to file a plan. Yet, unlike Atlanta, which was under less pressure but was already building public support for acceptance, New Orleans had not one white moderate group publicly supporting school desegregation. Since 1954, a few groups had tried but had failed even to promote a discussion of the issue. In 1958, a rabbi with a well-to-do congregation had organized an interfaith group of clergy to study race relations, but Jews were suspect on the issue and the group quickly collapsed. The Catholic hierarchy backed the efforts of another organization but this effort failed when the group was labelled "integrationist."

Another obstacle to moderate activity in New Orleans was the communism charge. The Southern Conference Educational Fund, an anti-segregation organization with headquarters in New Orleans, decided in 1955 to hold a forum on school integration. When they found one hundred sponsors, Mayor Morrison agreed to proclaim December 10–15, 1955, as Human Rights Week, and the school board granted permission for use of a school auditorium. But at the last moment the Young Men's Business Club passed a resolution urging a boycott of the forum because the leaders of SCEF were Communist. The school board rescinded its permission for use of the auditorium, and the mayor refused to proclaim Human Rights Week. When the respectability of the sponsors—mainly social workers and professors—was pointed out to the board, the school board offered to let the sponsors hold the meeting if they did not connect themselves with SCEF. The sponsors accepted this offer; the school board stalled, forced a postponement, and finally yielded. Nevertheless, the communism charge had severely jolted the sponsors and discouraged attendance at future forums, and the group eventually dissolved.

Another group, calling itself SOS (Save Our Schools), organized in 1959 but kept itself hidden until the announcement of the school board's postcard poll in April of 1960. SOS was immediately stigmatized as radical and integrationist because it was made up of the same people who had organized the earlier forum. SOS was composed of social workers, Tulane professors and their wives, and some lawyers and businessmen. No one in SOS was in the economic elite of the city, and SOS was full of Jews, integrationist Catholics, and non-southerners. Hence they were unable to attract the moderates of the city even though SOS strategy wisely emphasized open schools rather than integrated schools.

If the voices of moderation were silent, the voices of die-hard segregationism were plainly heard. The White Citizens Councils were organized by 1956. Besides holding mass rallies, the Councils were suspected of being the instigators if not the perpetrators of the endless obscene and threatening telephone calls to the board members and other moderates throughout each night.

There were, in addition, the words and actions of the governor and the legislature, clearly hostile to any position short of die-hard segregation. The position taken by the governor and his legislature were very largely determined during the elections in December of 1959 and January of 1960, elections held while the school board was under orders to produce a desegregation plan. The campaign was not one to give heart to the moderates or the school board. For the first time in over thirty years, the campaign for the governorship centered on racial issues. Ever since the rise of Huey Long in 1928, Louisiana state political campaigns, though one-party in name, were fought out along bifactional lines. The well-organized Long faction ran on an agrarian welfare-state program; the more amorphous anti-Long faction was a loose alliance of urban upper classes and rural planters who campaigned for good government—sound administration, a favorable atmosphere for business, and economy in government (see Key, 1949; Sindler, 1956; Havard *et al.,* 1963). But in the campaign for the first primary election (held December 5, 1959), the issue of racial segregation was forced into prominence by one of the eleven candidates, State Senator William Rainach. Rainach campaigned on an extreme segregation program, branding all the other candidates "soft" on this issue. (School board member Wagner campaigned actively for Rainach.) Mayor Morrison led the field with 33 per cent of the vote, Jimmie ("You Are My Sunshine") Davis had 25 per cent, Rainach 17 per cent, and the other candidates split the remaining 25 per cent. Clearly Rainach and his followers could have a lot to say about the outcome of the Morrison-Davis runoff election. Davis, a member of the anti-Long faction, had sung his way to a previous term as governor (1944–48) on an apolitical campaign of "peace and harmony" for friend and foe alike (see Sindler, 1956). Morrison had a solid base of support among the Negro voters of New Orleans and had thereby incurred the wrath of white supremacists. ("A vote for Morrison is a vote for integration.") Both began to bid openly for the Rainach voters. The runoff was unique in another respect; it was the first since Huey Long's election in 1928 in which no representative from either the Long or the anti-Long faction was in the race. The principal Long candidate, James Noe, finished fourth; Davis always appealed for cross-factional support, and Morrison was a loner who, despite his connection with the good government movement and thus with anti-Longism, had also built a base of support independent of either wing of the party. Thus the relatively stable bifactionalism of the past thirty years was obliterated, and the two candidates had little to offer the voter except to outpromise one another on streamlining the government and preserving segregation. In view of Morrison's record as a racial progressive, his effort to lure segregationist support was hopeless. Davis won easily, polling 54 per cent of the vote. The moderates in New Orleans—Morrison's personal friends—were treated to the disheartening spectacle of their good-government, reform mayor stumping the state for the votes of the segregationists while his city's school board was under court order to come up with a desegregation plan.

This should make clear the environment within which the four moderate segregationists on the school board were operating. Little wonder, then, that the board finally told Judge Wright in May of 1960 that they had no plan for desegregating the public schools. Viewed in its context, their statement can be seen as a moderate position; that is, it stopped short of refusing outright to come up with a plan. It was an admission of helplessness and a call for help. Help came from Judge Wright; he provided a plan himself (for integration in the coming fall), relieving the board members of the onus of having taken any initiative toward integration.[4]

SUMMER, 1960: THE CRISIS BREWS

But help would also have to come from the community. SOS came out publicly for open schools in late April of 1960, but this was expected from the radical SOS. On June 1, the city-wide PTA did come up with a resolution in support of keeping the schools open, but this was apparently a meeting dominated by liberals. A week later, at a meeting which drew a great deal of advance publicity, the open-schools resolution was voided and all school PTA's which persisted in supporting the resolution were threatened with expulsion. Five weeks rolled by without any help in sight. The feeling of helplessness that gripped the board was well illustrated in a desperate move they made at a school board meeting on June 20. By a vote of four to one, they passed a resolution asking Governor Davis to interpose the sovereignty of the state to prevent integration. Surprisingly, Emile Wagner was the dissenter. Interposition, which Wagner was later to herald as an easy way to keep the schools open and segregated, he now called "just about the harshest remedy that could ever be called into play. . . . The board has not completely exhausted other methods open to it" (*Times-Picayune,* 1960a). Rittiner agreed with Wagner "that calling on the Governor is a drastic measure, but I think the people of Orleans Parish should know what is ahead" (*Times-Picayune,* 1960a). Sutherland added that after six years of fighting integra-

[4]See *Race Relations Law Reporter* (1960). This was the first court-initiated integration plan in the United States.

tion they were running out of rope. After voting for the resolution, he added that if interposition failed, they would have to integrate or close the schools.

The first break in the wall of silence came two days later on June 22, when a new group was formed—the Committee for Public Education (CPE). Like the SOS members, CPE's members were doctors, lawyers, and young executives and their wives, but unlike SOS, CPE saw to it that none of its members had a liberal reputation. Indeed, CPE leaders made it clear that they disapproved of SOS. CPE was so precisely the answer to the school board's prayers that it seems likely that some members of the school board, Sam Rosenberg, or Judge Wright himself, were involved in organizing it. Some of the organizing of CPE was probably also done by the leaders of the Independent Women's Organization—the group that led the fight to reform the board.

During the tense months of May and June, 1960, members Riecke and Sutherland had had their fill, but Lloyd Rittiner rallied them and kept them from resigning. Rittiner's strength was partly derived from the fact that he had already made up his mind to support open schools; the others were still ambivalent. The formation of the CPE helped the other three moderates decide to stay and fight to keep the schools open.

The public stance of the CPE apparently gave heart to other moderates as well, for very shortly afterward the Episcopal clergy of New Orleans, the clergy of the United Church of Christ, and the pastors and elders from each of the forty-three Methodist churches in the New Orleans area all came out for open schools (see Breed, 1965, p. 136). The arrival of the new voices and others that followed in the summer helped to stiffen the resolve of the four school board members, but the support they most desperately wanted—from the mayor and the civic elite—never came. Their silence continued until months after the mob scenes began.

The summer of 1960 consisted of a running battle between the federal courts and the state of Louisiana. The legislature had already passed a host of bills to close the schools if necessary to preserve segregation. As Judge Wright put pressure on the school board to comply with his desegregation order, the legislature stepped up its own campaign at its regular session in 1960. One bill prohibited the granting of school funds to desegregated schools. Another gave the governor the right to close all the schools in the state if any one of them were integrated. A third gave the governor the right to close any school threatened with violence or disorder. The closest the legislature came to subtiety was Act 496, which laid out a procedure for integration: a school district could be integrated but not by its school board. When a district receives a court order, "the Governor . . . shall supersede such a school board . . . , and shall take over . . . the exclusive control, management and administration of the public schools . . . on a racially segregated basis until such time as the legislature shall . . . place into operation therein a plan of racial integration."

Armed with these statutes, State Attorney General Jack P. F. Gremillion filed suit against the school board in a state court. On July 29, the state court issued the requested injunction (*State of Louisiana* v. *Orleans Parish School Board,* 1960) against the school board to prevent it from integrating, basing its injunction largely on Act 496.

On August 13, Mayor Morrison, under increasing pressure from his friends and supporters to do something, finally uttered his first words on the subject, a tepid request that Governor Davis disclose how he would carry out his pledge to keep the schools open and segregated. "The human and economic effects of closed public schools," Morrison told the governor, "could have a heavy impact on the community well-being" (*New York Times,* 1960c). And a few weeks before school opened, Morrison came out more or less for acceptance of integration: "If we are going to lose the decision, inevitably, a small percentage of integration might be the answer in the situation instead of having lots of trouble and lots of mixing" (*Times-Picayune,* 1960c). Governor Davis, goaded into action by increased legal pressure from the NAACP, seized control of the school board with the following notice to School Superintendent James Redmond:

By Executive Order Number 1 . . . I have superseded the Orleans Parish School Board and have in my executive capacity as Governor . . . assumed exclusive control, management and administration of all the public schools in the Parish of Orleans . . . [as authorized by Act 496 of 1960].

The notice ordered Superintendent Redmond to open the schools on September 7 on a segregated basis.

The same day Governor Davis took over the New Orleans schools, a totally new aspect was given to the entire legal and political situation. Thirty white parents filed a new suit against Governor Davis and other state officials. It was an application for a temporary injunction restraining the governor and other state officials from obeying the state court injunction and the state statutes with respect to segregation.[5] The stated fear of the white parents was that, though the governor's notice to Redmond had specifically ordered the schools to be kept open, the governor would use the authority vested in him by the various acts of the legislature to close the schools. The filing of this case, *Williams* v. *Davis,* marks the first public action taken by white parents in recognition of the danger that the state's activities posed to the schools. The CPE played a key role in instigating the suit, searching out the white parents who would be willing to put their names to it and trying to find an attorney to handle the case. After several attorneys refused, Charles E. Richards agreed to handle the case. It must be mentioned here that many moderates were extremely fearful of harassment and even fearful for their lives; consequently, some of the important activists in CPE did their work secretly. One such person to whom we talked expressed the view, which he said was held by many in CPE, that the NAACP was deliberately "trying to lose the case" so as to force the schools to close and thus "to dramatize the issue." The white parents' suit was an attempt, not only to prevent the governor and the legislature from closing the schools, but also to keep the Negro plaintiffs from losing the case (whether by design or through ineptitude) and forcing the schools to close. Apparently, some individual Negroes had commented that if the schools were closed, the city would then wake up and see how important the schools were. (The CPE people also told us that some of the eco-

[5]Because this suit sought the same relief against the same parties, the court consolidated the two cases. From that point on, the two cases are virtually synonymous, going up and down the ladder together from the district court to the U.S. Supreme Court.

nomic leaders rationalized their own silence by saying that the legislature should close the schools and let the citizens see how much harm would be done—then the citizens would force the opening of the schools in quick order.) The CPE members, of course, were entitled to some normal feelings of paranoia. This misunderstanding of the NAACP strategy by some key CPE leaders clearly shows that the joining of the *Williams* and *Bush* cases in no way signified cooperation between the Negro and white plaintiffs, even though the two suits ostensibly sought the same relief. At no time in New Orleans did white moderates work with the Negroes.

Three days before the white parents filed their suit, a *New York Times* (1960c) dispatch from New Orleans quoted unidentified "sources high in legal circles" who believed NAACP's pleadings did not "provide the court with an adequate basis for cutting through the barrier thrown up by state officials." There is strong evidence that the filing of the *Williams* suit, which names the school board as one of the parties defendant and seeks to enjoin the board from obeying the state court injunctions, was in fact concurred in by the four moderates on the school board and given behind-the-scenes encouragement and support. This also would mean that Sam Rosenberg and even Judge Wright may have been consulted in the drafting of the *Williams* brief.

On August 27, a three-judge federal district court awarded judgment for the plaintiffs in both the *Bush* and *Williams* suits (*Bush* v. *Orleans Parish School Board; Williams* v. *Davis,* 1960a). Two days later, the court issued a sweeping injunction, striking down the key segregation acts of the legislature, nullifying the seizure of the school board by the governor, and ordering the board to get on with the desegregation of the schools.

If the Court thought its injunction was going to dispose of the case once and for all it was sadly mistaken, for much more was yet to come, but the events of the summer, culminating in the filing of the suit by the white parents and the strong, unyielding position taken by the federal district court, placed the school board members in a strong position. The *Williams* suit was vital, not only because it gave Skelly Wright the grounds to strike down the state school-closing laws, but also because it legitimated the school board's now "moderate" position. By mid-August of 1960, the CPE's work convinced the board members that if the legislature, the governor, and Leander Perez, the arch-segregationist political boss of neighboring St. Bernard Parish, could be persuaded to keep their hands off the New Orleans schools, the schools could be peacefully desegregated. Now, thanks to *Williams,* control of the schools had been returned to them. With the governor and others restrained from interfering with the schools, they were now ready to comply with Wright's orders. Accordingly, the four and Sam Rosenberg met privately at Rittiner's home and set up a Committee To Maintain Public Schools and named themselves to this committee. The purpose of this thinly disguised ruse was to permit themselves to have official meetings without having to have Emile Wagner present. At this private meeting they asked Rosenberg what to do, and he suggested that they go to Judge Wright and tell him that they now wanted to comply with his orders.

DESEGREGATION BY COMPUTER

The next day the four moderates met privately with Wright and told him that they and the school staff had made no preparation for desegregation but were now ready to comply with the court order. The schools were scheduled to open on September 7, little more than a week away, so the board members asked the judge if he could delay the start of desegregation until November 14. The delay would give them and the school staff time to devise a desegregation plan. But two other reasons were actually more important. The delay would mean that school would open on a segregated basis; desegregation in November would be by transfer and would be simpler than desegregation on opening day. Negro students would already be registered in a school and a relatively smaller number would go to the trouble of transferring. Finally, the board wanted desegregation delayed until after the November 8 election, when Matthew Sutherland, one of the moderates, was up for reelection. This idea, like the decision in March to conduct the postcard poll of parents, was Lloyd Rittiner's. A school board election at this time would be certain to center on the stand taken by the moderates; thus it would provide a good test of voter support for open schools. Despite the results of the postcard poll and despite the still impressive silence of the community leaders, Rittiner believed that the majority of the city would support them, and even the other moderates were more confident. Sutherland had come close to resigning a few months earlier; he was now ready to stand for reelection on an "open schools" platform.

Not even Emile Wagner knew that this meeting with Judge Wright had taken place, and no one knew the real reasons for the request for a delay. On August 31, when the four members formally went before Judge Wright to request the delay, the only reason given was to allow the school staff time to prepare a desegregation plan. The delay was granted (*Bush* v. *Orleans Parish School Board; Williams* v. *Davis,* 1960*b*). Attorney Rault resigned from his position with the school board, and Sam Rosenberg became once again the school board's only attorney. During the next few months, the four moderates and Rosenberg were practically living with one another, and much of their time was spent together in Judge Wright's private chambers.

Thus it happened that the public schools of New Orleans opened their doors on the usual segregated basis on September 7, 1960. The school board had two months to prepare for the long-dreaded desegregation, and they were busy months. Preparations included not only the setting-up of the machinery for selecting the Negro children and the schools, but also a feverish attempt to drum up support from the political and economic leaders of the city and to organize Sutherland's reelection campaign.

Trying to arrive at a legally acceptable way of limiting the number of Negroes who would be entering the white schools, the board and the superintendent adopted, on September 26, a four-step administrative process for considering applications for transfer. The plan, and all subsequent plans worked out by the school board and the superintendent, reflected their reform ideology; they wanted to make "objective," "scientific" decisions. "Objective" and "scientific" criteria had the further merit of freeing the board members and the superintendent from responsibility for the decisions made. To see the importance of this factor to the board members, we must keep in mind the enormous pressure on them. The four moderates had started to receive harassing phone calls from two to four in the morning. They were being referred to by the newspaper as the "four surrender members," and no one in a position of responsibility in the community had risen as yet to support them. Later, the board members were to deny responsibility for the details of their integration plan, both to the public and to the interviewer. More than one board member insisted, "We didn't select the schools and the children, the machine did."

A look at the plans devised by the board and the superintendent will indicate how carefully they tried to make the decisions mechanical.

Step one.—Consideration by four assistant superintendents of:

> Verification of information on application
> Proper age (birth certificate)
> Nearness of school to child's home
> Request or consent of parent and reasons assigned thereto
> Available room and teaching capacity of schools
> Availability of transportation

If the above factors were satisfactorily met, the applications were referred to the next step.

Step two.—Consideration by the Acting Director of Guidance and Testing, psychologists and psychometrists of:

> Scholastic aptitude
> Intelligence or ability
> Results of achievement tests

All information compiled about each applicant was referred to the third screening group.

Step three.—Consideration by the Assistant Superintendent for Instruction, the Director of Special Services, the Director of Kindergarten-Primary Education, psychologists, and visiting teachers of:

> Effect of new pupil upon the academic program
> Suitability of established curricula for pupil (in terms of grouping within the class)
> Adequacy of pupil's academic preparation or readiness for admission to school or curricula

Psychological qualification of pupil for type of teaching and associations

Effect upon academic progress of other students

Effect upon prevailing academic standards

Psychological effect upon the pupil

Home environment of the pupil

Maintenance or severance of social and psychological relationships with pupils and teachers

Step four.—Consideration by an administrative review team composed of the Superintendent, the First Assistant Superintendent, the Acting Assistant Superintendent for Instruction, and the school system's Medical Director of:

All information previously collected on each applicant

Choice and interests of pupil

Possibility or threat of friction or disorder among pupils or others

Possibility of breach of peace or ill will or economic retaliation within the community

All the factors in these lists were taken by the school board and the superintendent from the Louisiana Pupil Placement Act (regular session of 1960, Act 492). As can readily be seen, the Act was designed to make sure that no Negroes would be permitted to transfer. That any were permitted at all derives from the fact that the board had to find some, and it indicates that there must have been some "cheating" by the "machine." (The machine was also told not to find more than ten.) The factors listed in step four leave the "objective," "mechanical" realm and begin to involve subjective considerations. However, the administrative team seems to have followed faithfully all the objective tests in the first three screenings and not followed at all the subjective tests in the fourth screening. Certainly the schools chosen for integration hardly fit the criteria suggested in step four.

Finally, the school board was to consider the findings of the administrative review team and direct the superintendent to issue or not to issue a transfer for the pupil in question. However, the issue was so hot, and the desire on the part of the board to avoid responsibility for the choices so intense, that this part of the procedure was not followed. The board members urged Redmond not to release the names of the Negro children even to themselves. Of course, they were fearful of having the information released to Emile Wagner, who would then release it to the White Citizens Councils, but the four moderates could easily have obtained the information without letting Wagner see it; they simply did not want to know which Negro children and which schools had been chosen.

The elaborate administrative procedure thus had three principal advantages for the board: (1) It greatly limited the number of Negroes and the number of schools to be integrated. (2) It was a "correct" way of doing things, avoiding the subjective considerations typical of systems run by politicians. (3) It helped the board avoid personal responsibility for the decisions. The machine did it.

The board members were, meanwhile, actively trying to enlist the public support of the economic elite. Help in this enlistment came from an attorney who had long been the counsel for a very wealthy Jewish New Orleans family (a family which was known for its liberal proclivities but which, because Jews were suspect on the issue of segregation, had to work behind the scenes), and who had many contacts with the economic leaders of the city. At the end of September this attorney had succeeded in getting five of the very top economic leaders to meet with school board president Rittiner. They were not willing to be seen in public and met him at a private dining room. Rittiner argued, as many others had previously, that any chaos or disorder over the desegregation of the schools would be harmful to the city, and he called on these men to support publicly the board's efforts to achieve peaceful desegregation. But the business leaders replied with an ultimatum: they would offer their assistance only if the board would separate the first grades by sex and keep the toilets in the schools segregated by race. Rittiner saw nothing wrong with separating the first-graders by sex—all the New Orleans schools had at one time been so divided—but he rejected the idea of segregating the toilets. The meeting ended at this point, and these men did not come out in favor of peace until several months after desegregation.

On October 10, however, in an apparent attempt to meet these business leaders halfway, the board resolved to keep all integrated classes separated by sex. Other rules adopted by the board on October 10 included a rule that all accepted applicants must have test scores equal to or above the median for the school for which they were applying. Since the latter rule was crucial in determining not only which Negro children but, more important, which of the white schools would be integrated, it is important for us to understand exactly what the school staff meant by this rule and how they administered it. It had been a long-standing practice in the New Orleans public schools to give all children, white and Negro, the Metropolitan Readiness or Achievement Tests during their first week in first grade. This test was administered by the first-grade teacher and, as a matter of course, had already been administered to all first-grade children in the first week of school in September. The class median was based on the scores at each school's first grade for the previous five years. The 129 Negro children who had applied for transfers were assigned to testing centers where they were given additional tests; these were administered by psychologists who also reported on the behavior and dress of the children and their parents.

As the reader has no doubt noted, all the rules and procedures adopted by the school board and the superintendent pertained to the screening of the Negro applicants. There was absolutely no screening of the white schools to be integrated; in fact, the choice of the white schools was to be determined by finding a school whose first-grade class median was low enough to admit the Negro children. The consequence of this was that the white schools to be integrated were the worst possible choice.

Since both schools—William Frantz Elementary and McDonogh No. 19—were in the same general neighborhood, it was easy for segregationists to concert their activity. Of course, the decision to limit it to two white schools—another decision by the machine—also made it easy for the segregationists to concentrate their fire. In addition, the neighborhood was generally poor, with a concentration of white working-class and lower-class families living in housing projects, the groups most likely to be hostile to Negro advances. But Frantz and McDonogh No. 19 were bad choices for political reasons as well, for they were both in the most neglected section of the city, the ninth ward. The ninth ward was always the last to get street lights and the last to get paved streets. Politically, socially, and economically, the city has been dominated by the Anglo-Americans, who live uptown ("above"—

west of—Canal Street), and the Creole French, who live in the French Quarter. In the nineteenth century the area east of the French Quarter was the immigrant truck-gardening section of the city, composed of Germans, Italians, and non-Creole French. Though many of these people have achieved middle-class status, their section of town is still politically weak. Suddenly they discovered that two of their schools—and none in any other section of town—had been desegregated. To the residents of the ninth ward the decision seemed motivated by pure malice, and even upper-middle-class moderates were furious.

It is only necessary to add that the ninth ward of Orleans Parish is the next-door neighbor to St. Bernard Parish, which is under the political control of the wealthy racist, Leander Perez, and McDonogh No. 19 is itself only a few blocks away from the parish line. It was thus easy for Perez to hire pickets for the two schools and to make his own schools the haven for the white boycotters.

Had the board been willing to make a "political" choice of schools rather than a "scientific" choice, much of the difficulty could have been avoided. Board members told us that this conjecture was not merely hindsight, but they actually had been urged *at the time* to choose schools where Negro children would be likely to be accepted by the whites. The school board could easily have integrated almost any school it chose; Negroes have always lived in nearly every neighborhood of the city, even the most expensive. (One of the most militant Negro leaders of New Orleans, Mrs. Oretha Castle, lives between two ardent white segregationists.) Furthermore, in October, the PTA's of two schools in the Tulane University area actually volunteered to accept Negroes. Mrs. Mary Sand, president of SOS, said in 1961 that the open-school campaign had made little progress in the neighborhood of Frantz and McDonogh No. 19 "because we found few civic groups through which to work" (Third Annual Conference on Problems of Schools in Transition, 1961).

THE SUTHERLAND CAMPAIGN AND THE FIRST SPECIAL SESSION

While the school board and the staff were developing their screening procedure, the campaign for support for open schools and for Matthew Sutherland's reelection got underway. Election day was November 8, the same day as the Kennedy-Nixon presidential election. Of the five seats, only Matthew Sutherland's was being voted on at that time. Sutherland's reelection campaign was designed to put to the voters the stand taken by the four moderates. He would make clear that he was a segregationist but that he was going to keep the schools open even if they were desegregated. The moderates—including CPE and the now important Independent Women's Organization, which publicly came out for open schools on August 3—gave Sutherland their all-out support.

The extensive efforts to get the economic elite involved had a built-in deficiency. Who, after all, could exercise influence or exert pressure on the most powerful men in the city? The chief newspaper was published by a man who was himself a member of the great silent elite. Mayor Morrison was more vulnerable, since he had been a member of the good-government movement in New Orleans since 1936 and had thus received much political support from the people who were now appealing to him. Many of Morrison's closest friends and admirers are still bitter today over his response to their appeals. He absolutely refused to endorse Judge Wright's desegregation order or the board's decision to comply, and his few statements about the schools were ambiguous or tepid. Behind the scenes, he did contact the elites, but when they coldly rebuffed him—some refused even to discuss the subject with him, others were more polite—Morrison reportedly turned to two confidants and said, "Well, if those s.o.b.'s aren't going to do anything, I'll be damned if I'm going to stick my neck out!"

But the issue, especially as defined by CPE and SOS, could not be ignored indefinitely. SOS had first set the strategy back in April by coming out for open schools instead of urging integration. Observers of New Orleans have tended to minimize the contribution made by SOS because "they didn't come within a hundred miles of the power structure." But issue-defining is a key role and does affect the power structure. It was this emphasis on open schools rather than integration which permitted respectable elements of the community such as CPE to take a public stand in support of the board for the first time. During July and August various Protestant clergymen, a few union locals, IWO, and the Junior

Chamber of Commerce all came out for open schools. It must be emphasized that no white group made an effort in 1960 to win popular acceptance of Judge Wright's orders. Even those who spoke for keeping the schools open (except for SOS) stressed that they were for segregation. The school board itself did not switch from resistance to compliance until the issue changed from integrating the schools to keeping them open. The moderates were so effective in framing the issue in this way that by October the segregationists were compelled to say that what they wanted was to keep the schools segregated and open. And near the end of October the elite made their first tentative steps toward supporting peaceful desegregation.

During the month of October, reports were circulating that Governor Davis was going to call a special session to try to halt the New Orleans school desegregation. The five businessmen who had met with Rittiner in September journeyed twice to Baton Rouge to urge Davis not to interfere. These men had been important Davis supporters in the 1960 election, and Davis was aware of their economic power. They left his office under the impression that he had promised not to call a special session, but they, and others, told us that Davis never gives a direct answer to a question. They cannot be faulted for trying, but at a time when the school board was desperately in need of public support from the elite, this effort of theirs to help the board was kept secret.

On October 27, the school board announced that it had granted transfer permits to five Negro pupils. Their names were not revealed nor were the white schools identified. (The identity of the white schools was not known until the Negro girls arrived at school on November 14.) The next day Davis issued a call for a special session. Rumors quickly swept the city that Davis would interpose the legislature between the federal government and the school board. The New Orleans moderates seized on the call for a special session as one more sign that the schools were in danger of being closed. They renewed their effort for public support and finally succeeded.

On November 1, in a front-page editorial, the *Times-Picayune* (1960*d*) endorsed the candidacy of Matthew Sutherland:

Mr. Sutherland, in our opinion, has proved himself an ardent opponent of forced integration. He has backed every effort by the school board to have set aside court orders to end segregation. Nevertheless, opposition to Mr. Sutherland seems to be based on the school board's adoption of the state's placement law which was designed to meet the emergency that now exists. As far as we can see the board had no option. After losing some 35 appeals to the courts of one kind or another, the federal court order had to be recognized. The board wanted, of course, to keep the schools open and segregated. It has had to accept limited segregation [*sic*] under the pupil placement plan. It has no authority to close the schools if it wanted to. The legislature and the Governor can close the schools (if the closing is applied to the whole state). But none of Mr. Sutherland's opponents . . . have a definite plan to keep them open and fully segregated.

In response to this editorial, the principal opponent of Sutherland, John Singreen, a man endorsed and supported by the White Citizens Councils, wrote a letter to the paper on November 2 (*Times-Picayune,* 1960*e*). His letter indicates how the framing of the issue in terms of closing or keeping open the schools had put the diehards on the defensive.

The sole issue in this campaign is, are the voters willing to accept integragration now, or are they going to fight now for their rights. The four surrender members of the school board have already approved integration . . . and it will be a reality on November 14 unless each parent, each voter . . . make up their minds to fight for their constitutional rights. . . .

No one in official authority in Baton Rouge, nor anybody here, has mentioned closing the schools. . . .

Governor Jimmie Davis was elected by the people of Louisiana to keep the schools open and segregated. The people should trust the governor and the schools will remain open and segregated, and our own. . . .

Emile Wagner, who had publicly called upon the governor to remove the four "surrender members" of the board from office, endorsed Singreen and, referring to the postcard poll of parents, declared that Sutherland had "violated this mandate of the people." A few days later, Wagner, running as an unpledged elector in the presidential election, called for the defeat of both Nixon and Kennedy as a way of stopping such things as the integration order. Integration, he said, would be a disaster because tests had shown that "40 per cent of Negro students verged on moronic and ranged down to imbecile" (*Times-Picayune,* 1960*n*).

Sutherland persistently put to the voters the stand taken by the four moderates on the board. He reiterated his advocacy of segregation and ticked off the steps he had taken to defend the New Orleans school system from forced integration. But, he said, "we must face the issues as they are, not as we would have them to be. The question is, do we want public education or do we want economic chaos? . . . If we close the public schools, we will be depriving some of the people of an education, which is out of line with our democratic way of life" (*Times-Picayune,* 1960*g*). Seeing no other way to keep the schools open, he would comply with the federal court orders to desegregate, "but I would favor anything the legislature can do to keep the schools open and segregated" (*Times-Picayune,* 1960*g*). The last plank in this platform was a reliance on the Pupil Placement Act as a good way to limit integration. After fighting off forced integration for eight years, the board's moderates were now reluctantly going to admit a few Negro children, but only to keep the schools from being closed and only under conditions which would limit and control the number of Negroes. And if the legislature could come up with a way of keeping the schools open and segregated, they were all for it. In short, it was a tightrope act.

On November 4, the second break in the wall of silence occurred with the public endorsement of Matthew Sutherland by a committee of one hundred important business and professional men, headed by an executive committee of eighteen of the city's most influential citizens—the economic elite, at last. The endorsement, "for the future of our children and for the continued growth of New Orleans as a major industrial center in the South," made no mention of the fatal issue except for a brief reference to the closing of the schools: "Our struggle with the Soviet Union . . . makes it imperative that the education of our children not be stopped or interrupted . . ." (*Times-Picayune,* 1960*f*). The day before the election, this committee ran a three-quarter page ad in the

Times-Picayune (1960*m*) listing ninety-eight names and signed "The Business and Professional Men's Committee for Sutherland." The only message on the page was, "We believe that we and our children will all have a better future if Matt Sutherland is re-elected to the School Board." But the names were what was important.

On November 4, the legislature met, and everyone finally learned the details of Davis' legislative package. As soon as the bills were distributed to the legislators, the House voted to suspend the rules and sent the bills to the administration-controlled judiciary "B" committee. Only one New Orleans representative, Maurice Landrieu, objected on the floor to suspending the rules, and he was voted down 93 to 1. Another New Orleans representative, Salvador Anzelmo, described the administration "steamroller," "Twenty-nine bills were dumped on my desk, and within 15 minutes referred to a committee, without us having any opportunity to read or digest those bills" (*Times-Picayune,* 1960*i*). Anzelmo said many members of the House objected to the procedure but dared not speak up for fear of being branded integrationists.

Davis' package did hinge around interposition. Indeed, one bill went so far as to impose criminal penalties upon anyone, including any officer of the federal government, who attempted to interfere with the state's control of education. The rest of the legislative package was an arsenal of devices to prevent integration; their function was succinctly summarized by the three-judge federal court that ruled them unconstitutional a few weeks later (cf. *Bush* v. *Orleans Parish School Board; Williams* v. *Davis; United States* v. *Louisiana,* 1960*a*):

In order to forestall any effective integration order for this school year, present enrollment on a segregated basis is "frozen" and transfers are forbidden (Act 26); but, for the future, any school under an order to desegregate is immediately closed (Act 22), whereupon the local school board ceases to exist (Act 21); to carry out these directives . . . the state police are given additional powers and placed under the orders of the legislature (Act 16), and if demonstrators are needed, they may now be recruited among the students who are no longer compelled to go to school (Act 27); to assure that an integrated school does close, the new legislation provides that if it continues to operate it shall enjoy no accreditation (Act 20), teachers shall lose their certificates (Act 23), and the students themselves shall receive no promotion or graduation credits (Act 24). . . .

The New Orleans school board was mixed in its appraisal of the package. Sutherland and Rittiner said they would favor anything the legislature could do to keep schools open and segregated. "The only thing I am against," Rittiner said, "is the closing of schools. As an elected official I feel it is my duty to provide public education, if possible on a segregated basis but, if not, on an integrated basis" (*Times-Picayune, 1960h*). Shepard was more pessimistic; the bills looked to him very similar to ones the federal courts had already declared unconstitutional. If the governor was not able to produce anything new, Shepard saw pupil placement as the best course to follow. Emile Wagner, on the other hand, professed confidence that passage of the bills would keep the schools open and segregated, and he taunted his four colleagues, "It is to be regretted that the school board did not have more confidence in the governor. If it had it would not have walked hat in hand to a federal court and capitulated so that now it is bound by its word to the court to integrate" (*Times-Picayune, 1960h*).

At the committee hearings, statements by administration spokesmen made it abundantly clear that they really did not know how to keep the schools open and segregated and perhaps did not even know what they wanted to accomplish in the session. Representative Napper, who drafted the interposition bill, said in reply to a statement by the president of SOS, "Under no circumstances do we want to have another Little Rock in Louisiana. . . . [We] will do everything . . . to keep the schools open" (*Times-Picayune, 1960j*). Senator Kelly Gravolet from Perez' district expressed the same feeling when he said the session had only one purpose: to keep the schools open and segregated. "If interposition fails," he admitted, "schools will be either integrated or closed, but none of us wants them closed. We are hoping," he concluded, "to have six years more of litigation" (*Times-Picayune, 1960k*). However, Representative Risley Triche, Davis' floor leader in the House, blithely assured the state's parents that any pupil who did not attend school because of the school's closing would be considered by the state to have been legally attending school.

On November 6, the Louisiana House passed all twenty-nine bills, most of them by huge majorities, the interposition bill unanimously. In the Senate, the New Orleans delegation proved a little tougher, but all bills were passed in that chamber on November 8. The New Orleans Senate delegation was led by Robert Ainsworth,[6] Governor Davis' personal choice in 1960 for president *pro tempore* of the Senate, who bucked the administration because he felt the bills (especially Bill 18 to abolish the Orleans school board) were intended to upset responsible authority in New Orleans. Kelly Gravolet answered this charge with the following explanation: "Everybody here knows there is an injunction against the governor. If we do nothing the schools will be integrated November 14. The only way I can see that we could possibly have open and segregated schools on the 14th is by passing this bill" (Pinney and Friedman, 1963, p. 10).

Even though the legislation threatened to close the schools and was an attack on the right of New Orleans to home rule, neither Mayor Morrison nor the New Orleans delegation fought back. Only Landrieu voted against all seventeen of the bills affecting New Orleans; and only three other members opposed as many as half the bills. Morrison's two floor leaders, LeBreton and Casey, voted against only three and one, respectively. Vesich, the floor leader for the New Orleans Regular Democratic Organization, and three other delegates voted against two each; nine members of the House delegation from New Orleans supported all the bills.

However, when the legislature wanted to have an eight-man committee take over the New Orleans schools, Representative LeBreton introduced an amendment to have the committee be composed entirely of New Orleans legislators. "We've come a long way," said LeBreton, "toward getting our school board out of politics. I'm against only one thing—your taking our school board away from us" (*Times-Picayune,* 1960*l*). LeBreton was put on the legislative committee, but his amendment was defeated, and this is the issue which finally stirred Mayor Morrison. On November 8, he issued a statement to the press, which read in part as follows:

[6]Ainsworth is now a federal judge in New Orleans.

I have been shocked to learn that the House . . . rejected a proposed amendment by Orleans legislators seeking local control of its own affairs. . . .

It is just as wrong for Mr. Garrett [upstate Claiborne Parish] to try to run our Orleans school affairs as it is wrong for the U.S. Supreme Court to dictate to the people of Louisiana. . . .

It looks like home rule is taking another licking [*Times-Picayune,* 1960o].

It was stimulating to those in New Orleans to learn that Morrison could be shocked by anything that was going on in Baton Rouge. From his public statements, and the votes of his floor leaders, one would conclude that while he did not quite approve of a legislative committee's taking over the schools and closing them, he was not really outraged until he found that the committee would be composed of upstate legislators.

In sheer voting strength, a united New Orleans delegation could easily have been outvoted, but one wonders whether Governor Davis would even have attempted to go so far had official New Orleans presented a solid front of opposition. It is one thing to knock over a few representatives obviously acting on their own, but to beat down the united opposition of the mayor of the state's largest city, his political organization, and all his state legislators would have been a different matter. Even if Davis were to win, such an encounter might have cost him more than the issue was worth. The second special session was to provide a good illustration of the power New Orleans could exert in the legislature. A bill clearly aimed at Morrison would have made mayors and police chiefs subject to removal from office if they assisted in the execution of federal court orders (for example, by protecting children going to and from desegregated schools). This bill was attacked by mobilized New Orleans forces and was quashed in the committee.

The Louisiana Senate passed the bills and the special sessions recessed on election day, November 8—and the New Orleans voters rejected the diehard position and endorsed moderation by a wide margin. Sutherland received an outright majority, 56 per cent of the vote, and nearly doubled his nearest opponent, Singreen, who got 31 per cent. This smashing victory was the first public endorsement of the school board's policy of keeping the schools open.

DESEGREGATION WEEK

November 8 was also the end of the presidential election campaign. Until now, the federal government's involvement in the school desegregation situation in Louisiana had been limited to steps taken by the courts. Political observers generally believed that President Eisenhower's Attorney General, William P. Rogers, had been eager to enter the *Bush* case, but that Eisenhower and Republican strategists had feared that their entry into the case would raise the specter of Little Rock and cause the state to go for Kennedy. (It did anyway.) Rogers lost no time after the election, for on November 10, the United States District Attorney in New Orleans, M. Hepburn Many, a long-time Republican who reputedly hated Louisiana Democrats more than he hated integration, sought and obtained orders from Judge Wright restraining all Louisiana sheriffs, district attorneys, police chiefs, and mayors from interfering with federal court officers involved in school desegregation.

Thursday, November 10, was a busy day in Louisiana. On November 7, the legislature had created an eight-man legislative committee to run the New Orleans schools, and on the morning of November 10 four members of this committee arrived in the New Orleans school offices accompanied by armed state police. Risley Triche, floor leader in the House and chairman of the committee, retained Redmond as superintendent and ordered him to clear out all employees from the building. Many employees thought they had been fired. After stripping the school board of authority, Triche announced, "We are going to operate the schools the same on Monday as they are operating today. . . . There will be no change. . . . We know now of no transfer of students nor recommendations for transfer which have been approved" (*New York Times*, 1960*d*).

The legislative commission retained control of the schools most of that afternoon. Within a few hours attorney Charles Richards appeared in Judge Wright's court, at the request of the white parents in the *Williams* case, asking for a restraining order. Having no time for a hearing, Judge Wright issued temporary restraining orders and set November 18 for a hearing on the constitutionality of the statutes passed in the special session. Deputy U.S. marshals fanned out all over the state to serve copies of the orders on state officials, including the eight-man legislative committee.

By six o'clock that evening, Sam Rosenberg was able to tell the school board that, as a result of Wright's order, they were now in a position identical to the one they were in before passage of the acts of the special session. With this assurance, the board formally authorized the transfer of the five Negro girls into all-white schools. Emile Wagner was not present; he was meeting with the state sovereignty commission in Baton Rouge to map strategy.

That night Governor Davis announced that the special session was not over; it had only recessed, and he called it to reconvene on Sunday. In addition, he called a second special session to follow the automatic termination of the first. On Saturday, State Education Superintendent Jackson declared Monday the 14th, desegregation day, a state-wide holiday, and at 10 A.M. of Sunday the 13th, Judge Wright issued restraining orders against the holiday.

As Wright was issuing the order, the legislature was reconvening. Before television cameras, it replaced the special committee to run the New Orleans schools with the entire legislature, fired Redmond and Rosenberg for refusing to identify the Negro girls, and named an assistant sergeant-at-arms to proceed to New Orleans with a "legislative police force" and prevent desegregation. The idea behind replacing the eight-man committee with the entire legislature was to make it impossible for Judge Wright to issue restraining orders, since there was no legal precedent for enjoining an entire legislature. But that evening Judge Wright, who had been taking notes in front of his television set, did issue restraining orders against all members of the legislature. Perhaps even more significant than this shattering of legal precedent is the fact that this time the restraining orders were requested by the Orleans Parish school board—the four men who in June had panicked and asked the governor to interpose state sovereignty to prevent integration.

After Wright issued the restraining orders, Redmond called all the school principals (this was still Sunday night) and told them to open the schools on Monday and, despite the confusion, most teachers and pupils showed up for class. Not until 10 A.M. did anyone except Police Superintendent Joseph Giarrusso know which schools had been chosen. Then, four Negro girls (the fifth had withdrawn her application)—three at McDonogh No. 19 and one at Frantz Elementary—brought desegregation to the Deep South. It was only then that the citizens of New Orleans discovered that the two schools were in the ninth ward, the worst possible area in the city for such an experiment.

THE MOB IS ORGANIZED

The Negro girls were escorted to school by federal marshals, and as soon as the word spread, the parents of the white pupils came running to take their children home. Every white child was withdrawn from McDonogh No. 19, and all white children except two were withdrawn from the Frantz school. The two exceptions were the daughters of Mr. and Mrs. James Gabrielle and the Reverend Lloyd Foreman. (No white pupil ever returned to Mc-Donogh No. 19, except for one brief period in January of 1961. The father of the children who broke the boycott was then fired by Walgreen's and had to leave town when no one would hire him.) Led by the Gabrielles and Mr. Foreman, other parents brought their children back to Frantz, and the boycott of that school was never total.

On Tuesday the 15th, roving packs of truant teenagers tried to break into the two integrated schools but were repulsed by the police. Eleven arrests were made (but none of the eleven was given a jail sentence). That day the Young Men's Business Club had spoken out against the demonstrations, but at the same meeting the club voted to table a resolution expressing support of the school board. Then Governor Davis called on the people of New Orleans to stay calm. "I know feeling is running high in New Orleans," he said, "but I think it's timely . . . for me to suggest that the people restrain their emotions and above all things keep a cool head" (*Times-Picayune,* 1960*p*). That night, Willie Rainach, Leander Perez, and other segregationist leaders urged a mass rally of five thousand at the municipal auditorium to act. Rainach called for a scorched-earth policy (*Times-Picayune,* 1960*q*):

Bring the courts to their knees. . . . Let's empty the classrooms where they are integrated. A day lost can be made up; a week, a year lost is not fatal. . . . But once bloods are mixed, that is forever fatal.

But it remained for Leander Perez, the poet laureate of the evening, to provide the most stirring call to action. Calling for demonstrations against the NAACP, the Communists, the "Zionist Jews," Judge Wright, and "the real culprit, malefactor and double-crosser, the weasel, snake-head mayor of yours" *(Times-Picayune,* 1960*q*), Perez concluded:

Don't wait for your daughter to be raped by these Congolese. Don't wait until the burr-heads are forced into your schools. Do something about it now!

The next day the teenagers did something about it. A mob variously estimated at between one and three thousand swept through the New Orleans Civic Center and the state supreme court building, surged into City Hall, and then marched on the federal courts and the board of education building. Some New Orleans residents have tried to play down the events of this day and were irritated when we used the word crisis, but school board members and school staff admitted to being genuinely frightened at the sight of the mob steaming down Carondelet Street toward them. Pinney and Friedman (1963, p. 15) quote an account in the *Manchester Guardian Weekly* that described the mob as "the worst gang of thugs one has ever seen, even including some of the Mosleyites and the teddy boys of Notting Hill Gate." When the mob was turned away from the board of education building by police with fire hoses, it roamed through the business district throwing bottles and stones at Negroes in buses and cars.

That night Mayor Morrison went on television to call for an end to the violence. He stressed the damage that could be done to the image of New Orleans as "a thriving center of commerce and industry" if the "ugly irresponsible incidents such as took place today" continued. But it may not be surprising to add that Morrison also told his audience that his administration was still offering passive resistance to the Supreme Court. "I should like to repeat," he said, "that the New Orleans police department has not and is not enforcing the federal court order relative to school integration" (*Times-Picayune,* 1960s). He and the police, he explained, were only trying to maintain law and order.

After Morrison's talk, Negro teenagers went out on the streets seeking revenge for the stoning of Negroes during the day. It was a wild night. One Negro boy was charged with attempted murder for shooting at two white men downtown, one white man was shot by a roving band of Negroes, and many whites were attacked by Negro gangs. In all, police made 250 arrests that night, mainly of Negroes. The next day Morrison called a closed-door meeting of leading citizens to discuss the crisis. The meeting was attended by 160 business and professional leaders, who issued a statement calling on citizens to do their part to preserve peace and order. The statement, signed by most of the very top economic elite, commended the mayor, the police, and the city council for preserving law and order, and made absolutely no mention of the school board. Many others (including Superintendent Redmond) praised the mayor and his police superintendent for their "coolness" and their ability to prevent the spreading of the riots, but one has only to look at the police activity in Atlanta and other cities to see how attributes other than coolness can be used to prevent violence from getting started in the first place. The white demonstrators and troublemakers in New Orleans were justified in believing they were acting with the tacit approval and support of the community, the police, and the mayor. Neither the mayor nor the elite, in their calls for peace, had ever suggested that desegregation was not an intolerable disaster. Morrison told reporters and others the segregationists had the right to demonstrate at the two schools so long as they did not disturb the peace, but when they did disturb the peace, the police told the demonstrators that if they stood on someone's lawn instead of the sidewalk, the police would be powerless to stop them. When the police stopped one mob a block away from the school board office, a woman grabbed Police Chief Giarrusso and pleaded with him to let the mob continue: "Chief, help us, not the United States government." Giarrusso replied, "We'll help you if you do it in an orderly manner . . ." (*Times-Picayune,* 1960r).

THE PAYCHECK CRISIS

The state legislature and the governor apparently had learned that the school board had requested Wright to stop the legislative interference, for Risley Triche accused the board of complicity with the federal court and the NAACP, and on the first day of desegregation, the legislature addressed out of office the four "traitorous" members of the school board. The Louisiana Constitution permits the legislature to address out of office both elected and appointed officials "for any reasonable cause." The cause stated by the resolution was that the school board had created "a condition adverse to the best interests of the state of Louisiana and the parish of Orleans" (Pinney and Friedman, 1963, p. 14). By the time school opened the next day, however, Judge Wright had issued further orders putting the school board back in business.

The second special session of the legislature began on November 15, and the first act of this session was a concurrent resolution of both houses commending the parents who removed their children from the desegregated schools and pledging to them the support of the legislature in their "brave fight." Rumors spread quickly of impeachment proceedings against Judge Wright and criminal action against the school board. Lloyd Rittiner said that he expected to be arrested at any moment. What the legislature actually did was to declare all acts of the "now defunct New Orleans School Board" illegal and to warn all banks and businesses not to do business with, honor checks of, or make loans to the old school board. Further, they directed that the funds of the Orleans Parish school board be transferred to the legislature, and provided for a system of educational expense grants for children attending nonprofit, non-sectarian, non-public schools. It also fired Superintendent Redmond and Sam Rosenberg (again) for not disclosing the names of the Negro girls and the white schools they would attend. The charges of treason, applied to every legislator who dared even to question these bills, diminished the opposition to Davis' program. The tactics of Davis' floor leaders even forced Representative Landrieu to withdraw a modest resolution calling on state officials to use their influence to prevent violence and urging parents to express their indignation peacefully.

The attack on the school funds was by far the most menacing step the legislature had taken. In the previous school year (1959–

60) the state had provided almost $16 million of the school board's $28.7 million—55.6 per cent of the total revenue.[7] Of the remainder, 42.5 per cent came from local property taxes levied by the school board. Though it would appear that the legislature could thus hold up only 55 per cent of the school board's revenues, it could in fact hold up more than that, for the school board does not have the power to collect the local property taxes it has levied. These taxes are collected once each spring by the city. Consequently the board is forced each year to borrow money from banks to pay the operating costs for the school year, and the board cannot enter into these loans without state approval.

The immediately pressing need was a loan of $2,100,000 to meet the November 23 payroll. Not surprisingly, the State Bond and Tax Board refused to authorize the school board's request for this loan. One bank, the Whitney National, which continued to cash the school board's checks, was removed as fiscal agent for the state.

The schools were having other financial difficulties as well. In October, the board had had to reject a $10 million bond sale because the rates of the low bidder were the highest the board had ever received. A spokesman for the low bidder warned the board that the desegregation crisis might force them to pay even higher rates. The board rejected all bids and announced that its building program, already one year behind schedule, would be set back another year.

The financial pinch was so bad and the first week of desegregation had been so hair-raising that on Friday, November 18, the school board went before Judge Wright and asked him to delay desegregation until the state and federal governments settled the issue of sovereignty. This was the school board's thirty-ninth appeal of federal court orders. Sam Rosenberg told the judges (*Southern School News,* 1960):

From a practical point of view, the board is reaching a point that regardless of the orders of this court, we soon will be unable to operate. We are running out of money and the banks won't give us any. And rightfully so, probably—they don't know who's running the schools.

[7]Figures from New Orleans Department of Research, Census, and Planning (1960, p. 39).

The same day, the federal court heard two other requests, one by the plaintiffs in the *Williams* case for an injunction against further interference by the state, and another by U.S. Attorney Many for an injunction against state and local officials to prevent them from implementing the penalty provisions of the Interposition Act. The court took all three requests under advisement.

The state, sniping at the school board from all angles, got an injunction prohibiting integration on November 14 from the state court in New Orleans. But Sam Rosenberg was able to invoke a federal law to transfer this case to the federal court, where Judge Wright promptly nullified the state court decision. The state court refused to reactivate the case, and the Louisiana Supreme Court, on November 18, found the removal to the federal court improper but affirmed the lower state court's refusal to reactivate the case. This was the first setback for Davis in the state courts.

During the Thanksgiving vacation week, Leander Perez threw open the public schools of St. Bernard Parish to the pupils who wished to boycott the two desegregated schools in New Orleans. Six hundred students accepted the offer. The two desegregated schools had a total enrollment of 1,019 pupils, and in January, Redmond attempted to find out where they were. He discovered that 601 were in schools in St. Bernard, 132 were in various other public and private schools, and apparently 286 children were receiving no education whatever. The legislature later reimbursed St. Bernard Parish for the expense involved in educating the 601 pupils.

On November 22, Redmond announced that the school system could not meet its teacher payroll since its application for a loan had been turned down by the state, but on the next day the legislature authorized the payment of all Orleans Parish school employees except the administrative staff and the teachers at the two desegregated schools. The teachers at Frantz and McDonogh No. 19 were not paid until after Christmas.

On November 30, the three-judge federal court in New Orleans announced its decision on all the matters that had come before it during the month. The state attorney general rested his sole defense on the Interposition Act; the court ruled it and the rest of the legislature's package unconstitutional. Once again, the court enjoined over seven hundred state and city officials from interfering with desegregation. The district court turned down the request of the school board to have desegregation delayed. On December 12, the U.S. Supreme Court upheld the district court's decision (*Bush* v. *Orleans Parish School Board; Williams* v. *Davis; United States* v. *Louisiana,* 1960*b*). The decision of November 30, though by no means the last decision in the case, was the climax to the legal battle. With the collapse of interposition, the rest of the segregation package had nothing to stand on.

The battle between the federal courts and the state of Louisiana was now utterly predictable, and many were wondering when Davis and his floor leaders would cease beating the dead horse. In all, Governor Davis called five special sessions, extending all the way to February 26, 1961, but at each succeeding session fewer and fewer significant acts were introduced. The oratory in these sessions grew more heated, and the denunciations of Judge Wright, the Supreme Court, the federal government, and the school board grew more vehement, but after November 30, 1960, it was assumed that any act the legislature passed to interfere with the school desegregation would be struck down by the federal courts. In all the federal court decisions in the eight-year history of the case, there was never so much as a single dissenting opinion. Eventually, even the legislature revolted against Davis when he proposed, on December 17, a one-cent sales tax increase to finance the start of a grant-in-aid private school program.[8]

THE BATTLE AGAINST THE BOYCOTT

Perhaps because legislative interposition had failed, the street disturbances in New Orleans grew more intense after November 30. The real battle was now being fought in the streets of New Orleans.

At McDonogh No. 19 and especially at Frantz a crowd of housewives gathered daily. One indication of the ninth ward syndrome was the sign carried by one demonstrator: "If you are poor, mix; if you are rich, forget about it; some law!" The mob's main purpose was to harass the whites who were breaking the boycott. Two paragraphs from the Louisiana State Advisory Committee's

[8]This part of the story, centering on fiscal policy in Louisiana, is not fully germane to this study. For the interested reader, the story is documented by Pinney and Friedman (1963) and in the *Southern School News* (1961*a, b*).

(1961, p. 16) report to the United States Commission on Civil Rights effectively describe the street disturbances.

During the last days of November, Reverend Lloyd Foreman and Mrs. James Gabrielle, who had continued to take their children to the Frantz school, were subjected to abuse and physical violence by the mob in front of the school. This, coupled with the fact that several parents in the Frantz school area had appealed to S.O.S. for help in returning their children to school, led to the organization of a volunteer "carlift," run by parents from the uptown section of New Orleans, which transported the children to school in relative safety. The "carlift" began on December 1. The car carrying Yolanda Gabrielle was stoned and manhandled by the mob. Later in the week, it was pursued for two miles by a truck which had tried to ram it. Until Wednesday, December 7, the drivers and the women who escorted the children into the school were subjected to the vilest sort of shouted abuse from the daily-assembled crowds . . .

The parents were subjected to an organized telephone campaign of threats and abuse. Their houses and other properties were stoned, as was one of the mothers of a child at Frantz. The jobs of the fathers were threatened; four of them lost their jobs. . . . The volunteer drivers were threatened with death, arson, disfigurement . . . in a concerted telephone campaign. . . . With the exception of a couple of juveniles alleged to have stoned Mrs. Marion McKinley [mother of white children at Frantz], no one connected with the demonstrations was arrested, nor was the mob in front of the school dispersed or told to move on.

On November 29, press reports indicated that the police permitted a mob of four hundred to follow Mrs. Gabrielle and her daughter home from school. At home, their windows were smashed, but, according to the account of an SOS member (Wisdom, 1961), the family was unable to get police protection until "a wire service man called headquarters and promised to print a story on police indifference." Mr. Gabrielle, who worked for the city, was harassed by frequent reports given to him by his supervisor that his wife had been shot. Each time, as he went home to find her safe and then come back to work, he was told he couldn't keep his job if he was continually running home. Gabrielle finally resigned, and when he was unable to get another job, the Gabrielles left New Orleans in mid-December.

The high point of the back-to-school movement was December 6, when a total of twenty-three white children attended Frantz. The number was never again to climb that high, for at this point the Citizens Council renewed its efforts to enforce the boycott. A new wave of threats, stonings, and other harassments began and immediately pushed the number back to eight. Two families reported that their windows were broken nine separate times. Another parent, Everett Poling, removed his child after threats on his family and the slashing of his tires. On December 8, the Citizens Council distributed a list of all the volunteer drivers, describing their cars and showing their telephone numbers. This stopped the carlift. Starting with December 9, the federal marshals began transporting the white children who wanted to attend Frantz. But the pressure generated by the threatening telephone calls was too effective; the number of whites attending Frantz was kept at ten or fewer for the remainder of the school year.

As part of the campaign to perfect the boycott, Emile Wagner sued Redmond to obtain the names of all the pupils enrolled at Frantz. The state court ordered Redmond to give the names to Wagner (*Wagner* v. *Redmond,* 1960). But he did not get the names until February of 1961, when the Louisiana Court of Appeals affirmed the decision (*Wagner* v. *Redmond,* 1961).

The sidewalk in front of Frantz school had become an international spectacle with a huge press and television corps. Many national papers carried a running box score on the number of whites attending Frantz. The main attraction was a group of women whom the reporters called "the cheerleaders," who showed up each day to pass their latest press clippings around and lead the assault. John Steinbeck, who made a point of going through New Orleans in his "search for America," described the scene this way (Steinbeck, 1963, pp. 255–56):

The crowd was waiting for the white man who dared to bring his white child to school [Rev. Lloyd Foreman]. And here he came along the guarded walk, . . . leading his frightened child by the hand. . . . The muscles of his cheeks stood out from clenched jaws, a man afraid who by his will held his fears in check, . . .

A shrill, grating voice rang out. The yelling was not in chorus. . . .
The crowd broke into howls and roars and whistles of applause. This is
what they had come to see and hear.

No newspaper had printed the words these women shouted. It was indicated that they were indelicate, some even said obscene. On television
the sound track was made to blur or had crowd noises cut in to cover.
But now I heard the words, bestial and filthy and degenerate.

The words written down are dirty, carefully and selectedly filthy. But
there was something far worse here than dirt, a kind of frightening
witches' Sabbath. Here was no spontaneous cry of anger, of insane
rage . . . no principle good or bad. . . . The crowd behind the barrier
roared and cheered and pounded one another with joy. . . .

What does Steinbeck mean by saying that "there was something
far worse here than dirt?" Partly he is reminding us that what is
wrong is that this is civilized New Orleans—after watching this,
he adds, "I could no more have gone to Galatoire's for an omelet
and champagne than I could have danced on a grave." But the
other reason why this scene is incongruous (like a picture that was
"distorted and out of drawing") is that the mob was not acting out
of rage, it was merely a collection of housewives entertaining
themselves. And why shouldn't they? They were not doing anything illegal, as far as the police were concerned.

In November, Morrison blamed the street disturbances on
"outside agitators" such as Rainach and Perez. In December, he
found a new scapegoat—the press. The screamers were obviously
enjoying their press clippings and their performances on television, and Morrison claimed that the performance of the crowd
was purely for the benefit of reporters and television cameramen.
On December 4 he asked for a three-day moratorium on press
coverage of the school protests. This request, he said, "comes
from the heart of a public official who has spent most of his life
trying to build the economy and the good name of New Orleans."
He went on to explain that the "impression" of turmoil created by
the press coverage is bad for New Orleans business, "and it is a
damage that we are suffering *completely without fault on our part*"
(*New York Times,* 1960*f* [italics added]). When the reporters refused to stay away, he asked them to form a small pool to cover
the story. The reporters said they would form a pool if he would

reduce the number of demonstrators proportionately, but Morrison refused.

The question of whether the reporters were the cause or the effect of the trouble stirred our New Orleans respondents as did few other questions. The members of the economic elite whom we interviewed were vehement in their denunciations of *Time,* the *New York Times,* Huntley and Brinkley, and the press in general. If that rabble had kept out of our good city, they seemed to say, we could have handled our problems with a minimum of difficulty. The economic elite and other "moderates" told the interviewer they saw *Time's* newsmen and the television cameramen rehearsing the crowd on how and when to yell. An article in *The Nation* the following year by a reporter who had been there (Opotowsky, 1961) agreed with Morrison; he cited the New Orleans coverage as one of the many examples of newsmen, by their very presence, making the news. He believed that, had it not been for the reporters, the mob might have dispersed after its first outburst.

To the people who had to endure the hatred, the jeers, the stoning, and the loss of jobs, there was more than an "impression" of turmoil in New Orleans. The broken windows in the houses of the people who dared send their children to school attest to something much more real than Morrison and the economic elite were willing to admit existed. The windows were not broken in front of reporters, the men were not fired from their jobs in front of the television cameras, the threatening phone calls were not made to newspapermen. It seems very likely that the intense feeling of our respondents toward the reporters is simply a reaction to guilt. These men did not make any effort to stop the street scenes—now they would like to believe that they should not be blamed, that either the press exaggerated the story or else really caused the whole trouble.

This is a critical point in the New Orleans story. Morrison's attempt first to blame Rainach and Perez and then the press is part of his refusal to accept any responsibility for the school problem. ("We are suffering completely without fault on our part [*New York Times,* 1960e]." "My job is to maintain law and order . . . not to run the schools [Pinney and Friedman, 1963, p. 17].") Incredibly, he made these statements while street disturbances were keeping children from attending public schools in his city. His efforts were directed, not at stopping the trouble, but at keeping the press from reporting it.

In mid-December, with tourist trade off because of the bad publicity, rumors spread that the city's famed Mardi Gras would not be held. Morrison's action on this issue provides an interesting contrast to his non-involvement in the schools. First, he announced that that year's Mardi Gras (to be held in February) was definitely on, and, indeed, would be the biggest ever. To counteract the effect the unfavorable publicity might have on the Mardi Gras, Morrison wrote to all major cities saying that there was no friction in New Orleans and urging people to come to New Orleans.

Every year the first important Mardi Gras event is the "landing" and parade of the Zulus, a group of Negroes who wear blackface, hand out coconuts, wear grass skirts, and, in general, dress and act like savage buffoons.[9] With the Mardi Gras coming in the midst of white segregationist threats to the school system, many leading Negroes felt Negro participation in the Mardi Gras, and especially the Zulu parade, would be demeaning. Calvin Trillin, in an article in the *New Yorker,* describes the Negro efforts to boycott the Mardi Gras in general and to stop the Zulu parade. He reports (Trillin, 1964b, p. 42) that an advertisement in a Negro weekly in Louisiana presented a petition signed by 27,000 that read:

We, the Negroes of New Orleans, are in the midst of a fight for our rights and for a recognition of our human dignity. . . . Therefore, we resent and repudiate the Zulu parade. . . .

Under pressure from leading Negroes, the Zulus reluctantly voted to cancel the parade. Morrison was fearful that word of the Zulu cancellation would add fuel to the rumors that the Mardi Gras would not be held or give tourists the impression there was a possibility of racial strife in the city. When Morrison talked to the Zulus, they explained their own eagerness to have the parade but

[9]If the reader is bothered by this interpretation of the Zulus, he should recall that only seventy years ago the "Coon shows" playing in New York City included titles like Dat Watermillyon, and The Gentlemen's Coon Parade ("you'll find no common second-class nigs/in the Gentlemen's Coon parade" [Osofsky, 1963, p. 38]).

told him they feared hostile acts by both resentful Negroes and segregationist whites. Morrison and the police chief guaranteed the Zulus that they would be fully protected, and they were. A huge contingent of zigzagging motorcycle police kept the Zulus completely isolated from the audience that lined the route. A friend of Morrison's told the interviewer that Morrison thought it was a great joke on the Negroes and others who had criticized his failure to protect the white children who wished to attend Frantz school.

THE ELITE ACTS

In December, a page-one story in the *New York Times* under the byline of Claude Sitton was headlined "New Orleans Rift Takes Trade Toll." This fact, Sitton reported, was apparent in Morrison's public utterances and in the private remarks of business and civic leaders. Business leaders declined to speak for the record but privately estimated hotel and restaurant trade to be about 20 per cent off the customary rate. Hotel cancellations averaged higher than 25 per cent. One New Orleans executive said, "Canal Street merchants told me that their business for November—as of [November 25]—was the worst in memory, even including the depression," with sales down as much as 40 per cent (*New York Times,* 1960e). Sitton learned that business leaders were greatly disturbed, but most "reluctant to make any public attempt to resolve the problem apparently out of fear that this might bring economic sanctions from the Citizens Councils. . . ." The *Times-Picayune* did not carry this part of the story, and a New Orleans reporter told us that New Orleans newspapermen read out-of-town papers in order to keep up with economic developments.

Like Morrison, the *Times-Picayune* could be strongly provoked by any threats to the Mardi Gras. When the American Veterans Committee in New York suggested that tourists avoid the Mardi Gras while the turmoil in New Orleans streets continued, the *Times-Picayune* (1960t) in an editorial on December 14, called the A.V.C. a socialistic, bigoted organization. It continued thus:

Admittedly, New Orleans is caught in racial tensions. That, however, is a situation not of our own making. It was thrust upon us illegally and incited callously by extraneous forces that care not a whit what harm is done the city. . . .

The city has conducted itself commendably during these trying times and has preserved its dignity. . . .

But the economic pressures finally stirred the business leaders. On December 14, the same day the above editorial appeared, 105 business and professional men of New Orleans signed a three-quarter page advertisement in the *Times-Picayune* appealing for an end to threats and street demonstrations and for support of the school board. The ad said all the things that had been unsaid for four long weeks. Indeed, the ad said things that needed to be said before desegregation began; in other cities, such statements were made to prevent a crisis. It seems incredible that the elite did not forsee the economic consequences of the strife and lawlessness in their city. An article by Dykeman and Stokely (1960) quotes an unnamed southerner as saying:

Several months ago a business leader from Little Rock came to New Orleans to talk with some of the merchants and industrialists about the potential for damage to business that lay in this school situation. Many of the businessmen wouldn't even discuss the subject with him and the rest were very cool to the case he was trying to make for preparation to avert crisis.

At any rate, by December 14, they had learned for themselves, and the ad signaled the end of the economic elite's passivity.

The day after the statement by the businessmen, the Citizens Council held another mass rally in the municipal auditorium, but this one was poorly attended, attracting only one-fourth of the crowd that had attended the November 15 meeting. The statement of the businessmen was roundly denounced, and following the rally the businessmen began to receive threatening phone calls. At the rally, Dr. Emmett L. Irwin, chairman of the Council, brought to the stage seven little white children, four of them dressed in blackface. On signal, the children began kissing, and Irwin told the audience, "That's just a little demonstration of what integration means. Is that what you want?"

Many other problems remained unsolved. On December 22, the legislature adjourned without releasing funds for the salaries of four thousand teachers and other employees of the Orleans school system. December 23 was supposed to be payday. When the legislature adjourned, legislative leaders said that the various federal court orders had tied the hands of the legislature and made it impossible to release the funds. Some of these funds were released in January, but again not for Redmond, Rosenberg, or the teachers at Frantz and McDonogh No. 19. Federal court orders directed at various banks released some money. (Despite the earlier court orders directing the banks to release funds held on deposit, the banks had refused to honor paychecks written on these deposits.) A wealthy woman in St. Louis sent a considerable sum to pay the teachers at Frantz and McDonogh No. 19, and a wealthy woman in New Orleans contributed another sum to help with the salaries. In January, the new involvement of the businessmen provided another financial boost. With the State Loan Board still refusing to sanction loans in anticipation of local taxes, Mayor Morrison appealed to property owners to pay their taxes in advance (they were not due until June). Leading businesses, including the city's public utility and the newspapers, responded and paid in advance—one more sign that the business leaders were no longer content to sit and watch the school system get shot down. Nevertheless, the financial condition of the school system was still weak when the 1961–62 school year began.

As we noted, throughout January and February, the legislature continued to create new school boards for Orleans Parish, and Attorney General Gremillion continued to fire Sam Rosenberg. In January, the school board got a kick in the pants from yet another source. The Louisiana School Boards Association, of which Matthew Sutherland was the president, had voted in December to support the governor and the legislature in the school crisis. In January, two days before Sutherland's term as president of the Association was to expire, he and the three other moderates on the Orleans school board were ousted from the Association by a vote of 210 to 9. The legislature promptly passed a resolution thanking the Association.

All along, however, the board members and the superintendent believed that all their difficulties, bad as they were, could be handled if the mayor and the leading businessmen would only support the board's efforts. Throughout the troubled months, the women in CPE, IWO, and the League of Women Voters had worked unceasingly to involve the economic elite. It was the women who had obtained the signatures for the ad endorsing Sutherland and for the December 14 ad. On January 30, the efforts of the women, plus the financial difficulties of the downtown businesses, culminated in a huge testimonial dinner at the Roosevelt Hotel for the four board members and the superintendent. A total of 1,650 citizens came to the dinner to pay tribute to the sacrifices the school board had made to preserve public education in New Orleans.

One of the organizers of the meeting made a short address in which he said a recent *New York Times* editorial had asked, "Where are the southern moderates?" This gathering, said the speaker, is our answer; we are here. Introducing the main speaker, Harry Kelleher, a prominent attorney who is one of the top members of the economic elite, the master of ceremonies said, "If the face of the mob on Carondelet Street is our worst face, our speaker tonight represents our best face—the aspect with which we would like to face the nation and world at this time" (*Times-Picayune*, 1961). The things Kelleher said were incontestable. They should have been said in public long before then. But to hear a member of the elite say these things in public was like the end of a nightmare, "We are confronted now with the question of whether we believe our public school system is worth preserving. . . . We must consider whether we believe in due process of law . . . , and second, whether we believe in public education. This country and the South cannot afford to go backward." Citing the gallant fight (thirty-seven appeals to the courts) of the board to resist desegregation, Kelleher said the four men "have stood steadfast and discharged their full duty to us and to the children of this community. It behooves all of us to support these four honorable men. . . . We owe them our everlasting gratitude" (*Times-Picayune*, 1961). The relief and the exhilaration felt by the board members can be seen in the brief speech of thanks delivered by board member Riecke (*Times-Picayune*, 1961):

We believe . . . very strongly that the people of New Orleans elected us to the school board not only to administer business affairs of the school system but to improve and perpetuate public education in the city of New Orleans. . . .

We are going to do exactly that, come hell or high water. . . .

With the help of the taxpayer, and with the help of good citizens like you who are supporting us, we cannot fail.

One must recall, to get the significance of this public dinner, the atmosphere during the height of the crisis. One board member told us that old friends would pass him in church and furtively whisper to him, with their eyes averted, that he was doing a good job. He told these friends the best thing they could do for him would be to speak to him openly on the street, but this they refused to do. Another school board member told the interviewer two businessmen had phoned him during the height of the crisis and said they would like to meet him at a restaurant in the French Quarter and discuss ways of helping the board. He was overjoyed and replied that if he could just be seen having lunch with them that would be the biggest help they could give. But they were having none of that; they would arrive at a different time and meet him in a private room. At lunch, they offered to try to get the banks and the legislature to release the money needed for teachers' salaries, and they made a genuine effort to do so even though they failed. But the school board member was correct: what he needed most from them was a public affirmation of support. Only with that could the board begin to solve its problems. The behind-the-scenes talks were to no avail; the problems could not be solved until the governor, the legislature, and the mayor and people of New Orleans knew that the power structure of the city was standing firmly and openly behind the school board.

The January testimonial finally provided the needed public display of confidence and support. From that point on, though the boycott was still effective, though the school system's finances took another year to straighten out, the school board and the superintendent knew their problems, serious as they were, were manageable. The worst of the crisis was over.

16

Why New Orleans?

Why did violence occur in New Orleans and not in other cities? Several different kinds of explanations could be made. First, there is the "national climate" theory—that southern school integration took many communities to the brink of violence, and that, as school integration moved into the Deep South, some school system would go over the edge—if it had not been New Orleans, it would have been somewhere else. The three major crises—Little Rock, New Orleans, and Birmingham—were neatly spaced at three-year intervals. Does this suggest that 1960 was a year for trouble, and that New Orleans happened to be unlucky?

We do not believe this to be a useful explanation. First, the early incidents of violence—Sturgis, Clinton, Mansfield, and Little Rock—each occurred because of a new and unexpected factor, each demonstrated some new principle, and each set an example for other cities. From Clinton, police learned the danger of the traveling provocateur. From Mansfield, we learned that the state could intercede to prevent voluntary integration, and from Little Rock, we learned what lay in store for the state that tried to fight the federal courts. From Virginia, we learned that southerners would not tolerate disbanding the public education system, and that private schools simply would not work. But there was nothing new about New Orleans. No rational person could look at New Orleans and believe that school integration could be avoided by the same old mobs and pickets that had been used in Little Rock. Furthermore, people in New Orleans and Atlanta knew the price that Little Rock had paid in its unsuccessful attempt to find some way around the *Brown* decision. Nor can we accept the idea that New Orleans had to be violent just because it was the first city to desegregate in the Deep South. New Orleans had a history of desegregated colleges to accustom it to desegregation. In any case, even if 1960 was a time to expect trouble, this hypothesis

This chapter written by Morton Inger.

does not explain why New Orleans did so little to prepare for it, while Atlanta, which did not desegregate until 1961, was already taking steps to ease the process.

A second possible explanation for New Orleans is that the segregationist activity centered around mass demonstrations of great magnitude, which were beyond control from the start. This also seems implausible. If it were the case, then there are certainly many southern cities where segregationist opposition would be even greater, and the large rural areas of the South should have been consumed in a bonfire of segregationist activity.

A third possible explanation is a purely political one—that the political leadership at the state and federal level was responsible. At the state level, this at first seems quite plausible. We have seen that the state legislature passed a long list of rather ingenious bills. But it must be remembered that nearly all this legislation was voided by Judge Wright before it could have any lasting impact. The state was unable to compel the closing of the schools, to enforce the boycott, or to provide funds to support private schools for the boycotters (although they did reimburse Leander Perez' parish later).

In Louisiana the state was limited to little more than a harassing rear-guard action. We do not believe that this in itself would have been sufficient to create and maintain a year-long boycott. In addition, we should recall that the relationship between New Orleans and the state was a two-way interaction. Even when it became fairly obvious that the state legislature was trying to disrupt the New Orleans schools without any hope of actually preventing desegregation, the New Orleans delegation, Mayor Morrison, and other local political leaders made only a token fight. Georgia could have harassed the Atlanta schools in the same way (and Atlanta represents a smaller portion of the Georgia population than New Orleans does in Louisiana). Again, why New Orleans and not Atlanta?

Peltason, Muse, and others have noted that at various times the federal government was slow to take action to prevent school desegregation crises. We might apply this consideration in explaining the crises in other cities, but it is more difficult to apply it to New Orleans. The United States Justice Department could have entered the New Orleans case much earlier. But on the other hand, Judge Skelly Wright acted with astonishing speed in invalidating various efforts of the state to interfere. And federal marshals escorted the Negro girls to school every day and, beginning with the ninth of December, escorted the white pupils as well. The federal government did as much or more in New Orleans as it did anywhere else. Furthermore, the federal police role is by definition reactive—it could only appear after a crisis had begun.

Fourth, we can advance the hypothesis that the New Orleans crisis resulted from a chance accumulation of various factors and that there is no general explanation. This is the sort of explanation which reads: *if* New Orleans had not had Leander Perez next door, and *if* Morrison had not wanted to run for governor, and *if* the school computer had not picked out schools in Ward Nine for desegregation, and *if* Archbishop Rummel had not broken his hip, and so forth. While this explanation makes some sense—there is a good deal of chance in any action—it does not strike us as a particularly good explanation. The list of accidents is not so very long. Catholic schools do not always desegregate before the public schools do, so that cannot be the major factor; and we can find similar qualifications for the other *if*'s. Summing all the accidents does not give us the impression that 1960 was an unlucky year for New Orleans. And some of these accidents cannot be treated as mere chance occurrences. Recall that several of our informants claimed that they had opposed the use of the computer to choose white slum schools and had been overridden in the decision-making process.

One way to demonstrate that there was more than chance involved in 1960 is to contrast the behavior of the actors in 1960 with that in 1961, when the second year of desegregation began. In 1961 the school board again employed the computer. This time, when the computer again produced the names of slum schools for desegregation, the program was changed until the school board could get some schools that it wanted—in this case, schools in the silk-stocking area where support for desegregation was greatest. In addition, in 1961 the police were under orders to disperse crowds, rather than merely to prevent violence. Finally, the civic and economic elite in the city purchased an advertisement, calling for peaceful desegregation, before school opened. If we contrast this ad with the three statements made in 1960, we see that the civic elite was out in full force in 1961 for the first time. In the course of our interviewing, we asked twenty-two respondents to designate those persons most influential in local decisions. This yielded a list of fourteen men.

Table 16.1 reveals that the leaders signed the ad supporting Sutherland and the ad supporting peaceful desegregation in 1961, but they did not sign the ad calling for support of the school board in 1960. The contrast between 1960 and 1961 is clear. The 1960 ad supporting the school board did not come until December, when the boycott was two months old and business was hard hit, yet the ad still lacked the signatures of most of the top leaders.

The changed approach of the school board, the police, the mayor, and the civic elite in 1961 seemed to pay off. The newly desegregated schools had only minor difficulties, and the Frantz enrollment soared to 100 (out of a capacity of 575). Five Negroes and fifteen whites enrolled at McDonogh No. 19. The continuing boycotts at Frantz and McDonogh No. 19 are really not surprising; these children had been in other schools with little or no tuition, and for many of them there was no real advantage to transferring back.

We think that the events of 1961 indicate that the situation in 1960 was controllable and that something more than mere accident, or a coincidence of several accidents, caused the difficulty.

What hypotheses do seem to be reasonable explanations, then? First, we must consider that some of the difficulty arose because of the behavior of the school board. They maintained a head-in-the-sand attitude for over four years, when they could have been letting the public know that desegregation was coming. It was not until the beginning of July, 1960, that the board members decided to work to keep the schools open. Yet even during the school board election, as late as the first week of November, board members were pledging their full cooperation to Governor Davis if he could keep the schools open and segregated. Though the board held little hope for Davis' efforts (Sutherland cautioned the voters on the necessity of facing the issues "as they are, not as we would have them to be"), the board members nevertheless did not say

Table 16.1 Number of Signatories and Number of Leaders Signing Four Statements

Date	Statement	Number of Signatories	Number of Leaders (Out of Possible Ten)[a]	Comment
Nov. 7, 1960	Supported Sutherland's reelection[b]	98	6	Made no mention of desegregation or of school board
Nov. 17, 1960	Deplored violence[c]	160	7	Praised mayor for preserving law and order, but made no mention of school board
Dec. 14, 1960	Deplored violence and called for support of school board[d]	105	1	Boycott now two months old; Mardi Gras threatened
Aug. 31, 1961	Called for peaceful desegregation in compliance with orders of federal courts	315	9	Before school opened

[a] Of the fourteen who were mentioned twice, four are not included here. One was Leander Perez, one was the mayor (and mayors do not sign such petitions), one was the *position of president* of the Chamber of Commerce, and the fourth was a known liberal who was supporting the drive to get the signatures.

[b] The November 7, 1960, ad for Sutherland was markedly brief, giving no hint either of the crisis in the city or of the stand taken by Sutherland. It said, "We believe that we and our children will all have a better future if Matt Sutherland is reelected to the School Board."

[c] The November 17, 1960, statement praising the mayor for preserving law and order was issued at the request of the mayor and came the morning after riots and violence had erupted on the streets.

[d] The December 14, 1960, ad was the first call for the support of the school board by an elite body. The one top leader on the ad was the single most influential member of the elite.

flatly that desegregation was unavoidable. And on November 18, after the first week of desegregation, the school board once again asked the federal courts to delay desegregation. Although it is impossible to demonstrate, we think that had the school board acted earlier, the rest of the community would have had more time to make adjustments and begin to build a save-the-schools movement.

Second, the school board could have avoided the fiasco caused by their choice of schools to integrate. Even if we dismiss as mere Monday-morning quarterbacking the claims made by various respondents that they had expressed their opposition to the computerized selection, the fact remains that the school board had ample reason to know that there were more favorable alternatives. They had been invited to send Negro students to two silk-stocking schools, and they had rejected the invitation. They knew that their main support groups, SOS and CPE, had been unable to organize in the ninth ward. The school board members told us that they had refused to intervene in the selection of schools and had ordered the use of the computer because they did not want to have a part in deciding who would have to suffer integration. In other words, this was part of the syndrome: first refusing to believe that integration was coming, then refusing to draw a plan, so that Skelly Wright played school administrator in addition to his other roles in this crisis, and finally refusing to have anything to do with selecting the schools.

But the board did look for ways to build public support. First, the parents were polled to see whether they preferred "a small amount of integration" to closing the schools. The reader might object that the school board should have been telling the voters that schools would be open rather than asking their opinion, but we interpret the referendum as a shrewd maneuver to build support. On its face, it looks as if the "loaded" questions should have received a favorable response. Why did they not? The best explanation we can offer is that the questionnaire was administered too early.

The postcard questionnaires were sent out April 22, 1960. At that time there was simply no public discussion of the issue. It was not until May 16, 1960, when Judge Wright issued his decision setting the date for September, that the city became aware of the immediacy of the issue.[1] Six months later, after prolonged public discussion of the issue, Sutherland ran on a save-the-schools platform and won reelection. Of course he was an incumbent and had a well-organized campaign; even so, it seems hard to believe that an electorate deeply committed to closing the schools would have supported him. This leads us back to our initial point: the school board should have taken a public position earlier. Even if the initial reaction to their position had been hostile, an early stand would have generated earlier the kind of public discussion which eventually led to Sutherland's victory in November. Had the postcard poll been conducted after some public discussion instead of before it, Rittiner's faith in the attachment of New Orleans parents to the public schools might have been borne out.

Of course the school board received very little help from the other actors in the community. Morrison did nothing; the economic elite did nothing; even "the Girls" were slow to organize. The save-the-schools campaign reached its peak with the testimonial dinner, when the boycott was in its third month. The school board had made private overtures to all these people without success. This brings us to our principal hypothesis—that the New Orleans crisis arose from a general failure of community leadership, resulting in a breakdown of social control over the masses. The school board, the mayor, and the civic elite all shied away from taking action. To make a more general statement, we propose that the New Orleans civic elite has always been reluctant to become involved in local politics, and that this withdrawal contributed not only to the crisis, but also has tended to produce the kind of mayor, and the kind of school board that New Orleans had in 1960.

The civic elite's withdrawal from the school desegregation controversy is important primarily because these men have power and at the same time are much more insulated from public opinion

---

[1]Breed's (1965) measurement of space devoted to the issue in the *Times-Picayune* supports the word of our respondents on this point. In February of 1960 there was no space whatsoever devoted to the subject; in the first half of May there were only sixty column inches. But in the fifteen days following Wright's order, there were 320 column inches, and the number increased thereafter. In Atlanta, by contrast, the story was front-page news in 1958.

than are the elected officials. Their power takes several forms: they have the money with which to influence political campaigns and to influence public opinion, they have personal influence over many leaders in the community, and they hold the positions of highest prestige, especially in a southern city. Other people have power, but most of them are also vulnerable—ministers can be fired, politicians defeated, and anyone who is an employee can lose his job.

If the civic elite had decided early enough to support peaceful desegregation, they could have taken several steps. The *Times-Picayune* could have supported peaceful desegregation and the save-the-schools movement. An advertising campaign could have been conducted (Dallas businessmen, for example, bought advertising space on streetcars). The elite could have persuaded ministers to make public appeals for peace. Our respondents who were close to Morrison reported that he would definitely have made a public statement if he had had support from the top leaders. The businessmen could have made it clear to Morrison that they did not want—indeed, would not tolerate—street disturbances that would damage business in the city. In turn, Morrison could have had the police disperse the demonstrators and arrest those who resisted. (In Atlanta, police permitted no crowd to gather in front of the desegregated schools. The few who refused to move on were arrested and given jail sentences. That ended the loitering.) The top businessmen could have offered jobs and job security to those white parents who wanted to send their children to school. Many would-be demonstrators would have been deterred had they seen their employers listed as leaders in the save-the-schools movement. Above all, the economic elite could have let the board know that they could support them if the school board would begin the public discourse by taking an early stand. The economic elite, most of them supporters of Governor Davis, could have put some public pressure on Davis to stop interfering in the New Orleans school situation. Again, these are all obvious steps, which in other cities have ordinarily led to a chain reaction and to a strong community consensus in favor of peaceful desegregation.

Why did the New Orleans elite fail to act? The first and most obvious hypothesis is that there is a power vacuum—that leadership is diffuse, fractionated, and invisible and therefore difficult to coordinate. This does not seem to be the case, however. We asked twenty-two respondents (including school board members, other actors in the desegregation crisis, and those they named as community influentials) to name the city's influential men. We found a surprising amount of agreement. One man was named by twenty of the twenty-two respondents, and six of these respondents immediately named him as the single most influential person. Another man was named eleven times, two were named seven times, and one was named six times.

In addition, there is a strong grapevine connecting the top elites to one another. From the interview data available to us, we believe that a full-scale study would indicate that New Orleans has a power structure similar to that described by Hunter (1953) as existing in Atlanta. To some extent our sample is biased since it includes many respondents who were involved in school desegregation. But we do not think that the list of influentials consists of an elite specializing in race relations. The leaders identified by this listing include those responsible for the present efforts to attract industry to Louisiana. Most important, as we have already stressed, these men did not specialize in race relations; they were not involved in the school desegregation struggle. Although we did not systematically attempt to study other issues, we collected enough incidental information to indicate that the men listed as influential did have influence.

We find a similar pattern in two other racial issues. In 1963, Negroes were threatening to hold public demonstrations because they were not allowed to sit on the benches in the public park. The mayor (Schiro) refused to meet with the Negroes—he had a meeting to attend, he said. But the man who was at the top of our list of influential citizens called the mayor out of the meeting and ordered him to meet with the Negroes. The mayor did. In 1962, 1963, and 1964, Negro leaders made extensive efforts to get the mayor to appoint a public biracial committee to handle racial problems. Many moderates (including some of the elite) backed this proposal. The mayor let it be known that he would favor such a committee if he could get the backing and participation of the city's top influentials. But because two of the top men on our list opposed the formation of such a committee, no such committee was formed. (Meanwhile, the governor of Louisiana, elected originally as a segregationist, saw fit to form a state biracial committee; so now New Orleans is lagging behind the state of Louisiana in at least this one principal aspect of racial relations.)

Thus, not only do the men on our list have the reputation of being influential, but when they wanted the mayor to do something, he did it. When they opposed something the rest of the community wanted and the mayor was willing to go along with, it did not get done. When these men would not endorse peaceful desegregation, the city did not have it. And when these men backed peaceful desegregation, the city had peaceful desegregation. So apparently there is a power structure. But we hypothesize that the power structure does not want to wield influence in New Orleans.

First, there is a general withdrawal of the elite from politics. This may seem strange, since Morrison was elected on the basis of a reform vote and was generally seen as a reform mayor interested in economic development. And Morrison certainly had the support of the economic elite. But in contrast to other southern cities, the economic leaders did not play a prominent role in his election. He was not a candidate chosen by the elite, nor was he a member of their group. If the economic leaders had wished to recruit a candidate to run against Mayor Maestri in 1946, it is unlikely that they would have chosen Morrison. He was from the right section of town (the uptown silk-stocking section) and he had "good breeding"—he was the scion of a 150-year-old Creole family. But a handsome thirty-four year old playboy who moves in a fast crowd is hardly the type of candidate business leaders generally seek to represent their interests in the city government. One must keep in mind, in trying to understand why Morrison was drafted for the position, that no one else wanted to run and that Maestri was considered to be a shoo-in. No one, of course, knew what "the Girls" could accomplish. And no one knew what they were getting when they elected Morrison. What they got was a nonlocal, a man with a burning ambition to become president some day. With his city in crisis in the late 1950's and in 1960, Morrison was pursuing the governorship of a segregationist state and taking the stance that he thought would enhance that personal goal. By contrast, the mayor of Atlanta was completely a local with little time for anything but the city's business and no ambitions beyond the mayor's office.

Oddly enough, though Maestri was Long's man, the anti-Long business leaders seemed quite content with him and even praised the wisdom of those who declined to battle him. All it took was a little conservatism on Maestri's part to wed the anti-Long economic elites of New Orleans to the machine that, throughout the thirties, had plundered the city and destroyed self-government in New Orleans. The New Orleans economic elites withdrew from the political battlefront for two decades, until after Morrison was elected by the clubwomen.

The failure of the elite to play major roles in politics is equally pronounced in the school board elections. When the Independent Women's Organization began its drive to reform the schools, they were unable to find any man who would run for the board, and had to elect Mrs. Jackie Leonhard instead. Later on they were also to recruit men, but in general these were men active in the middle-class associations, rather than in the circles of the elite.

Related to this withdrawal from politics is the fact that the elite seem to have only a mild interest in such matters as economic development. The drive to develop the Port was spearheaded by Morrison, and one respondent remarked that in that effort Morrison brought the economic leaders together in a concerted campaign for economic development for the first time. It is of course difficult to know why New Orleans has been unable to attract new industry, but whatever the reason, New Orleans does not have a strong "booster" spirit or any strong organizations committed to attracting industry.

Without this strong interest in economic development, the proponents of peaceful desegregation could gain little leverage by threatening the elite with "another Little Rock." In Atlanta, the mayor hired a management consultant firm to produce a report on the failure of new plants to move to Little Rock, and the report was a best-seller among the elite. In New Orleans, a Little Rock businessman was brought into the city, only to discover that no one wanted to hear him.

Finally we arrive at the conclusion that, whatever the reason, the New Orleans elite is simply more traditional than the elite of Atlanta or Baton Rouge. In many ways, New Orleans is dominated by its old wealth. In an effort to pursue the implications of this, we asked six members of the civic elite—including three of the four men most frequently named as influentials—how long they had lived in New Orleans and how they felt about the city. Four of the six volunteered the information that their family had been in New Orleans for over a century. In response to the second question, two of them added that "money means little in New Orleans," and they unanimously praised New Orleans for its "way of life"—its "pleasant and gracious" set of social relations. If they were critical of New Orleans, it was only of the climate, and the one man who complained that the city was resistant to change was also the one man who was not named as one of the elite.

In some of these interviews, we brought up the subject of Atlanta and Houston—New Orleans' two rival cities. (In 1920, New Orleans was larger than Houston and Atlanta combined; if present trends continue, however, it will soon be the smallest of the three.) It was here that the comment that money was unimportant in New Orleans became relevant. The two rival cities are considered to be not truly southern; they are money-grubbing, ruled by the nouveau riche, and made repugnant by their brashness and boosterism, their lack of culture and civility. As one top influential put it, "Yes, but who'd want to live there?"

In cities like Atlanta and Houston, money and achieved status count for everything. But in New Orleans, being a native and coming from a good family count for everything. New Orleans is thus an anachronism—a traditionalist society in mid–twentieth-century America. We find attitudes in New Orleans which were prevalent in the traditionalist societies of the nineteenth-century South, the most obvious of which is a resistance to new ideas and new values. Since new values are brought in by new wealth and by outsiders, the economic elite of New Orleans is predictably not as hospitable to new industry as the elites in other southern cities. We saw a dramatic illustration of this point when we learned of some real estate speculators and contractors with ambitious plans for downtown New Orleans. They were either northerners or came from working-class origins, and thus they found New Orleans a very unfriendly city.

A second attitude inherent in the traditionalist ideology is aloofness from politics and governmental affairs. To the nineteenth-century capitalist, business was more important than government (unless he wanted to buy a city streetcar franchise). A third attitude typical of the southern traditionalist is so obvious that we might almost overlook it here—racial prejudice. We can report that the economic elite of New Orleans scored low on our civil rights liberalism scale. But we may find a more concrete example of the ramifications of prejudice in the elite if we recall that the *Times-Picayune* (whose publisher and editor were both listed as influentials) could not decide which would be a worse disaster— integration or closing the schools. Another of the top leaders refused to support the school board because the school toilets would be unsegregated.

There were three groups of people in New Orleans who had power that could have been used to prevent the breakdown of social control, and each of these groups used too little influence too late to prevent the crisis. The school board waited until the last possible moment to begin a campaign to keep the schools open, and even then they were hesitant to commit themselves. The elected officials kept a minimum amount of law and order and used little of their influence on the state legislature. The civic elite did not act at all on the issue of race until January, although it did lend its support to the Sutherland campaign. For each group there is an explanation: the school board was insecure and conservative on racial matters, Mayor Morrison had an eye on the governor's mansion, the civic elite was traditional and aloof from civic activity and politics. Furthermore, these are not three random factors that happened to coincide. The school board was weak because it did not include the first-line civic elite (such as those who serve in Columbus), the second-line elite (as in Montgomery), or even the third-line elite (as in Atlanta). If Morrison was ambitious, it must be added that only one who was ambitious would have been willing to undertake a last-minute campaign against the Maestri machine.

New Orleans is politically disorganized almost to the point of having a power vacuum. The one well-organized group with money, prestige, control over communications, and technical skill is the civic elite—and it has taken little more than a casual interest in city politics. The city had been reformed, true; but the most powerful political organization behind this reform was a collection of women's clubs.

17

The Correlates
of Peace

Up to this point, we have analyzed New Orleans as if it were a single case study, with only casual and unsystematic references to other cities. In this chapter we shall try to defend some of our hypotheses about New Orleans by making systematic comparisons between it and the other six cities in our sample.

In Chapter 14, we suggested that the typical southern school system that desegregated in the period after massive resistance tried to do four things: to delay desegregation, to avoid being labeled integrationist, to promote a favorable climate for peaceful desegregation, and to prevent intervention by the state. New Orleans does not differ very much from the other southern cities in our sample in two of these areas. It did attempt to prevent state intervention, and it delayed desegregation as much as possible. New Orleans does differ in its handling of the other two problems, however. First, the school board members went to greater lengths to maintain their reputation as segregationists. Second, the city failed to produce a local climate favorable to peaceful desegregation.

A MEASURE OF ACQUIESCENCE

We shall continue to call our main variable acquiescence, just as we did in our study of the North. But it should be clear that we are now studying a different issue—that acquiescence will be defined differently and will correlate with other variables in new ways. Acquiescence will have two components: first, willingness to desegregate (or willingness to take the risk of being labeled integrationist), and second, ability to mobilize the community to maintain law and order.

Among the three cities that were the first in their state to desegregate—Miami, Atlanta, and New Orleans—it seems clear that Miami was the most willing to accept integration and New Orleans the least so. Montgomery and Baton Rouge were both faced with the issue soon after disorder had resulted from desegregation in the first city in their state. Montgomery's suit was filed in 1964, and its school board did not appeal the first decision handed down. It is not clear whether Montgomery would have been successful in delaying desegregation by appeals, but in any case it did not bother and desegregated only a few months after the suit was first filed. Baton Rouge, on the other hand, delayed desegregation through a long series of appeals, so that it did not integrate any schools until four years after New Orleans. But Baton Rouge did mobilize a campaign to defeat the school board members who had been appointed when the board was packed by Governor Davis. Thus we would rank Montgomery as more willing to desegregate than Baton Rouge, and Baton Rouge higher than some other cities. Columbus and Jacksonville were faced with a much less difficult decision. Both cities desegregated late and were in states that had had no previous difficulty. Columbus was under instruction from the federal government to desegregate or lose a considerable amount of "impacted area" money. This was a relatively new situation in the South, and Columbus did not know precisely what the government would do if its bluff were called. Thus we could expect Columbus to stall a bit before surrendering. Jacksonville was less willing to comply; it managed to delay a court decision with repeated appeals.

It is difficult to put all this together in a rank ordering, but after considerable staff discussion, and a good deal more disagreement than we faced in ranking the northern cities, we produced the ranking shown below:

Willingness To Desegregate	First City in State	Second City in State	"Later" City
1	Miami		
2–3	Atlanta	Montgomery	
4–5		Baton Rouge	Columbus
6–7	New Orleans		Jacksonville

The ranking places those cities which had the most violence at the bottom. Columbus took only routine steps to prepare for integration, although the support of the county political leaders was recruited; Jacksonville mobilized very little public support; we have already seen how much difficulty New Orleans had. On the other hand, Baton Rouge, Montgomery, and Atlanta all went to considerable lengths to insure that desegregation would be peaceful. (Miami seemed to feel—correctly—that there was little danger of violence there, so its preparations were not as extensive.) All this indicates that we can treat acquiescence as approximately unidimensional—that whatever factors cause a school board to accept desegregation easily also lead to the successful mobilization of the community. Thus our final ranking will be: Miami most acquiescent; Atlanta and Montgomery tied next; Baton Rouge and Columbus tied for fourth place; Jacksonville sixth; and New Orleans seventh.

SCHOOL BOARD CHARACTERISTICS
AND ACQUIESCENCE

In the North, we found the best correlate of acquiescence to be the board member's attitudes toward civil rights and the civil rights movement. A similar scale of liberalism was constructed from interviews with thirty-nine southern board members, 65 per cent of the total number. As in the North, we made no attempt to interview most of the others; there were only a small number of refusals. As in the North, those board members who were not interviewed were rated on liberalism so that a median score for the entire board could be developed. Unfortunately, the staff's efforts to predict the liberalism of southern board members were much less successful than their predictions of the northerners—Q was only $+.52$ between the staff's ratings and actual scores. However, the actual scores on the attitude scale ranged over a wider segment of the scale, so the medians are still fairly reliable. The liberalism score ranges from 0 to 15; the medians for each board range from 11.5 in Miami to 2.0 in Montgomery.

The rank-order correlation between school board liberalism and acquiescence is a rather poor .44, indicating that liberalism has little to do with acquiescence in at least some of the cities. Of course, the obvious reason why liberalism is not a better correlate is that the school board is not autonomous in making decisions about desegregation; some of these boards were directly under the influence of political and economic leaders. But before turning to these influences, let us see how much we can explain by looking at two other characteristics of school boards.

Given the way we have described the problems confronting these school boards, it seems logical that civil rights liberalism is not the only important attitude variable. The school board that decides to press for peaceful desegregation need not agree that desegregation is desirable, but it must take considerable risk; it must be willing to alienate the "rednecks," to run the danger of social ostracism or even physical attack. This suggests that the attitude that we have called "conflict tolerance" will correlate with acquiescence. The two components of conflict tolerance are a willingness to disagree with one's constituency and a belief that disagreements are not simply a matter of misunderstanding.[1] Both these attitudes are correlated with liberalism, just as they were in the North. In addition, both seem to be characteristics of the kind of board member who would be willing to act to insure peaceful desegregation despite real or imagined personal risks. Such a board member recognizes the necessity of sometimes making unpopular decisions and the legitimacy of conflict and disagreement.

The third board characteristic that should correlate with acquiescence is socioeconomic status. In the North we found that board members of high status were more liberal. We also think that board members of high status are in less danger of losing their prestige (and hence are more willing to take risks) and are better able to mobilize community support for their position. Unfortunately we cannot readily test this hypothesis, because most of the school boards are very similar in social status. The boards of Baton Rouge and Jacksonville are obviously of lower status, but the other five boards are quite close to each other. The median incomes of the members of the five higher status boards are all

[1]The questions on which this scale is based are in agree-disagree form: (1) A politician's first duty is to represent the views of his constituency. (2) A school administrator's job is to give the community the kind of school system that the public wants. (3) If people really understood the issues, there would be no disagreement over school policy. (See Chapter 11 for the discussion of the scale.)

between $25,000 and $30,000. Most of these board members are attorneys, bankers, or businessmen; a few are physicians and dentists. Thus all five of the boards seem to be made up of men who are of fairly high status but generally are not influential outside the area of education. (Only Columbus has any members who are recognized as generally influential.)

With only seven cases it is difficult to unravel the interrelationships between conflict tolerance, social status, civil rights liberalism, and acquiescence. In Table 17.1 we present the rank ordering of the boards by conflict tolerance, socioeconomic status, civil rights liberalism, and acquiescence. In Table 17.2 we present the matrix of rank-order correlations between the four factors.

As Table 17.2 indicates, civil rights liberalism correlates poorly with the other three variables, while the other three correlate moderately well. Conflict tolerance, at the individual level, is a good predictor of liberalism; therefore we particularly expect the correlation between conflict tolerance and liberalism at the

Table 17.1 Ranking of School Boards of Southern Cities, by Conflict Tolerance, Social Status, Civil Rights Liberalism, and Acquiescence

City	Conflict Tolerance	Social Status	Civil Rights Liberalism	Acquiescence
Atlanta	1	1	2	2.5
Montgomery	2	4.5	7	2.5
Columbus	3	2.5	4	4.5
Miami	4	2.5	1	1
Jacksonville	5	6	3	6
Baton Rouge	6	7	5	4.5
New Orleans	7	4.5	6	7

Table 17.2 Rank-order Correlation between Conflict Tolerance, Social Status, Civil Rights Liberalism, and Acquiescence of School Boards

Scale	Social Status	Civil Rights Liberalism	Acquiescence
Conflict tolerance	.69	.24	.69
Social status		.51	.69
Civil rights liberalism			.44

With seven cases, a correlation of .71 is necessary to reach the 0.5 level of significance (one-tailed test).

board level to be very high. In reality, it is not. The apparent problem is that civil rights liberalism is affected by the culture of the region in which the city is located. In Figure 17.1 we plot conflict tolerance against liberalism, identifying the cities, and we see that the deviations are systematic. The two Florida boards are more liberal than we expected, the two Louisiana boards are slightly more liberal, the two Georgia boards more conservative, and the Alabama board much more conservative. The obvious explanation is that these four states vary in climate—Florida being most liberal, Louisiana next, Georgia third, and Alabama last—and that a board with a particular predisposition toward liberalism would be more liberal if it were transplanted into a more liberal state. If our hypothesis is correct, it explains why liberalism is such a poor predictor of acquiescence, for acquiescence was partly defined relative to state norms. Once we make this assumption, the other correlations become more plausible. The correlation between social status and race liberalism is only .51 (again with systematic deviations by state), and social status correlates reasonably well with conflict tolerance (R = .69). This suggests that some combination of liberalism with either conflict tolerance or social status would yield a better prediction of acquiescence. In Figure 17.2, we

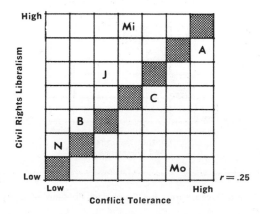

A–Atlanta; B–Baton Rouge; C–Columbus; J–Jacksonville; Mi–Miami; Mo–Montgomery; N–New Orleans.

Figure 17.1 Conflict Tolerance and Liberalism

show the plot of conflict tolerance and liberalism against acquiescence. Even here, with two of our predictors of acquiescence combined, the rank-order correlation is only .67.

These correlations are not very high, and we suspect that there is some other factor operating here. The figure suggests that we should consider the role played by the civic and political elite groups. The correlation would be perfect if it were not for Montgomery and Baton Rouge,[2] and these are the two cities where the civic elite's intervention in school desegregation was most obvious. The less autonomous is the action of the board, the less accurately do the board characteristics predict the outcome.

This brings us to our first hypothesis: that conflict tolerance, high social status, and liberalism are school board characteristics that produce acquiescence, to the extent that school desegregation is a school problem rather than a community-wide problem and that the board is autonomous in making decisions on desegregation.

[2]The remaining five are in the following order: Miami, Atlanta, Columbus, Jacksonville, and New Orleans, which agree with the acquiescence ranking.

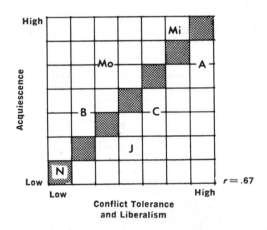

A–Atlanta; B–Baton Rouge; C–Columbus; J–Jacksonville; Mi–Miami; Mo–Montgomery; N–New Orleans.

Figure 17.2 Acquiescence and the Combined Ranking of Conflict Tolerance and Liberalism

THE INFLUENCE OF THE CIVIC
AND POLITICAL ELITE

So far, we have seen one reason why New Orleans had difficulty with the school desegregation issue; compared to the other cities in our sample, it had a school board that was more conservative (ranking above only Montgomery) and that scored lowest in conflict tolerance. The New Orleans board did move slowly and to some extent timidly, but this does not sufficiently explain the entire catastrophe. The board did make an effort. Meanwhile, the school board in Montgomery, which is also conservative, experienced no difficulty. While the civic and political leaders in New Orleans did nothing, those in Montgomery came in, uninvited, to make sure that desegregation came off smoothly.

Let us take a look at the seven cities again, this time concentrating on the role of the civic and political elite. There are two basic questions here. First, to what extent did the elite participate in the decision? Second, what was the ideological position of the elite?

Columbus

Columbus has the most traditional economy of all our cities. The major industries are locally owned and have been established for nearly a century. The owners and managers of these industries constitute a well-organized leadership group, which has considerable influence on local politics. The Muskogee County school board is appointed by the grand jury and is made up of men of uniformly high status. When asked to name the local influentials, four board members named thirty persons, and seven of these persons were school board members.

Race relations in Columbus are generally considered good, despite the fact that a leading civil rights leader was shot to death in Columbus a few years ago. The power structure of the white community is mirrored in a group of five Negro civic leaders, so that many civil rights issues are handled through contact between these two groups. Columbus has never had a strong direct-action civil rights movement.

In the school desegregation issue, the most important fact about Columbus is that it is the site of the huge Fort Benning army base. During the first part of 1963 the federal government began pressing for desegregation of impacted areas. First, the Justice Department prepared to file suit and let a copy of their brief get into the hands of the school board. Second, the Department of Health, Education, and Welfare sent a representative to meet with the board and inform them of the federal government's intention to construct a high school on the military base and withdraw military children (and therefore federal funds) from the school system if it did not desegregate. The school board representatives agreed to desegregate in September of 1964—fifteen months after the meeting. During the next three months, the board leadership persuaded the other members to support desegregation, and a plan was unanimously adopted in September, 1963.

It is hard to know how much choice the school system had. It could have accepted the loss of federal funds. Or it could have attempted to delay desegregation further, although it is unlikely that such a delay would have had much success.

The Muskogee County school board, with its excellent ties to a strong civic elite, had little difficulty maintaining social control during desegregation. It also had little difficulty dealing with non-legal federal intervention, a situation which was relatively new in the South. On the other hand, the Columbus school board was very reluctant to desegregate and delayed action for what would seem to be the longest period of time possible. The most plausible explanation for this is that the Columbus civic elite is more tradition-oriented, and more strongly opposed to integration, than the elite in some of the other cities.

Jacksonville

Jacksonville did not desegregate until 1963—four years after Miami, and after eight smaller school systems in the state had done so. The court suit was not pushed aggressively, and the board took every delaying action possible. When desegregation came, the board took some limited action to insure peaceful desegregation. When one Negro mother sought to send her child to a "cracker" school, the school system attempted to dissuade her, without success. Her home was then bombed. This was the only incident of violence.

There are interesting similarities between the Jacksonville and New Orleans situations. In both cases, the school board resisted integration as much as possible and wished to avoid taking an active role in insuring peaceful desegregation; and in both cases the political and civic leaders stayed clear of the school desegregation issue. Indeed, we have the impression that if Jacksonville had been the first city to desegregate in Florida, and if the Florida state legislature had attempted to intervene, the crisis might have been worse there than in New Orleans.

If we examine the Jacksonville school system and its relationship to local politics, we see immediately why the school board played a passive role, and why the city does not have the sort of civic elite that Atlanta and Montgomery have.

Jacksonville's government has a certain flavor of the late nineteenth century about it. There is a very weak civic elite in the city. Despite several reforms, the government retains an archaic, formal structure. For example, in 1964 the following bodies were involved in school decision-making: the school board, composed of five members elected from wards in partisan elections; the superintendent of schools, who was also elected on a partisan ballot; and the board of school trustees, composed of three members elected at large (partisan). After these three bodies prepare a budget, it is approved by the county budget commission and then by the county commissioners. Non-instructional employment is handled by the city's civil service commission, which is also an elected body. In addition to this complex structure, the electorate is politically immature. For example, when one of the school board members ran for the assessor's office on a platform of raising taxes, the Negro vote (traditionally a source of support for increased taxes in the U.S.) was delivered to his opponent.

Although the recently reformed Duval County school board was moderately liberal, it had relatively little influence over political leaders and, because the superintendent was elected, little influence over the school system itself. In 1965, the financial difficulties of the schools became so intense that the schools lost their accreditation. Following this the school board was enlarged, the superintendency was converted to an appointive post, and a general reform of the tax-assessment process was begun.

There are several possible explanations for the unusual political structure of Jacksonville. One is that Jacksonville has been for many years a major railroad center, and the railroads are heavily committed to maintaining low taxes. Several respondents felt that the heavy intervention of the railroad interests in local politics was a fundamental factor in maintaining Jacksonville's political style.

New Orleans

There is no point in repeating our previous discussion of New Orleans, except to note several points. First, the school board is a reform board, but the reformers were not directly part of the civic elite—the Girls draw much of their strength through voluntary organizations, rather than through the direct use of community prestige. There is a clear civic leadership group, but it proved to be quite conservative on racial matters. Consequently, New Orleans did not form a public biracial committee, and the civic elite did not lend their support to efforts to keep the schools functioning.

New Orleans, like Jacksonville and Columbus, has a traditional elite. In Columbus this has resulted in a patrician control of government, but in New Orleans and Jacksonville it has led to a bifurcation between the elite as a class and politics, which is mass-based.

Montgomery

Montgomery tends to have a tradition of mass politics, but it is not as extreme as either New Orleans or Jacksonville. Several members of the school board have ties to the civic and political elite, but the elite is not generally able to control all the school board seats or the mayor's office. The main division in local politics is between the high status South Side and the low status and rural East Side. The economic leaders have had relatively little influence on race relations, with the result that race relations have not been very good in Montgomery. The city became famous first for the long bus boycott, then as the scene of the mauling of the freedom riders who attempted to integrate the bus station.

Finally, attempts to integrate the city parks led to their being closed down. One of our informants, a prominent businessman, commented that the government "listened to advice from the wrong persons" when it closed the parks. In 1964, however, Montgomery had learned its lesson, and several prominent businessmen organized a biracial commission. The white members of the commission in effect took charge of school desegregation. All three of the city commissioners (including the mayor who had closed the parks and the police commissioner who had been accused of permitting the freedom riders to be attacked) served on the biracial commission. Under the leadership of the business elite, a very thorough campaign was undertaken to insure peaceful desegregation, and Montgomery received favorable national publicity for its efforts.

Atlanta

Atlanta has earned a reputation as the leader of the new South. It is frequently said that the main reason for Atlanta's achievement is the successful coalition of the business leadership and the Negro voters against the "rednecks" and the state legislature. While Atlanta may not have as definite a power structure as New Orleans, it is considerably more visible. In one interview, a leading governmental adviser answered our query for the names of influentials by asking his secretary to "bring in the power structure list." In part this is self-consciousness due to the existence of Floyd Hunter's study of the city, but it is also a reflection of the political style. The school board was reformed in the late 1950's, and new board members were elected and a new superintendent hired. The board members represent the interests of the civic elite but are not in themselves top influentials in the city; consequently the schools did not receive much attention from the elite until desegregation. The school board delayed desegregation through appeals until 1961, but it was still the first city to desegregate in the hard-core area of Mississippi, Alabama, Georgia, and South Carolina. Although the inside story of who influenced whom is unknown, it seems clear that Atlanta business leaders and Mayor William B. Hartsfield were in close contact with Governor Ernest Vandiver, who was a committed segregationist.

The result was the appointment of a commission, headed by Atlanta banker John A. Sibley, which lobbied successfully throughout the state for "local option"—meaning in this case that the state would not interfere in Atlanta's school system. This was the major hurdle. In addition, Atlanta citizens had already organized HOPE (a save-the-schools committee similar to SOS of New Orleans, but with more influence), and the police, clergy, and Chamber of Commerce all committed themselves to preserving the peace.

All this fits with Atlanta's basic orientation toward race relations, which springs from the attitude that good race relations are necessary in order to attract new industry. (Atlanta leaders usually express this by saying "we are too busy to hate.")

Miami

Miami desegregated voluntarily, although a suit was in court at the time. Governor Collins had privately urged several Florida school boards to desegregate in order to prevent the courts from deciding that the state pupil placement law was meaningless and ruling it illegal, but none of the boards agreed to do so. However, in 1957, the Miami school board was expanded from five to seven members, and the governor, who makes appointments to vacancies on the Miami board, appointed two moderates. Governor Collins appointed one other moderate before desegregation, and after desegregation one of the seats was captured by a committed liberal, apparently with Collins' blessing.

Thus we see that Miami resembles a northern board in that the board is autonomous but with its political outlook determined by the appointment process. The board has close ties to liberal members of the civic elite, but the elite seems to be more pluralistic in structure than in the other southern cities.

Baton Rouge

Much of what was said about Atlanta applies to Baton Rouge as well. The city is in the midst of an economic boom, and the business leadership of the city is committed to maintaining economic growth. The state legislature attempted to prevent integration by enlarging the school board from seven to eleven members. The four new members were appointed by the governor and were die-hard segregationists. They served until the next school board election, at which time a revolt was organized, and these members were defeated and replaced by four men committed to keeping the schools open. The Baton Rouge representative who had introduced the bill to pack the school board was also defeated by a combination of Negro and middle-class white votes. This was the last effort of the state to interfere with the school desegregation issue in Baton Rouge. In March, 1963, the board was ordered to desegregate. On April 4 a declaration of principles entitled "The Law Is Clear" was published in the Baton Rouge *Morning Advocate*. The paid advertisement bore four hundred signatures, including most of the business, professional, and labor leaders, and made a direct appeal for peaceful desegregation in order to maintain the economic boom. At the same time, a biracial commission was formed. Like the commission in Montgomery, and unlike that in New Orleans, it was a public body. The white members of the biracial commission have close connections to the men who would probably be designated as top influentials in Baton Rouge.

INTERPRETATION

Admittedly, we have dismissed many factors in presenting this brief comparison, but we think that we have seen, as we did in the North, that the civic elite is an important factor. In the North, city government is more pluralistic, and the civic elite has relatively little direct influence on school integration. However, in these southern cities (with the possible exception of the two cities in Florida) it is relatively easy for the economic leaders to exert a great deal of influence on this decision. In part this difference between desegregation in the North and in the South is a difference in the nature of the issue. Southern school desegregation involves a single decision, with a narrow range of alternatives. But there is also a real difference between the structures of the northern and southern cities. In none of the northern cities would a respondent produce a power structure list.

Thus the question is not can the elite influence the desegregation decision, but does it want to do so? The answer seems to be quite simply that these elite groups differ in ideology. Recall that in the North, we talked about a common denominator—peace, prosperity, reform, and welfare—around which the elite in any city could unify. The implication was that an executive could move from one city to another and be immediately at home in civic affairs. This is probably not the case in the South. One New Orleans leader made it clear that he felt that Atlanta was pursuing false values in throwing away the traditions of the South to make money. The New Orleans leadership is a group which would constitute the society rather than the civic elite in a northern city.

Another way the difference in the values of these southern cities appears is in the integration of the city into state politics. Atlanta makes no bones about its permanent conflict with the state. An Atlanta mayor would not consider for a moment the possibility of running for governor, nor would he have much chance of election. But mayors in both New Orleans and Jacksonville have run for the governor's office. A mayor cannot represent the interest of a major city which is concerned with economic development and at the same time accept the traditional southern values and develop the rural and small-town support necessary to run for a state office. Of course, if New Orleans were completely traditional in outlook, there would have been little objection to Morrison's running for governor. But a group of New Orleans leaders did attempt to dissuade him. (This group was nicknamed "the Coldwater Committee.")

Unfortunately, we do not have the data necessary to rank the cities in the traditionalism of their civic elite groups, and we will only divide the cities into three broad categories. Columbus, Jacksonville, and New Orleans fall on the traditional side, since family background plays an important role, and interest in economic development a less important role, in the activity of the elite. Miami, Baton Rouge, and Atlanta, on the other hand, are cities with a developing or modernizing elite. Montgomery does not fall definitely into either category, and we shall leave it in an intermediate cell. The access which the elites have to the school board is a less important factor; it can be roughly measured by simply taking the socioeconomic status of the board: the higher the status, the closer the board's ties to the elite. In Table 17.3 we have ranked the cities by placing the modernizing elite cities at the top and the traditional elite cities at the bottom, and then, within each group, placing the boards of higher status at the top. We shall refer to this variable by the cumbersome title "elite ideology and influence." As Figure 17.3 indicates, this seems to be a better predictor of acquiescence than any of the school board characteristics that we considered earlier.

This brings us to our last question: Can we determine any factor that will predict whether a city will have a modernizing or a traditional elite? The answer is that we can, but the factor is a trivial one; modernizing cities are experiencing economic growth, while traditional cities are not. The census provides us with two measures of development. A growing economy will require a growing labor force and will tend to attract better-educated workers.

Table 17.3 Ranking of Cities, by Elite Ideology and Influence

City	Ideology	Status Rank
Atlanta	Modernizing	1
Miami	Modernizing	2.5
Baton Rouge	Modernizing	7
Montgomery	Intermediate	4.5
Columbus	Traditional	2.5
New Orleans	Traditional	4.5
Jacksonville	Traditional	6

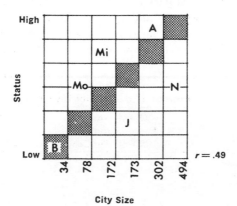

A–Atlanta; B–Baton Rouge; J–Jacksonville; Mi–Miami; Mo–Montgomery; N–New Orleans.

Figure 17.3 Size of City and Social Status of Elected School Board (1940 Population, in Thousands)

These two measures—the growth rate of the metropolitan area and the educational level of the population—are given in Table 17.4.

The two Florida cities have quite high growth rates, of course, but even here Jacksonville's is much lower than Miami's. Since many of these new residents are not members of the labor force, or are employed in servicing retired persons, Jacksonville's growth rate does not necessarily indicate a large increase in industrial employment. Montgomery's high educational attainment, like that of Baton Rouge, is partly a reflection of the number of government employees—both cities are state capitals. However, even if this were corrected in some way, it is unlikely that the educational level would drop to that of New Orleans or Columbus.

CORRELATES OF BOARD RECRUITMENT PATTERNS

We have one additional question that should be raised: What are the community characteristics that produce liberal, conflict-tolerant, or high status boards? Unfortunately we do not have a good answer to this question, but we can make the following points: Columbus, the only appointed board in the sample, is high in status and in conflict tolerance. If it is not as high in status as Atlanta's board, this is partly because even the top elite of a small city like this one may not hold extremely high economic positions, and partly because it is a large board with a rural representation. While we do not have data on other cities, it seems likely that

Table 17.4 Growth Rate and Educational Level of the Southern Cities

Classification of Elite	Growth Rate of Metropolitan Area, 1950–60 (Per Cent)	Education (Median Number Years of Schooling)
Modernizing:		
Baton Rouge	45.5	11.9
Miami	88.9	11.5
Atlanta	39.9	11.1
Intermediate:		
Montgomery	21.8	11.2
Traditional:		
Jacksonville	49.8	10.8
Columbus	27.8	9.6
New Orleans	26.7	9.5

most southern appointed boards would be influenced by the elite. Few southern cities have political parties strong enough to make the appointment of low status professional politicians possible. The southern cities resemble the two west-coast cities in our northern sample, in that there is no sharp distinction between professional politicians and the civic elite. Thus, even if appointments were made on a strictly partisan basis, they would probably include some persons of high status, as Lawndale's board does.

Suppose, then, that we drop Columbus from the sample and look at the six elected boards. In general, large cities tend to have boards of higher status: the correlation is .49. (In order to allow for the stability of political style and the fact that school board candidates are usually middle-aged with long-term local residence, we have used the 1940 population.) The two large cities of high status are Atlanta and Miami, while the two large cities of lower status are New Orleans and Jacksonville. Both Atlanta and Miami have reformed their school boards in the last decade, replacing appointees of lower status with persons closer to the civic elite. In addition, both cities have what we have called modernizing elites. In contrast, although New Orleans and Jacksonville have also undergone reform, in neither case were their resulting boards of particularly high status. The reformers in New Orleans and Jacksonville slated businessmen who had organizational involvements that would give them grass-roots political support, but who were not intimately connected with the civic elite (there are exceptions, of course, but this is the general pattern). In Atlanta the original reform movement included top leaders, and the reform resulted in appointees of high status; later, these same leaders backed the schools during a successful desegregation campaign. We should recall here that the original reform in New Orleans was led by that peculiar political body called the Girls, whose contacts with the elite were more limited; the movement had its base in the middle-class grass roots. The result was a board quite different from Atlanta's, with members who were of slightly lower status, were not as closely tied to the elite, and showed less conflict tolerance.

This suggests that three factors explain the presence of a board of high status: city size, the presence of a modernizing elite, and whether the board is appointed or elected. After excluding Columbus (the appointive board) and combining elite ideology and city size into one scale, our rank-order correlation with status is .70 and our rank-order correlation with conflict tolerance and civil rights liberalism combined is .77. Thus we do have at least a partial explanation for the differences in the school boards.

SUMMARY

In the North we saw that the school desegregation issue was complex and ambiguous, that the school board tended to be autonomous, and that community characteristics tended to affect the outcome of the integration issue only through the way they affected the recruitment and organization of the school board. The particular school desegregation issue that occurred in New Orleans—desegregation as required by a federal court order during what we called the post–Little Rock period—was in some ways a much simpler issue. It was (or should have been) clear to the participants that the schools were going to be desegregated. A decision made by a southern school board during this period was not a decision at all. In addition, the issue was of such overriding importance that it is hardly surprising to find that the more influential community leaders took control, directly or indirectly, in several of our cities. All this would make southern school desegregation a dull issue, if it were not for violence. In 1965, when the number of Negro students in desegregated schools jumped markedly without violent repercussions, there were few newspaper headlines.

For these reasons, our analysis has produced a set of factors in explaining the way different communities handled integration in the South which is quite unlike the factors we produced for the North. In the North, we saw evidence that higher status communities, because of their less tightly organized decision-making processes, were less likely to acquiesce to Negro demands. In the South, white collar cities were more likely to desegregate efficiently, because, we think, such cities are the ones with the most new industry and the most interest in economic development. These are the cities with strong school boards and with the most progressive elites.

Despite the fact that the southern issue was simpler—or perhaps because of it—we did not succeed in presenting as satisfactory an explanation of community differences. The partial explanation that we have offered is shown in Figure 17.4. The rank-order correlations shown in this flow chart indicate that the ideology of the civic elite is the dominant factor in determining whether the city will acquiesce peacefully to the desegregation order, and that the composition of the school board is less important. As in the North, higher status boards and liberal boards are more acquiescent.

In a larger sense, there is a parallel between the northern and southern analysis. In both cases we found a general relationship between political style and the outcome of the school desegregation issue. Although we are unable to pursue this problem in the present research, there seems to be reason to expect that this same political style will show up in comparative analyses of other issues.

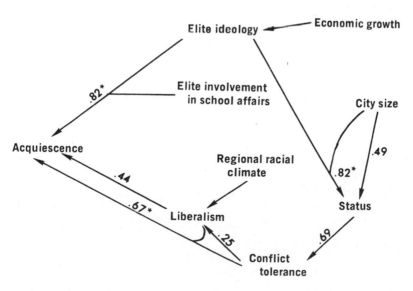

*Combined ranks of two factors.

Figure 17.4 Rank-order Correlations for Seven Southern Cities

Part IV

The Community and the Civil Rights Movement

18

The Civil Rights Movement
in Northern Cities

Up to this point, we have said very little about the civil rights groups in the fifteen cities which we studied. Mainly, this is because their action is of little relevance to the task at hand—explaining differences in community action on school desegregation. In the North, the civil rights movement has little power to get its will, and whether it is fiercely militant or carefully moderate is of little importance to the overall outcome. In the South, the burden for initiating litigation rests on the movement, but almost any southern city can put together a handful of plaintiffs, a lawyer, and a small amount of money for a suit. In many southern cities, school desegregation becomes the province of a small group of men, while the greater part of the movement goes on to other issues.

Despite the fact that it is not directly relevant to the issue, our attention was repeatedly drawn to differences among cities in the structure and style of the civil rights movement. Some cities are much more militant than others; some seem to have different goals from others; and some have harmonious movements while others seem badly fragmented. While we were not able to undertake the sort of study of these differences that is needed, our interviews with the top civil rights leaders in these cities do suggest some factors that might account for these differences. The next two chapters review our findings, first for the northern cities, then for the southern ones. It is unfortunate that we do not have the data to permit a thorough analysis of the civil rights movement. In many ways, it is as fascinating a topic as is the school board; and we present these two chapters in the hope that it will encourage

First draft by Gerald A. McWorter.

others to undertake the large-scale comparative study which is needed.

We have already observed (in Chapter 10) that a resistant school board provokes civil rights activity; but we also saw that a good deal of the variation in civil rights activity was not accounted for by the behavior of the school board. Civil rights movements vary in that some were more anxious to demonstrate and were able to mobilize the community for demonstrations, while others were reluctant to demonstrate and less succcessful in doing so. Our first task is to develop a ranking of the cities on their willingness or ability to take direct action.

Civil rights activity falls into four general categories, which can be conveniently summarized in a 2×2 table (Table 18.1). First, action can be taken either through formal and regular channels for protest, or it can be taken in the form of extralegal or even illegal demonstrations; second, the action can be merely expressive, designed to call the school system's attention to the demands or develop public support for them, or it can involve sanctions brought against the board, either by the use of legal authority or by embarrassing or inconveniencing the school system. There are some fine lines here, of course; a public march through the central business district can be merely expressive if it is held on Sunday afternoon; it can involve the use of sanctions if it winds up snarling rush-hour traffic or discouraging shoppers. Table 18.1 indicates the four types of action with examples of each.

In Table 18.2 we have listed the eight cities, commented on the amount of action taken under each of these headings, and

Table 18.1   A Typology of Civil Rights Activity

Type of Protest	Channels of Protest	
	Formal	Extralegal
Expressive	Action designed to publicize grievances: reports, speeches, testimony at board hearings	Action designed to publicize grievances using direct-action techniques: marches, demonstrations, rallies, vigils
Sanctioning	Action designed to compel schools to act: suits, petitions to state or federal authority	Action designed to inconvenience or embarrass system: inconvenient street demonstrations, boycotts, sit-ins

Table 18.2 Civil Rights Activity Ranking

City	Activity (Score in Parentheses)					Total Score	Acquiescence Rank	Net Score (Propensity To Act)
	Formal Expressive (Testimony, etc.)	Formal Sanctioning (Suits, etc.)	Extralegal Expressive (Demonstrations)	Extralegal Sanctioning (Boycotts, etc.)	Other			
Bay City	Noisy (3)	Suit filed (2)	Sit-ins, marches, vigils (4)	Two boycotts (6)		15	7.0	8.0
Buffalo	Somewhat noisy (2)	Petition to state (2)	Small demonstration (1)	One boycott, one unsuccessful boycott (4)(0)		9	5.0	4.0
San Francisco	Somewhat noisy (2)	Two suits filed; one settled (3)	Sit-ins, picketing (3)	–		8	3.0	5.0
St. Louis	Somewhat noisy (2)	Out of court; one suit filed (2)	Large demonstration (2)	One small boycott, one threatened (2)		8	2.0	6.0
Newark	Some noisy, but some quiet (1)	One suit settled out of court (3)	Demonstration at one school (1)	One small strike (2)		7	4.0	3.0
Lawndale	Somewhat noisy (2)	Suit threatened (1)	– (0)	– (0)	Election campaign	7	6.0	1.0
Baltimore	Quiet (1)	One suit threatened (1)	– (0)	– (0)		2	0.5	1.5
Pittsburgh	Quiet (1)	–	– (0)	– (0)		1	0.5	0.5

Note: Formal expressive scores range from 0 to 3; "noisy" refers to testimony that is provocative and backed with delegations, etc. Formal sanctioning ranges from 0 to 4; a score of 4 would be given to a suit that is carried all the way through court. Buffalo received only a score of 2, since a petition to the state requires less local effort. Extralegal expressive ranges from 0 to 4 and is based upon the extensiveness of activity. Extralegal sanctioning refers only to school boycotts in these data; a score of 3 is given for each city-wide boycott, and a score of 1 for each localized boycott. Newark receives a score of 2 for its "strike," where the students did not return to school until the issue was settled.

assigned a numerical value to the amount of action; the sum of these four numerical scores is a rough indicator of the total amount of civil rights activity. However, this does not give us a good measure of propensity to take action, since much depends upon whether the school system has provoked action by refusing to acquiesce. Ideally, one should use regression procedures to control for this, but as usual the quality of our data and the number of cities involved makes sophisticated techniques rather inappropriate. What we have done is to list in the next to last column the rank of the city on the acquiescence scale, beginning with 0 for the most acquiescent city and ending with 7, and subtract this rank from the action score; the result gives us a measure that is primarily dependent upon the amount of civil rights activity, but that compensates slightly for school system acquiescence. (The introduction of acquiescence does not affect the final scores very much.) We shall call this "propensity for action."

Approximately four civil rights leaders who had been involved in the school issue were interviewed in each city. In large measure it was up to these men to decide when the movement would take action, and therefore we would expect to find that the patterns of action in each city are mirrored in the attitudes of this leadership. This proves to be the case.

The most commonly discussed attribute of civil rights leaders is militancy. An agree-disagree attitude questionnaire was administered to civil rights leaders, similar to the one used for school board members. The one question that seems to capture best the meaning we wish militancy to have is, "Too many times Negroes have compromised when they could have made more progress if they had held out a little longer." There are three other questions which are correlated with this one, and these four together make up what we will call a militancy scale (Table 18.3). The first three items are not surprising, since they all reflect a willingness to take action and a belief that demonstrations are the most effective way to get results. The last item—disagreeing that "the average white man really wants the Negro to have his rights"—is more interesting. Taken together, they suggest that the militant believes there is little to be gained from appealing to the better nature of whites and therefore the only hope is to make discrimination unpleasant or costly, so that whites will give in out of self-interest. From these data, a militancy scale was developed for each city.

It is clear, despite the limitations of our data, that the most active movements have the most militant leaders. In Figure 18.1 we see that the average militancy score correlates very highly with the activity scores generated in Table 18.1.[1] In fact, the correlation is perfect, but we can assume that this is partly a statistical fluke. Our wisest conclusion is that the correlation between militancy and propensity to act is high but by no means perfect.

Having established a connection between activity and the attitudes of civil rights leaders, we are now ready to take the next step and try to determine what kinds of movements recruit militant leaders. We shall assume that militancy is an attitude that the leader brings with him to office, rather than a response that he has developed from his experience as a leader. (In extreme cases the behavior of the white leadership will certainly influence his attitudes, but if it were simply a learned response, the civil rights leaders would be most militant in the least acquiescent cities, and this is not the case.) Some movements recruit more militant leaders than others. Why?

[1]The cities were divided into four groups. The average militancy scores are highest in St. Louis (2.52) and Bay City (2.40); next highest in Buffalo (1.76), San Francisco (1.72), and Newark (1.60); and lowest in Baltimore (1.32) and Pittsburgh (1.32). No militancy scores were obtained for Lawndale; the interviewers rated it between Newark and the two lowest ranked cities.

Table 18.3 Militancy Scale

Opinion Item	Militant Response
1. Too many times Negroes have compromised when they could have made more progress if they had held out a little longer	Agree
2. Unless you dramatize an issue through mass protests and demonstrations it seems that there is scarcely any progress made	Agree
3. It is sometimes better to have white resistance to Negro requests, because then you have a basis for bringing the overall problem to the public's attention	Agree
4. The average white man really wants the Negro to have his rights	Disagree

Measures of association (Q) between the items:

	2	3	4
1	.45	.73	.89
2	—	.62	.69
3	—	—	.54

In Table 18.4 we have reported some of the correlations between militancy and some background characteristics. The table indicates that, in this group of leaders, the militants are young and slightly better educated, but have lower incomes and are long-term residents of the city (rather than migrants from the South). This fits with one popular conception of the militant, who is sometimes pictured as a young native northerner who is of marginal social status despite his educational attainment. The conventional explanation for this is that the young, high status Negro leader experiences the greatest status discrepancy; the more obvious his ability to get ahead, the more glaring is the fact that as a Negro his social status will also be low regardless of his occupational attainment. Two of these factors, income and age, suggest that the city with militant leaders must have a recruitment process that permits people of low social status to enter and rise to a position of power on the basis of their ability. This also fits the everyday image of the movement—the militant civil rights movement has an open, achievement-oriented leadership structure. This suggests that if a movement has considerable competition for leadership, and a large number of organizations to provide leadership training,

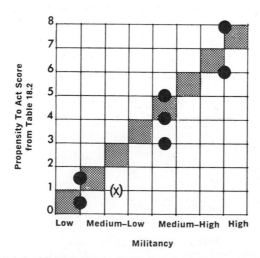

Note: (X) has only an estimated militancy score.

Figure 18.1 Militancy and Propensity for Civil Rights Activity

there will be more opportunity for the young, low status, but skilled person; hence the movement will become more militant.

But it also seems reasonable (indeed, it is part of the conventional wisdom) that competition among civil rights groups leads to increased militancy as the groups bid against each other for followings. Thus we have two reasons to hypothesize the next step in our chain of causation: *The more internal competition in the civil rights movement, the greater its militancy.*

None of this is original or surprising, of course, but it serves as a preamble to asking what types of communities will develop high levels of civil rights activity. We can now modify the question to ask what types of cities will have internal competition in their civil rights movements. One general hypothesis comes to mind; there will necessarily be competition between groups if there are alternative bases for power. If, for example, one civil rights group has access to financial support, and another access to "troops," there will be a natural bias toward conflict between the two groups. In the North, of course, all civil rights groups are underfinanced, so this is not a real conflict; but in the South one can easily imagine one group with access to local support (the NAACP) competing with another with access to northern money and participants (such as SNCC). In two cities in our northern sample there is this kind of competition between the political machine and the civil rights movement. St. Louis and Newark both have strong Negro

Table 18.4 Militancy and Background Characteristics

Characteristics	Per Cent Militant	N
Age:		
Under 35	73	11
35 or over	40	15
Education:		
Advanced degree	57	14
B.A. or less	45	11
Residence:		
In city over 15 years	78	9
Less than 15 years	31	8
Income:		
Under $10,000 per year	75	12
Over $10,000 per year	45	11

Note: Only years of residence yields a correlation significant at the .05 level (two-tailed test); age is significant at 10 per cent and income at only the 20 per cent level.

political organizations which are patronage-based. These machines have control over access to political office and hence are able to hold the loyalty of a large number of persons who might otherwise be active in civil rights movements. More important, since their power base lies in patronage and control over political rewards, they can tolerate a disagreement with the civil rights movement. Finally, they are able to exercise considerable influence over the local NAACP branches. Under these conditions, avenues for access to non-political civil rights groups become much more open, the pressure to organize groups to compete with the NAACP increases, and leadership passes into "deviant" hands—young persons and white liberals. In both Newark and St. Louis the NAACP was rather conservative on the schools issue and wound up splitting with other civil rights leaders. In contrast, in the other cities the battle between moderates and militants occurred within the NAACP, or else the NAACP cooperated with the other groups, even when there was disagreement.

A review of the case studies suggests that the highest level of conflict was in the two machine cities and that conflict was also high in San Francisco and Bay City. The obvious common factor in these latter two cities is that they both have high status Negro populations.

This brings us to our second hypothesis, that competition in the Negro community, like competition in the white community, stems from high levels of political participation and hence from high social status. This is of course the argument which we advanced in Chapter 13 to explain the low cohesiveness of school boards in high status cities, and it is consistent with explanations of other community characteristics (see, for example, Hawley, 1963; Pinard, 1963).

Table 18.5 gives two indicators of the socioeconomic status of the Negro community, which are combined into a single ranking. In Figure 18.2, the correlation of status with militancy is negligible (.3). However, two of the cities in the upper left corner of the chart are the two machine cities. If they are deleted, the correlation rises to .6 among the remaining six cases. Although the correlation is still not high enough to be persuasive, it is consistent with our expectation.

We observed in Chapter 10 that the school board is accustomed to receiving demands from groups asking the school system to solve, within its present policy framework, a specific problem in a specific school, and school integration is not this type of issue. In the North, the civil rights movement tends to ask for the establishment of new policy—opposition to *de facto* segregation. Furthermore, the demand is not only novel, it is vague, in the sense that it is unclear precisely why segregation is bad, how and when it should be eliminated, and when it could be said that the task was finished. The civil rights group does not usually specify any particular school, but rather speaks on behalf of the entire Negro community. Thus the demands are *abstract, diffuse,* and *city wide* in base. This is the "ideal type" of civil rights movement, and actually this description of the goals of the movement fits only Bay City in our sample. The other cities fall on a continuum, at the other end of which we would find a city where the civil rights movement demanded, on behalf of the parents of one school, that the board stop gerrymandering and redraw a particular boundary in a certain way. Obviously, this sort of demand is much easier for the board to understand and hence to deal with. (No city fits this description very well, but this might apply to the initial activity in Newark, the opposition to the building of Vails-

Table 18.5   Ranking of Social Status of Negro Population

| City | Socioeconomic Status | | |
	Per Cent White Collar	Per Cent High School Graduates	Combined Ranking, SES
San Francisco	27	40	1.0
Bay City	17	37	2.0
Lawndale	18	32	3.0
Pittsburgh	14	25	4.5
Buffalo	11	22	7.0
St. Louis	15	24	4.5
Newark	11	22	7.0
Baltimore	15	19	7.0

Combined ranking for socioeconomic status ranking is based upon: per cent white collar + per cent high school graduates.

burg High School.) In Table 18.6 we have ranked seven cities on these three criteria. (Baltimore was excluded from the ranking because the civil rights groups played almost no role in determining the goals of the movement.)[2]

As Table 18.6 indicates, the three criteria go hand in hand. Together, they come close to reflecting what is meant by the symbolic-welfare distinction. At one extreme, groups are asking for a commitment on the part of the board to the symbols of racial equality; at the other extreme, the movement asks for a specific action to affect a particular group.

In the last column of Table 18.6 we have listed the Negro socioeconomic status ranking of the cities. The rank-order correlation is virtually perfect. This is not especially surprising. A large middle-class population means that the city has many eyes turned to the mass media, to the national civil rights values. It also means that the population has a large group of Negroes whose real deprivations are not so serious and who can concern themselves with symbolic wounds. (Of course, even a high status population is

[2]The reader may wish to refer back to Chapters 8 and 10, to the discussion of symbolic and welfare goals.

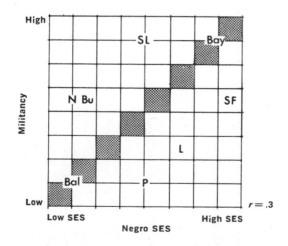

Note: Initials indicate name of city.

Figure 18.2   Status of Negro Population and Militancy

Table 18.6 Comparison of Civil Rights Goals in Seven Cities

City	Initial Demand	Did It Stress General de Facto Segregation?	Was It Diffuse?	Was It Oriented to Entire Negro Community?	SES Rank
San Francisco	*De facto* segregation statement and establishing school board study committee	Yes	Yes	Yes	1
Bay City	*De facto* segregation statement	Yes	Yes	Yes	2
Lawndale	Integrate Woodside High	Partly	Partly	Yes	3
Pittsburgh	Relieve overcrowding at one school; integration plan	Partly	Partly	Partly	4
St. Louis	Preserve West End integration; desegregated bussing	No	Partly	No	5
Newark	Integrate Vailsburg High	Only slightly	No	No	6.5
Buffalo	Integrate Woodlawn Junior High	Only slightly	No	No	6.5

only high in comparison to other Negro communities—the median family income for Negroes in the high status cities is only slightly over $4,000.)

Taken together, we now see two different ways in which a high status population produces intense conflict. The Negro community's more diffuse leadership and more middle-class values produce a movement that is diffuse, competitive, militant, and symbol-oriented; meanwhile the general presence of high status persons in the community tends to produce weak political parties and a less cohesive school board. This description seems to fit all three of the high status cities in our sample—Bay City, San Francisco, and Lawndale. But like nearly every other finding in this study, this one must be considered tentative until the other large American cities are studied.

SUMMARY

We have isolated only two community characteristics that seem to influence the civil rights movement. First, we have argued that cities with entrenched political machines should tend to produce highly militant civil rights movements, and that high status Negro communities should have more militant movements—and we have also seen that the amount of civil rights activity depends very strongly upon the militancy of the movement. Finally, we have also documented the rather unsurprising hypothesis that high status Negro populations will produce civil rights movements that are more symbol-oriented, in that they will make diffuse demands on the school board involving the whole city and place heavy emphasis upon *de facto* segregation.

19

The Civil Rights Movement
in Southern Cities

In the preceding chapter, we argued that high status Negro communities in the North generally had a more militant civil rights leadership, were more active in civil rights, and held goals that were more diffuse and symbolic. We have sufficient data from six southern cities—Atlanta, Columbus, Jacksonville, Miami, Montgomery, and New Orleans—to permit us to try a partial replication of these findings. While there is no important contradiction between the northern and southern data, there are some differences; indeed, we did not expect the pattern of relationships to be exactly the same in both parts of the nation. First of all, Negroes are still excluded from political office in most of these cities, so that the role of politics in shaping the style of the civil rights groups will be different. Second, the school integration issue is itself different. With a clear legal situation, there is no need to demonstrate or threaten retaliation at the polls; given enough time one small boy and his lawyer can desegregate a southern school system. But most important, the hostility toward Negroes in the South is so intense that local variations in the behavior of whites can have a very important effect on the behavior of the civil rights movement, and other correlations become of secondary importance.

THE NEGRO COMMUNITY AND THE GOALS OF
THE CIVIL RIGHTS MOVEMENT

In the North it is frequently the case that school integration is the *cause célèbre* of the civil rights movement—much of the energy of the movement is poured into the schools issue, and the whole

First draft by Gerald A. McWorter.

340

ideology of the local movement is reflected in its behavior on this single issue. This does not occur in the South. School desegregation is set aside for the NAACP lawyers, while the rest of the movement becomes involved in a host of other issues—lunch counters, bus stations, employment, voting, a variety of "welfare" projects, and so forth. Under such conditions, it is difficult to characterize the civil rights movement as symbol- or welfare-oriented solely on the basis of its behavior in the school desegregation issue. However, we can contrast those cities that did nothing except push for court-ordered desegregation with those that went farther. We can divide the cities into three groups:

Group 1: *Desegregation plus "integration" goals.*—In this group we place the three cities that have filed a second suit or taken some other action to increase the amount of integration: Atlanta, Columbus, and Miami

Group 2: *Desegregation plus welfare goals.*—In this category we place Jacksonville. Although the Jacksonville civil rights groups have not been greatly concerned with the extent of integration in their desegregated school system, they have been concerned with such welfare issues as building new Negro schools, fair treatment of Negro teachers, and the inclusion of Negro representatives on citizens' committees working to improve the quality of the public schools.

Group 3: *Desegregation only.*—The two cities in this group, New Orleans and Montgomery, have so far expressed little interest in anything beyond the initial desegregation of the schools.

In the North, the high status cities held the most symbolic goals, and in the South we see that the two high status[1] cities (Atlanta and Miami) fall into Group 1, by having integrationist goals and generally going beyond desegregation. The two cities in Group 3 have the lowest status and Jacksonville in Group 2 is intermediate in status. The only exception to the correlation is Columbus. One possible explanation for this deviant case is that, because Columbus desegregated under pressure from the federal government, the plaintiffs did not have to go through an emotion-

---

[1]As in the North, status is measured by the percentage of the population who are high school graduates and the percentage who have white collar jobs.

ally and financially exhausting suit to obtain desegregation; thus it was easier for them to file a second suit.

Whatever the explanation for Columbus, the data generally support our interpretation of the northern data. We would expect the high status community to have the most elaborate set of goals with regard to schools, and in general to place more emphasis upon the schools and upon school integration, and this seems to be the case. Or to put it another way, the middle-class–dominated community can afford to put aside the pressing welfare needs of the community to focus on school integration as a way to build the new South.

LEVEL OF CIVIL RIGHTS ACTIVITY

In comparing the amount of civil rights activity, three basic questions can be asked: (1) When was the suit filed? (2) How aggressively was the case pursued? (3) Did the civil rights leaders help protect the students during desegregation?

By these criteria, the civil rights groups of Atlanta and Miami were most active. In both cities an organized campaign was mounted to find plaintiffs, the attorney handled the cases aggressively, and the civil rights groups continued to press the schools after desegregation.

At the other extreme, Montgomery did not file suit until 1963, at approximately the same time that Birmingham became the first city in Alabama to desegregate. It was difficult to keep a corps of parents and students involved, even though the case took only a year. Columbus also had difficulty recruiting plaintiffs. More important, relative to other cities in the state, Columbus was late in filing suit even compared to Montgomery. Despite the fact that Atlanta desegregated two years before Birmingham, Columbus did not file until shortly before Montgomery did.

In addition to the way the cities differed in their handling of the suits, there are other differences. In Atlanta, the civil rights movement engaged in direct demonstrations over the integration issue. In Jacksonville, the post-desegregation campaign included a school boycott. And in all the cities except New Orleans, the civil rights groups made an effort to protect students on the first day of desegregation, or at least worked with white officials to prevent disorder.

On the basis of this information, we have ranked the six cities from most active to least active (Table 19.1). The appearance of Montgomery in last place on the list indicates that there is no necessary relationship between the level of civil rights activity on one issue or at one time with the level on other issues at other times. Montgomery was the scene of some of the most important civil rights activity in the South only a few years earlier.

We probably do not need to give warning that this ranking is one of the most problematic of any we have presented thus far. There is at best a fine distinction between the amount of activity in New Orleans, Columbus, and Montgomery.

Some of these cities have until very recently had such oppressive anti-Negro sentiment that civil rights activity was highly dangerous. It is hardly surprising that the leaders of Miami and Atlanta should feel relatively free to press a desegregation suit, while those in Columbus and Montgomery should be reluctant. A ranking of cities from least anti-Negro to most would probably be approximately as follows: Miami, Atlanta, Jacksonville, Columbus, New Orleans, Montgomery.

Notice that this listing of degree of anti-Negro sentiment correlates strongly with the amount of civil rights activity; the most active cities have the least anti-Negro sentiment.

Table 19.1 Ranking of Cities, by Extent of Civil Rights Activity Concerning Schools

City	When Suit Filed	Difficulties in Pursuing Suit?	Helped Maintain Control over Demonstrations?	Other Action
1. Atlanta	Early	No	Yes	Demonstrations
2. Miami	Early	No	Yes	
3. Jacksonville	Moderate	Some	Yes	Boycott
4. New Orleans	Early	Yes	No	
5. {Columbus[a]	Late	Yes	Yes	
{Montgomery[a]	Moderate	Yes	Yes	

[a]Tied.

COMPETITION

In the North we saw that the most active cities also had the most competition for leadership. In the South, a series of sociometric questions were used to give us a picture of the structure of the civil rights leadership. In describing civil rights leadership in the South, we are also describing the Negro community leadership, since any Negro community leader can almost always be considered a civil rights leader as well.

Most communities, unless they are very small, have a diffuse leadership rather than a power structure. In the Deep South, the diffuse and unstructured Negro community leadership is most often also the leadership of the civil rights movement, so that the civil rights movement in these communities also lacks a power structure. This seems to be the case in our two most southern cities, Montgomery and New Orleans. At the time of the Montgomery bus boycott, Martin Luther King and his immediate aides represented a leadership structure, but these men have all left the city to work in the national movement.

Negro leader and civil rights leader are also synonymous in Columbus, but the leadership of the movement there is not diffuse simply because the Negro community itself has a true power structure. In the two previous generations, Columbus had a monolithic structure led by one man. When the second such leader died, leadership passed into the hands of a tightly knit group of five men. Our interviewer attended one of the *daily* meetings where these men thrash out community problems. One of the group is in direct contact with a representative of the white leadership in Columbus, and a civil rights demand tends to take the form of a quiet conversation between these two ambassadors. The Negro leaders are powerful and are willing to use their power on occasion. (When one department store refused to go along when the others opened their lunch counters, a quiet boycott was organized, which nearly bankrupted the store before it capitulated.)

The other three cities tend to have civil rights specialists as northern cities do. In Miami, this results in a monolithic leadership similar to that in Columbus. The leader is a charismatic Episcopal priest, a long-time NAACP leader on the local and national levels. Flanked by many secondary leaders he has been able to keep the civil rights leadership centralized into one major thrust.[2]

The two remaining cities are each divided into two organized factions, and we shall call them dichotomous cities for this reason. Jacksonville has a powerful Negro political organization; its leaders are fairly conservative. The NAACP is controlled by a militant reform faction which is heavily committed to demonstrations. Atlanta, the other dichotomous city, is split by a conflict between the generations which permeates the political arena, the NAACP, and the leadership of the city's seven Negro colleges.

In Table 19.2 we compare the leadership structures of the six cities with their militancy and the extent of their civil rights activity in school desegregation. Since Jacksonville, like St. Louis and Newark in the North, has a civil rights movement whose goals conflict with those of the Negro politicians, we would expect it to be the most militant city. Jacksonville's civil rights leaders are no more militant in their attitudes than are the leaders of Atlanta and Montgomery. But Jacksonville did organize a city-wide, three-day boycott during its battle with the school system, and we do not know of any boycott lasting this long in any other city,

[2]His concept of the leader's function is evidenced by his decision to step down from the presidency of the NAACP because his image was too acceptable to the "boys downtown." His feeling is that a major Negro leader should be unpredictable enough to present a threat but reasonable enough to win the confidence of his white counterparts. He feels he has now dealt with them so long that he has become too predictable.

Table 19.2 Leadership Structures, Militancy, and Action

City	Status of Negro Community (1 = High)	Leadership Structure	Militancy	Level of School Desegregation Activity (1 = High)
Specialized leadership:				
Jacksonville	3	Dichotomous	High	3
Atlanta	1	Dichotomous	High	1
Miami	1	Monolithic	Medium	2
General leadership:				
Montgomery	4	Diffuse	High	5
New Orleans	4	Diffuse	Low	4
Columbus	6	Monolithic	Medium	5

North or South. We would expect the three cities without specialized civil rights leadership to be less militant, and here the glaring exception is Montgomery. We think that the militancy of Montgomery is a result of the city's ties to the national civil rights movement and its history as a leader in the southern civil rights revolution. If we hypothesize that cities with specialized civil rights leadership will have more civil rights activity than others, and cities whose leadership is monolithic will have less, we find that our hypothesis is supported (R = .78).

POLITICAL PARTICIPATION AND LEADERSHIP STRUCTURE

It is interesting that there is a perfect relationship between the leadership structure and the way in which the Negro community participates in local politics. In both of the diffuse cities (Montgomery and New Orleans), Negroes are virtually excluded from political leadership; in the two monolithic cities (Columbus and Miami) they are informally co-opted into the political arena; and in the two dichotomous cities (Atlanta and Jacksonville) they hold formal or semiformal positions in politics.

Of course it is not correct to say that Negroes are completely excluded from politics in New Orleans and Montgomery, but compared to the other cities they are in a different position. In New Orleans, which may elect a Negro state legislator in the near future, there is little relationship between Negro and white political leaders—they tend not to see each other. Less than one-fifth of the Negroes in Montgomery were registered in 1958,[3] and Negro political activity there was handled by the civil rights groups. In Columbus and Miami, the Negro community leaders are consulted about political matters on a regular basis. In Jacksonville, Negroes are directly involved in the local political machine, and in Atlanta, Negroes hold a variety of elected offices—a city council post, two school board seats, and (since redistricting) seven seats in the state legislature.

The type of political participation Negroes may take in a city

[3]The Southern Regional Council found that at most 9.4 per cent of the registered voters were Negro. In 1960, Negroes made up 34 per cent of the voting-age population. If two-thirds of all whites were registered, this would mean that approximately 18 per cent of the Negroes were registered.

almost determines the Negro leadership structure. In a city which places Negroes in formal political positions, there is inevitable conflict within the Negro community; one ambitious leader finds himself in conflict with others as he competes for a party or governmental office. Conversely, without politics and the divisiveness which necessarily accompanies it, there is not much reason for conflict. To be sure, it is possible for people to disagree over ideological issues—this is part of the conflict between the generations in Atlanta—but even here there is not really very much disagreement among Negro leaders.

It seems plausible that in a city such as Columbus or Miami, with high informal contact between Negro leaders and white political figures, the Negro leadership must be monolithic in structure: the Negro community must have a spokesman, and this in turn requires a defined leadership group. The two diffusely organized cities, on the other hand, do not need a single spokesman. Negroes are not communicating with whites on basic problems.

COMMUNITY SOCIAL STATUS

We are left with one variable to consider—socioeconomic status. There is a strong interrelationship in a Negro community's socioeconomic status, type of leadership structure, and amount of civil rights activity. Looking again at Table 19.2, we see that the higher the social status of the Negro community, the more likely the city is to have a specialized civil rights leadership and the less likely it is to have a monolithic structure. The only city out of place is Jacksonville, which has a dichotomous leadership not because the status of its Negro community is high but because of the presence of a political machine.

This would lead us to predict that the high status cities, having a specialized leadership and more competition for leadership positions, would be more militant, but unfortunately we cannot test this hypothesis very well. As noted earlier, the militancy of Jacksonville can be explained by the presence of a political machine, and the high militancy scores of Montgomery can be attributed to the fact that Montgomery is the birthplace of the Southern Christian Leadership Conference. That leaves only four

others to test the hypothesis on. While it is true that Atlanta (the
city of highest status) is the most militant, and New Orleans
(third of the four in social status) is the least militant, so that the
correlation is in the right direction, this cannot be considered useful evidence. The correlation of social status with level of civil
rights activity is high, however, and this is what we would expect.
The correlation in Table 19.2 is .94.

SUMMARY

We have found a pattern of positive correlations between five
variables: cities in which the political participation and social
status of Negroes is high tend to have competition for civil
rights leadership, are more militant, and have a greater amount
of civil rights activity. Three of these variables were used in the
northern analysis, and the correlations between the three (status,
militancy, and action) were positive there also. As we commented
at the beginning of the chapter, the South is different from the
North, but the South does not contradict any of our northern
findings.

But we cannot combine this set of positive correlations into a
single persuasive theory. One obvious line of argument is to say
that high status cities have a larger supply of leadership and the
resources for a more elaborate organizational base. These factors lead to a more complex leadership structure (especially if the
leadership roles are specific to civil rights activity), which in turn
attracts more militant candidates for leadership and inspires
higher levels of action. This argument seems sound on its face
and is almost identical to the conclusions we drew about the North.
But it ignores the unignorable differences in the racial climate
of these cities. It is just as easy to argue that a progressive city
attracts Negro high school and college graduates (or at least does
not banish them) and, being progressive, invites Negroes into the
political arena, which complicates and divides the Negro leadership structure, which in turn creates room for more militant
civil rights leaders who organize more civil rights activity.

Part V

Conclusion

20

School Desegregation: North and South

Possibly the commonest judgment held about school integration is that intense conflict is unavoidable because, as is true of most racial issues, Negroes want a good deal and whites are too prejudiced to give it to them. It seems to us that this statement contains four factual errors. First, intense conflict is avoidable. Our own data indicate, for example, that some of the northern cities experienced only a brief flurry of picketing, and school desegregation in the South is so tame as to be uninteresting. Second, the statement makes the assumption that conflict is to be expected when a racial issue is raised. In fact, many racial issues have been raised and resolved in northern cities without a battle. As we said in the Introduction, war is news and peace is not. Hence national publicity was given to Governor Wallace's 1964 "northern campaign," to the Cadillac and Bank of America employment demonstrations in San Francisco, to such "non-events" as the World's Fair stall-in (New York), and to such demonstrations of white prejudice as the repeal of open occupancy by referendum in California. But this is hardly a fair picture. For example, the Gallup poll has indicated that white voters support President Johnson's civil rights legislation; fair employment and fair housing legislation have been passed in a number of states (and an attempt to prevent Illinois fair housing legislation failed to get the question onto the ballot). Our data indicate that the civil rights leaders are not in general asking for anything that whites will object strongly to. We have observed that civil rights leaders must often be content with little more than token integration plans, and if they have not been content, they have at least been quiet about it. And we have seen that bussing Negroes into white schools is now common practice in most of our cities with at most a short-lived white backlash.

Thus we do not see any reason why school integration issues should be riddled with conflict—the Negro demands are not unreasonable, whites have shown a willingness to accept school integration, other racial issues have been handled peacefully, and some cities have avoided serious controversy over schools. Yet northern cities have experienced more controversy about school integration than they have in any other area of racial change. Why is the school issue the difficult one?

We think the reason for this is that compared to other racial issues in northern cities, the parties to the school integration controversy have chosen to keep their dialogue on a highly ideological level. We have seen that conflict has more often broken out over ideological issues than over the actual details of the integration plan. Once the board and the movement have agreed in principle, both sides have demonstrated more flexibility and willingness to compromise. In turn, we see two reasons why the school integration issue should be more ideological. One is the high autonomy of school boards; the other is the symbolic orientation of the civil rights movement.

First, the autonomous school board, which participates in a narrow range of decisions, has less to lose from social conflict than does a mayor, who must make decisions in a whole range of issues. The mayor must decide what combination of decisions over the several issues which he must handle will maximize his chances for reelection and further the goals he holds for the city. He is very likely to decide that all-out war over a racial issue, and the subsequent permanent loss of the Negro vote, is dangerous. On the other hand, the school board is likely to have only one issue—school integration—which is of public importance. If it loses the white vote, it cannot regain it by making a decision in some other area which will please this group. Further, if the school board member is politically ambitious, he can make school integration into an attention-getting device; thus social conflict is not necessarily to the disadvantage of the school board member. In the eight cities studied here, mayors interceded in support of the civil rights movement twice; no mayor took a public position in opposition to integration.

Second, the autonomous school board is only indirectly responsible for the day-to-day operation of the schools. The school system is the one department of government that has gone farthest in separating policy-making from administration. Thus the school board is not under much pressure to make pragmatic decisions, especially in areas of policy innovation. The pragmatic decision in this case would be to acquiesce to the civil rights demands in order to avoid disrupting the normal operation of the schools. But the school board cannot balance these two values against each other because the normal operation of the schools is not its direct responsibility, but the superintendent's. The school board's task is only to make policy. Thus the whole structure of the school decision-making apparatus tends to make the board focus upon the school integration issue as a matter of policy, and hence as a largely ideological question.

We have presented in this study a statement of the goals of the civil rights movement as highly symbolic in orientation. We have presented a rationale for this set of goals which makes them appear quite reasonable, but the fact remains that a more welfare-oriented approach would also seem reasonable. There are probably a number of reasons why the civil rights groups have made this choice. First, a welfare orientation would plunge the movement into the difficult task of trying to evaluate the quality of education, and would make it very difficult for the NAACP to fall back on its area of greatest experience, legal redress. In addition, the precedent of the southern school cases is handy, and many civil rights leaders are committed to demonstrating that racial discrimination is as real in the North as in the South.

Moreover, a welfare-oriented concern for Negro school achievement falls into the trap of raising the issue of innate racial inferiority. If the school system chooses to grant that Negroes do not on the average learn as well as whites and then cites cultural deprivation as the reason, the implication of innate inferiority is clear. This is a very frightening issue, simply because many Negroes, very likely including civil rights leaders, are unconsciously afraid that there is truth here. Thus we think there is some pressure on the civil rights leader to stay with the issue of segregation, rather than open this Pandora's box, where he may find evidence that his worst fears are true.

However, the school integration issue can be transferred from North to South easily only if there is evidence that the schools are in fact intentionally segregated. What happens when there is little or no evidence of *de jure* segregation? There is still one more test the school system can be put to; they can be asked to demonstrate not merely that they have not segregated the schools, but that they personally approve of integration—this leads to the development of the *de facto* segregation issue. By continuing to focus on schools despite the change in the type of demand made, the civil rights movement has chosen to fight a battle on unique terrain. The *de facto* school segregation issue is possibly the only case where the movement intentionally sacrifices its strongest weapon, the ability to reveal publicly that the enemy is intentionally discriminating against Negroes. On the other hand, they have the opportunity to win a major moral victory by forcing a public body to commit itself, not merely to non-discrimination, but also to intentional integration and to the principle that public bodies should go out of their way to help Negroes achieve equality.

The school board must face this new demand with very little help available to it. The board cannot depend upon the superintendent, whose narrow orientation is an invitation to extensive controversy. The educational profession has not taken a position that could guide an individual school system. The federal courts have not made decisions that give guidance to the school boards, and the federal government has taken no action. The only help the school board has received in the form of a guideline for policy has been from state governments. A number of states have passed legislation committing school boards to a policy of furthering integration, and in particular, New York's state commissioner of education has played a very active role in bringing the practices of local boards into line with this policy. We saw in the case of Buffalo that Commissioner Allen's intervention had an important effect on the behavior of the board. Although we have no data, it seems likely that the same sort of thing is happening in other states as well. The effect of the state's intervention is to resolve the ideological issue and leave the contesting parties with the simpler problems of negotiating the details of the settlement.

The school integration conflict has some parallels with labor-management negotiations—not the present highly structured and rather tame contract negotiations, but the recognition battles during the first part of this century. At that time there was no common acceptance of the principle of collective bargaining. The factory owner was faced with an unprecedented demand, and it was largely up to him to decide whether it should be considered legitimate. If he chose to deny the legitimacy of the workers' demand, the result was sometimes a long and blood-drenched strike. The issue was redefined with the passage of the Wagner Act and the establishment of the National Labor Relations Board. In the desegregation of southern schools, the federal government played a strong role, which apparently redefined the issue in a similar way and prevented overt social conflict. The federal government may eventually play some sort of lesser role in the North, possibly serving as a mediator of disputes. One can imagine the NAACP and the school board agreeing to bring in a federal mediator just as they presently agree to the appointment of a bi-racial citizens' committee or to calling on the state commissioner of education.

Thus we see a distinct possibility that a national climate of opinion will develop that will narrow the range of alternatives open to school boards and hence dampen considerably the conflict they are now facing. We also see the possibility that the civil rights movement will become more welfare-oriented in its approach. The federal government has here set one guideline by redefining a part of the civil rights revolution as a war on poverty. In addition, the continued emphasis of the schools on compensatory education is an invitation to the movement to engage in a dialogue in these terms. Finally, the new civil rights groups have stressed grass-roots organization. Since the people in the neighborhoods seem to be more welfare-oriented, this will also have an impact on their orientation. Whether this will lead to more or less conflict with the schools is hard to say. On the one hand, it will prevent the present ideological problems; on the other hand, as we pointed out earlier, the welfare-oriented civil rights movement may demand much more in the way of results. One possibility is that there will be great pressure for the publication of achievement test scores, just as there was pressure for publication of racial censuses of schools.

If these changes occur, how much of our analysis of the differences between cities will remain valid? It is a truism that the conditions which lead to successful resolution of one issue will not necessarily lead to resolution of another issue, and a more welfare-oriented issue, or an issue which requires coordination with the demand of the state or federal government, would in many ways be different from what northern schools have faced until now, just as school desegregation in the South is different from northern school desegregation.

21

Community Structure and Community Decision-Making

The goal of our research project was to analyze, from a political perspective, one issue as it occurred in fifteen different cities. In the pursuit of this goal we have found ourselves involved in several different types of analysis.

First, we have written nine case studies of cities dealing with the desegregation conflict.

Second, we have defined the two issues of school integration. We found this necessary because, in terms of decision-making, there is little resemblance between school integration in a northern city and court-ordered desegregation in a southern city. In analyzing the issue in the North, we tried to determine who has been leading the campaign for integration and what they seem to want. We also tried to determine what the school superintendent, the voter, and the school board member think of the demands made upon them. In the South, where the issue is crystal-clear, we considered the perspective taken by the white southern leadership and the ways this perspective has changed from 1954 to the present.

Third, we have been forced to consider the question of how a school board (which is a particular kind of small, formally organized group) makes decisions. After analyzing the school board itself, we examined the process by which a government recruits its school board members. This is, of course, one rather special case of the general topic concerning how governmental offices are filled. But in the course of answering that question, we had to look at one of the most complex issues in the study of American local government—the phenomenon of the businessmen and others who, without holding formal office, make up a civic elite that influences the government's actions.

Having performed this analysis of the school board, we then conducted a similar study of the civil rights movement. In its most general form it is the same sort of analysis, since it deals with the same three questions—who occupied the decision-making offices, what influences were brought to bear on them, and how were they recruited to office—but the details of the analysis are quite different. The school board is a formally chartered part of the government; the civil rights movement functions almost as if it were a part of the Negro community's government, but it is informally organized and has no legal authority. We looked both at cities where the civil rights movement is a rather peripheral part of the Negro leadership structure and at cities where the civil rights leadership is virtually identical to the civic elite of the Negro community.

Out of all of this we have tried to draw out some ideas to explain the ways in which different economic bases and different types of populations or governmental structures make cities different in their decision-making styles. Since there are summaries at the end of each analytical chapter, we will not try to repeat all the findings or list all the hypotheses we have put forward. However, it may be worthwhile to mention some of the more intriguing and suggestive hypotheses here.

1. In both the North and South, we began by assuming that civil rights leaders would be concerned almost exclusively with placing as many Negro students as possible in integrated schools. This is an important concern, but it is not the single overriding goal of the leadership in either the North or the South. In both areas, the main goal seems to be persuading, or forcing, the school board to make the strongest possible commitment to the concept of racial equality. And in either area a school board can demonstrate this commitment without desegregating every school, while a school board which permits a large amount of integration may be attacked if its public position does not live up to its actual behavior. In a word, the civil rights movement is more symbol-oriented than we expected it to be.

2. We also began the study with the basic assumption that the school integration decision would be a complex, bargaining ar-

rangement, the result of rather elaborate negotiations, threats, and counterthreats. Obvious though this assumption may be, it is not a good way to approach the problem. We found instead that in most cases the school board members first responded to the issue by acting according to their predispositions about civil rights; liberal boards tended to integrate; conservative boards did not. By increasing the pressure, the civil rights movement might be able to exhort some minor additional concessions or to escalate the conflict into an all-out battle, but it could not change the overall tone of the board's behavior.

3. It is commonly assumed that school superintendents exert much more influence over the policy of the school system than does the school board. Our data show the precise opposite: the school board sets the tone of the integration decision and the superintendent plays a less important role.

4. The politically appointed school board members are more conservative on racial matters and express other attitudes which we summarize as an unwillingness or inability to tolerate conflict. In general, their behavior makes it understandable why minor party officials are sometimes called "party hacks."

Counts (1927) demonstrates clearly that at the time of his writing school boards drew very few of their members from the laboring class that made up the bulk of the population. Counts makes it clear that his research is motivated by the assumption that the businessmen who are so heavily overrepresented on school boards would not represent the interests of the workers in the way that workers would if they were able to serve on school boards. Today the radical voices of the civil rights movement pick up a related theme and discuss the "white power structure." However, our data indicate clearly that the members of the white power structure and the business class are the ones most willing to break with traditions and to innovate in order to meet the demands of the most oppressed group in our society. The finding is really not so surprising. Furthermore, we see no reason to accept Counts' assumption—that putting working-class men on school boards will eliminate the school system's middle-class bias. When we examine a school board made up of professional politicians with close ties to the working class, we do not see a different educational philosophy in operation. It may well be that all school systems operate with a heavy bias in favor of the middle class. But if this is true, more will need to be done than simply appointing a "proletarian" school board to change this.

5. We have also seen some evidence that the level of internal conflict within the school board is a factor in determining how far the board will go to satisfy the civil rights movement: the conflict-ridden board has difficulty taking action.[1]

6. It is not surprising that the composition of the school board should reflect the political style of the city. What is surprising is that the role of the civic elite is one of the most important components of this political style. The hypothesis which best describes this is somewhat different from those advanced by other students of local government. The power structure theorists argue that the holders of wealth and social status exercise rather definite power and are informally organized into a power structure, at the pinnacle of which is one man, a small group, or two or three competing leaders. While this might describe New Orleans, Columbus, or Atlanta, we did not find such a power structure in the northern cities. There are too many cases of important decisions being made by men who were obviously not key influentials, and there are even cases in which extremely important men were defeated. Instead we have hypothesized that the civic elite comprises a loosely organized class, whose members operate as individuals seeking goals which the members of this class agree upon.

In some of the southern cities, and most of the northern cities, the civic elite either do not or cannot exert much influence on the school desegregation issue. Yet school desegregation is an issue that is often of great importance to the whole community; when it is mishandled it can result in a great deal of social conflict, even to the point of crippling the schools and influencing the whole political alignment of the city. Hence, evidence that the elite have no direct influence in this area seems to give strong support to the

---

[1]This hypothesis was developed in our northern analysis. It cannot be easily tested with our southern data, so we cannot say how important this factor is in the South.

"pluralist" school, the political scientists who have argued against the power structure concept.

This is not, however, the same as saying that the elite have no influence, for their indirect influence in establishing the political style of their city is of great importance. In particular, the civic elite does exercise an important role in managing the policy regarding school board appointments: we think the existence of reform boards can be attributed to continued pressure by members of the elite over a period of years.

In general, school boards are reformed in cities that have an active civic elite; and these are the cities where high income families have not moved to the suburbs and where strong political parties provide a structural channel for elite influence.

7. In the North, then, the question is, "How much influence do the elites have?" In the South, however, the more important question is, "What is the ideological position of the elite?" We could find no evidence that the elite of New Orleans failed to act out of weakness; indeed, New Orleans has a more organized and visible elite structure than several of the other southern cities. But this power structure is committed to traditional values and is oblivious to the social costs of trying to maintain those values.

8. We have found evidence in three test cases (out of four) that the higher the social status of the community, the more prone it is to controversy. In the North there is less consensus among the school board members of high status cities (resulting, we suspect, from the fact that the boards are more heterogeneous, since board members are recruited in a variety of different ways to satisfy the many and various pressures exerted by an articulate community), and this means that even liberal boards will be less acquiescent and more prone to conflict. We also found that higher status Negro communities are more militant and hold more symbolic goals. In the South, we found that higher status Negro communities develop more elaborate goals and organize more civil rights activity. To sum these three cases up, high status communities pour more energy into decision-making, and this participation greatly encourages conflict and provides support for extremist positions. In the fourth case—southern school boards—we did not

find this pattern. We attribute its absence to the existence of what we think is a more important variable: high status communities in the South have a white civic leadership that is committed to progress, and this is of sufficient importance to override the higher participation level of the citizenry.

9. Closely related to social status is the level of political party organization. High status cities tend to have weaker political parties, and this in turn tends to magnify the effect of citizen participation, since the elected official is not insulated from the voter. Without political parties to freeze the voter's loyalty, each interest group represents a serious bloc of fickle voters who must be appeased.

Several methodological problems have plagued our study, the most serious being the small sample size. This predicament has had its usual effect—making it impossible to find significant differences—but more important, it has often prevented us from distinguishing between two factors, each of which seems perfectly capable of explaining the dependent variable. The problem is that we have been unable to control for one variable while looking at the effect of a second. This same problem has bothered other students of local government, and the usual solution (which is the one we take here) has been to construct a typology. A typology enables us to make the most fundamental distinctions between cities. By dividing cities into some small number of groups and constructing a typology, we are making an *a priori* commitment to regard certain factors as most important, others as less so. For example, Williams and Adrian (1963) divide their four cities according to the kinds of values the cities display in their decision-making process. Agger, Goldrich, and Swanson (1964) classify cities according to what we might call the general structure of the political decision-making group. In either case, the authors' assumption is that with only four cases, the best one can do is to pull out the fundamental differences between the cities. Finer distinctions can only be hinted at. Another way one can build a typology is by determining what seems to be the most important factor, then determining the second most important factor, and cross-tabulating them to build a 2×2 table. This is the approach used by Alford (1964) and is the approach we used in analyzing our northern cities. In principle one can build as complex a typology as he wishes by adding additional factors until there are no cases left.

We also used another typology in preparing this report—one which is centered around the historical development of the relationship between the political party leaders and the holders of high social status. We have not formally presented it because it remains too vague for careful discussion. However, we should point out that some of our cities seem presently to represent some of the historical stages through which New Haven and Chicago have gone, according to Dahl (1961) and Bradley and Zald (1965). For example, we think that, despite the presence of Fort Benning, Columbus remains in some ways a patrician city similar to New Haven in the eighteenth century, when the established elite of that city took on the task of government. In other ways, Columbus resembles the New Haven of the early nineteenth century, or Chicago in its early days, when the leading industrialists maintained control of the government. New Orleans and Jacksonville, on the other hand, seem reminiscent of New Haven or Chicago at the end of the nineteenth century. The economic elite is still active in local politics and may even have one of its own members in the mayor's office, but since working-class politics have become important, the extent of the elite's influence has been only minor. Interestingly enough, at the turn of the century, politics was also the politics of Lincoln Steffens, in whose time business participated in politics primarily out of narrow self-interest, and this description fits Jacksonville better than any of our other cities. After the turn of the century in New Haven, and a little later in Chicago, politics became strictly a working-class affair, with ethnic "ex-plebes" holding the major elected offices. This is the case today in Buffalo, Bay City, and Newark. Finally, Dahl refers to Richard Lee, the mayor of New Haven at the time of his study, as one of the "new men" who can appeal across class lines to the rapidly growing "good government" vote. This description would certainly fit Mayor Tucker of St. Louis or the last two mayors of Atlanta, and such new men would fit into the political style of Baltimore, Pittsburgh, and, in some ways, even Miami.

Dahl argues that these stages are the result of the changes in New Haven's economy and population composition—that first industrialization, then class conflict, and finally the death of class conflict are principal factors in explaining the end of each of the three preceding eras. Parallel to this, the change in New Haven's politics has partly affected the structure and the values of the business community. Businessmen first took control from the patricians, then were forced out by the working-class vote, and finally have begun to return in quasi-governmental roles, armed with a new ideology of consensus rather than conflict.

The parallels between Dahl's historical analysis of New Haven and our own cross-sectional analysis tend to confirm our belief in the utility of a concept like political style. We expect to find differences in the various types of decisions a local government must make, but we think that these differences will not be enough to override the similarities. The similarities are present because the structure of decision-making is not very complex in the cities we have studied. In each case, the four important actors are the elected officials, persons or groups with special interests, the citizenry, and the civic elite.

In cities the size of New Orleans, there are no special interests which can exert overwhelming power in a variety of issues, and interest groups are generally either organized on a temporary basis to struggle with a particular issue, or else they are very fluid organizations which can change easily from one point in time to the next. (For example, we do not believe that one can accurately predict the behavior of an NAACP chapter merely from knowing its behavior ten years earlier.) For this reason, we can expect to find a strong correlation between the behavior of the interest groups and the character of the population segment which is its base.

This is not as true for the elected officials, since the formal structure of government does persist from one time period to the next. For example, a city which had weak political parties twenty years ago is likely to have weak parties now. And the type of party determines in large measure the extent to which the elected officials listen to the voters. If parties are strong, the political leaders know they can maintain a stable voting bloc despite temporary divisions on particular issues; if parties are weak, any issue—no matter how temporary—may serve to realign the electorate. It is probably true that the composition of the electorate eventually determines the structure of government, and in this sense there will be at least a weak correlation between the behavior of the elected officials and the character of the electorate.

Similarly, there should be a relationship between the civic leaders' ideology and interest in local politics and the response of the elected officials. This pattern will derive partly from the nature of the civic elite—their personal orientations toward their community, for example—but it will also derive from the historical pattern of their interaction with politicians. If politics has been based on ethnic rivalry and machine-style organization, the members of the elite will have little to offer the government, and if their overtures are resisted, they will become apathetic. The point is that these four factors—the electorate's attitudes, the electorate's relationship to the government, the civic elite's ideology and internal organization, and the elite's relation to the government— are all interrelated; the behavior of each modifies the behavior of the others. Furthermore, these four factors are the major determinants of the way in which the government will respond to any particular issue. The interaction of these four factors determines what we have called the political style of the city and what Williams and Adrian (1963) have called the values which the government endorses. Of course, in any particular issue there are incidental or even accidental factors which are important, but these factors are best understood in the context of the political style.

In the South, this political style is translated into the willingness or ability of the civic and political leaders to exercise direct social control. In the North, the way in which political style explains the outcome of the desegregation process is much less obvious. We have said that the government's relationship to the electorate, on the one hand, and to the civic elite, on the other, are the components of political style. But in the northern school desegregation controversy, neither the electorate nor the civic elite plays an important role.

The decision about school integration is one of the most important to be made in any city, and we find that the powerful men of the city either do not choose to influence this decision, or attempt to and are unable. Yet at the same time, we find that cities that have influential civic elites have school boards that act *as if* they were being influenced by the elite. The reason for this consistency is that the influentials exert their influence indirectly by acting to set a style of politics for the city. It is this political style which overrides the actual formal governmental structure to produce a school board which then takes actions appropriate to the style.

Appendix 1

The Selection of the Sample of Northern Cities

The universe from which the sample of northern cities was selected is all cities between 250,000 and 1,000,000 in population having 10 per cent or more of its population Negro and located outside of those states in the Confederacy in the Civil War. The universe was limited to cities with 10 per cent or more of the population Negro, so that there would be some assurance that the issue of school desegregation had been salient in the community. Cities over 250,000 were chosen by the definition of the study as being "large" cities. Cities over 1,000,000 in population were eliminated—partly because the issue in these cities would probably be too complicated to fit into a comparative framework, but primarily because we felt that those five cities had been studied already by others. The twenty cities in the universe include six border cities (in Oklahoma, Missouri, Kentucky, and Maryland), five northeastern cities, seven midwestern cities, and two in the West.

With this universe established, the sample was selected on the basis of three variables—geographical location, size, and proportion of the population Negro. Location was considered relevant because of possible cultural factors, i.e., in the contrast between border states and the rest of the North, or between West and East. The politics, economics, and social structure of cities is thought to vary by size, and thus this variable was introduced. The relative proportion of the population Negro is thought to affect the system of politics and leadership within the Negro community and the relationship between the Negro and white segments of the community. Further, it was decided to select the sample of cities i matched pairs in order to increase the range of comparative variables which could be analyzed. The size of the sample is eight cities.

The first step was to divide the cities into border cities and northern cities. There are six border cities and fourteen northern cities. The decision was then made to select one matched pair of border cities and three matched pairs of northern cities. Thus two graphs of population size by percentage Negro were constructed, one with border cities on it (Figure A-1.1) and one with northern cities on it (Figure A-1.2).

In Figure A-1.1, with the use of the principle of least distance between cities in a pair, the cities are easily divided into three pairs as indicated on the graph—St. Louis and Baltimore, Louisville and Kansas City, Oklahoma City and Tulsa. The pair selected randomly was St. Louis with Baltimore.

The selection of the three pairs of northern cities was begun in the same manner. Since we had already drawn a pair of large cities with large Negro populations, it was decided to draw three more pairs which would include small cities with large Negro populations and both large and small cities with small Negro

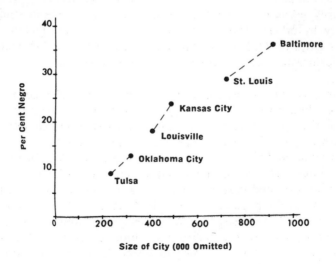

re **A-1.1**   Border Cities Graphed (City Size by Per Cent Negro)

populations. The fourteen cities were divided into the four quadrants shown in Figure A-1.2, and the cities were paired within each quadrant as much as possible. City A in the upper right-hand corner could not be paired with any other city and was in the same quadrant as St. Louis and Baltimore, so it was eliminated; we then found that if we eliminated City F, the remaining twelve cities could be paired as shown. In every case a port city was paired with another, and inland cities were paired with each other. Since it was necessary to conceal the names of two of these cities in the report, they will not be identified here.

In the initial drawing the pairs D-E, G-H, and K-L were selected. However, we decided that the pairs drawn had several problems; first, our preliminary contact with informants in cities G and H left us uncertain whether racial issues had ever come up in the schools; second, we felt that we were overrepresenting one region of the country, since G, H, K, and L are all in the western New York–Pennsylvania–Ohio area. Finally, it was decided that an additional western city would be useful. For these reasons, cities G and H were dropped and cities M and N added.

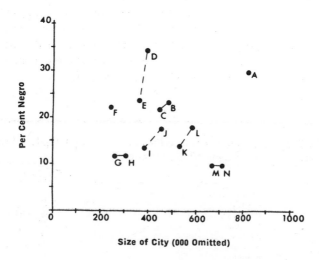

Figure A-1.2 Northern Cities Graphed (City Size by Per Cent Negro)

Appendix 2

Measuring School Segregation

In all eight cities a racial census of the pupils by school has been made. From this it is possible to derive several different indices of the extent of school integration. The index we have chosen to use is the percentage of the Negro elementary school population in schools that are over 10 per cent white in enrollment. This percentage varies from 8 per cent in St. Louis (before the increase in bussing of Negro students) to 70 per cent in San Francisco, as shown in Table A-2.1.

We noted in Chapter 10 that there is little or no relationship between the number of Negro students in integrated schools and the attitude of the civil rights movement toward the school system. This is to be expected, since the extent of segregation in the schools is largely outside the control of the school system. The most ambitious program of school integration in this sample is probably that in St. Louis; and it has increased the percentage of Negroes in school with whites by only 6 per cent.

Table A-2.1 Percentage of Negro Elementary School Pupils in Schools Which Are over 10 Per Cent White, for Each City

City	Per Cent
San Francisco	70
Bay City	57
Pittsburgh	48
Lawndale	37
Newark	28
Buffalo	20
Baltimore	17
St. Louis	8

Figures A-2.1 and A-2.2 indicate the roots of school segregation. In the first figure we have plotted the index of school integration against the Taueber coefficient of residential segregation (K. Taueber and A. Taueber, 1965). The Taueber coefficients are indices of dissimilarity between the location of the Negro and white populations, and they approximately indicate the percentage of the population which would have to move in order to disperse Negroes equally throughout the city. We have used the complement, 100-T, in Figure A-2.1. In Figure A-2.2 we have added a second factor, the size of the Negro school population. In general, the number of Negroes in integrated schools will be related to the number who live on the periphery of the ghetto, and the length of the periphery increases proportionately to the square root of the population, so we have used the square root. The correlation is not very high in Figure A-2.2, and we are tempted to try to determine how much of the deviation might be attributed to school policy; but most of the deviation results from the fact that the

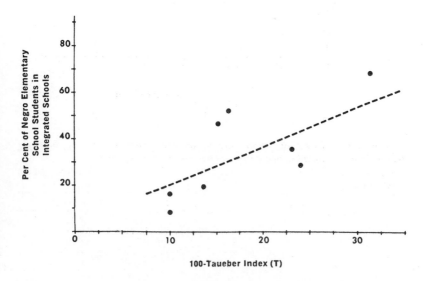

Figure A-2.1 Extent of School Integration and Index of Residential Segregation

more irregular the shape of the ghetto, the greater will be its periphery in relation to its area. For example, three of the four cities which fall above the regression line have more than one Negro ghetto; the four cities below the line have the bulk of their Negroes concentrated in a single residential area.

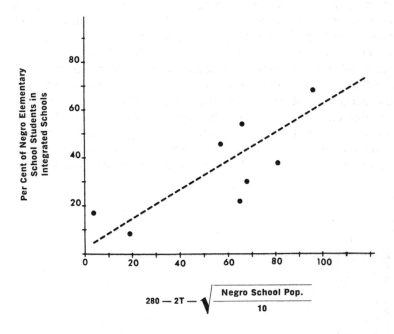

Figure A-2.2 Extent of School Integration and Index Combining Size of Negro School Population and Degree of Residential Segregation

References

AGGER, R. E., GOLDRICH, D., and SWANSON, B. E. *The rulers and the ruled: Political power and impotence in American communities.* New York: John Wiley, 1964.

ALEXANDER, G. J. "Buffalo." In U. S. CIVIL RIGHTS COMMISSION, *Civil rights report: Public schools in the North and West, 1963.* Washington, D.C.: U.S. Civil Rights Commission, 1963.

ALFORD, R. *Party and society.* Chicago: Rand McNally, 1964.

BAKER, J. E. The selection of superintendents of schools by boards of education. Unpublished Ph.D. dissertation, University of Chicago, 1952.

BANFIELD, E. C. *Big city politics.* New York: Random House, 1965.

BANFIELD, E. C., and WILSON, J. Q. *City politics.* Cambridge, Mass.: Harvard University Press, 1963.

BLOSSOM, V. *It has happened here.* New York: Harper, 1959.

BRADLEY, D. S., and ZALD, M. N. From commercial elite to political administrator: The recruitment of the mayor of Chicago. *Amer. J. Sociol.,* 1965, **71**, 153–67.

BREED, W. The emergence of pluralistic public opinion in a community crisis. In A. W. GOULDNER and S. M. MILLER (Eds.), *Applied sociology.* New York: Free Press of Glencoe, 1965.

Brown v. *Board of Education of Topeka.* 1955, 349 U.S. 294.

Bush v. *Orleans Parish School Board.* 1956, 138 F. Supp. 337.

Bush v. *Orleans Parish School Board; Williams* v. *Davis.* 1960a, 187 F. Supp. 42,45.

Bush v. *Orleans Parish School Board; Williams* v. *Davis.* 1960b, 5 Race Rel. L. Rep. 669.

Bush v. *Orleans Parish School Board; Williams* v. *Davis; United States* v. *Louisiana.* 1960a, 188 F. Supp. 916, 928. `

Bush v. *Orleans Parish School Board; Williams* v. *Davis; United States* v. *Louisiana.* 1960b, 364 U.S. 500.

CAMPBELL, E. Q., BOWERMAN, C. E., and PRICE, D. O. *When a city closes its schools.* Chapel Hill: University of North Carolina Press, 1960.

CARMICHAEL, O., and JAMES, W. *The Louisville story.* New York: Simon and Schuster, 1957.

CLARK, K. B., and CLARK, M. P. Racial identification and preference in Negro children. In T. M. NEWCOMB and E. L. HARTLEY (Eds.), *Readings in social psychology.* New York: Henry Holt, 1947.

COLEMAN, JAMES S., *et al. Equality of educational opportunity.* Office of Education Report OE-380001. Washington, D.C.: Government Printing Office, 1966.

COUNTS, G. S. *The social composition of boards of education.* Chicago: University of Chicago Press, 1927.

CRAIN, R., KATZ, E., and ROSENTHAL, D. *The politics of community conflict.* Indianapolis: Bobbs-Merrill, in press.

DAHL, R. *Who governs? Democracy and power in an American city.* New Haven: Yale University Press, 1961.

DAVIS, J. A., and BRADBURN, N. H. *Great aspirations: Career plans of America's June 1961 college graduates.* Report No. 82. Chicago: National Opinion Research Center, September, 1961. (Multilithed.)

DAVIS, W. H. "St. Louis." In U.S. CIVIL RIGHTS COMMISSION, *Civil rights, U.S.A.: Public schools, cities in the North and West.* Washington, D.C.: U.S. Civil Rights Commission, 1962.

DAWIDOWICZ, L. S., and GOLDSTEIN, L. J. *Politics in a pluralist democracy.* New York: Institute of Human Relations Press, 1963.

DOLCHER, L. A time of worry in "the city care forgot." *The Reporter,* 1956, **14** (March 8), 17–20.

DYKEMAN, W., and STOKELY, J. Integration: Third and critical phase. *New York Times Magazine,* 1960 (November 27), pp. 24–25, 111–113.

ELDERSVELD, S. J. *Political parties: A behavioral analysis.* Chicago: Rand McNally, 1964.

ERSKINE, H. G. The polls: Race relations. *Pub. opin. Quart.,* 1962, **26**, 137–48.

FESTINGER, L., SCHACHTER, S., and BACK, K. *Social pressures in informal groups.* New York: Harper, 1950.

FOWLER, I. Local industrial structure, economic power and community welfare. *Soc. Problems,* 1958, **6**, 41–51.

FULLER, H. New Orleans knows better. *New Republic,* 1959, **140** (No. 7, February 16), 14–17.

GIFFIN, R. *Sturgis, Kentucky: A tentative description and analysis of the school desegregation crisis.* ("Field Reports on Desegregation in the South.") New York: Anti-Defamation League of B'nai B'rith, n.d.

GOODMAN, M. E. *Race awareness in young children.* Cambridge, Mass.: Addison-Wesley, 1952.

GRIFFIN, J. H., and FREEDMAN, T. *Mansfield, Texas: A report of the crisis situation resulting from efforts to desegregate the school system.* ("Field Reports of Desegregation in the South.") New York: Anti-Defamation League of B'nai B'rith, n.d.

HANSEN, C. *Miracle of social adjustment.* New York: Anti-Defamation League of B'nai B'rith, 1957.

HAVARD, W. C., HEBERLE, R., and HOWARD, P. H. *The Louisiana elections of 1960*. Baton Rouge: Louisiana State University Press, 1963.

HAWLEY, A. Community power and urban renewal success. *Amer. J. Sociol.*, 1963, **68**, 422–31.

HAYS, B. *A southern moderate speaks*. Chapel Hill: University of North Carolina Press, 1958.

HOLDEN, A., VALIEN, B., and VALIEN, P. *Clinton, Tennessee: A tentative description and analysis of the school desegregation crisis*. ("Field Reports on Desegregation in the South.") New York: Anti-Defamation League of B'nai B'rith, n.d.

HUNTER, F. *Community power structure*. Chapel Hill: University of North Carolina Press, 1953.

HYMAN, H. H., and SHEATSLEY, P. B. Attitudes toward desegregation. *Sci. Amer.*, 1956, **195** (6), 35–39.

———. Attitudes toward desegregation [seven years later]. *Sci. Amer.*, 1964, **211** (1), 16–23.

KAPLAN, H. *Urban renewal politics: Slum clearance in Newark*. New York: Columbia University Press, 1963.

KEY, V. O., JR. *Southern politics*. New York: Vintage, 1949.

KILLIAN, L. W. Community structure and the role of the Negro leader-agent. *Soc. Inq.*, 1965, **35**, 69–79.

KIMBROUGH, R. *Political power and educational decision making*. Chicago: Rand McNally, 1964.

LEVY, C. School desegregation in Warren County, Virginia: A case-study in the mobilization of restraints. Unpublished Master's thesis, University of Chicago, 1961.

LOUISIANA STATE ADVISORY COMMITTEE. *The New Orleans school crisis: Report of the Louisiana State Advisory Committee to the United States Commission on Civil Rights*. Washington, D.C.: Government Printing Office, 1961.

MILLS, C. W., and ULMER, M. *Small business and civic welfare*. U.S. Senate Document No. 135 (Serial No. 11036). Washington, D.C.: Government Printing Office. 1946.

The municipal yearbook, 1963. Chicago: International City Managers' Association.

MUSE, B. *Virginia's massive resistance*. Bloomington: Indiana University Press, 1961.

———. *Ten years of prelude*. New York: Viking, 1964.

NEW ORLEANS DEPARTMENT OF RESEARCH, CENSUS, AND PLANNING. *Facts and finances, 1959–1960*. New Orleans: Department of Research, Census, and Planning, New Orleans Public Schools, 1960.

New York Times, 1960a (May 8), p. 7.

New York Times, 1960*b* (May 8), p. 67.

New York Times, 1960*c* (August 14), p. 56.

New York Times, 1960*d* (November 11), p. 25.

New York Times, 1960*e* (November 28), p. 1.

New York Times, 1960*f* (December 5), p. 38.

OPOTOWSKY, S. The news mob. *The Nation,* 1961, **193** (September 30), 203–5.

OSOFSKY, G. *Harlem: The making of a ghetto.* New York: Harper, 1963.

PELTASON, J. *58 lonely men.* New York: Harcourt, Brace, and World, 1961.

PETERS, W. *The southern temper.* New York: Doubleday, 1959.

PINARD, M. Structural attachments to and political support in urban politics: The case of fluoridation referenda. *Amer. J. Sociol.,* 1963, **68**, 513–26.

PINNEY, E. L., and FRIEDMAN, R. S. *Political leadership and the school desegregation crisis in Louisiana.* (Eagleton Institute of Politics, "Cases in Practical Politics," Case No. 31.) New York: Eagleton Institute of Politics, 1963.

POIS, J. *The school board crisis: A Chicago case study.* Chicago: Aldine Publishing Company, 1964.

Race Relations Law Reporter, 1959, **4**, 583.

Race Relations Law Reporter, 1960, **5**, 659.

RECORD, W., and RECORD, J. C. *Little Rock, U.S.A.* San Francisco: Chandler, 1960.

SHOEMAKER, D. (Ed.) *With all deliberate speed.* New York: Harper, 1957.

SINDLER, A. *Huey Long's Louisiana.* Baltimore: Johns Hopkins Press, 1956.

Southern School News, 1960 (December), p. 10.

Southern School News, 1961*a* (January), pp. 8, 11.

Southern School News, 1961*b* (February), p. 6.

State of Louisiana v. *Orleans Parish School Board* (Civil District Court for Parish of Orleans). 1960, 5 Race Rel. L. Rep. 659.

STEINBECK, J. *Travels with Charley: In search of America.* New York: Bantam, 1963.

STERNLIEB, G. Is business abandoning the big city? *Harvard Bus. Rev.,* 1961, **39** (1), 6–12, 152–54.

TAUEBER, K., and TAUEBER, A. *Negroes in cities.* Chicago: Aldine Publishing Company, 1965.

THIRD ANNUAL CONFERENCE ON PROBLEMS OF SCHOOLS IN TRANSITION. *Conference before the U.S. Commission on Civil Rights.* Williamsburg, Va., February, 1961.

Times-Picayune, 1960*a* (June 21), p. 1.

Times-Picayune, 1960*b* (June 26), Sec. 2, p. 2.

Times-Picayune, 1960*c* (August 21), p. 16.

Times-Picayune, 1960*d* (November 1), p. 1.

Times-Picayune, 1960*e* (November 2), p. 10.

Times-Picayune, 1960*f* (November 4), Sec. 2, p. 7.

Times-Picayune, 1960*g* (November 5), p. 5.

Times-Picayune, 1960*h* (November 5), p. 19.

Times-Picayune, 1960*i* (November 6), p. 21.

Times-Picayune, 1960*j* (November 6), p. 22.

Times-Picayune, 1960*k* (November 6), p. 23.

Times-Picayune, 1960*l* (November 7), Sec. 3, p. 20.

Times-Picayune, 1960*m* (November 7), p. 22.

Times-Picayune, 1960*n* (November 8), Sec. 3, p. 18.

Times-Picayune, 1960*o* (November 8), p. 20.

Times-Picayune, 1960*p* (November 16), p. 2.

Times-Picayune, 1960*q* (November 16), p. 19.

Times-Picayune, 1960*r* (November 17), p. 6.

Times-Picayune, 1960*s* (November 17), Sec. 2, p. 11.

Times-Picayune, 1960*t* (December 14), p. 12.

Times-Picayune, 1961 (January 31), p. 2.

TIPTON, J. H. *Community in crisis.* New York: Columbia Teachers College, 1953.

TRILLIN, C. *An education in Georgia.* New York: Viking, 1964*a*.

———. The Zulus. *New Yorker,* 1964*b*, **40** (June 20), 41–119.

VIDICH, A. J., and BENSMAN, J. *Small town in mass society.* New York: Doubleday, 1958.

Wagner v. *Redmond.* 1960, Civil District Court for Parish of Orleans, No. 386-056.

Wagner v. *Redmond.* 1961, 127 So. 2nd 275.

WILLIAMS, O. P., and ADRIAN, C. R. *Four cities.* Philadelphia: University of Pennsylvania Press, 1963.

WILLIAMS, R. M., JR. *Strangers next door.* Englewood Cliffs, N.J.: Prentice-Hall, 1964.

WILLIAMS, R. M., JR., and RYAN, M. W. *Schools in transition.* Chapel Hill: University of North Carolina Press, 1954.

WILSON, J. Q. *The amateur Democrat.* Chicago: University of Chicago Press, 1962.

———. *Negro politics.* New York: Free Press of Glencoe, 1965.

WISDOM, B. Letter from a New Orleans mother. *The Nation,* 1961, **193** (November 4), 353.

Index

ABOUT NORC

The National Opinion Research Center is a non-profit social research institute, founded in 1941 and affiliated with the University of Chicago since 1947.

The Center maintains a professionally-trained interviewing staff to conduct national surveys on a wide variety of topics, using representative cross-sections of the population, quota cross-sections, and samples of special populations.

Recent research includes studies of race relations, occupational prestige and social stratification, public political participation and attitudes, the components of happiness, educational needs, and career choice.

Staff members of the Center are skilled social scientists, many of whom also hold appointments in one of the academic departments of the University. NORC's Survey Research Service provides sampling, interviewing, and data processing facilities for other social scientists, and offers consultation on research design. In addition, the Center administers a formal training program for graduate students in the social sciences and related fields.

The research activities of the Center are financed through grants from and contracts with private foundations, government agencies, and colleges and universities. NORC is governed by a Board of Trustees chosen from among prominent social scientists, educators, and laymen interested in social research.

National Opinion Research Center
6030 South Ellis Avenue
Chicago, Illinois 60637